Methods and Models

At present, much of political science consists of a large body of formal theoretical work that remains empirically unexplored and an expanding use of sophisticated statistical techniques. Although there have been some noteworthy efforts to bridge this gap, there is still a need for much more cooperative work between formal theorists and empirical researchers in the discipline. This book explores how empirical analysis has been and should be used to evaluate formal models in political science. The book is intended to serve as a guide for active and future political scientists who are confronting the issues of empirical analysis and formal models, as well as a basis for a needed dialogue between empirical and formal theoretical researchers in political science. Once combined, these developments presage a new revolution in political science.

Rebecca B. Morton is Associate Professor of Political Science at the University of Iowa. Professor Morton's articles have been published in numerous publications such as the *American Political Science Review,* the *American Journal of Political Science,* and *Journal of Law and Economics.*

Methods and Models

A Guide to the Empirical Analysis of
Formal Models in Political Science

REBECCA B. MORTON
University of Iowa

CAMBRIDGE
UNIVERSITY PRESS

CAMBRIDGE UNIVERSITY PRESS
Cambridge, New York, Melbourne, Madrid, Cape Town, Singapore, São Paulo, Delhi

Cambridge University Press
32 Avenue of the Americas, New York, NY 10013-2473, USA

www.cambridge.org
Information on this title: www.cambridge.org/9780521633000

First published 1999
Reprinted 2000, 2002, 2005

A catalog record for this publication is available from the British Library

ISBN 978-0-521-63300-0 hardback
ISBN 978-0-521-63394-9 paperback

Transferred to digital printing 2008

Contents

Acknowledgments

This manuscript began when I was asked to write a paper for the 1996 annual meeting of the American Political Science Association on the use of laboratory experiments to test formal models. In the process of writing that paper, I realized that the more general question of empirical evaluation of formal models needed study before I could truly understand the role played by experiments. I found it surprisingly enjoyable to explore this complicated subject. Many of my colleagues and friends have helped me refine my ideas in the process and discover the examples used in the book. Moreover, I believe that a book on how a discipline should conduct research is a much better product if constructed with help from scholars active in the field, those currently confronting issues that the book attempts to address. I benefitted tremendously from the suggestions and comments of readers of earlier drafts, particularly from the anonymous referees. In particular, the views of Charles Cameron, Daniel Diermeier, Avinash Dixit, Scott Gates, and Gary King on the proper relationship between theory and empirical models were extremely helpful in clarifying my own thoughts on these issues. Kelly Kadera and Ken Kollman were patient with my attempts to understand computational models. Gary Cox, Rod Kiewiet, Douglas Madsen, Elizabeth Martin, Jonathan Nagler, Keith Poole, and Charles Shipan read (and supplied extensive comments on) various parts of the manuscript. Invaluable observations for the project were also provided by Michael Alvarez, Timothy Amato, David Austen-Smith, Frank Baumgartner, Jenna Bednar, John Brehm, Daniel Carpenter, Elisabeth Gerber, Jonathan Katz, Arthur Lupia, Nolan McCarty, John Moloney, Harry Paarsch, Tom Romer, Andy Sobel, Gerald Sorokin, Kaare Strom, and Margaret Trevor. I am grateful to my graduate students – Kevin Chlarson, Ebru Erdem, Aaron Fate, Robert

ix

Frederick, Jingyan Gao, Alice Gilchrist, Ha Lyong Jung, Kristin Kanthak, and Peter Moore – who used the manuscript for class discussions. Finally, this book would not have been possible without the steady friendship of my sister, Renda Goss; the constant support and assistance of my mother, Mildred Bradford; and the patience of my daughters, Renda and Charlotte.

PART I

Introduction

CHAPTER 1

Political Science's Dilemma

1.1 The Problem

1.1.1 *Sophisticated Methods without Theory*

Political scientists have become adept at applying – from economics and other disciplines – exciting new statistical methods to analyze data. Even more noteworthy, political science "methodologists" are making their own contributions to the development of statistical techniques used in the discipline. As Bartels and Brady (1993) argue, many now expect political science graduate students in the field of methodology to use high-level econometric texts and to be versed in nonlinear estimation procedures, generalized least squares, ordered probit analysis, maximum likelihood, and so forth.

Yet this increase in complexity is not without costs. As the use of methodological techniques in political science has advanced, researchers have found that often their empirical study leads to more questions, questions that need theoretical input. However, because little existing theory is relevant or because the well-developed theory that does exist seems unconnected to the empirical issues, typically the response is to use more sophisticated methods or data gathering to answer the questions without reference to a fully devel oped theory. But these new methods often lead to still more questions, which in turn result in the use of more sophisticated methods to gather or analyze the data. The connection to theory seems to get lost in the methodological discussion. Rarely do researchers take the empirical results and rework the theoretical framework that began the discussion.

Example: Are Incumbents Spendthrifts? Consider the progression of research on the effects of campaign expenditure levels on voter choices in elections. After campaign spending data became available in 1972, political scientists began to examine the extent to which campaign spending affects the number of votes a candidate receives. This is an important research area for political science – for academic reasons and also in terms of public policy. Campaign spending legislation is a perennial issue in the U.S. Congress. Understanding the effects of campaign spending on electoral outcomes is critical for understanding the possible effects of the legislation. In particular, will limiting campaign spending advantage incumbents or challengers or neither? Research on the effects of campaign spending levels on vote totals can help us answer this important question.

Early empirical research on the effects of campaign spending were simple empirical investigations based on a basic hypothesized "vote production function," where votes were assumed to be a function of the level of spending. These studies found an interesting empirical anomaly: campaign spending by challengers increases their vote totals, but spending by incumbents has the opposite effect. Of course, this result may be simply due to the simultaneity of choices; that is, incumbents will spend more the more strongly they are challenged, and the more strongly they are challenged the worse they are likely to do electorally. So the first methodological advance in this literature was to control for challenger spending. Nevertheless, under a variety of empirical specifications, researchers found that incumbent spending had only small (often insignificant) positive effects on incumbent votes, whereas the effect of challenger spending on votes for challengers was significant, large, and robust (see Glantz, Abramowitz, and Burkhart 1976; Jacobson 1976, 1978, 1980, 1985, 1987, 1989).

Green and Krasno (1988) argued that this empirical result was a consequence of using an inappropriate statistical estimation technique. Since the relationship between campaign spending and votes may hold in both directions (i.e., candidates may receive more contributions and hence spend more as their expected vote totals increase), they contended that empirical analysis using ordinary least-squares regression techniques – which allow for a causal relationship in only one direction – yields biased and inconsistent estimates because the explanatory variable (campaign spending levels) is correlated with the error term in the regressions (see Johnston 1972). Green and Krasno provided another methodological advance to tease out the effects of campaign spending on vote choices. They used a two-stage least-squares estimation procedure in which incumbent campaign spending in the previous election becomes an instrumental variable for incumbent campaign spending in the election considered, thus avoiding the possible endogeneity problem. Contrary to the earlier results, Green and Krasno found positive and (what they considered to be) significant effects of incumbent campaign spending on votes for incumbents.

But the methodological debate did not end there. Jacobson (1990) critiqued the analysis of Green and Krasno. He raised a number of issues; but in particular he criticized their linear specification, arguing that campaign spending probably has diminishing marginal returns and that the assumed linearity leads to inaccurate results. Jacobson then presented new empirical results of his own using the two-stage regression technique and allowing for nonlinearity. Discussing his specification choice, Jacobson noted: "Theory provides no guide in choosing the appropriate transformation to measure diminishing returns to campaign expenditures. . . . I therefore used the Box–Cox procedure to find the appropriate functional form" (1990, p. 338). Jacobson also maintained that the cross-sectional approach used in the previous studies was inappropriate because the research question is a dynamic one: whether vote choices are affected by campaign spending during the election process. He provided additional evidence – using poll data on voter choices compared with aggregate spending levels – and found that incumbent spending does have less of an effect than challenger spending.

The dialogue on methods continued with Green and Krasno's (1990) response to Jacobson. They provided more data supporting their results, argued that Jacobson misinterpreted the existing empirical results (i.e., Jacobson focused on the marginal effect of campaign spending whereas Green and Krasno emphasized the total number of votes generated from the spending), and questioned Jacobson's new empirical study on poll data. Green and Krasno suggested that, since Jacobson used aggregate spending data for elections rather than separate measures for the different periods of elections, his analysis was not truly dynamic. In answer to this criticism, Kenny and McBurnett (1992) presented an empirical study of one Congressional election with data on campaign spending over time coupled with survey data on voter choice; they found that incumbent spending does not have a significant effect on voter choices although challenger spending does. Even more interestingly, Kenny and McBurnett found that campaign spending has the greatest effect on those who do not actually vote in the election.

The debate has not ended. Ansolabehere and Snyder (1996) have provided a new methodological wrinkle to the debate. They first argue (as pointed out by Grier 1989) that the two-stage estimation process is not necessary, since spending is a function of expected rather than observed votes and since there is no simultaneity bias in ordinary least-squares estimation processes when the dependent variable is actual vote shares. Ansolabehere and Snyder contend that instead there are biases in the ordinary least-squares estimation due to omitted variables that affect expected vote totals directly and indirectly through effects on observed levels of spending (as noted also by Levitt 1994 and Gerber 1994). They remedy this problem by constructing an instrumental variable from factors that affect the cost of raising money for spending in the estimated vote production function. The construction of the instrumental variable led them to collect a much more expansive data set on these factors. Ansolabehere and Snyder find that the effects of both incumbent and challenger spending are significant and of similar magnitude.

In summary, the early results on incumbent campaign spending's effects on voter choices led to more sophisticated methods (ordinary least-square regressions replaced by two-stage least-square regressions, which was then replaced by ordinary least squares with an instrumental variable) and more comprehensive data gathering (aggregate cross-sectional data replaced by individual-level dynamic data, which was then replaced by more expansive cross-sectional data on candidates' personal and political backgrounds).[1]

Incumbent Campaign Expenditures and Voters: Theory? I do not mean to suggest that researchers in this debate are unconcerned with theory. Jacobson provides a nonformal theoretical justification for his result that incumbent spending does not matter. He posits that voters typically know less

---

[1] There have been attempts to relate some of the empirical work in this context to formal models of the relationships between contributors and candidates; see for example McCarty and Rothenberg (1996), which is discussed in Chapter 8. Mebane (1997) argues that the equilibria in this relationship are inherently nonlinear and render problematic the empirical estimations that do not allow for nonlinearity. However, this literature "black boxes" the relationship between voters and contributors.

These empirical studies have spawned further empirical analyses of related questions with the same spiraling of sophisticated methodology. For example, Goldenberg, Traugott, and Baumgartner (1986) suggest that incumbents may use campaign spending to deter the entry of quality challengers. But in cross-sectional empirical studies, Krasno and Green (1988) and Squire (1989) find little effect. Box-Steffensmeier (1996) presents new evidence – using a more detailed data set coupled with a more sophisticated methodology (duration analysis with time-varying covariants) – that suggests incumbent spending does have a deterent effect. One exception to the emphasis on data and methods is Epstein and Zemsky's (1995) game theoretic model of the interaction between incumbents and challengers. However, they too black-boxed the relationship between campaign spending and voters; their model is referenced in Box-Steffensmeier (1996), but just how the data analysis relates to the game theoretic model is not explained.

about challengers. He then argues that challenger campaign spending can positively influence voter views of challengers, whereas incumbents are already well known and so their campaign spending has less of an effect on voters' views. However, there are some problems with this seemingly plausible explanation. For example, if incumbent spending may relay information on challengers then incumbent spending also could have an informational effect. Alternatively, if incumbent spending has no effect on voter decisions then why do incumbents spend money? In any event, this theoretical explanation has received little attention in the empirical literature on the effects of incumbent campaign spending. Similar nonformal theoretical arguments are made by Green and Krasno in contending that campaign spending levels are an endogenous variable and by Jacobson in calling for a dynamic rather than cross-sectional empirical study.

Yet there has been no attempt (of which I am aware) to take the theoretical explanation Jacobson offers with respect to incumbent campaign spending, develop it further, assess other empirical implications that can be evaluated, and tie the theory to the incumbent campaign spending results. For example, if the informational story is correct then we would expect campaign spending's effects on voter choices to work through changes in voter information and evaluations about the candidates. This suggests an empirical specification where voter evaluations of the candidates and uncertainty in their evaluations are functions of campaign spending and where voter choices are a function of the evaluations and degree of uncertainty. Such theory-influenced specifications have not been considered.

Furthermore, Green and Krasno (1988, 1990) provide no alternative explanation of voter behavior. Ansolabehere and Snyder (1996) do refer to some existing formal models (to be discussed in Section 1.1.2) which assume that campaign spending provides voters with information, but they do not explain the relationships among these theories, Jacobson's nonformal theoretical justification, and their own empirical specification. Without an alternative theory of the underlying vote production function, it is not possible to compare other empirical implications of the two theories – a comparison that could illuminate how voters are influenced by incumbents' campaign spending. Thus it is difficult to take the empirical results on campaign spending effects and use them to build a greater theoretical understanding of why voters may or may not be influenced by the spending. The theory cannot be used as a guide in the specification of further empirical analysis.

Researchers were intrigued with the original empirical result that incumbent spending mattered less than challenger spending, and they wondered if the result was robust with respect to various changes in specification; this question spawned a lengthy and extensive methodological debate. More than 20 years of research on this issue has shown that incumbents may not be spendthrifts if we are careful in how we measure the relationship between spending and votes. But the connection to the original theoretical question – that is, how incumbent campaign spending affects voter choices – was lost in the empirical exploration. Why voter choices may be affected by spending of either candidate and how that relates to the empirical research are still open questions.

A General Problem for Political Science? The debate over the effects of incumbent campaign spending is just one example of methodological work in political science that needs theoretical guidance. In their review of the state of methodology, Bartels and Brady maintain that:

Statistical inferences always rest upon the assumptions embodied in a specific statistical model. In an ideal world, the specification of a model would be determined by strong theoretical expectations, together with accumulated knowledge of the measurement processes generating our data. But real political research is more often marked by very considerable uncertainty about which explanatory variables may be relevant, their functional forms, and the sources and nature of stochastic variation and measurement error.

Ironically, as political methodologists have become more sophisticated, fundamental problems of specification uncertainty have become increasingly pressing. . . . [C]omplex simultaneous equation, factor analysis, and covariance structure models have become increasingly commonplace in various areas of political science. In most respects, this increasing complexity is well and good; but one costly side effect of complexity is to multiply the number of difficult, and often arbitrary, specification decisions upon which any empirical result depends. Too often we lack the strong theory necessary to specify clearly how observable indicators are related to latent variables, or which variables in a structural equation are exogenous and which are endogenous. "We are left with a plethora of loosely related, partially contradictory models in a single substantive area; one analyst's key endogenous variable is assumed by a second to be exogenous and totally ignored by a third, with substantive consequences that are completely unclear to all concerned" (Bartels 1985, p. 182). The result is that, even after we have estimated our complex models, we remain – or at least, we should remain – much less confident in our estimates of causal effects than classic statistical theory would lead us to expect. (1993, pp. 140–1)

Bartels and Brady call for "strong theory" as a guide for empirical specification. They are not precise about what they mean by this, but they do cite the application of spatial voting theory to empirical studies of voting as an example of how strong theory has been used in political science to organize empirical exploration. The implication is that strong theories are precise, theoretically derived statements about the expected relationships that the empirical analysis is designed to uncover. Bartels and Brady seem to suggest that political scientists need explicitly developed theoretical reasons for positing estimating models, and that explicit theory should play more of a role in specification issues of empirical research.

1.1.2   *Strong Theory without Data*

I believe that we political scientists *have* been developing "strong theories." With the increase in sophisticated methodology there has been a concurrent rise in the use of formal modeling techniques, which have provided explicitly derived strong theories. An important transformation has taken place in political science: a move from a focus on nonformal, largely inductive theorizing to formal deductive modeling using mathematics. Indicative of this trend is the expanding number of published articles using mathematics for theoretical purposes only – with no empirical testing or data analysis in the article. Also noticeable has been the growth of interdisciplinary journals publishing theoretical papers on political science questions; examples include *Public Choice, Journal of Theoretical Politics, Economics and Politics,* and *Journal of Law, Economics, and Organization.* Part of the rise in formal models in political science has been an increased focus on "rational choice" models from the discipline of economics.

Nevertheless, many of these explicitly derived formal models have neither been used for empirical study nor empirically evaluated. A number of formal modelers have pointed out that much formal modeling remains untested. For example, Palfrey remarks:

Many of the predictions and theoretical findings that emerge from such analyses [formal models in political science] are couched in terms of variables and parameters that are extremely difficult to measure using either of the traditional data methodologies (surveys and historical data) . . . [and] very little serious testing of these formal theories was undertaken. The result was a situation in which model development far outpaced model testing. This imbalance is undoubtedly one major source (perhaps *the* major source) of the early skepticism and controversy about the usefulness of the formal approach to studying political processes and political behavior.[2] (1991, p. 1)

---

[2] Palfrey speaks in the past tense, before the advent of laboratory testing of formal models, which he argues has lessened the imbalance. This is true, but much of the imbalance remains.

Likewise, Enelow and Morton observe:

We believe the dichotomous relationship among empiricists and theoreticians in political science has developed largely because few public choice political scientists have tried to blend empirical work with formal theory and those who have usually are testing a model that mainstream political scientists find uninteresting. The emphasis among political scientists in public choice in the last twenty-five years has been on development of pure theory, so much so that many non-public choice political scientists believe that public choice people (and economists in general) rarely do empirical work. (1993, p. 88)

Campaign Spending and Voters Redux. Parallel with the empirical research on campaign spending just discussed, a few researchers have attempted to formally model the relationship between voter choices in elections and campaign expenditures. This literature began with trying to understand how voter choices may be affected by campaign spending in a general model of electoral competition with interest groups, campaign contributors, and voters. Early theoretical explorations of the subject were made by Brock and Magee (1978). Austen-Smith (1987), Cameron and Enelow (1992), and Hinich and Munger (1989) all assume that voters are risk-averse and uncertain about candidates' positions. Campaign spending somehow reduces the uncertainty and, given risk aversion, voters' expected utility from a candidate increases with campaign spending, resulting in an increased probability of the candidate's winning. These models run into difficulties because voters and campaign contributors alike are motivated by the policy positions that the candidates advocate. Candidates are therefore (theoretically) drawn to centrist positions, which reduces the incentives for contributors to provide resources – and the candidates' incentives to acquire them – as they converge in positions. Additional assumptions (e.g., that policy has asymmetric effects on either voters or contributors that prevent the candidates from converging) must be made to explain observed candidate divergence and positive campaign spending. Simon (1998) presents a formal model where candidates allocate a fixed budget of campaign expenditures over a set of issues and where voter preferences are a function of the weights that candidates give to issues in campaign advertising, weights that are based on psychological models of voter preference formation supported by experimental research.[3]

---

[3] Alvarez (1997) develops a Bayesian decision theoretic model where voters are assumed to acquire information during campaigns through campaign advertising and where candidate and interest-group behaviors are assumed to be exogenous. There is also a large number of

The approach of assuming that campaign advertising is informative has been criticized by modelers (including myself; see e.g. Morton and Cameron 1992; Austen-Smith 1997) for not explaining how voters are able to use political advertising to become more informed about candidates' positions. Thus, from a modeler's perspective, these models are only a step beyond the vote production approach. An alternative approach models the interactions between candidates, voters, and interest groups as a signaling game where campaign spending can serve as a signal or endorsement to voters by an interest group or groups of the candidate's type. (In these models, the signal is about candidate type in a nonpolicy dimension where all voters and interest groups prefer high-quality types; see e.g. Austen-Smith 1991; Cameron and Jung 1992; Gerber 1996a; Grossman and Helpman 1996; Potters, Sloof, and van Winden 1997; Prat 1997). This approach assumes that campaign advertising itself is noninformative. That is, the observed campaign spending on advertising may be informative to voters about interest-group knowledge of candidate types, but the advertising context provided by the spending is uninformative. Moreover, in many of these models, additional restrictive assumptions are necessary to derive outcomes in which candidates' spending actually does reveal information to voters.

Relationship to the Empirical Literature on Spendthrift Incumbents. I have discussed briefly some formal models of campaign spending and voter choices that could be used to explain the vote production functions seen in the empirical literature on incumbent campaign spending. Yet the theoretical research has generally had little interaction with the empirical one. To my knowledge, neither the models that assume campaign advertising is informative nor the ones that take a signaling approach have been used explicitly to consider whether incumbent campaign spending has a different effect on voter choices than challenger spending as in the general empirical literature just reviewed. In theoretical models, the election is for an open seat and no candidate is the "incumbent" per se. Voters vote prospectively based on their estimates of candidate positions and/or types. The effect of incumbency in the context of this literature appears to remain unexplored.

empirical and experimental studies of the relationship between voter information and campaign advertising (Alvarez 1997; Ansolabehere et al. 1994; Basil, Schooner, and Reeves 1991; Brians and Wattenberg 1996; Faber and Storey 1984; Garramone 1984, 1985; Iyengar and Ansolabehere 1995; Just, Crigler, and Wallach 1990; Merritt 1984). However, to my knowledge none of these models or empirical work has been related to the debate over the effects of incumbent campaign spending levels on voter choices.

I do not mean to suggest that the modelers are completely unconcerned with the empirical relevance of their works. It would be incorrect to suggest either that empiricists are uninterested in theory or that theorists are ignoring empirical reality. For example, Prat (1997) argues that there are stylized facts from the empirical literature that a model of campaign advertising must explain: (1) campaign advertising is paid for by interest groups with preferences distinct from the median voter, (2) campaign advertising provides little "hard" information, and (3) campaign advertising increases a candidate's electoral prospects. Simon (1998) uses empirical evidence to support his model of voter choices. Some have evaluated empirically the conclusions from formal models with candidates, interest groups, and voters that assume a vote production function (e.g. McCarty and Rothenberg 1996; Mebane 1997; Snyder 1990). However, the modelers typically use simple examples from the empirical world to "illustrate" how their conclusions may fit reality, or at best they perform limited tests of some of the conclusions from the models, ignoring other conclusions and possible alternative models.

Both research lines (empirical and theoretical) have tended to follow questions generated by the previous research with little overlap across the divide. In the empirical literature, researchers take an existing empirical formulation and add either a new variable, a new statistical technique, or a new data set to re-examine previous results while continuing to black-box the relationship between spending and votes in a "vote production function." Modelers, for their part, have generally built their models by altering and generalizing the assumptions made by others in earlier models. There has definitely been an attempt to understand what is going on in the vote production function, but no attempt has been made to connect that understanding with the question that has drawn empirical focus: Is incumbent spending less effective than challenger spending? The two literatures combined have considerably added to our understanding of how campaign expenditures may affect voter choices, but they seem to follow their own independent paths.[4]

This is, as I noted, just one example of how parallel research in sophisticated empirical analysis and theory may be conducted simultaneously, addressing research questions that are "close" but with different aims. At present, political science consists of (a) a large body of formal theoretical work that remains unexplored empirically and (b) an expanding use of sophisticated methodological techniques to analyze empirical data that is used

---

[4] I suspect that it is only a matter of time before an enterprising modeler/empiricist bridges this particular gap.

with nonformal theorizing as a foundation. Although there have been many noteworthy efforts to bridge the gap, there is still a need for much more cooperative work between formal theorists and empirical researchers in political science. These developments are potentially the basis for a new revolution in political science.

1.2   Source of the Dilemma

To comprehend the current state of political science research and prospects for a new revolution in political science, it is important to appraise the past. I will start my brief historical look with the first revolution in political science, the "behavioral revolution." In my review I note the following important caveat: my discussion is idiosyncratic, and it generalizes across researchers among whom significant differences exist and makes distinctions between groups that are usually considered to be similar. I take this approach to highlight developments that subsequently proved crucial for the progress of political science. In my review I will first discuss how the behavioral revolution affected political science and led to an increased emphasis on empirically based inductive theorizing. I then examine how – despite the significant advances in our understanding of politics that resulted from research out of the behavioral revolution – we began to reach limits in the knowledge of politics to be gained via the behavioral research program. This led to increased use of sophisticated methodology and formal modeling techniques and, as a result, a distance between empirical political science and formal modeling that I hope to shorten.

1.2.1   The Behavioral Revolution

What was the behavioral revolution?[5] I begin with the period between the two world wars. At this time, political science was largely dominated by a descriptive institutionalist perspective, with few attempts to generalize and derive explicit theories of politics. Political theorizing of the time used casual bits of observations about how elites and masses act out their political lives. Of course, there were some remarkable exceptions, particularly the group of political scientists working with Charles Merriam at the University

---

[5] For more information on the behavioral revolution, see Dahl (1961), Simon (1985), Truman (1968), and Wahlke (1979).

of Chicago, but for the most part political science lagged behind the behavioral sciences.

While political science concentrated on institutional and casual description, significant movements were being made in both empirical estimation and theorizing in some of the other social sciences (economics, sociology, psychology, and anthropology). Two of these groups are especially noteworthy for the development of political science: (1) the Lewinians, who focused on laboratory experiments in group dynamics under the leadership of Kurt Lewin at the University of Iowa and MIT and his successor, Leon Festinger at the University of Michigan; and (2) Lazarsfeld's research program at the Bureau of Applied Social Research at Columbia University. Both research agendas were prominent for developing new empirical techniques (laboratory experiments and survey research, respectively).

Significantly, both of these research programs also encouraged the use of mathematics in theorizing. Lewin used matrix algebra for his theoretical analysis and enlisted a mathematics student at MIT, R. Duncan Luce, for assistance. Lazarsfeld held seminars that encouraged formal analysis (one of the presenters was Herbert Simon; others included theoretical economists William Baumol and William Vickery), published a volume based on these seminars, and hosted regular visits by game theorists Howard Raiffa and Luce. (See O'Rand 1992 for a review of both of these research programs.) During this period there were other notable efforts using mathematics in theory and empirical work in the behavioral sciences. In particular, see the work of Chapple (1940), Dodd (1948), Rapoport (1950), Rashevsky (1947), Richardson (1939), and Simon (1957); see also Arrow (1968) for reviews of these and other efforts. In summary, the behavioral sciences developed exciting data sources using new empirical techniques and began some theory building to explain the data generated. Most of the research focused on techniques and results of empirical investigations, but there was also some limited work on mathematizing and formalizing theory.

1.2.2   *Effects on Political Science*

A New Emphasis on Empirically Testable Theories. Some political scientists found the advances in data analysis in the behavioral sciences more exciting than descriptive institutional study. Survey research and experimental analysis allowed political scientists to ask questions that had not previously been considered, questions about individual political decision making and small-group interactions. It is interesting that the survey research approach received more attention than the experimental one. I suspect this is because it seemed straightforward to apply results from survey research to understanding such individual political decisions as voting and party identification, but many agreed with Truman's (1968, p. 558) assessment of the group decision-making experimental approach as having little external validity for understanding similar sized political groups (e.g., legislative committees) and even less validity for understanding larger group behavior. Experimentation has recently received increasing attention in political science, partly to evaluate formally derived models in controlled settings (see Chapter 4) and partly because experiments on individual decision making are viewed by some as useful for behavioralist questions.

Truman (1968) reviews the effects of the behavioral revolution on political science. He notes that the revolution caused a dichotomy in political science:

This influence has had the consequence of creating a divergence between what, for want of better terms, I have referred to as the "institutionalist" tendency in political science and the "political behavior" tendency. The differences between these two are genuine, lying in the character of their commitment to the discovery of uniformities, in their approach to political institutions, and to a lesser degree, in the types of data and technique with which they are concerned. (p. 559)

Truman maintains that it was not the advent of new data and techniques that led to differences between behavioralists and institutionalists; rather, it was their distinctive approaches to theorizing ("commitment to the discovery of uniformities") and to studying institutions.

Many political scientists today (and, I suspect, even then) would disagree with Truman's assessment of the value for political science of theories on individual behavior from sociology and psychology. Truman goes so far as to characterize the study of voting behavior as the "perhaps least important element in the political process." Nevertheless, Truman sees value for political science in the approach taken by the behavioral sciences toward theory. He argues that

theory in the behavioral sciences has become far more completely fused with empirical research and theorizing has become more self-consciously central to the concerns of investigators than was the case shortly after World War I. One has the distinct impression that the volume of taxonomic description of concrete phenomena has declined and that there has occurred an increase and general commitment to the discovery of uniformities, to the use of observation for the verification of hypotheses, and to the search for empirically supported generalizations. (1968, p. 549)

It is the approach to theory, more than the techniques or specific theories of the behavioral sciences, that Truman prescriptively sees as important in the long term for political science. He summarizes this view as follows:

I would fully accept the proposition that the advance of our discipline lies in the acceptance of generalization as its primary objective and of empirically testable theory as its principal method; that advance will lose no speed from a critical familiarity with both the techniques and the theories of the behavioral sciences, but it has much to lose, in my opinion, from an incautious attempt merely to project these into the realm of governmental institutions. (p. 559)

Truman anticipates criticism from behavioralists for his less than enthusiastic evaluation of behavioralist techniques and the value of their theories for political science as well as from institutionalists for his insistence on the value of empirically testable theory. His response to the expected criticisms from institutionalists is noteworthy: "there is nothing so practical as a well-developed and testable theory; . . . the choice lies not between an approach to such theory and no theory at all, but between an implicit and unexamined set of assumptions and an explicit theoretical effort" (Truman 1968, p. 559).

In my view, the evidence that the first revolution occurred is in the quietening of the debate between behavioralists and institutionalists. Surveys and other techniques borrowed from the behavioral sciences during this period are now standard tools used by political scientists. Purely descriptive institutional study is rare, and qualitative research is considered subject to the same procedures and analyses as more quantitative research (see King, Keohane, and Verba 1994). Furthermore, few political scientists would argue that developing empirically testable theory is not central to the discipline of political science. Although there are disagreements over the types of theories that we investigate and the meaning of "empirically testable theory," it is widely accepted that mere description – without the overarching aim of eventually understanding politics in a theoretical sense – is misguided.

Nonformal Theorizing Became the Basis for the New Empirical Analysis. Even as the importance of empirically testable theory and theory in general became a well-accepted dogma in political science, the behavioralist approach of searching for uniformities and regularities, particularly in individual decisions, resulted in an emphasis on nonformal over formal theories. The use of mathematics in theorizing did not become standard in political science and remained an approach used by a minority of researchers. The behavioralist tradition that came to political science with the first revolution was characterized by *nonformal* theorizing: neither precise in assumptions nor utilizing deductive logic or mathematics but instead based almost exclusively on generalizing from observable variables. Mathematics was seen as useful in empirical estimation but as inconsequential in theory development.

What stymied the trend toward developing more formal theories and using mathematics in theorizing? The answer is complex, but four factors are especially important. First, the mathematical theorizing was primarily in economics, whose paradigm of rational choice was no doubt a big hindrance to those trained principally in psychology and sociology. For example, James Coleman stated that distaste for rational choice approaches prevented him from becoming interested in game theory in the 1950s.[6] A second factor (somewhat related, since mathematical theorizing was primarily done by researchers in other disciplines) was that political scientists felt the modeling approaches ignored important empirical realities of the political world. Formal modelers working outside of political science often did not have sufficient empirical grounding to model empirical questions of interest to political scientists. The temptation to apply models developed in other fields without a careful understanding of the limits of such application sometimes led to theorizing that seemed little related to the real world of politics.

Third, the advent of new data and techniques may have fueled the idea that complex theorizing was not necessary, that what seems to be "unrestrictive" nonformal theorizing might better allow the data itself – newly available in a usable form – to reveal generalities and uniformities. Finally, the approach based on nonformal theory had early empirical success for understanding politics, particularly the American system. The combination of Michigan school voting behavior with the theory of transformative elections and the theory of pluralism provided a basis of nonformal theory that appeared to adequately describe the American political system from the late nineteenth century to the early 1960s. Hence, the first revolution in political science led to a more inductive, empirically oriented political science. What was called political theory, as a field, became isolated and highly normative, and it remained largely nonmathematical.

1.2.3 *Political Science Today*

Today's political science is different from the political science of the behavioral revolution. The recent rise in formal models and explicit deductive

---

[6] Quoted in Swedberg (1990). Surely this remains a barrier to the acceptance of much formal modeling in political science.

theories using mathematics is distinct from the tradition that came with the first, behavioralist revolution in political science. On the other hand, the increase in sophisticated statistical techniques is consistent with the behavioralist tradition in many respects because the use of these techniques is often accompanied by nonformal rather than formal theorizing. How did these changes come out of the behavioral revolution?

Sources of Today's Political Science.

Influence from Other Disciplines. The recent changes in political science have two main sources. First, as researchers in other social sciences – notably economics – continued the evolution of formal theorizing, some became interested in questions related to the study of politics. Hotelling (1929) argued that his model of spatial location theory could be applied to candidate locations. Bowen (1943), Black (1948a,b; 1958), and Buchanan (1954) began formal examination of voting. Downs (1957) expanded on this work to present a theory of party competition. Some of this research is concerned with the normative implications of social choices, such as Arrow's seminal (1951) work and Buchanan and Tullock's (1962) discussion of institutional design. Others took a more positive perspective, as in the analysis of Shapley and Shubik, whose paper on using game theory to measure power in committees was published in the *American Political Science Review* in 1954. Luce and Raiffa (1957) addressed issues of voting and presidential vetoes. By the late 1960s, many economists had begun to question the public finance literature's normative outlook of treating government as a maximizer of social welfare. Economists at the University of Virginia (later Virginia Tech and now George Mason), Carnegie-Mellon, the California Institute of Technology, and Yale began to seek interaction with political scientists interested in formal modeling. (This history is reviewed in Mueller 1997, pp. 1–20.)

Researchers from economics clearly had an influence on political science, but investigations in other disciplines also helped formal modeling to gain more of a foothold in political science. In an autobiographical essay, Dina Zinnes tells of her collaboration with mathematicians and engineers:

At about this time John Gillespie and I attended a rather far-out conference that had been designed to foster interdisciplinary research, principally between the more quantitative types and those doing historical case study analyses. Someone with either considerable foresight, or a great sense of humor, had invited historians, area specialists, quantitative types like John and myself, and engineers. The discussions were unbearable. The historical area types argued that everything was unique and therefore science in general but mathematical analyses in particular were impossible. The quantitative and engineering participants tried to show that what was unique from one perspective could share characteristics with other cases from another perspective and that analytical methods could provide some intriguing ways to answer questions of concern to the area specialists. When the level of boredom had hit a particularly high threshold, I began to engage one of the engineers in a private conversation. That was the beginning of a new way to think about hostility patterns and interaction processes.

The engineer was Jose Cruz, a preeminent control theorist, who, after hearing about our differential equation models of arms races, excitedly began to show us how these models could become the basis for a far more sophisticated approach. (1989, p. 91)

Interdisciplinary work and interactions during this period sustained political scientists interested in formal models at a time when their own discipline was skeptical at best.

Limits of Behavioral Empirical Research. The other major impetus for the recent changes in political science was a demand for new ideas. Empirical analysis from the behavioralist tradition began to reach the boundaries of knowledge that could be gained with existing nonformal theoretical approach and techniques of statistical estimation. Within American politics, in particular, a number of new developments caused the understanding built on nonformal theorizing to become insufficient. Some examples: the movement politics of the 1960s, split-ticket voting, the rise of independent voters, the declining influence of political parties, and the rise of the personal vote in Congress. With the existing behavioralist nonformal theorizing unable to explain these events, researchers in American politics responded by dividing into subfields specializing in particular areas: Congress, the presidency, public opinion, law and the courts, and so forth. Much research in these areas continues to work with the behavioralist approach, searching for empirical regularities with nonformal theorizing as a buttress.

In Chapter 2 I explore more expansively the relative values of formal versus nonformal models as the basis for empirical testing. My point here is that mining data for uniformities and regularities – both at the individual level using survey data and with other data sets devised using techniques from the behavioral sciences – is limited in how much can be revealed with nonformal theorizing as a basis. This research does provide valuable insights and a significant amount of new knowledge of politics; most notably, the accumulation of years of survey projects has made possible new aggregated data studies, as exemplified in the work of Campbell and colleagues (1960) and Carmines and Stimson (1981, 1989), for instance. But as long as the theoretical basis remains imprecise, the empirical search has meant continually finding new data or new ways to analyze old data. Ideally, in the scientific method as described in standard research texts, generalizations from empirical analysis lead to refinement of theories to be tested by new empirical analysis. To some extent this has occurred. Yet the behavioralist strategy of using nonformal theory as a basis for empirical research has constrained the development of more complete theories from the empirical results derived and thus also the knowledge to be gained from empirical study.

Reaction to the Limits: Searching for New Techniques. There have been two reactions to the limits of empirical study with nonformal models. One is to search for better statistical techniques in order to facilitate the search. The other is to go back to the theoretical drawing board and derive empirically estimable models from formal and specific theories with stated assumptions whose evaluation can yield more specific information than the evaluation of nonformal theories. A substantial portion of current empirical research in political science continues to search for uniformities with nonformal theorizing. Much of the heart of the development of more sophisticated statistical techniques has been the quest for better ways to deal with data problems that limit the ability of the empirical research to discover regularities and "empirical" laws. For example, how can researchers handle the fact that much data is at an aggregate level even though researchers would like to discover evidence on individual behavior? This question has produced significant work on how to manage the problem of "ecological regression" (see e.g. King 1997; Nagler 1994). I believe this work is path-breaking and significant, and I would hardly argue that it is atheoretical. Rather, my point is that such work continues in the behavioralist trend, that is, the search for better ways for the empirical world to reveal regularities or generalities on political behavior using nonformal rather than formal theories as a framework.

I recognize that there is a significant and growing body of empirical research in political science that has moved beyond the behavioralist approach and does attempt to test formal models. I use much of this research as examples in the chapters in this book. There is also work that seeks to derive new estimation procedures in order to better evaluate formal theories. For example, Alvarez and Nagler (1995) show that the standard statistical procedure used to examine voting – as well as the electoral predictions of spatial theory – are problematic when applied to elections with more than two candidates or parties; these authors provide an alternative estimation procedure. Thus, some of the collaboration between empiricists and theoreticians that I advocate is already underway. Even so, as contended by Bartels and Brady (see Section 1.1.1), nonformal approaches are still widespread in political science empirical inquiry.

Reactions to the Limits: The Search for Better Theory. The other reaction to limits of the behavioral approach is the quest for more specific theories of politics and thus for more empirically relevant theories among political scientists (and the resulting collaborative research with economists). Some political scientists saw that empirical research that does not lead to the building of more theory has limits in terms of the knowledge that can be derived. They sought methods of formalizing theories of politics. Consider Riker's discussion of his movement toward formal modeling:

This, then, was my state of mind in 1954. Despite my poor education in social science, I had begun to understand that, to be scientific, political science needed testable models about political phenomena – that is, refutable descriptive sentences. But no such theory existed. There were a few hints: Maurice Duverger had proffered what is now called Duverger's law about the relation between plurality voting and the two party system. . . . But aside from this so-called law and its rationalization with a nascent theory, there was very little empirical generalization and almost no theory. Because of this fact, I had been looking, somewhat randomly to be sure, for methods of constructing theory. I had looked, fruitlessly, at modern logic, and it was just at this juncture that I read the Shapley and Shubik paper and Kenneth Arrow, *Social Choice and Individual Values* . . . . These two works led me back to von Neumann and Morgenstern, *The Theory of Games and Economic Behavior* . . . . There I discovered what I thought that political science needed for constructing theory. (1992, pp. 208–9)

Riker's movement toward game theory – which has had important and long-reaching consequences for political science, as he assembled students and followers both in political science and in collaboration with economists – is not the only instance of formal models attracting political scientists dissatisfied with the empirical approach of the behavioralists dominating the discipline. Dina Zinnes at the Merriam Institute at the University of Illinois, Elinor and Vincent Ostrom at Indiana University, and G. R. Boynton at the

University of Iowa were also attracted to the mathematical formalization of political theories.

In summary, the recent changes in political science have two main sources: (1) the continued work on formal modeling in other social sciences with interest in questions of politics; and (2) the success and failure of the behavioral revolution. The behavioral revolution's success in emphasizing new techniques and nonformal theorizing as a basis for empirical work – and its failure to satisfy in terms of building new theory – led some political scientists interested in more complex specific theories to seek formal modeling techniques while leading other political scientists to pursue better techniques for data analysis.

1.2.4   *The Gap between Theorists and Empiricists*

Almost all disciplines in the social and natural sciences have dealt with the problems of linking theory and empirical analysis. In political science the history has been to emphasize one area over the other. Before the behavioral revolution, nonformal institutional descriptive theorists dominated the discipline; after the revolution, empiricists came to the fore. The behavioral revolution led to notable new empirical research that was largely based on inductive theorizing. A sizeable body of new research in voter behavior, for example, took as its goal a search for empirical laws arising from the data, and a massive amount of knowledge of individual political behavior has been learned from this research.

The behavioral revolution in political science resulted in an emphasis on an inductive approach (which I believe still has its effect on much empirical research in political science). Likewise, current political science research contains theoretical studies that are as much divorced from the empirical world as research of some early behaviorists is devoid of theory. As with the empirical work from the behavioral revolution, much can come from such "unempirical" models. Pure theory is valuable for two reasons: (1) it leads to more applied theory that can be empirically estimated and (2) it can provide prescriptive or normative analysis. Since my focus is primarily on positive rather than normative theory, I do not elaborate much in this chapter on the second benefit of pure theory except to note that a significant portion of social choice theory has been normative (I revisit the normative side of rational choice–based models in Chapter 3).

It is sometimes hard to explain the value of pure theory "mind-experiments," as Einstein called them, to the eventual development of more attractive realistic theory. As noted by Binmore:

When such mind-experiments are employed, as with Einstein, outside pure mathematics, it does not greatly matter whether or not the hypotheses on which they are built are realistic or even realizable. The purpose of the mind-experiment is usually to test the *internal logic* of a theory rather than to verify or to challenge its prediction. . . . The fact that a mathematical model with unrealistic hypotheses can be useful is not widely understood and such models are often treated with derision by "naive positivists." Such derision might equally well be directed at Einstein for postulating that Swiss tramcars might carry junior patent clerks to their work at the speed of light. (1990, p. 30)

I believe it is important to recognize that much applied research that has gained some popularity in political science is a direct descendant of pure theory mind-experiments. For example, consider the highly esoteric theoretical work on the lack of equilibria in majority rule voting, as exemplified in the famous papers of Kramer (1973), McKelvey (1976), Plott (1967), and Schofield (1978). This work led to a re-emphasis in understanding of the role of institutions in political decisions and how institutions can affect political outcomes (Shepsle 1979; Shepsle and Weingast 1981). The analysis out of the "new institutionalism," in contrast to the theoretical work that spawned it, often provides much in terms of empirically estimable theoretical predictions about the effects of different institutional rules. For example, the research of Denzau and Mackay (1983) demonstrates how open versus closed rules in legislatures can affect legislative policy choices.[7] I discuss in Chapter 2 how the pure theoretical work on strategic voting in social choice by Gibbard (1973) and Satterthwaite (1975) are the antecedents for the work of Cox (1997) examining the impact of comparative electoral systems on political representation, an issue that many political scientists find more interesting than social choice theory. Nevertheless, although I believe mind-experiments to be fundamental[8] and that the empirical analysis of applied research is limited, the emphasis on pure theory without empirical testing has led to a distance between empiricists and theorists in political

---

[7] Loosely, bills proposed by a committee in an "open rules" legislature can be amended by any member, whereas bills proposed by a committee in a legislature under closed rules cannot be amended. Closed rules give committees gatekeeping power and decrease the probability that the status quo will be changed.

[8] See Tetlock and Belkin (1996) for essays on the role of thought experiments in comparative politics.

science, as noted by Palfrey and by Enelow and Morton in the foregoing quotations.

Thus, at present there is a large amount of empirical and theoretical research in political science that is highly sophisticated. The expansion in statistical techniques has led to a set of complex tools available for standard empirical questions in political science and the need for specialists in methods and methodology. On the other side, formal theoretical work has outpaced empirical testing. The repercussion is that political science has many experts in the use of the latest technology of statistics working with data to understand politics out of the behavioralist, inductive tradition, as well as formal modelers, with less knowledge of the latest in empirical estimation, seeking deductive knowledge of politics. While there are a few notable scholars in the discipline who are "switch hitters," capable in both areas, this is far too rare.

My opinion is that solving this problem will involve examining the question of just how to empirically evaluate formally derived models in general. Two developments in political science – the increase in formal modeling and the accompanying rise in sophisticated statistical techniques to analyze data – each have value in and of themselves. However, political scientists now need to systematically think about how they are going to use these new tools together. The researchers quoted in this chapter indicate that both methodologists and formal theorists in political science believe that there is a need for greater incorporation of formal models in empirical analysis. As Bartels and Brady summarize, "there is still far too much data analysis without formal theory – and far too much formal theory without data analysis" (1993, p. 148). I believe that the following question poses the principal dilemma for future political science research: How can political scientists merge the expanding use of methodological tools to analyze data with the increasing use of formal modeling techniques in theorizing? My goal in this book is to help bridge this gap – to provide a framework for the empirical analysis of formal models.

1.3   Goal of This Book

1.3.1   *Bridging the Gap*

I aim to explore, in a straightforward manner, how empirical analysis has, can, and should be used to empirically evaluate formal models in political science. The book is intended to be a guide for active and future political scientists who are confronting the issues of empirical analysis with formal models in their work. I wish for this book to serve as a useful basis for a needed dialogue between empirical and formal theoretical researchers in political science. As long as empirically focused political scientists and formal theorists in the discipline talk past each other, the scientific knowledge of politics will be limited. As noted previously, this book attempts to help bridge the gap between these two approaches.

1.3.2   *Non-Goals of the Book*

There are two things this book is *not* intended to achieve. First, this book is not an attempt to defend rational choice–based research per se. It is true that a considerable portion of the book does address the empirical evaluation of rational choice–based formal models and how their use is justified, but my goal is to focus on the empirical analysis of these models as formal models in general. The book is thus not limited to rational choice–based models. I present and evaluate a number of formal models that use psychological or behavioral theories of individual behavior or that can be considered *non*rational choice (Brown 1993; Carpenter 1996; Kadera forthcoming; Kollman, Miller, and Page 1992; McKelvey and Palfrey 1996; Offerman 1996; Signorino 1998; Westholm 1997). A significant portion of Chapter 5 addresses experimental tests and alternatives to expected utility theory, the standard conception of "rational choice" in political science.

There are rational choice–based nonformal theories and works that I do not discuss *because* they are nonformal. In my view, nonformal rational choice–based models – though quite useful in general and satisfying to some of my own biases and predilections – are as limiting in our ultimate research exercise as any other nonformal model. Thus the analysis in this book concerns the empirical study not of rational choice–based models (which may be nonformal) but rather of formal models (which may or may not be rational choice–based).

Second, this book is not a text on methods techniques or formal modeling. There are a number of noted texts in both these areas and it would not be possible to cover the vast material on these subjects. Nevertheless, it is impossible to discuss empirical evaluation of formal models without defining some commonly used concepts and terms such as equilibrium, noncooperative game theory, and so on. I provide intuitive explanations of these terms when they arise as well as references to sources where these concepts are described more expansively. And because some of the material is necessarily mathematical, I do attempt to provide accessible explanations of concepts that are beyond the training of many existing graduate programs in political science.

1.4   Examples in the Book

Since this book is designed as a practical venture, I present many examples drawn from the political science literature. The examples are biased toward American politics and voting models, partly because much of the empirical work testing formal models has been in these areas and partly because these are areas with which I am most familiar. I also use a number of examples drawn from my own research in large part because I feel I can present these examples more clearly than others.

I emphasize examples from very recent research in political science, typically articles and books published in the last five years. My reasoning is that it is best to present examples that illustrate state-of-the-art formal models and empirical analysis from the perspective of the discipline as a whole. Thus my examples omit some interesting and significant early empirical analysis of formal models, and for this I apologize. Because of space limitations I am not able to give as comprehensive a review of examples as I would like, and I tend to emphasize work from research articles rather than books. Owing to the broader readership of books, journal articles often contain more detail on the formal models than is found in books. Still, for some of the more interesting empirical analyses based on formal modeling, the following books are recommended: Aldrich's (1995) work on political parties; Dion's (forthcoming) study of the U.S. Congress; Kiewiet and McCubbins's (1991) work on delegation; Krehbiel's (1991) research on legislatures; Laver and Schofield's (1990) and Laver and Shepsle's (1996) studies on parliamentary democracies; and Bueno de Mesquita and Lalman's (1992) analysis of war.

It is my conviction that one of the more important ways that formal models can be analyzed empirically is through the use of laboratory experimentation. In Chapter 4 and in a number of examples I discuss the advantages and disadvantages of such experiments versus empirical analysis using naturally occurring data. However, because I view experimentation as such a serviceable vehicle for testing formal models, I have edited a volume of papers on experimental testing of formal models that illustrate examples of many of the arguments made in this volume; I hope that readers interested in experimentation will find the edited volume (Kanthak and Morton 1998) useful and interesting.

In presenting the examples in this book, my outlook is slightly different from what would be found in a literature review on the area of study from which the example is drawn. That is, I do not attempt to critique any literature in a general sense. Thus, there are aspects of the examples that I ignore, and the versions I present are simplified. I hope that readers who find the examples interesting will consult the original works from which they are drawn. In some sense my desire is to whet appetites rather than satisfy them. I also do not go into much detail on the formal modeling solution techniques or the empirical estimation procedures *except* when I believe that these factors are important in understanding choices that are made in empirical analysis of formal models. I attempt to provide references to texts on formal modeling and empirical estimation, when relevant, for readers who would like more details on these techniques. At times I may make critical evaluations of the examples in their role as either theory or empirical work, but the reader should always bear in mind that my evaluation of an example is limited to one purpose and is hardly a complete measure of its source's value to the literature. I apologize in advance for my limited appraisals. Finally, in the examples I attempt to retain the notation used in the original source.

1.5   Plan of the Book

In the next chapter I discuss what is meant by a formal model. I explain how false or unverified assumptions are crucial to formal modeling, and that formal models differ from nonformal models in that the assumptions are stated explicitly and predictions are derived from these assumptions. I discuss how mathematics and formal approaches have two advantages over nonformal modeling in social science. First, I show that mathematics allows a researcher to check more carefully the logic and consistency of a theory and also may produce unexpected or counterintuitive results. Second, I argue that formal models have advantages in empirical research since they make more precise predictions about the real world. Formal models allow for empirical evaluation of assumptions and for a larger number of predictions as compared with nonformal theorizing.

Chapter 3, which is coauthored with Elizabeth Martin, examines the diversity of formal models that are used in political science. Since rational choice–based and game theoretic models constitute a significant portion of this research, much of the chapter concerns this approach. However, formal models that use assumptions of "almost rational choice" and "boundedly rational choice" are also explored. Psychological process models used in political science are examined as well as models that make assumptions about aggregate behavior without making explicit assumptions about the individual choice process. Some of the mathematical techniques that are used in formal models are also reviewed briefly.

Following the examination of formal models in Chapters 2 and 3, in Chapter 4 I present an overview of my approach to the empirical analysis of formal models. Before empirical analysis of a formal model begins, a researcher must determine (a) the extent to which she wishes to view her model as a complete version of reality in the empirical analysis and (b) whether the model is deterministic or has random or stochastic aspects. The answers to these questions determine the type of empirical analysis that the researcher conducts. I also divide standard empirical analysis of formal models into three types: analysis of assumptions, predictions, and alternative models. Each type of empirical study plays a unique role in the evaluation of a formal model.

The next four chapters (Chapters 5–8) examine and assess the appropriateness of the three different types of empirical analysis (assumptions, predictions, and alternative models) of formal models. In each chapter I present examples to illustrate how the type of study can be conducted as well as a summary of the implications of the examples for empirical evaluation of formal models. In Chapter 9 I consolidate these implications in a set of suggested "steps" and I return to the goal of the book – to lead to a new, second revolution in political science. I conclude with my vision of this new political science.

1.6   Using the Book

I hope that this book will lead to a cooperative alliance between empiricists and modelers in political science; thus, an important audience for the book is professional political scientists. I also hope it will be used in graduate classes as the foundation of courses on the topic of using formal models in empirical work or of general courses on research design – supplemented by journal articles, working papers, and other books in particular substantive areas of interest. The early chapters (2 and 3) present information on the nature of formal models and can be emphasized for students without prior exposure to this area or omitted for students with knowledge of formal modeling. The entire book (or relevant chapters) can also serve as reading material in courses on methods or formal modeling. An advanced undergraduate class in political science research can be organized around the book, which can also function as an introduction for other social scientists who desire information on current political science research in the intersection of formal models and empirical analysis.

PART II

Formal Models in Political Science

CHAPTER 2

What Makes a Model Formal?

2.1   There Are Many Different Types of Models

Political scientists, like all social scientists, use the term "model" frequently, but not always consistently; the same individual might use the term to mean different things in different settings. In order to understand the terms "model" and "formal model," I first consider model building as part of the process of scientific inquiry.

2.2   The Scientific Process and Model Building

2.2.1   *Observations about the Real World Suggest Research Questions*

My presentation of the scientific process is idealized. In this ideal process, research begins with observation and experiments about the nature of the real world. One point of view is to think of the real world as being governed by a "data generating process" (DGP), that is, the source for the data observed about the real world.[1] These observations range from the quite uncomplicated and simply described to the highly sophisticated in need of

---

[1] Some call the data generating process the "true model." This term is an oxymoron since models are not true by definition, and thus I chose not to use it. My presentation of model building is based largely on that outlined in Maki and Thompson (1972) and the other references cited there. Some of my names for the concepts are a little different; Maki and Thompson call the data generating process a "logical model" and a "nonformal model" a "real model." They also label all formal models "mathematical" models (even if not expressly mathematical) and do not discuss pure theory, applied formal models, or empirical or computational models. I have changed the names of the concepts to terms more familiar to political scientists and have discussed the other modeling terms as well.

complex statistical study. The key is that the observation in some way reveals a question or problem about the real world (the data generating process) to be answered, something that a researcher does not understand and desires to understand. For example, a researcher may wonder why some ethnic groups live cooperatively in some jurisdictions but are unable to do so in others. Or, the researcher may observe that juries who must reach unanimous verdicts sometimes make decisions that seem obviously wrong to outside observers.

The observation may be coupled with some prior theorizing or model building that has not been successful or does not satisfactorily explain the observation. For example, Banks and Kiewiet (1989) note prior empirical research showing that incumbent members of Congress are rarely defeated, which typically deters strong challengers. However, weak challengers often enter such races (and run ineffectual campaigns). Banks and Kiewiet see this empirical regularity as a riddle that existing theory does not explain: "This pattern of competition, however, is a puzzling one. Formal models of competition as well as common sense indicate that weak opponents are deterred more readily than strong ones. Here, however, strong challengers are deterred from challenging incumbents while the weak are not. How can that be?" (1989, p. 1000). That is, why is it that weak challengers, who are more likely than strong challengers to lose against an incumbent (all other things equal), enter these races while strong challengers sit out? Banks and Kiewiet thus began their research with an empirical riddle that seemed contrary to prior theorizing.

2.2.2   *Nonformal Model Building as a Start in Answering Research Questions*

At some point, researchers like Banks and Kiewiet begin to imagine how the results they observe could be explained, and so begins the mental process of modeling. Of course, there is no fine line at which model construction truly originates. But there is a moment when a researcher moves from an emphasis on data gathering based on previous theorizing to a focus on mental evaluation of building new theory. Oftentimes the researcher who begins to theorize is not the same one who made the prior observation. The observation may have occurred some period of time before the theorizing, and the data may have been gathered for an entirely different purpose than to answer the theoretical question or problem that is the subject of new theorizing.

For instance, Banks and Kiewiet's (1989) analysis is based on the empirical analyses of Leuthold (1968), Huckshorn and Spencer (1971), Mann and Wolfinger (1980), and Jacobson and Kernell (1981).

At the theorizing stage, a researcher may begin to form conjectures about what she believes is going on in the real world and how the DGP works. The conjectures are based partly on intuition and partly on observation and the recognition of similarities that may imply relationships among aspects of the real world. The conjectures may also arise from a loose application of previous theorizing. The researcher then reworks these conjectures into more precise statements about the real world. In this, a researcher necessarily must make some approximations and decisions regarding which concepts to investigate and what to ignore. This stage is called *modeling* because the researcher is engaging in abstraction. The way the real world is represented cannot be entirely realistic, since the researcher has to some degree employed idealization, identification, and approximation in devising the model. However, the model is *nonformal* because (a) it is expressed in terms of real things, rather than in abstractions or symbols, and (b) it does not involve statements that are derived or deduced from assumptions. The nonformal model is usually presented as a direct hypothesis or set of hypotheses about the real world and the real things that the researcher is interested in explaining. The researcher may use a simple diagram or graph to represent these ideas. The researcher may stop at this point, using hypotheses that arise from nonformal modeling as a basis for further empirical study.

Banks and Kiewiet (1989) report on some of the nonformal explanations from existing empirical research for the puzzle they pose. This early research focused on the costs and benefits of running for office and argued that the costs may be lower and the benefits higher for weak challengers than strong challengers. These nonformal models presented the costs and benefits in "real" terms, and the researchers engaged in empirical analysis to see if these real cost and benefit parameters explain the actual data. For instance, Jacobson and Kernell (1981) argue that weak candidates are less likely to be required to give up another position to run and thus the cost is lower. Maisel (1982) emphasizes that weak candidates run to use the campaign as a forum to present their views on issues. Others note that lawyers may see campaigns as ways to increase their legal practices through publicity.

Yet Banks and Kiewiet contend that the empirical results based on nonformal theorizing are unsatisfactory. That is, if the benefits for running are higher for weak than for strong challengers then weak challengers should more often run in open-seat races. The nonformal theorizing and the empirical results, though useful and informative, are limited in their explanatory power. In particular, Banks and Kiewiet (1989, p. 1002) argue that it is hard to explain why results seem to imply that challengers ignore the probability of winning in their choices:

> For strong candidates a consideration of the relevant probabilities generally leads to an obvious course of action; knowing that they are far more likely to win an open seat than to defeat an incumbent, they will be inclined to wait for the incumbent to step aside. Previous research has suggested that weak candidates who challenge incumbents, on the other hand, have deluded themselves into wishfully thinking that their probability of winning is much higher than it actually is (Leuthold 1968; Kazee 1980; Maisel 1982).

In the opinion of Banks and Kiewiet, more must be going on than simply a misunderstanding of the probabilities by weak challengers or differences in costs and benefits that depend on challenger type. In their view, the existing work is too simplistic. It does not capture the complexity of the entry choice facing challengers and how the probability of winning may be endogenously determined. Banks and Kiewiet devise a formal model in which they consider these complexities explicitly and thereby derive the probability of winning for the challengers.

2.2.3   Formal Model Building

A nonformal model becomes a formal model when a researcher expresses the real-world situation in abstract and symbolic terms in a set of explicitly stated assumptions. Theoretically formal models need not necessarily be mathematical (although they almost always are). But only when a formal model is expressed mathematically and solved using the techniques of mathematics do we call it a mathematical model. The appeal of mathematics for formal modelers is discussed later in this chapter. In devising a formal model, whether mathematical or not, the researcher moves away from direct hypotheses depicted in real-world variables and toward assumptions that incorporate abstract and symbolic terms. For instance, here are some of the assumptions made by Banks and Kiewiet (1989).

- There are three possible candidates: an incumbent, C_I, and two potential challengers, C_1 and C_2. The two challengers differ in quality (labeled as q_1 and q_2 for challengers C_1 and C_2, respectively), and $q_2 > q_1$.

- The candidates are risk-neutral and hence seek to maximize their probability of winning the election.
- If re-elected, C_I will retire after one more term in office.
- At time $t = 1$, both C_1 and C_2 will decide whether to run in a primary election that will choose a candidate to run against C_I in a subsequent general election; at $t = 2$ they will decide whether to run in a primary election that will choose a candidate to run for the open seat.
- ". . . (1) each challenger can run in only one general election, and (2) if either challenger wins at $t = 1$, the other will not challenge their incumbency at $t = 2$" (p. 1003). Note that a challenger defeated in a primary at $t = 1$ can run in the primary again at $t = 2$ if the incumbent is not defeated in the general election at $t = 1$.

Banks and Kiewiet clearly create an "unreal" situation in the model since in most elections many of these assumptions are either unverified or false. Nonetheless, formal modelers hope their assumptions can logically and consistently capture at least the important aspects of the situation under study. This is the stage of formal modeling. Formal models have explicitly stated assumptions about reality which are used to derive predictions about reality. Formal models are deductive, because conclusions proceed from the assumptions. Assumptions are crucial components of formal models because they become the agreed-upon premises for all subsequent arguments.

2.2.1 Choosing a Formal Model

Assumptions in a Formal Model. There are a number of different formal models that could have been used by Banks and Kiewiet. For example, they could have assumed a larger number of potential challengers. They could have assumed that challengers had policy motivations (as in Calvert 1985) beyond winning. How is this choice to be made? The answer relates to the question at hand. I suspect that Banks and Kiewiet assume three candidates in order to make the model tractable and because they believe that the results are largely unaffected by expanding the number of candidates.[2] Also, formal modelers like to begin with the simplest possible model that can capture the research question before building to a larger, more general, and perhaps less tractable model. I also surmise that Banks and Kiewiet assume that candidates maximize their probability of winning in order to focus

---

[2] How formal modelers justify assumptions is discussed in more detail in Chapter 5.

on the effect of probability motives on candidate entering decisions and to "stack the deck" against the entry of low-quality challengers. Allowing for different entry motives would cloud the analytical results.

Some of the assumptions in formal models are considered to be true – or there is a large amount of evidence that they are true. For example, in most Congressional races there is typically an incumbent (as Banks and Kiewiet assume), and most races become open-seat when the incumbent retires. A model of bargaining between a legislature and an executive assumes that both exist in a governmental structure. Such assumptions are not problematic since it is well known that incumbents and governmental structures with executives and legislatures do exist. Banks and Kiewiet (1989) also assume that the probability that either candidate wins in the open-seat race is higher than when a challenger faces an incumbent, something that we have empirical evidence to support. Undoubtedly, a number of assumptions in formal models are not regarded as suspect and do not raise many objections from researchers.

Nevertheless, many assumptions of formal models are either not directly verifiable or blatantly false. For instance, the incumbent in many Congressional races plans to stay in office for many more terms, and it is highly uncertain when he or she will retire. It is unknown whether candidates for office are risk-neutral or not.[3] Banks and Kiewiet also treat the Congressional election in isolation, ignoring the fact that there are other Congressional races as well as other races for other offices that might influence voter and candidate choices. Though potentially controversial, such assumptions are necessary to study complex phenomena. Formal models thus typically begin by describing the world in simplified form. Most models of legislative and executive conflict, for example, may ignore the structural features of bicameralism and committees, as well as the influence of the judicial branch. Similarly, many models of elections may – like Banks and Kiewiet's – overlook some of the details of candidate nomination procedures, the role of political parties, and the media. A useful common assumption is *ceteris paribus* (all other things equal): aspects of the real world that could have an effect on the outcome are held constant during the analysis. For example, a sudden outbreak of war might conceivably make a low-quality challenger more desirable than a high-quality challenger owing to characteristics whose importance was previously viewed by voters as negligible.

---

[3] However, some have argued that risk taking is an attribute of many candidates for elected office; see Rhode (1979).

The ceteris paribus assumption helps us focus on relationships between the variables in a model without having to worry about strange possibilities and extremely unlikely events.[4]

Complexity in a Formal Model. These examples indicate the difficult choices that must be made when developing a formal model. A formal model, as an abstraction from reality, *must* make some false assumptions – but which ones? Imagine the task of building a tabletop model of the Brooklyn Bridge in New York City. Should all of the ornate architectural details of the towers be included? Should the model of the bridge be placed over water moving at a given speed or a fluctuating speed or only a mirror representing the water? Should the model be made of the same material used to construct the bridge or simply be made of plastic?[5] These judgments depend upon what the modeler is interested in learning. For example, if she wishes to have a three-dimensional view of the bridge for an artistic evaluation then the architectural details of the above-water portion of the bridge are most important. In contrast, if her purpose is to examine how the bridge affects water flow and currents, then the underwater structure is significant and the bridge should be part of a general model of the water flow. In designing formal models, researchers face the same types of decisions. Hence, formal models should be evaluated in terms of what is and is not included and their relationships to the problem examined. Finding how the choice of abstraction affects the results of the model can be as important as discovering its logical implications.

Consider the simple Hotelling–Downsian model of two-party competition (the antecedent for Banks and Kiewiet's), which predicts the convergence of candidates to the policy position most preferred by the voter whose preferences are at the median of the distribution of voter preferences. This famous model makes many assumptions that are known to be false, such as the existence of only two candidates and the requirement that everyone must vote. Other assumptions are "suspect" rather than false and have generated much debate. How realistic is it to assume that candidates or parties care only

---

[4] Nevertheless, the mind-experiment of imagining the effects of a sudden outbreak of war on Congressional races can allow a researcher to think through some counterexamples to and limits of the theory. For instance, challenger quality might be interpreted differently by voters if unexpected war occurs. Thus, in general, challenger quality may not be independent of the term of the legislature and may vary over time.

[5] King et al. (1994, p. 49) make a similar analogy between a social science model and a model airplane. They also make the point that "good models abstract only the right features of the reality they represent."

about winning? How realistic is it to posit that voters evaluate candidates or parties along a single dimension over which the voters have single-peaked preferences? In the years since the Hotelling–Downsian model became popular in political science a large literature has developed whose principal aim is to explore how relaxing these assumptions changes the basic conclusions of the theory.

The title of a paper by Randy Calvert (1985), "Robustness of the Multidimensional Voting Model: Candidate Motivations, Uncertainty, and Convergence," emphasizes that his paper is a quest of determining how theoretically robust the Hotelling–Downsian spatial model's predictions are to changing the assumptions of candidate motivations. Calvert investigates whether changing the assumption of candidate motivations means that the convergence prediction fails. He finds that convergence is still likely *if* there is certainty about the identity of the median voter, but if there is uncertainty and candidates are policy-minded then they pick divergent positions. In a similar exercise, Palfrey (1984) relaxes the assumption of two parties in the Hotelling–Downsian model and adds a third party that enters after the two major parties have chosen their positions. He also finds that divergence of the two major parties' platforms is theoretically predicted, since these parties recognize that convergence can lead to fewer votes for them and a win by the third party.

Modelers face a constant tension over how complex to make formal models. The more general the assumptions made, the more realistic the model can become *and* the more difficult to solve. Fortunately, significant advances in computer technology have helped a good deal in the difficulties of solution; however, general models have other costs as well. Typically, the more general the assumptions of a model, the less clear its predictions. For example, Calvert (1985) relaxes two assumptions – of candidate motivation and candidate knowledge of voter ideal points – and finds that, in this case, it is possible that candidates diverge in policy positions, which is *not* a result of relaxing either assumption alone. Suppose this Calvert model were to incorporate entry by a third candidate, as in Palfrey's work. In such a hybrid model it would be even more difficult to determine what could be causing policy divergence of the two major candidates. Is it the change in candidate motivations or the anticipated entry of a third candidate? How relevant is uncertainty in this case? The implications for the empirical world and what it means to evaluate such a complex model become less clear. Models with stark and simple (yet false) assumptions thus have some attractive features for modelers. Such models are easier to solve, and they can make clearer and more precise predictions.[6]

2.2.5   *Nonformal versus Formal Models*

I have emphasized that the formal model of Banks and Kiewiet (1989) is based on a number of restrictive assumptions. One source of puzzlement among formal modelers is the belief by some in political science that non-formal models make less restrictive assumptions than formal models and that, because of this, nonformal models have advantages over formal models in empirical study. Imprecision is argued to have an advantage over precision because ambiguity is assumed to be more general and flexible than exactness. This is often an unstated assumption when political scientists evaluate the usefulness of formal models in empirical analysis. Consider the following discussion of King and colleagues on the role of formal models in political science.

Formality does help us reason more clearly, and it certainly ensures that our ideas are internally consistent, but it does not resolve issues of empirical evaluation of social science theories. An assumption in a formal model in the social sciences is generally a convenience for mathematical simplicity or for ensuring that an equilibrium can be found. ... Indeed, some formal theories make predictions that depend on assumptions that are vastly oversimplified, and these theories are sometimes not of much empirical value. They are only more precise in the abstract than are informal social science theories: they do not make more specific predictions about the real world, since the conditions they specify do not correspond, even approximately, to actual conditions. (1994, p 106)

The point of this discussion is that some formal models – such as Arrow's (im)possibility theorem – are not directly applicable to the real world but rather serve as foundational pure theory and thus should not be interpreted as a statement by the authors that nonformal theorizing is preferred in all cases. Moreover, King and colleagues use formal models to illustrate points in their work. However, their remarks do express the viewpoint of some

---

[6] This discussion has highlighted the fact that assumptions are often false by necessity. In empirical evaluation of the derived predictions of formal models it is sometimes desirable to control for model assumptions that likely are false, in particular the ceteris paribus assumption. I will further discuss the merits and demerits of control in Chapter 4. Along with the empirical study of predictions, empirically evaluating assumptions is also relevant and important. Empirical analysis of assumptions can lead researchers to better theory and understanding of how well a model can yield useful predictions of the real world. I will show how this can be true in Chapter 4.

political scientists concerning formal versus nonformal models in empirical applications.

This reasoning can be confusing to political scientists who work with formal models. That is, many formal modelers take pride in incorporating key features of the environment in their work and attempt to generate falsifiable predictions. Why is there a presumption that nonformal models are better for empirical analysis? The confusion stems from differences in views on nonformal modeling. Because formal modelers and nonformal modelers look at nonformal models differently, there is a misunderstanding over which is "better." There are two ways to look at nonformal models: as unexpressed formal models or as loose frameworks for empirical analysis. I next examine both views and the implications of each.

Unexpressed Formal Models. The way most formal modelers approach a nonformal model is to presume that the nonformal model is just a formal model that is not explicitly presented. As Arrow suggests, the argument is that "There is really an identified model in the minds of the investigators, which, however, has not been expressed formally because of the limitations of mathematics or of language in general" (1968, p. 667). Some political scientists who are nonformal modelers also seem to have this view. They approach formal models as follows: a formal model can be devised to show any result; hence a prediction that follows from a formal model tells us little because it is always possible to devise another formal model that makes a contrary prediction. Thus the formal model is not necessary – we can simply assume that one exists. This is the implicit view of a social scientist who argues that he could always "put" a formal model in his research without affecting the research or analysis.

From the perspective that nonformal models are just unexpressed formal models, the criticism that formal models are less empirically useful strikes the formal modeler as strange. First, unstated assumptions in nonformal models *cannot* be empirically evaluated as the assumptions of formal models can be. Although many of the assumptions of formal models are extremely difficult to verify empirically or are known to be false, stating them explicitly at least allows for the possibility of empirical analysis. Unstated assumptions are unknowns that cannot be evaluated, empirically or otherwise. Second, when predictions of formal models are empirically studied, researchers can gain information on the reasonableness of explicitly stated assumptions (indirect evaluation); this is not possible when evaluating predictions of nonformal models based on unstated assumptions. Third, researchers who empirically estimate a formal model that embodies an explicit dynamic process gain more information about reality than what is possible from empirically evaluating a nonformal model that offers predictions about outcomes only, with no predicted dynamic structure. Formal models are therefore *more* empirically useful than nonformal models that are merely viewed as unexpressed formal models.

Loose Frameworks for Empirical Research. There is an alternative perspective on nonformal models that may explain why some political scientists believe nonformal models to be more serviceable for empirical testing than formal models. In this perspective, nonformal models are imprecise because there does *not* exist a particular underlying unstated model in the investigator's mind. How then does nonformal modeling work? Nonformal modelers have some ideas about expected empirical relationships. These ideas may come from previous empirical research, introspection, or theoretical arguments in other areas. The researcher believes her ideas could be based on many different possible assumptions. By not specifying which underlying assumptions are thought to be relevant, the researcher considers herself indifferent with regard to the assumptions. Empirically examining nonformally derived ideas then involves choosing data the researcher believes are relevant and using sophisticated statistical techniques that are as "assumption-free" as possible to analyze the data.

This perspective regards models as frameworks whose purpose is to allow data gradually to reveal themselves to the researcher. The deliberate avoidance of formal modeling implies the researcher believes that the more imprecise the framework, the more likely that careful statistical analysis will convey the underlying structure of the real world. Imprecision is here considered a virtue because it appears to put fewer a priori restrictions on the data and thereby on the underlying real world the researcher wishes to discover. In this view, starting with a formal model with explicit assumptions about reality makes it harder for the data to "speak" for itself. Obviously, this perspective on the role of models and assumptions takes an inductive approach to theory, whereas the approach taken by formal modelers is deductive.

I believe that most formal modelers view nonformal models as coming from the first view and that most nonformal modelers view nonformal models as coming from the second. Thus, while formal modelers see obvious advantages to using a formal model for empirical research, nonformal modelers see obvious advantages to working without a theoretical construct. Formal modelers view empirical work based on nonformal modeling as atheoretical, whereas nonformal modelers see formal models as a limited and restrictive base on which to place empirical research.

Resolving the Conflict in Perspectives. Is it possible to reconcile these two positions? The inductive view that nonformal models are better than formal models relies on strong beliefs about the ability of researchers to measure the right data about the real world precisely and neutrally. It relies on strong faith in a researcher's competence to use statistical methods to analyze data objectively and with little error. But data analysis makes all sorts of usually tacit assumptions, and researchers are increasingly reaching the limits of their abilities to loosen these. This is the point made by Bartels and Brady (1993), as quoted in Chapter 1.

Although there is certainly a place for data analysis based on nonformal theorizing, ultimately researchers must begin to formally and explicitly explore the deductive logic of the evidence that arises. Empirical analysis that never builds toward an explicit set of assumptions and predictions about the real world is no better than pure description, just as formal modeling that never leads to empirical exploration is no better than a mathematical exercise (I discuss pure theory in more detail shortly). Whereas both deductive and inductive modeling play roles in increasing our understanding of social situations, neither alone is sufficient. Almost any research design or methods book used in political science would argue that researchers need *both* inductive and deductive research. The suggestion is that nonformal analysis will lead to an improved understanding of reality and then be used to construct more precise theory, which itself will be tested further. Eventually this process will lead to a better understanding of the underlying DGP (although that understanding may never be perfect).

Nonformal modeling has an important place in political science. Nonformal models can yield empirical evidence for assumptions and help researchers gain insight into potential relationships worthy of further investigation using formal models. As the discussion of the process of model building and the choosing of assumptions emphasizes, descriptive observational knowledge of the real world is critical in devising effective formal theory. One reason, I believe, why formal models have not been popular in political science is that some formal modelers begin with an insufficient knowledge of the empirical world of politics. Nonformal modelers are correct in criticizing formal modelers who merely take a model developed to explain competition between firms (in the market for private goods) and assume that the same model describes political competition. Political competition is inherently different; for instance, in political competition preference differences over policy are crucial whereas such differences can safely be ignored in many models of economic competition. There are definite advantages from working with models from other disciplines, but it is vital that the modeler know the situation in an empirical sense and not simply how to model. Empirical research gathered from nonformal modeling is necessary, just as (ultimately) formal theorizing is necessary. Thus, nonformal and formal models can be complementary. I next present an example of how the two approaches to modeling can work together.

An Example: Duverger's Law.   An excellent case of formal and nonformal models allowing us to gain complementary insights that can be combined into an improved explanation of political behavior is offered by the comparative study of electoral systems. As Cox (1997) points out, two literatures have developed in this area, one formal and one nonformal. On the nonformal side is the famous study of Duverger (1953), who argued that in simple "plurality rule" electoral systems (winner-take-all elections) voters vote strategically (i.e., sometimes voting for a party that is not their first preference in order to achieve a better electoral outcome); this results in two-party systems. On the other hand, voters do not vote strategically in proportional representation or "majority required" voting systems, which yields a multiple party system.[7] Subsequent work by Leys (1959) and Sartori (1976) argued that strategic voting does take place in voting systems that are more complex than simple plurality rule, but that there is a difference in the ability of strategic voting to reduce the number of electorally successful parties. Following this research, further empirical work has examined the effects of electoral system differences on the number of parties and voting behavior; see Taagepera and Shugart (1989) and Lijphart (1994). This empirical research is not atheoretical; however, the underlying model that is being tested is not explicitly developed as in a formal model.

---

[7] Majority-required voting systems are those that require a party or candidate to receive a certain percentage of the vote (usually 50%), not a mere plurality, in order to win. If no candidate receives at least that percentage then a second election, or *runoff*, is held between the two who received the most votes.

On the formal side, a related question has also led to significant research. Arrow's theorem considers the possibility that social choice systems can lead to an aggregate outcome when the true preferences of voters are known. To what extent we expect voters to reveal their preferences sincerely is thus relevant. Gibbard (1973) and Satterthwaite (1975) show that, in almost any voting system, there are incentives to vote strategically. A large body of formal theory has examined (a) the extent to which simple plurality rule (with strategic voting) can lead to a two-party system and (b) the extent of strategic voting in proportional representation and majority-required elections; see Cox (1997) for a review.

Cox notes that the nonformal, largely empirical literature and the formal, mainly theoretical literature developed almost parallel to each other. He presents an interesting comparison of the merits of the two approaches.

If one compares the Gibbard–Satterthwaite theorem to the Leys–Sartori conjecture, the theorem wins hands down in terms of rigor and precision. But it is not as useful to political scientists as it might be, because its conclusion is politically ambiguous. The theorem merely alerts one to the possibility that there may be strategic voting under any democratic electoral system, while saying nothing about either the political consequences of that strategic voting, or about how much strategic voting one should expect. In contrast, the Leys–Sartori conjecture focuses on a particular kind of politically relevant strategic voting – the kind that acts to reduce the vote-weighted number of parties – and says something specific about which systems will have a lot and which a little. This greater relevance presumably explains why political scientists who study electoral systems are more likely to use Sartori's distinction between strong and weak systems than they are to cite the Gibbard–Satterthwaite theorem. (1997, pp. 11–12)

Cox's goal is to combine these two approaches: to develop applied formal models that address the issues that concern political scientists and to test his predictions empirically. One may ask how this work improves on what is already known from existing empirical studies. Cox argues that elections are often a type of game in which groups of voters must coordinate strategies to achieve outcomes, and he proposes a set of assumptions that can lead to the outcomes conjectured by the nonformal modelers. However, this cannot be the end of the research enterprise, as Cox knows; there is more to theorizing than simply explaining known results. In addition, Cox tests his formally derived conclusions against further empirical evidence, and he builds on both formal and nonformal traditions in comparative electoral systems to present new theory *and* new empirical research.

This example demonstrates the value of both nonformal and formal modeling for increasing our understanding of politics. Ultimately, we wish to work with theory that is as well developed as a formal model, but empirical research that is based on nonformal models is still essential. Even so, the presumption that nonformal modeling is always an equal (or sometimes better) basis for empirical analysis than formal modeling is wrong. Formal models can be superior when conducting empirical research, particularly when addressing questions of concern to scholars in the discipline. Nevertheless, nonformal modeling remains more attractive to political scientists as a basis for empirical research. I suspect this may be due in part to a lack of knowledge of the power of formal models in guiding empirical work, a shortfall this book hopes to alleviate. Chapter 8 discusses how researchers can empirically compare formal and nonformal models.

2.2.6   *Applied Formal Models versus Pure Theory*

In Chapter 1 I note that sometimes a researcher may devise or work with a model that is not intended as a literal description of anything in the real world (or only in a very generic sense). Theorists usually call these types of models "pure theory"; models designed to be more directly and empirically applicable to the real world are called "applied theory." Pure theory models may describe a reality that is unlikely or almost impossible to imagine. Early spatial voting models (e.g., those of Gibbard and Satterthwaite cited previously) are good examples of pure theory in political science: individuals are characterized only by a set of preferences over alternatives – given only by numbers that do not represent any real political issue – and the voting choice is free of agendas or other institutional constraints.

As Cox's work shows, the exercise of pure theory modeling plays a significant role in building applied theory. For another example, consider a more recent applied model, the Baron–Ferejohn legislative bargaining model. This model has been used to explain the effects of legislative voting rules (Baron and Ferejohn 1989a), committee power (1989b), pork-barrel programs (Baron 1991a), government formation (Baron 1989, 1991b; Baron and Ferejohn 1989a), multiparty elections (Austen-Smith and Banks 1988; Baron 1991b; Chari, Jones, and Marimon 1998), and interchamber bargaining (Diermeier and Myerson 1994).

The Baron–Ferejohn model is based on earlier bargaining models of Stahl (1972), Krelle (1976), and Rubinstein (1982). These early models describe an exact bargaining process that one is unlikely to observe in any real-world context. The typical model assumes that there are two players (call them players 1 and 2) who must reach agreement over an outcome within a given set of outcomes; if they do not reach agreement then they will receive some fixed known outcome. Generally the two players are bargaining over how to divide a pie (representing a fixed sum of money) between themselves. If they cannot agree, then neither player will receive any of the pie. The players bargain by making alternating offers over time. Player 1 first makes an offer on how to divide the pie. Then player 2 chooses whether to reject or accept the offer. If player 2 rejects, then player 2 makes a counterproposal, which player 1 can accept or reject. If player 1 rejects then he can make yet another proposal for player 2 to consider. The game continues until one of the offers is accepted. There is no limit in the game to the number of offer periods; that is, the game has what is called an "infinite horizon" and could conceivably go on forever if offers are continually rejected. (See Osborne and Rubinstein 1994 for more detail.)

The Rubinstein bargaining model was never intended to be used in a *direct* empirical study of bargaining in a specific real-world case (or set of cases), and it is pointless to think of empirically estimating or evaluating that model with naturally occurring data. This particular model can be empirically evaluated using laboratory experiments if we relax the assumption of an infinite time horizon.[8] Such an analysis can provide the theorist with important data on the extent to which, in the stylized bargaining environment, individuals behave as predicted by the theory. This is one reason why experimental analysis has begun to play such a significant role in the development of formal theory; in some cases it provides the only empirical check on such theory.[9] But not all purely theoretical models are amenable to laboratory study without significant changes to the original theory.

Nevertheless, the Rubinstein bargaining model does have empirical relevance to the real world when it is adapted as an "applied" model. The Baron–Ferejohn model, for example, takes the pure Rubinstein alternating bargaining model and applies it to the bargaining process that can occur in legislatures by extending the number of actors and incorporating a voting rule to determine when a proposal is accepted. Other variants of the model add more specific empirical relevance to the real-world case(s) that the theorist wishes to consider. For example, Austen-Smith and Banks (1988) add elections to consider the interaction between electoral and legislative outcomes.

---

[8] See Chapter 7's review of Boylan et al. (1991) for a discussion of how to design an experiment evaluating a formal model with an infinite time horizon.

[9] There is actually a large literature on experimental analysis of these types of alternating bargaining models and on simpler versions such as the ultimatum game; see Roth (1995) for a review of the literature.

These applied formal models can be more directly used in the empirical study of naturally occurring data. Without the initial purely theoretical study of bargaining by Rubinstein and others, this later applied theoretical work would not have been possible. Similarly, applied theoretical models (like Banks and Kiewiet's) are possible only because of early purely theoretical work on choices in stylized games that involve risky situations.

2.2.7   *Solving a Formal Model*

After the situation is transformed into a formal set of assumptions expressed in abstract terms, the system is then studied or "solved" for predictions, which are presented as theorems, propositions, or just "results." Solving a model means exploring the implications of the set of assumptions. Solution concepts typically depend on the formulation of the model. Some types of solutions and predictions that come from formal models are discussed in later chapters. The solutions of formal models are typically stated as propositions or theorems about the variables in the models. As noted in Chapter 1, working through the formal model often involves mind-experiments that are quite divorced from the reality that was the original impetus for the research. Sometimes the way to see how to solve a model is to attempt to find counter-examples, even if such examples are highly unlikely ever to occur.

How do Banks and Kiewiet solve their model? First of all, the model needs some additional assumptions about the probabilities that the candidates can win the election. Banks and Kiewiet assume that the probability of winning the general election is a function of challenger quality (higher challenger quality increases the probability that a challenger wins) and a number of incumbent-specific variables as well as a random variable. Thus they can solve for the plurality of votes that a challenger can expect to receive as a function of these variables. Because the plurality is partly a function of the random variable, they can then derive a continuous function that represents the probability of winning the general election for a given challenger. They assume that only one challenger can face an incumbent in a primary. They then derive a function for the probability that C_2 wins a primary contest with C_1 as the other candidate (note that the probability that C_1 wins is just 1 minus the probability that C_2 wins).

Recall that the point of Banks and Kiewiet's formal model is to understand why, when an incumbent is running for re-election, often only a low-quality challenger enters although the probability of success is exceedingly low.

Thus, the researchers wish to determine under what conditions their derived "probability of winning" functions lead to that specific outcome. Banks and Kiewiet's (1989) model is a game theoretic one, in which it is assumed that the outcome for each player is a function of (i) the choices made by that player and (ii) the choices made by the other players. We call this situation "strategic." A solution concept often used in game theory is the idea of Nash equilibrium. Intuitively, in a Nash equilibrium each player's strategy or choice is optimal given the choice or strategy of the other player(s).[10]

Banks and Kiewiet's objective is to discover whether a Nash equilibrium exists in which a low-quality challenger, maximizing his probability of winning, enters a race against an incumbent while a high-quality challenger, maximizing her probability of winning, does not. They show that this is indeed possible. Using figures (based on Congressional election data) from Gary Jacobson on actual probabilities of winning, Banks and Kiewiet demonstrate that these equilibria do exist for real-world cases. They explain the result intuitively as follows:

the strong challenger has a dominant strategy: wait to run for the open seat. Regardless of what the weak challenger does, the strong challenger's probability of getting elected is higher than if he or she were to run now. Because of the slim chance of winning a contested primary, the weak challenger's best strategy is to run whenever the strong challenger is not running and thus sail through the primary unopposed. The weak challenger would of course prefer the strong challenger to run now against the incumbent, while he or she waited to run for the open seat. The young lawyer knows, however, that the strong challenger will wait for the open seat regardless of what he or she does. (1989, p. 1007)

2.2.8   *Numerical versus Analytical Solutions*

Banks and Kiewiet are able to solve their model analytically and thus show under what conditions an equilibrium or solution exists. In my discussion of model building I noted that there is often a trade-off between designing a model that (a) is complex enough to represent reality adequately for the research question at hand, yet (b) is also solvable and yields clear and concise insights. The greater the number of variables included in a model and the more general the assumptions about choices and strategies of actors

---

[10] See Morrow (1994) for a discussion of Nash equilibria and game theory as applied to political science. Gates and Humes (1997) also present examples of how to apply game theory to particular political science situations, using more detail than my presentation here of the Banks and Kiewiet example. Game theoretic models are compared with other modeling techniques in Chapter 3.

in the model, the more difficult the model can be to solve. That is, solving formal models can involve complex mathematics, and in some cases solutions require intricate and challenging calculations that may even be theoretically impossible. Technological advances have helped significantly in our ability to solve complicated mathematical models and allow us to achieve a greater level of complexity and precise solutions. For instance, Richard McKelvey (at the California Institute of Technology) and Andrew McLennan (at the University of Minnesota) have devised a computer software program, GAMBIT, for solving games. Other researchers have found software programs such as Mathematica and Maple quite useful in solving formal models. When researchers solve a model using mathematics, the solution is said to be *analytical* in that we have results that hold for all possible values of variables in the model.

Computational Models. Sometimes a researcher cannot (or chooses not to) solve a formal model analytically for all possible values of parameters in the model and instead uses computers to derive numerical solutions for a set of parameters via simulations. A formal model solved in this way is called a *computational* model. In some cases it is mathematically impossible to solve the model in terms of all possible values of variables and parameters. There have been significant advances in the technological capacity to solve models analytically, but limits to that capacity still remain. Thus, a researcher can sometimes solve a model only by *specifying* values for the parameters and then deriving specific solutions for the numerical values in the simulations – solutions to the model for the particular cases of the parameter values specified.

When it is unclear whether a model is solvable analytically, researchers may choose to solve it numerically using simulations. Some models that are used in political science may have analytical solutions that are unknown; in such cases researchers use computer simulations to provide predictions and suggestions about the existence and location of the analytical solutions. The simulations provide numerical solutions given the assumptions used to design the simulations. That is, in simulations the researchers set parameter values and solve for outcomes or predictions given these assumed values. By running a large number of cases with variations in the assumed values of the parameters, the computational model can provide a set of numerical solutions, which are solutions for the given values of the parameters as well as special cases of the analytical solution of the formal model. We are thus solving the model for specific cases rather than providing a general analytical solution. Computational models have also been used in political science as a basis for empirical analysis. For example, Kollman, Miller, and Page (1998) consider how their model of adaptive parties measures against empirical realities, and Kadera (forthcoming) analyzes how simulations of her differential equation model of power relationships fit real-world data.

The value of models that have not been solved analytically is a debated issue among formal theorists. Such models do not generate precise analytical predictions and so are seen by some as much less useful owing to this limitation. That is, the predictions of numerical solutions are not general solutions for all cases but are only for the cases simulated. Thus, the formal model has not been solved for general predictions for all possible cases. Some make a distinction between computational models that can be solved analytically and those that cannot. These researchers contend that the first focus should be on solving a model analytically, and that only when this has been conclusively shown to be impossible should we use computational models. Others argue that working with analytically unsolved theory is constructive in understanding the real world, since the models can more closely approximate real-world complexity. That is, if researchers limit themselves to models that can be solved analytically, they will have to ignore and simplify important details in assumptions. Models that can only be solved using computational methods are believed by some to have a wider range of applicability and to more closely mirror the real world. These researchers therefore believe that such numerically derived predictions are more realistic and useful than the analytical solutions of simpler models.

I believe (a) that it is a mistake to limit our theorizing and empirical study to analytically solvable models and (b) that computational models can be a useful complement to analytically solved models. For one thing, it is sometimes difficult to determine in advance whether a model truly is analytically solvable until an attempt is made. Simulations of models that are not evidently solvable can be useful in achieving eventual analytical solutions. For another, working with an analytically unsolvable model can provide insight into the real world that is unattainable if research is restricted only to models with analytical solutions. The numerical solutions are "true" solutions for the numerical values of the parameters and/or initial conditions in the models. Empirical analyses of the predictions derived from simulations are serviceable in helping work toward an increased understanding of the real world when the results are used as feedback for subsequent theoretical and empirical study, much as the empirical analysis based on nonformal theorizing can have considerable value for research that follows.

The difficulty in empirical work based on an analytically unsolvable model lies in determining which complexities are important and how the model's "predictions" are direct functions of all its assumptions. When analytical solutions are not possible, the ability to make these determinations depends on the results from simulation designs and researchers' own conjectures in assigning numerical values in the simulations. The researcher can work with a more complex model whose assumptions might better represent the real world, but he introduces other restrictive assumptions when solving the model by numerics rather than analytics. Important theoretical predictions may be ignored or could turn out to be false in important cases that would be captured if the model were solved analytically because of the restrictions used in deriving the numerical solutions. Empirical work based on analytically unsolved models should be carefully evaluated as a consequence, and the assumptions used to derive numerical solutions should be explicitly considered in terms of their relationship to reality – just as the assumptions used in an analytically solved model should be evaluated cautiously.

Simulations and Analytically Solved Models. The foregoing discussion suggests that work with computational models and simulations is more of a complement than a substitute for empirical analysis based on analytically solved models, yet simulations and work with computational models do play important roles in empirical understanding even when researchers use analytically solved models. First, as noted previously, simulations can be useful in solving a formal model. Conducting a simulation can often lead a theorist to an analytical solution. Second, simulations can serve as demonstrations of how a formal model works. For example, in their model of legislative coalitions, Groseclose and Snyder (1996) use a simulation to demonstrate how coalition size varies with the reservation values of the legislators. Such a simulation becomes a useful presentation device, much as researchers use graphs and figures to illustrate results from formal models. Third, simulations can be used to consider the anticipated effects of policy changes. Gilmour and Rothstein (1994), for instance, use simulations of a formal model to estimate the effect of term limits on Congressional party balance. Cameron, Epstein, and O'Halloran (1996) similarly use simulations to investigate the effects of redistricting plans on minority representation.

Finally, simulations can be coupled with experimental work as in Axelrod's (1984) famous tournament over strategies in prisoner's dilemma games, which involved both an experiment and a simulation. That is, he asked a number of noted researchers to submit strategies for a two-person repeated prisoner's dilemma game (this game is discussed in greater detail in Chapter 6) and then used simulations to test which strategy survived against randomly generated choices of the other player in the game. He found that cooperative strategies were much more likely to survive than noncooperative ones. There are other cases where part of an experimental design is a simulation; for example, in evaluating Calvert's (1985) model of candidate location decisions, I simulate voter decisions while using real subjects as "candidates" (Morton 1993). I find that, as Calvert predicts, subjects will diverge in their choices when their payments are tied to their location choices in a two-candidate location game in which subjects do not know the ideal point of the electorate's median voter.

Simulating some of the decisions or actors in an experiment can allow a researcher to lessen the cost of the experiment. Artificial actors can also increase a researcher's control in the experimental design, resulting in a more direct test of the predictions of the model about the choices of the actors who are not artificial – in this case, the candidates. In these experiments the subjects were told that the voters were artificial actors simulated by a computer, but this procedure is not always followed. In some experiments, such as Bohm's (1972) research on public goods provision, subjects were told that there was a large group of other subjects making contribution decisions when this was not the case (public good games are discussed in more detail in Chapter 6). Deception such as Bohm's involves a loss of control over the experiment and can be problematic for future experiments when subjects as a population have reason to discount the truth of instructions and experimental setups in general. Thus, simulations can be useful for experimental study but must be carefully incorporated. I believe that deception should be avoided as much as possible.

2.2.9   *Empirical Analysis of Applied Formal Models*

Relationship to the Formal Model.   Once the results of an applied formal model are derived, either by analytically or numerically solving the model, researchers then empirically evaluate the model's predictions against the outcomes observed in the real world (this process is examined in Chapters 6 and 7). Again, the researcher who conducts the empirical analysis of the model may or may not be the same researcher who devised the model. A researcher uses an empirical or statistical model to conduct the empirical analysis. Under ideal conditions, when the formal model is mathematical, the empirical model estimated is the same as the formal model or is derived from the formal model explicitly. However, this is rarely the case in existing empirical studies of formal models. For instance, Banks and Kiewiet do not provide a set of equations that are an explicit empirical model derived from the mathematical formal model; instead they analyze the predictions of the formal model through a number of empirical estimations or examinations. Thus, their empirical analysis, like almost all empirical analysis of formal models in political science, involves empirically evaluating the predictions of the model and simultaneously a large number of auxiliary assumptions about the random error, the functional form of the empirical estimation, and the inclusion of various control variables outside of the theory. The links (and disconnects) between formal and empirical models are explored in more detail in Chapter 4.

Researchers know that a given formal model is not the only possible one that can be used to represent the real-world situation under study. Hence an empirical model may be devised to compare the predictions of one formal model against alternative models in explaining real-world outcomes (this strategy is addressed in Chapter 8). A researcher may find that empirical results reveal that one formal model is clearly superior to others. However, researchers often find that the outcome of the comparative study is less conclusive and that they should therefore revise a model, incorporating or discarding different aspects (these techniques, too, will be detailed in Chapter 8). Or a researcher may choose to accept a combination of several models as a framework for understanding the real-world questions of interest.

As discussed previously, a researcher may devise an empirical model to evaluate hypotheses or conjectures arising from the stage of nonformal modeling. A researcher may also attempt to evaluate empirically a hypothesis of an unsolved formal model; in this case the model is used as a framework or *heuristic* for empirical study. For example, we might use a game tree or payoff matrix to present the choices faced by challengers in electoral competition without explicitly solving for the choices the model would predict (in equilibrium, given the model's assumptions). As a first step in devising a formal model, this type of research can be useful.

Sometimes researchers take the preliminary exploration as a basis for empirical study, just as they use hypotheses derived from nonformal models in empirical research. But this type of empirical study should not be confused with an empirical evaluation of the unsolved and more general theoretical model. That is, if the formal model is not solved either analytically or numerically, then a researcher has no idea what the predictions of the model are. A researcher whose empirical study is based on an unsolved model makes conjectures about empirical outcomes that are no different from hypotheses based on nonformal modeling. Because the model is unsolved, no amount of estimation can tell us if it's supported by the data. Therefore, empirical analysis of this type should be distinguished from the empirical evaluation of formal models.

Banks and Kiewiet's Empirical Analysis. In order to evaluate their model empirically against real-world data, Banks and Kiewiet restate their results in the form of empirical predictions. They conduct two analyses using simple empirical models. The first analysis focuses on one of the model's premises: that low-quality challengers enter partly because they recognize they are unlikely to win if they wait and face a high-quality challenger in a primary for an open seat. Thus, assessing the truth of this "recognized" likelihood serves to test one of the premises of the model and its results. Banks and Kiewiet examined Congressional nomination contests between 1980 and 1984 to find that weak challengers won only 11.2% of primaries when faced with strong challengers.

The second empirical analysis conducted by Banks and Kiewiet was to evaluate the model's prediction that "weak candidates are less likely to enter primary elections that are also being contested by strong candidates" (1989, p. 1010). They evaluate this prediction by comparing the percentage of elections in which at least one weak challenger is running in primaries with no strong challengers versus primaries with a strong challenger. They also compare the number of weak challengers in primaries with no strong challengers versus primaries with a strong challenger. They further divide their comparisons by party and by whether an incumbent was running or the race was an open seat. All the comparisons (except for the number of weak Republican challengers in open-seat races) support the model's prediction.

It may seem that we evaluate models only to compare their assumptions or predictions with the real world, but much more goes on in the empirical analysis of formal models. That is, although formal models make predictions that researchers wish to compare with the real world, in many cases these models are designed also to enable empirical tests of questions to which the model itself does not give precise answers. For instance, a model may predict that an independent variable will have a negative effect on a given dependent variable, but researchers may be uncertain as to the size of this effect. An empirical analysis of the model would (1) tell if the prediction is supported *and* (2) provide new empirical information on the size of the prediction; thus, it can answer a question that the theory poses. Banks and Kiewiet note that their analysis provides new information: in a surprising number (over one third) of open-seat primaries, strong candidates failed to enter. The authors suggest this may be due to a large number of weak challengers or to incumbents that unexpectedly drop out of the race. They also explore the implications of their analysis for the nature of candidates actually elected in Congressional races.

2.2.10 *Further Theoretical and Empirical Study*

Canon's Critique. After the initial empirical study of an applied formal model – whether using an empirical model directly derived from a mathematical model or one devised (as in Banks and Kiewiet) to evaluate predictions or assumptions – the research process typically continues in two ways: refining the theory and expanding the empirical analysis. As I have noted, the Banks and Kiewiet mathematical model is not used to directly derive an empirical or statistical model for estimation and evaluation, as with much of the current empirical analysis of formal models. In Chapter 4, I discuss how their model might be adapted in order to connect more closely the theoretical to the statistical formulation.

The Banks and Kiewiet (1989) model also takes a simple situation that Canon (1993) argues applies in only a small number of actual electoral contests. Canon claims that a more general model with less restrictive assumptions is more empirically relevant than Banks and Kiewiet's model. For example, he reasons that, since Banks and Kiewiet ignore national trends in electoral success, they fail to recognize that the probability of a weak challenger winning the general election might be greater when a strong challenger enters the primary (i.e., when the incumbent is weak due to exogenous national factors) than when a strong challenger does not enter the primary. Canon also contends that if the number of potential weak and strong candidates are increased, the probability assumptions made by Banks and Kiewiet will no longer hold. Canon presents empirical evidence from Congressional electoral outcomes of a larger data set (1972 to 1988), including cases where there is a larger number of candidates. He finds that the probability of a weak challenger winning an open seat when a strong challenger runs is *higher* than the probability of defeating an incumbent without a strong challenger in a race (4.3% versus 1.4%).

Canon proposes that a more general model of weak challenger decisions – with less restrictive assumptions than in Banks and Kiewiet's model – would be more applicable to the research question. Canon does not solve the more general model for precise equilibrium predictions but, as in empirical research based on nonformal models, he uses his conjectures about the predictions as the basis for additional empirical study of weak challenger entry (Canon calls weak challengers "amateurs"). That is, he conjectures that amateurs are of two types, experience seeking (Maisel-like) and ambitious (strategic Banks–Kiewiet-like), and that experience-seeking amateurs will enter different sorts of Congressional races than ambitious amateurs. He hypothesizes that experience-seeking amateurs will enter races that strong challengers do not enter whereas ambitious amateurs will enter races that strong challengers have also entered (using the strong challenger entry as a signal of incumbent weakness). In his empirical analysis, Canon defines ambitious amateurs as "those who have not previously held office but (1) enter an election after another candidate is already running; (2) received at least 40% of the vote in a previous congressional race; or (3) are celebrities. . . . An experience-seeking amateur is the first amateur who enters a primary that is not contested by an experienced candidate (and also does not meet the second and third conditions)" (1993, pp. 1130–1).

Canon's Results. Canon presents empirical evidence that supports his hypotheses about the predictions of a more comprehensive model. Characteristic of modern political science research, his study uses advanced methodological techniques to statistically estimate an empirical model based on his conjectures. Canon estimates a multivariate logit regression model for the existence of experience-seeking amateurs in Congressional elections, 1972–88. Logit is used since the dependent variable is either 1 for the existence of an experience-seeking amateur in an election and 0 otherwise (see Aldrich and Nelson 1984 or King 1989 for a discussion of logit). He finds that experience-seeking amateurs are less likely to run in races where the incumbent was hurt by redistricting and more likely to run in races where the incumbent received a sizeable electoral victory in the previous election, which he contends suggests nonstrategic behavior on the part of these amateurs. Canon uses the generalized "event count" model (developed by King 1989) for the existence of ambitious amateurs because the distribution of the dependent variable in this case (number of ambitious amateurs) is highly skewed. He chooses this method over alternative estimation procedures because it allows for the number of ambitious amateurs to be correlated. Canon concludes: "The contrast between ambitious and experience-seeking amateurs is stark. Ambitious amateurs are more likely to run when incumbents are more vulnerable (as indicated by scandal, a strong challenge in the primary, or relatively low vote in the previous election), or when the challenger's party's normal vote is high" (1993, pp. 1134–5). As with other empirical analysis, his estimation is a simultaneous test of his conjectures and his assumptions about the data and the error terms that arise when using either the multivariate logit model or the event count model.

Canon's research is illuminating, and it demonstrates that the entry decisions of weak challengers are more complex than the simple first formal model proposed by Banks and Kiewiet. Solving a formal model that incorporates the less restrictive assumptions advocated by Canon might be the next step in this research: discovering if the conjectures he makes about the model's predictions are correct. Of course, the theoretical expansion should be accompanied by a thorough empirical evaluation of the predictions of the more general formal model. Canon's empirical analysis ignores the interdependency of candidate decisions in a game theoretic model by using single-equation estimations. In Chapter 4, I present an example of how estimating equations might be derived from a more general model.

It is important to recognize that Banks and Kiewiet's model is an attempt to set up the simplest interesting model capable of examining the research question that arose from observations. It is often easier to generalize to a more complicated model once the basic points of the simple model are grasped than to wade through the data with a very general model at the beginning. Banks and Kiewiet's model and empirical study were thus the first steps toward reaching more comprehensive theoretical and empirical studies.

2.2.11   *Models and the Scientific Process: A Summary*

Figure 2.1 presents an idealized (and oversimplified) view of the scientific process. The depiction is stylized and ignores the fact that some theoretical structures may never be empirically evaluated or devised for empirical study. Also, many researchers doubt whether it is possible to actually devise

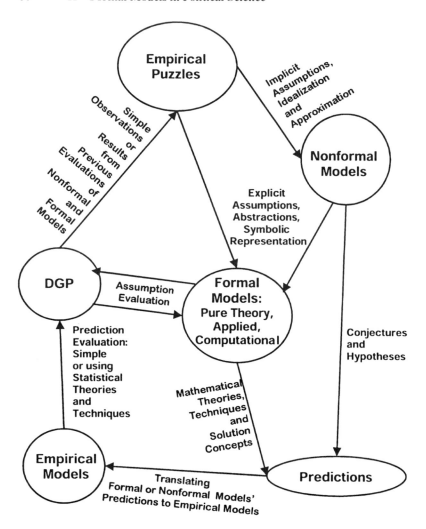

Figure 2.1. Idealized view of scientific process.

a formal model that comes close to matching the DGP. Moreover, we often continue to accept theories that are rejected by empirical work or to reject theories that are supported.

This perspective of the scientific process helps to illuminate the different ways that the term "model" is used. These can be summarized as follows.

Nonformal Model – a set of verbal statements about the real world. These statements involve idealization, identification, and approximation, but are given in terms of real observables rather than symbols or abstracts. The statements may be presented in a diagram or graph. Sometimes these statements are directly tested as hypotheses about the real world.

Formal Model – a set of precise abstract assumptions or axioms about the real world presented in symbolic terms that are solved to derive predictions about the real world.

- *Mathematical model* – a formal model, presented in mathematical symbolic representation, that is solved using mathematical theories and techniques.
- *Computational model* – a formal model presented in computer languages and solved numerically using computer simulations for given numerical values of parameters. The solutions are then used to derive predictions based on the assumed values of the parameters as well as the other assumptions in the formal model. The predictions can also be used as a basis for empirical evaluation.
- *Pure theory* – a formal model that is designed not to be empirically estimated using real-world data but rather to represent a highly stylized version of the real world. Sometimes these models can be modified and empirically evaluated using controlled laboratory experiments, and often they are the basis for applied formal models.
- *Applied formal model* – a formal model that is designed (a) to provide predictions that can be used as a basis for hypotheses about the real world or (b) to be directly evaluated empirically.

Empirical or Statistical Model – a set of equations used for (a) empirical estimation of an applied formal model's parameters or (b) to evaluate a hypothesis or set of hypotheses about the real world derived from either a formal or nonformal model.

Clearly, the goal of model building in the social sciences is to eventually arrive at the DGP. But even the conception of the DGP, or "reality," involves abstractions. Social scientists typically leave out many aspects (e.g., cosmology, chemistry, biology) as irrelevant to their purposes. These are judgments or prior assumptions that are never likely to be tested. Some social scientists believe that the world is too complex to be captured in one all-encompassing model, even when limited to explaining issues relevant to social science. From this perspective, social scientists aim to discover the nature of the real social science world, which may never actually be expressed as a complete comprehensive model that explains all of that reality. The best social scientists might do, in the opinion of these researchers, is to devise a "toolkit" of a set of models that can be used to understand specific situations in the real social science world.

My view is that the relevant distinction is between long- and short-run achievements. In the short run, the toolkit approach seems to be how most political scientists conduct research and has increased our understanding of the real world. But in the long run, as researchers add to the toolkit or figure out ways to advance and combine features of existing models (as the electric drill with detachable bits allowed for old hand-powered drills and screwdrivers to be combined), research does move toward more comprehensive general models.

The connections between formal models and empirical models is an important subject, one that merits exploration beyond that just provided – particularly in a book about the empirical analysis of formal models. Chapter 4 discusses these links more extensively and other general issues in the empirical evaluation of formal models. First, though, I investigate more thoroughly the use of mathematics in formal models.

2.3   Mathematics in Formal Models

Once the assumptions of a formal model have been explicitly stated, the implications of these assumptions are explored using deductive reasoning. Many errors can be made in this stage if formal models have inconsistent assumptions or are used to derive fallacious results (see Phelan and Reynolds 1996 for a nice nontechnical discussion of the problems of deduction). It is partly because of the tendency to make these errors that formal modelers find mathematics an attractive vehicle in modeling. Why is that so? The language of mathematics presents an easy way to be precise about assumptions and, most notably, to derive the results. It is because mathematics makes modeling less difficult that formal theorists are drawn to it. It is paradoxical that a tool that nonformal modelers see as complicating actually has the opposite effect. A more basic reason for using mathematics in formal models is that mathematics is the only language available for keeping track of simultaneous and multicausal interactions among several entities. Words can neither describe these sorts of relationships completely nor be used to solve for the consequences.

2.3.1   *Income and Voting*

Two Nonformal Models. Consider the following two nonformal models about the relationship between income and voting.

1. When a voter's income increases it becomes more costly for him to take time away from work to acquire information about candidates and to vote. Because his opportunity cost of voting is high, he will vote less frequently as his income rises.
2. A major function of our government is to redistribute income across voters, imposing burdens on high-income taxpayers and conferring benefits on low-income taxpayers. The party in control of the government determines the extent of redistribution, and the parties differ in the amount of redistribution they propose. Thus the "stakes" that a voter has in an election depend on whether her income is high or low. That is, if a voter has a low income then the difference between the parties for that voter is higher than for a voter with a more average level of income. And if a voter has a high income then the difference between the parties for that voter is higher than for a voter with a more average level of income. An increase in income for high-income voters can make their stakes higher and the outcome of the election more important, whereas an increase in income for low-income voters can make their stakes lower and the outcome of the election less important. Because the gains from voting can be higher or lower with increases in income, it is unclear whether increases in income cause voters to vote less or more frequently.

These two nonformal models appear to be inconsistent. Acceptance of both arguments seems to lead to very unclear predictions of the relationship between income and voting. The first one makes a precise prediction, increases in income cause voters to vote less, while the second seems to imply that the effect of more income on voting depends on one's income. One reaction to these inconsistent predictions is to conduct an empirical analysis and see which nonformal model better explains the observed relationship between income and voting. Another alternative would be to attempt to reconcile the two verbal arguments in a consistent way and to make precise predictions about the relationship between income and voting.[11]

A Formal Model. The problem can be solved by considering how these two arguments can be combined with explicit assumptions in a formal model of voter turnout. By using mathematics, precise predictions about the relationship between income and turnout can be derived. First consider how to make these arguments part of a formal model of turnout. I will construct a simple formal model based on the one presented in Filer, Kenny, and Morton (1993). In this model I make the following assumptions.

1. The costs of voting are positively related to the income level of an individual.
2. The benefits of voting are a function of the position of a voter in the distribution of income in the population: If a voter's income is below the median income in the population then the benefits from voting decrease with a rise in the voter's position on the *distribution* of income; if a voter's income is above the median income then the benefits from voting increase with a rise in the voter's position on the distribution of income.
3. Voters vote if the benefits from voting are greater than or equal to the costs of voting.
4. All other factors that affect the costs and benefits of voting are assumed to be constant.

Notice that these assumptions illustrate a number of the features of formal models discussed previously. Most significantly, the model makes many false or unverified assumptions. First, it overlooks the fact that the benefits from voting may also be a function of the probability that an individual's vote is decisive; the well-known paradox of not voting is ignored in the framework. That is, since the probability that any one vote will decide the outcome of an election is small, the expected benefits from voting for

[11] The interested reader may wish to compare this section with the discussion in Green and Shapiro (1994, pp. 65–6). They present these arguments as independent models of the relationship between income and voting and consider these arguments to be inconsistent.

investment reasons are also likely to be negligible, regardless of income.[12] The model assumes also that the benefits and costs of voting are separable, which may not be true. Finally, the last assumption is the ceteris paribus one: other factors that could affect voting are unchanging.

Stating the two arguments as part of the assumptions in a formal model allows a partial reconciliation of the inconsistency. That is, the effect of a change in income on whether a voter will vote will depend upon (a) the change in the costs and benefits and (b) which is greater for the individual, given his or her income and position on the income distribution. However, the model is still in an imprecise form and does not yield clear predictions. What does it mean to say that the costs of voting are positively related? Do they increase at a constant, increasing, or decreasing rate as income increases? Similar questions abound for the relationship between a voter's position on the income distribution and the benefits from voting. Once these two terms are put together, can the model be solved for an income level at which the costs and benefits are equal? Is there only one such income level?

Mathematics in the Model: The Costs of Voting. Mathematics can be used to make the formal model precise and derive specific predictions. Let y_i represent voter i's income and let C_i equal i's cost of voting. The first assumption states that the cost of voting is a function of y_i, which can be mathematically expressed as $C_i = f(y_i)$. The first assumption argues further that C_i is increasing in y, that is, the first derivative of C_i with respect to y is positive: $dC_i(y_i)/dy_i > 0$. This is a general mathematical statement of the assumption. However, in order to solve for an exact solution to our model, I further assume that the $C_i = ky_i$; that is, I assume the cost function to be linear and that the marginal cost of voting is constant and the same across voters, $dC_i(y_i)/dy_i = k$.

The additional specificity will make solution of the model easier but needs to be considered carefully. How might I justify this additional specificity? In particular, I could have assumed that $C_i = ky_i^2$. Then $dC_i(y_i)/dy_i = 2ky_i$. Why would I think that the linear representation is more accurate than the

---

[12] See Riker and Ordeshook (1968). In Filer et al. (1993) the paradox is avoided by assuming that the voters vote as groups of like-minded citizens and that the decision to vote is made at this group level rather than the individual level. Thus the probability of having an impact on the electoral outcome is expected to be significant enough to induce positive turnout.

quadratic? I could argue that the principal costly component of voting is the time spent on voting, which is probably unaffected by a change in income (the position taken in Filer et al. 1993). But this is an unproved assumption that must be evaluated cautiously. I could also make k voter-specific – that is, let $C_i = k_i y_i$, where each voter's marginal cost of voting is different. These are all modeling choices that may or may not affect the outcome. The important point is that by forcing myself to be precise about the relationship mathematically I am also forcing myself to be explicit about the assumptions that I am making.

Mathematics in the Model: The Benefits of Voting. For specifying the second assumption, let B_i represent the expected benefits of voting and let Y represent the total income of all voters, $Y = \sum_{\text{all } i} y_i$. The second assumption is that the benefit of voting is a function of y/Y, which can mathematically be expressed as $B_i = g(y_i/Y)$. But this function is complex: for low incomes, B_i decreases as income increases; for high incomes B_i increases as income increases. That is, the second assumption is that the effects of redistribution are greatest when a voter has a low or high income relative to the overall distribution of income (I am holding total income, Y, constant). So, depending on a voter's income, increases in income can have differing effects on B_i. How can this be formally expressed? First I can let y_m equal the median level of income in the population. I can express the second argument by assuming that

$$\frac{dB_i(y_i/Y)}{d(y_i/Y)} \begin{cases} < 0 & \text{for } y_i < y_m, \\ > 0 & \text{for } y_i > y_m. \end{cases}$$

Again, in order to derive a exact solution I will need to specify a particular benefits function. I could assume that the benefits from voting are a quadratic function of y_i/Y, that is, $B_i = a(y_i/Y - y_m/Y)^2$. Then

$$\frac{dB_i}{d(y_i/Y)} = 2a\left(\frac{y_i}{Y} - \frac{y_m}{Y}\right).$$

Again, the specification used here must be carefully evaluated in terms of the underlying assumptions made about income redistribution by the government. In Filer et al. (1993) the assumed relationship is derived from underlying assumptions about the tax schedule of the government, and the relationship then depends on the extent of the progressiveness of the tax schedule.

Solving the Model. The third assumption is that voters compare the benefits of voting with the costs of voting when they make their voting decisions. Mathematically, this assumption can be stated as follows: voter i votes if $B_i \geq C_i$ but does not vote otherwise. The two functions can be combined (using the linear cost function). For the parameters of the cost and benefit functions chosen, voters with incomes below or equal to y_L/Y and above or equal to y_H/Y are expected to vote because the benefits for them are greater than the costs, whereas voters with incomes between y_L/Y and y_H/Y will abstain since the costs of voting outweigh the benefits for these voters. (Here, of course, the subscripts L and H denote "low" and "high," respectively.) The probability of turnout can be expressed as a function of y_i/Y.

Predictions of the Model. So how then will an increase in income affect the decision to vote? First, if an individual's income increases with a general increase in everyone's income – so that y_i/Y does not change – then only the costs of voting will increase and hence the probability that all individuals will vote decreases. If an individual's income rises relative to Y (i.e., if the individual's position rises on the income distribution) then the answer is more complicated, depending on that individual's income in relation to y_L/Y and y_H/Y. An individual's propensity to vote will increase with an increase in y_i relative to Y if $2a(y_i/Y - y_m/Y) > k$, that is, if the increase in benefits from voting from the increase in income are greater than the increase in costs (holding Y constant). So, for $y_i < k/2a + y_m$, an increase in income decreases the propensity to vote; for $y_i > k/2a + y_m$, an increase in income increases the propensity to vote. This threshold level of income is greater than the median level of income: $k/2a > 0$. Note that, even if we had assumed the cost of voting to be given by a quadratic relationship, the results of the analysis would still be the same. Thus, in some cases the choice of functional form is not crucial, and the linearity assumption is a "harmless" simplification in this context.

The two arguments combined make two precise predictions about the relationship between voting and income: (1) an increase in income accompanied by an equivalent increase in all income will decrease the propensity to vote; (2) an increase in income that raises an individual's position on the overall income distribution will decrease the propensity to vote for individuals below a threshold income level but will increase the propensity to vote for individuals above the threshold level. Thus, the two arguments in the nonformal model are *not* inconsistent.

Mathematics and the Prediction. The mathematical representation of the two verbal arguments makes their relationship clearer and allows for the derivation of specific exact predictions that can then be empirically evaluated. The model provides precise statements about the empirical relationship between voting and income. More complex functions of the benefits and costs of voting might be more realistic, but they would result in the two problems noted before: solving the model would become more difficult and the predictions would likely not be as clear.

This caveat aside, mathematics provides for an advantage in solving models deductively, as the example shows. Mathematics allows a researcher to keep track of the simultaneous interactions of the model. Furthermore, mathematizing the arguments makes it easier to understand how to evaluate empirically the two different arguments on the effects of income on voting. Rather than posit that the two nonformal arguments are independent and somehow test to discriminate between them, the mathematical model's specific predictions can be compared more fruitfully with reality. In Filer et al. (1993), the authors examine voting turnout using pooled cross-sectional time-series data. They use county turnout data for the presidential election years 1948, 1960, 1968, and 1980 matched (respectively) with census data for the years 1950, 1960, 1970, and 1980. They measure the effect of income on the costs of voting by using the time-series data on changes in absolute income; they measure the effect of income on the benefits of voting by using the cross-sectional data on changes in a voter's position on the distribution of income.

Because the theory predicts a nonlinear relationship between position on the income distribution and turnout, the researchers use a spline estimation procedure to allow for a nonlinear relationship. The results support predictions that are derived from the two arguments reconciled in the mathematical model. Turnout first declines with position on the income distribution and then increases. Turnout declines with absolute changes in income over time. Of course, the empirical model estimated by Filer and colleagues incorporates additional assumptions about the randomness in the data as well as "control" variables that are not in the formal model – such as educational attainment, the urbanness of the counties, and so forth. Thus their empirical analysis simultaneously considers a host of auxiliary assumptions in "operationalizing" the formal model. Again, I will discuss this issue in Chapter 4.

2.3.2   *Formal Models and Intuition*

There is a vital feature of formal modeling and the use of mathematics in formal modeling that I have not yet considered. Namely, the exercise of formal model building and solving often leads to results that are unexpected or "counterintuitive." Usually this happens because intuition does not allow for considering *all* the complexities of a situation. I illustrate how this can occur with two examples.

The Line-Item Veto and Government Spending.

A Formal Model. Casual theorizing about the line-item veto has suggested that a president who wants to spend less than Congress can use the line-item veto to achieve a lower total budget than with only an all-or-nothing veto. The nonformal reasoning is that use of the line-item veto could lower spending on selected items, leading to an overall lower budget. This casual logic, however, is incomplete. It implicitly assumes that Congress will not act strategically and that budget proposals under the different veto systems will be the same. But Congress is likely to make different budget proposals under the different veto systems. As Carter and Schap (1990) show, it is possible that the overall budget could be higher with the line-item veto – even when the president wishes to spend less than Congress on all spending issues – owing to the strategic nature of the Congressional budget process.

To illustrate Carter and Schap's argument, assume that there are two types of spending upon which Congress and the president must agree. Let x and y be the spending levels on two publicly provided goods. Assume that Congress and the president each have spending preferences that are symmetric about a single ideal point. Congress' preferences can be graphed as in Figure 2.2, where the point C is Congress' ideal position. Congress' utility decreases monotonically as spending levels move away from this point. Congress' utility can be depicted by drawing indifference curves that represent policy positions equidistant from point C, such as the circle I_C. Congress is indifferent between all the spending combinations on I_C. Spending-level combinations inside I_C provide Congress with higher levels of utility whereas spending level combinations outside I_C provide Congress with lower utility. Imagine that, for every point in xy space, there is a corresponding indifference circle.

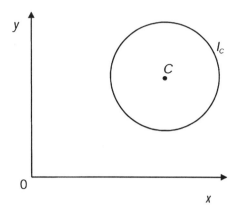

Figure 2.2. Congressional spending preferences.

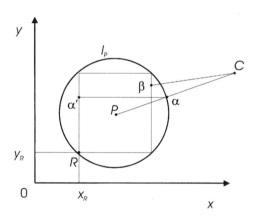

Figure 2.3. All-or-nothing veto versus line-item veto.

The president's spending level preferences can be similarly drawn as symmetric about a single ideal point, P. Figure 2.3 shows the president's and Congress' ideal points, with the president preferring lower levels of spending on both publicly provided goods. I need also to specify the "reversion" level of spending and so assume that – if the president vetoes Congress' budget proposal – spending levels will be at point R, spending on good x will be x_R, and spending on good y will be y_R. I assume that a president who is indifferent with regard to the reversion and proposed spending levels does not veto; I also assume that Congress cannot override a veto.[13]

Note that I_P is the president's indifference curve, which shows the spending combinations the president finds equal in preference to point R. Under an all-or-nothing veto, the president will veto any bill outside the circle. Consider now Congress' decision problem when the president wields an all-or-nothing veto. Congress knows that a proposed spending combination that falls outside of I_P will be vetoed. If Congress' ideal spending level is inside of I_P then Congress can simply propose its ideal point. But if Congress' ideal spending combination is outside of I_P, as in Figure 2.3, then Congress will propose the closest spending level to C that is on I_P, which is α in the figure.

The Effect of a Line-item Veto.   What happens under the line-item veto? With the line-item veto, the president is guaranteed a spending-level combination at least as good as those along the boundary of the inscribed rectangle in Figure 2.3. That is, suppose Congress proposes α under the line-item veto. The president can veto the additional spending on x, resulting in a spending combination that is at point α', which is closer to his ideal point than is α. Thus, in order for a proposed spending combination to be (line-item) "veto proof" it must be as close to the president's ideal point as the corresponding spending combinations when spending levels on only one dimension are vetoed (represented by the rectangle). Under the line-item veto, then, Congress will propose a point that is on the rectangle but as close to Congress' ideal point as possible; this is point β. Note that in this case β denotes a slightly greater total spending combination than α. Thus, the line-item veto does not necessarily result in lower total spending than the all-or-nothing veto. Of course, I could construct examples in which the line-item veto does have the intuitively predicted effect. Nevertheless, the formal model of the process shows that there could be no general result that the line-item veto reduces spending. The formal modeling forces consideration of various aspects of the situation and sometimes yields results that intuition fails to recognize.

---

[13] I can justify making many of these assumptions as complexities that do not change the qualitative results. For an analysis of presidential vetos, see Tien (1996).

Voter Information and Preference Extremity. For another example of how casual and nonformal reasoning can sometimes be incomplete, consider the problem of voter acquisition of information about candidates. Intuition might suggest that voters are more likely to be informed about candidates the more extreme the voters' preferences, since extreme voters may have more intense preferences over issues. Yet, it is possible to show – with some simple and standard assumptions about voter preferences and information – that the opposite is likely to hold. Consider a simple formal model of voter acquisition of information about candidates that incorporates the following assumptions (see Lasley 1996).

1. Policy is unidimensional; that is, it is given by $\pi \in [0, 1]$.
2. Voters have single-peaked preferences over policy. Specifically, the utility of voter i from policy is given by $u_i(\pi) = A - |\pi - \pi_i|$, where π_i is voter i's ideal policy preference. Assume that the median of the distribution of ideal points is equal to 0.5. Voters are assumed to vote sincerely for the candidate whose position is expected to be closest to their ideal point; abstention is not allowed.
3. There are two candidates, A and B. Assume that A is the incumbent, that her policy position is known to be π_A, and that $0 < \pi_A < 0.5$. Candidate B is the challenger, and his policy position π_B is expected to be a random draw within the range denoted by $[0.5, 1]$. The expected value of the challenger's policy position is thus 0.75. Voters can discover the exact position of the challenger by paying a fixed cost of c.
4. Voters acquire information that could possibly change their voting decision, and the anticipated difference in utility between the two candidates is greater than the cost of information acquisition.

The assumptions imply that voters with ideal points below $\pi_A/2 + 0.25$ and above $\pi_A/2 + 0.5$ will not acquire information about the challenger, since their voting decisions will not be changed with the information acquisition. Thus, contrary to intuition, extremist voters on the left of the policy space will not acquire the information.

This simple model is highly stylistic and, as I have repeatedly emphasized, makes false or unverified assumptions about voters, candidates, and policy. Relaxation of these assumptions may easily result in a different conclusion that is not counterintuitive. Nevertheless, the model helps illustrate how nonformal theorizing about the relationship between voter preferences and information acquisition may be misleading; that is, intuitions may not always be correct. Intuition is limited and does not typically allow consideration of all the possibilities. By using a formal model to carefully specify preferences and how voters acquire information, a researcher can better evaluate her intuition. This is not possible if she works only with nonformally presented arguments.

Some researchers may find this analysis unsurprising because they believe that formal models can be devised to show *any* result. This may be true in theory, but in practice it is more difficult to find models that are both solvable and empirically viable. Oftentimes the modeling process reveals results that the researcher never anticipates.[14]

2.4   Conclusions

In summary, I argue that formal models are critical for effective political science research. Formal models help researchers think through theory in a logical and consistent manner and yield better empirical investigations because they have explicit assumptions and specific predictions that are based on these assumptions. Choosing the assumptions of formal models is important and a researcher must be careful that the assumptions are logically consistent and capture the important aspects of the real-world issues to be examined. By stating assumptions explicitly, a researcher can reconcile apparent conflicts in nonformal theories and can sometimes discover counterintuitive results that nonformal reasoning is not always capable of reaching.

Nevertheless, empirical analysis from nonformal modeling is still a vital part of the study of the real world, and the empirical research that arises from nonformal modeling can ensure that formal theoretical efforts are appropriately grounded in the real world situation of interest. Similarly, computational models play a complementary role to analytically solvable formal models in deriving predictions when a researcher chooses to work with

---

[14] Another example of a formal model that shows a problem with a commonly accepted intuitive argument can be found in Shotts (1997a,b). Shotts uses a game theoretic model to analyze the effects of majority/minority district requirements on policy outcomes in the House of Representatives. Many claim that these requirements will increase the number of conservatives elected to the House and thus lead to more conservative policy outcomes as conservative gerrymanderers group liberal voters in liberal districts. Shotts shows instead that more liberal policy outcomes are expected. That is, conservative gerrymanderers are constrained to draw districts that elect more liberal minority representatives while liberal gerrymanderers can satisfy the constraint without decreasing the number of liberal representatives. Thus, the number of liberal representatives in the House increases even though conservative gerrymanderers attempt to maximize their own representation.

models that are too complex to be solved analytically. Yet a researcher must be careful that the computational process does not result in theoretical predictions that prove to be inaccurate because the cases analyzed were inappropriate. Likewise, choosing inappropriate assumptions in devising an analytically solvable model may result in predictions that are problematic.

CHAPTER 3

The Variety of Formal Models

Coauthored with Elizabeth M. Martin

The discussion so far has centered on common characteristics of formal models. There are, however, a number of differences among classes of formal models in political science. The primary difference concerns assumptions about behavior: (1) rational choice or "economic man"; (2) models of human behavior from the behavioral sciences such as psychology (or psychology and economics combined), called "almost rational choice" or "boundedly rational choice"; or (3) no particular theory about individual choice processes. Models also differ in the extent to which the actors act strategically (as in some game theoretic models) or nonstrategically (as in decision theoretic models). Some models examine aggregate rather than individual behavior. Finally, the formal models in political science also vary in the mathematical techniques that are used.

This chapter examines the large variety of formal models used in political science and how they differ. We first consider rational choice, variations of rational choice, and game theoretic models. Then we review psychological models and models of aggregate behavior without explicit individual choice assumptions. The chapter concludes with a discussion of mathematical techniques.

3.1 Rational Choice–Based Models

3.1.1 *Rational Choice as an "As If" Assumption*

What Does Rational Choice Mean? In one sense, rational choice is about as nebulous a concept as one can imagine. Fundamentally it is very simple: actors have goals and make choices in order to achieve these goals.

75

Researchers who work with rational choice models are often amazed that anyone could find such an innocuous assumption problematic. One common criticism is that rational choice implies a focus on selfish, individualistic behavior. Yet there is nothing in this assumption that implies selfish behavior – the goal may be altruistic. Some political scientists may be surprised to learn that there is actually now a large literature in the field of economics that incorporates altruism in rational choice models; see Rose-Ackerman (1996) for a review and the discussion of behavioral game theory later in this chapter (Downs 1957 discusses altruistic motives). And there is nothing in the rational choice assumption that is necessarily individualistic – the actors in many rational choice–based models are not individuals but groups such as legislatures, firms, interest groups, regulatory agencies, and countries. Rational choice modelers accordingly find the criticism of rationality perplexing. How could this assumption be so problematic? How can anyone dispute that people, either as individuals or groups, make choices to achieve particular ends? Do political scientists who dislike the rational choice assumption really believe that all behavior is random?

Ah, but here we are underplaying what the rational choice assumption can imply. In conjunction with other aspects of a model, the rational choice assumption often suggests much more than the simple goal maximization story that rational choice modelers tell undergraduates. Consider, for example, what rationality means for expectations. A researcher who assumes that individuals make rational decisions is assuming that they are unbiased processors of information. This information processing may require the researcher to assume that individuals make complex calculations, even in what may seem a simple model. Suppose an incumbent is facing re-election. Assume that voters have preferences over the state of the economy and will vote for the incumbent if they believe that he will make good economic choices in the future. Voters know the outcomes of the economic policies they have observed during the incumbent's term in office; however, they do not know the extent to which the observed beneficial outcomes are attributable to the incumbent's ability to manage the economy or simply to favorable random shocks to the economy. In a rational choice–based model, the voters would be assumed to know the distribution of the random shocks and the probability that the incumbent was a high-quality manager of the economy. They would know the process through which economic policy affects the economy. Consequently, the rational voter would be able to infer an incumbent's ability and vote for an incumbent whose expected quality is higher than a randomly drawn challenger.[1] Assuming that a voter makes rational choices means that the voter uses all information available in order to make choices to maximize her satisfaction, including calculations about the workings of the economy, the behavior of incumbents, and so forth.

Sometimes these calculations seem well beyond the capability of the average individual, especially if the model is game theoretic. Game theory is used to analyze situations in which individual decisions are strategic, that is, in which the outcomes that one individual or group faces are functions of the decisions of other individuals or groups.[2] In contrast to decision theoretic models, where individuals are assumed to make decisions under the additional assumption that their decisions do not affect the decisions of others, in game theoretic models an individual is assumed to know her decision will impact the decisions made by others and vice versa. The calculations that researchers then perform to determine rational choices in a game theoretic setting can require the use of high-powered computer equipment and/or knowledge of matrix algebra and integral calculus. Even the most ardent supporters of the rational choice assumption do not claim that individuals actually make these calculations. The standard defense is that individuals behave *as if* they make the calculations. The situation is often argued to be analogous to the professional tennis player who does not know the physics of hitting the ball but still manages to do so very well. The assumption of rational choice is not meant to be an accurate description of how the brain works; rather, the assumption is that individual choices are made "as if" the brain does work in this way.

Is Rational Choice Rational? How useful is rational choice in this role? The experimental evidence that rational choice assumptions have difficulty explaining behavior in some situations of risk is well known among political scientists (see Kahneman and Tversky 1979 and the discussion in Chapter 5). Moreover, many rational choice–based modelers, including Aldrich (1993), have argued that – in very low-cost, low-benefit situations such as deciding to vote – rational choice models are probably not very good at explaining behavior. Fiorina argues that "citizens voting in mass elections neither bear the full consequences of their decisions nor have much impact on the outcomes. The combination of these two features of large elections means that

---

[1] For formalized presentations of the moral hazard and adverse selection problems in elections, see Banks and Sundarum (1993).

[2] Not all game theoretic models assume rational choice, as we will discuss later. Also, the next section describes game theory as used in political science in more detail.

any conception of voting behavior that is instrumental in nature is highly suspect" (1997, p. 403). If the rational choice assumption is such an inaccurate description of how individuals really "think" and if it fails to explain behavior in simple experiments and decision situations, then why do many modelers persist in making the rational choice assumption?

One of the best answers for this question is given by the economist Alvin Roth (forthcoming). Roth first discusses the concepts of rational economic man and psychological man. He points out: "Psychological man doesn't have preferences, at least not in the sense that economists customarily think of them. Rather he has a collection of mental processes. And different descriptions of options, different frames and contexts, and different choice procedures elicit different processes." Roth then discusses a third type of model of man:

consider for a moment the class of models of individual choice that seem to be suggested by recent research in brain science and clinical pharmacology. *Neurological man* doesn't (even) have a fixed collection of mental processes, in the sense of psychological man. Instead, he has biological and chemical processes which influence his behavior. Different blood chemistry leads to different mental processes; e.g. depending on the level of lithium (or Valium or Prozac) in his blood, he makes different decisions (on both routine matters and matters of great consequence – even his life and death). . . . One can then ask the neurobiologist's question: What accounts for the [psychologist's] "reluctance to abandon the [psychological] model, despite considerable contrary evidence"? The psychologist's answer (as imagined by this economist) might go something like this: "No one really supposes that an individual's mental processes are fixed and never change. But this is a useful approximation. It breaks down for people who have lithium deficiency, and who (therefore) exhibit abrupt cycles of manic and depressive behavior. But it helps us explain a lot of the phenomena which concern us, without requiring blood tests of our subjects. And, while we are fully persuaded that real people have blood chemistry and brain processes, the compelling evidence that the neurobiologists have assembled on this point does not address the question of how often decisions are affected by normal variations in blood chemistry and processes in ways that can be predicted without reference to blood chemistry. (We note that even analysis at the level of blood chemistry is only an approximation to the underlying quantum mechanical processes of the brain.) Finally, the blood chemistry model doesn't seem to bring a lot of explanatory or predictive power to bear on the questions we try to study, like why people exhibit preference reversals." . . . My point, of course, is that with the natural substitution of terms, an economist's answer to this question could look a lot like the psychologist's.

Roth argues that rational choice should be viewed not as a complete model of how individuals think but rather as a useful approximation of how individuals make decisions in many situations, much as the psychological model can be a useful approximation in many other situations. While we also work with rational choice models and assume that individuals behave "as if" they maximize according to these principles, we still believe it is useful to evaluate the assumptions behind rational choice. Evaluating assumptions and analyzing the dependence of results on assumptions are crucial steps for building better theory, as discussed in Chapter 5. Evidence of when these approximations break down in their predictive capacities can be, as Roth notes, "enormously useful, even when it is not the sort of evidence that causes the approximations to be abandoned. To know that utility maximization may be a weak guide to choices among alternatives with 'similar' expected values, or to choices involving probabilities near zero or one, can only enhance the actual (as opposed to the apparent) usefulness of the approximation."

3.1.2 Rational Choice as Prescription

Models that use rational choice assumptions also play a normative role in political science; that is, these models have a dual interpretation as both predictive models and normative models of behavior. While the emphasis in this book is on formal models that are positive and hence designed to be predictive models, a significant portion of rational choice modeling in political science is normative at heart. Social choice theory, for example, focuses on the normative question of how to design an aggregation mechanism for social choices that meets certain desirable criteria (see e.g. Sen 1970). Similarly, work on comparative features of electoral rules by Myerson (1995) has a normative dimension. Some political scientists equate rational choice–based models with positive political theory, a very inaccurate description of a significant portion of the literature. Because some political scientists do not recognize that rational choice models sometimes have a normative or prescriptive purpose, they may undervalue the benefit of what they see as nonempirical theorizing. For example, if the normative aspects of Arrow's (im)possibility theorem are ignored then its value is significantly lessened. Arrow's undertaking was to characterize the process by which social choices can be made. His research considered whether a social choice rule exists that will satisfy a set of normative criteria. Arrow (1951) clearly specifies that the focus of his theoretical work is normative and prescriptive. He does not attempt to devise a positive description of what collective choice is like in the real world but rather describes what a fair collective choice rule *can* look like. To a lesser degree, the analyses of Downs (1957) and Olson (1965) are concerned with normative as well as descriptive questions. Riker's *Liberalism against Populism* (1982) makes a number of normative judgments. Much of the seminal work on rational choice in political science is normative, and its value is underestimated by those who focus only on testable implications.

3.1.3   *Myths of Rational Choice*

Rational Choice and the Level of Analysis. There are a number of myths in political science circles about rational choice–based models. Some we have already dismissed; for instance, rational choice–based models do not necessarily assume self-interested behavior (some rational choice models attribute altruistic or fairness motives to individuals). Another myth is that rational choice–based models are always individualistic, yet many rational choice–based models examine the behavior of groups of individuals rather than the individuals themselves. For example, Filer and colleagues (1993) examine the voting behavior of groups, not of individuals. These inaccurate generalizations about rational choice arise in part from the desire of many rational choice modelers to derive endogenously – from rational choice–based individual behavior – an explanation for altruism, norms of cooperation, or group rationality (see e.g. Fearon and Laitin 1996).

Rational choice–based models generally assume that the behavior of a group or collective is deducible from its individualistic parts. As Arrow notes:

The rejection of the organism approach to social problems has been fairly complete, and to my mind salutary, rejection of mysticism. But as usual, in these problems, there is something to be said for at least the possibility of a collective basis for social theorizing, if not taken too literally. Much of our casual observation and much of our better statistical information relate to groups rather than individuals. We may therefore be led to generalize and form a theory whose subject is the total behavior of a group. So long as it is understood that such a theory is really a resultant of certain as yet unanalyzed laws of individual behavior, no harm will be done, and the greater convenience of empirical analysis on groups will be highly beneficial. (1968, p. 641)

Again, in Filer et al. (1993), the authors argue that the group decision is based on an unspecified process through which the individuals in the group rationally choose the group decision (the argument is that the group uses selective social incentives to motivate voters). Thus, when rational choice modelers look at decision making at the group level, they usually argue that the decisions are explained by (unmodeled) rational decision making at the individual level.

Purity and Rational Choice. A third myth is that a "pure rational choice–based" model exists. All rational choice–based models contain some assumption or assumptions of nonrational choice behavior. That is, because rational choice–based models are abstractions from reality, like all models they ignore details of the real world. Rational choice–based models need to assume that the actors in their models also ignore these details – a nonrational assumption. All rational choice–based models make, in some way, what are called *ad hoc* assumptions about the individuals or the situation analyzed. For instance, Filer et al. (1993) make the ad hoc assumption that other, unanalyzed factors that could affect voting decisions – such as education, which may actually be related to income – are constant.[3] Thus, it is not a pure rational choice model. And as noted previously, the actors' choices are not explicitly derived from rational choice calculations because the internal choices within groups of voters are not examined. Similar assumptions are made in some models of the interactions among political parties, legislatures, committees, the presidency, and the bureaucracy. There is a constant tension between expanding the assumption of rationality to incorporate these details while keeping the model simple enough that it can be solved and yield useful predictions.

The nonexistence of a pure model of rational choice obviously has implications for the meaning of testing rational choice theory. Rational choice is a *paradigm*, a set of assumptions used to approximate individual and (sometimes) group behavior. When we use rational choice in models, however, our models include ad hoc assumptions and so are always imperfect empirical analyses. There is no way to completely evaluate the concept that rational choice best describes behavior as a whole. Yet there is a large body of experimental research suggesting that, in some situations, behavior is not "rational," especially when (as in voting) the costs and benefits are low. Does this mean researchers should discard the paradigm? Such a decision will not rest on these results or on any other empirical analyses of specific rational choice–based models but instead on the overall performance of the

---

[3] However, education level is controlled for when the model is empirically tested, so the model is changed when it is estimated.

paradigm as an approach in comparison to alternative paradigms. The empirical evaluation of formal models that are rational choice–based is one step in evaluating the paradigm, but this step alone does not constitute an empirical evaluation of the rational choice paradigm.

3.2   Game Theoretic Models

3.2.1   *Types of Game Theoretic Models*

Game theory has become popular in political science largely because of its attractiveness as a mathematical language for modeling strategic interaction between individuals or groups of individuals. A situation is *strategic* when the actors make choices knowing that their choices might affect the choices of other actors, and so on. Many situations in political science are likely to be strategic; examples include candidate election entry and policy location decisions, arms-treaty negotiations between countries, and executive–legislative relations.

Although a complete discussion of game theory is beyond the scope of this book, a few fundamental concerns are important for understanding the empirical testing of game theoretic models.[4] First, there are two types of game theoretic solution techniques that are used in political science: cooperative and noncooperative. The terms "cooperative" and "noncooperative" can be misleading to non–game theorists. That is, these terms may be misinterpreted to mean that noncooperative game theorists are not interested in cooperation, which is definitely not true. In cooperative game theory, it is possible for actors to make binding commitments outside the game. Thus, cooperative outcomes are not endogenously derived but instead are assumed to occur as a consequence of actor choices within the game. Noncooperative game theory does not make this assumption. In noncooperative game theory, the solution to the model must be immune to deviations by individual actors or players. That is, an outcome cannot be a solution to a noncooperative game if an individual can optimize by choosing a different strategy.[5] Fearon and Laitin (1996) offer an excellent illustration of how noncooperative game

---

[4] A significant number of game theoretic texts are now available. Morrow (1994) is especially useful for a presentation of the techniques of game theory within the context of political science. Gates and Humes (1997) present case studies of how game theory can be applied to political science questions.

[5] In coalitional game theory, as discussed by Osborne and Rubinstein (1994), deviations are examined at coalition or group levels rather than the individual level.

theoretic models can help explain cooperation. They present a social matching game (based on prior work of Calvert 1995; Ellison 1994; Kandori 1992; and Milgrom, North, and Weingast 1990) to explain how interethnic cooperation can be sustained over time despite a high potential for ethnic conflict and limited interaction across ethnic groups. Because noncooperative game theory can be used to explain cooperation as an endogenous choice, it has received greater attention from theorists in the last two decades. For a discussion of cooperative game theory, see Myerson (1991).

3.2.2 *Solutions in Game Theory*

A second important issue in game theory is how we interpret the solutions to the games we analyze. In noncooperative game theory there are two ways to think about the solution to a game that are sometimes confused. The first is the "deductive" approach. In this interpretation, the game is considered as an isolated, one-shot event, and game theorists assume that each player believes the other players are rational and uses only the principles of rationality to deduce how these other players will behave. The calculations in a complex game can become quite complicated and time consuming, even for game theorists with computer aid. Binmore (1990) calls this viewpoint on game solutions "eductive," emphasizing the education that may be required for actors to make the often extremely difficult choices implied. In political science, researchers typically solve game theoretic models by following the deductive approach.

Political science game theoretic modelers may solve games using the deductive approach, but this does not mean that they necessarily believe the players are making choices according to this interpretation. Again, researchers generally think of the players making choices "as if" they are using the deductive approach. A modeler who argues that players are making choices "as if" they were deducing them according to the principles of rationality is using the alternative interpretation of the game solution: the "steady state" or "evolutive" view. Osborne and Rubinstein describe this view as follows:

The *steady state* ... interpretation is closely related to that which is standard in economics. Game theory, like other sciences, deals with regularities.... The steady state interpretation treats a game as a model designed to explain some regularity observed in a family of similar situations. Each participant "knows" the equilibrium and tests the optimality of his behavior given this knowledge, which he has acquired from his long experience. (1994, p. 5)

Note that the term "equilibrium" refers to the solution of the game that the modeler is examining. Thus, while modelers solve a game as a one-shot situation and look for the solution according to the principles of rationality, their interpretation of how the players actually make choices is typically according to the evolutive view. Even so, just how the steady-state solutions emerge – and whether the solutions deduced from assumptions of rationality constitute steady-state solutions – are much-debated questions in game theory. As discussed in what follows, a number of researchers have modeled repeated games with adaptive or boundedly rational agents in order to derive steady-state solutions.

3.3   Rationality Relaxed

3.3.1   *Individual Choice Models*

Nonlinear Expected Utility and Prospect Theory. Related to the myths about rational choice is a lack of knowledge among political scientists of the extent that many theoretical economists now use what Roth terms "almost rational" and "nonrational" models of choice. As noted before, rational choice can involve complex calculations. In particular, an important question concerns how rational decision makers make choices in situations of risk or uncertainty. *Risk* is generally understood to mean that the outcomes are unknown but have known probabilities; with *uncertainty,* the probabilities are unknown. For risky situations, assuming rational choice typically involves the application of expected utility theory, which was formulated by von Neumann and Morgenstern (1944) in order to model games where information is imperfect. For uncertain states, rational choice modelers usually follow the approach of Savage (1954). Both formulations present a set of axioms about individual preferences that are used to derive utility functions characterizing the individual's decisions in risky and uncertain states. Almost from the inception of expected utility theory and subjective expected utility theory (Savage's approach), researchers have questioned the axioms' empirical support; see for example the work of Allais (1953) and the discussion in Camerer (1995). Kahneman and Tversky's (1979) experiments showing violations of the independence axiom of expected utility theory are one example of this evidence. Chapter 5 reviews the axioms of expected utility and some of the experimental evidence on violations of the axioms.

As a consequence of experimental evidence suggesting that the axioms of expected utility theory are sometimes violated, a number of researchers have proposed alternative theories on how individuals make risky decisions that relax some of the axioms of expected utility theory. Prospect theory, developed by Kahneman and Tversky (1979), is one example. Other alternatives devised by economists include Chew (1983), Fishburn (1982), and Machina (1982, 1989). These approaches are what Roth calls "almost rational choice." Chapter 5 reviews some of these alternative approaches, including prospect theory. Prospect theory has been applied in a limited way to some political science questions (reviewed in Chapter 5), but there is no political science research that uses other alternatives to expected utility theory that have been developed in economics. Moreover, these "almost rational choice" approaches have been little used in game theoretic models.

Bounded Rationality, Learning, Evolution. Additional work by game theorists in economics and other social sciences has incorporated what Roth calls "nonrational" choice assumptions, or what Morrow (1994) labels "bounded rationality." In essence, nonrational or boundedly rational models assume that individuals ignore information available to them in making their choices and thus do not necessarily make the choices that would maximize their utility or satisfaction. One implicit argument for using boundedly rational models is that individuals have cognitive limits that affect their ability to process all the information available and thus make decisions that are less than fully rational. The difficulty with operationalizing this idea is deciding which information individuals are able to process. How stupid should researchers assume that the decision makers are? If the research question involves single decisions, then assuming that individuals are boundedly rational seems to admit any observation as theoretically supported; it seems almost tautological to say that individuals are boundedly rational. Therefore, when assuming that individuals in a model are boundedly rational, it is important that there be a precise expectation about the choices that are refutable.

Bounded rationality can be interesting when used to understand behavior in situations that are repeated. As we have noted, modelers often think of players in games behaving "as if" they choose fully rationally; that players choose strategies that have worked over the years in similar games; and that player choices *evolve* toward those that are fully rational. Thus, a number of game theorists have looked at repeated games with boundedly rational players to determine if, by repetition, the players reach the strategies that are deduced using principles of rationality. Morrow (1994, pp. 308–11) reviews some of the approaches that have been used (see Fudenberg and Levine 1997 for a fuller explanation of these approaches). He presents three illustrations from game theory in which the actors make choices that are boundedly rational: fictitious play, finite automata, and evolutionary game theory. In these three cases the actors are assumed to make decisions that are less than fully rational in a game that is played repeatedly, and the principal theoretical question is: What strategies emerge in the long run or steady state? In fictitious play, the actors make choices in each round that are "best replies" or optimal in response to the distribution of choices of the other actors in the previous rounds; in finite automata theory, the actors are assumed to have strategies that respond to a limited number of previous strategies, or finite history of the past; and in evolutionary models, players change their strategies over time through adaptation and imitation (see Boylan and El-Gamal 1993). One aim in these models is to determine whether the equilibria that game theorists discover through deductive theorizing with assumptions of rationality emerge also in repeated games with boundedly rational agents. So far, the results of this research are inconclusive.

Morrow (1994) points out that all three of these approaches have limitations that may be problematic as models of individual behavior. That is, why is it reasonable to assume, as in fictitious play, that the actors do not use rationally all the information available to them? Why would they respond to the distribution of strategies rather than attempt to forecast the actions of the other player more accurately? Why do finite automata "forget," and how should modelers judge how much forgetfulness is reasonable? How should researchers model explicitly adaptation and imitation in evolutionary models; is not some imitation perhaps a rational choice that will vary with the player and the situation?

Morrow and others believe that game theoretic models with bounded rationality have no fewer difficulties than those with full rationality. However, it should be emphasized that the focus of most economists and game theorists who work with bounded rationality models is to explain the process through which steady-state equilibria (solutions) are achieved by attempting to model formally the evolutive process that most modelers believe underlies rational choices. In some ways these exercises are still very much mind-experiments that attempt to understand how choices in simple situations may evolve over time. In many cases the point is not so much to argue that bounded rationality prevents actors from making rational choices but rather to determine what choices are made in steady-state equilibria as boundedly rational actors choose over time. Do these choices converge to those predicted by full rationality or by solving a game using the deductive approach? Similarly, others have begun to consider the process of learning in games. Much of the research on learning and bounded rationality is also coupled with experimental exploration of choices in simple repeated one-shot games.[6] Researchers working from this perspective see the goal as deriving evolutive predictions of equilibria (solutions) rather than using inductive predictions that are then argued to be "as if" they are evolutive. Since this is an ongoing research project and since the results are, as Morrow (1994) correctly notes, still limited, political scientists should be extremely cautious about assuming that bounded rationality models are superior to fully rational ones. The implications of this highly theoretical analysis for applied game theoretic work in political science are at present unclear.

Bounded Rationality in Political Science. Nonetheless, some work using bounded rationality has been applied to political science questions. For example, Carpenter (1996) compares three different models of bureaucratic decision making, one of which assumes that the actors process information in a boundedly rational method; this is discussed in more detail in Chapter 8.

Kollman and associates (1992) present a computational model that uses adaptive, boundedly rational agents in a repeated game to analyze the policy location decisions of political parties. They assume that there are two parties and a set of voters with preferences in a multidimensional ideological space. They assume that one of the parties is an incumbent party at given policy positions on the issues. The other party then chooses positions in order to win more votes than the incumbent party in an election. The challenging party has incomplete information about voter preferences although it can commission a number (up to 40) of polls of voters regarding different possibilities before choosing positions for the election. The challenger party is constrained in the number of issues on which it can change positions and in how far that change can be from its previous position. After

---

[6] See for example Crawford (1990), Miller and Andreoni (1991), Roth and Erev (1995), and the review in Sunder (1995). Fudenberg and Levine (1997) review the literature on learning.

the challenger party chooses a position, an election is held; the party that receives the most votes becomes the incumbent, and the process is repeated. The researchers also examine parties that care about the policy enacted as well as winning. Voters in the model vote and respond to polls sincerely.

How do Kollman and colleagues model the aforementioned limit on the parties' ability to make rational choices? As the authors note, there are many possible alternatives, perhaps an infinite number of ways. They examine three models of boundedly rational parties: random adaptive parties (RAPs), climbing adaptive parties (CAPs), and genetic adaptive parties (GAPs). RAPs randomly generate a fixed number of positions and choose the one that performs best in the polls. CAPs take their initial positions, try out small deviations from these positions in polls, and then change to positions that are successful. GAPs adapt a population of platforms using a genetic algorithm (i.e., they test out a set of platforms in order to discover interactions between these platforms). This process is described as follows:

The genetic algorithm generates new platforms using three procedures. It begins with the random creation of, say, 12 platforms. The first operator, reproduction, randomly selects (with replacement) 12 pairs of candidates from the list and reproduces only the preferred member of the pair. The resulting candidates are then randomly arranged in pairs to which the cross over operator is applied. During crossover, the candidates randomly decide (with probability 50%) whether or not to trade positions on a few issues. If they decide to switch, they exchange groups of positions. Finally, the mutation operator allows each candidate to alter positions randomly on an issue or two. (Kollman et al. 1992, p. 932)

The authors claim (p. 932) these approaches describe three different views of the campaign process. The RAP version captures a "smoke-filled-room selection process"; CAPs "represent parties that select a candidate and then adapt the candidate platform to the electorate's views by testing alterations with focus groups and speeches"; and GAPs "represent parties whose potential candidates shift positions both by borrowing from competitors and by testing their own alterations." Kollman and associates use a computational approach to solving the three models and thus present numerical solutions for given parameters over a period of elections. As in other research based on boundedly rational agents, the researchers consider whether these agents, over time, reach convergent positions as predicted in static spatial voting (e.g. Hotelling–Downsian) models of candidate competition. They find that convergence is likely in their numerical simulations but varies with the amount of information that the parties have, a similar conclusion to that reached by Calvert (1985), who shows that convergence is less likely when parties are ideological and have incomplete information on voter preferences. Kollman, Miller, and Page have also used their model of party competition as the basis for empirical research on American presidential elections (Kollman et al. 1998).

Behavioral Game Theory. As with the axioms of expected utility theory, a significant body of experimental research in economics has studied the behavior of subjects in game situations. Davis and Holt (1993) and Kagel and Roth (1995) review this literature. Similarly, some experimental work in political science has focused on evaluating game theoretic models. In many cases, the highly rational game theoretic models' predictions are supported in the laboratory, as in Morton (1993). As noted in the previous chapter, Morton confirms Calvert's (1985) prediction that candidates who are motivated by policy concerns and do not know the location of the ideal point of the median voter will diverge in policy positions, although if these candidates are aware of the median voter's ideal point then their positions will converge. However, despite the general experimental success of game theory, notable anomalies have occurred in a number of experiments where subjects' decisions appear to be affected by factors that theoretically should not matter. For example, in Morton (1993) the subjects' choices show a greater degree of error in early rounds of the experiment than in later rounds, which suggests a learning factor that the highly rational game theoretic model ignores. Also, the subjects' positions are more convergent than predicted by Calvert's (1985) theory. These anomalies are evidence that something else is going on that the model cannot explain without modification.[7]

Camerer (1997) contends, based on similar results in other experiments, that highly rational game theory does not work well as a descriptive theory of human behavior. He also contends that the alternatives of boundedly rational, adaptive, or evolutionary models are also unsatisfactory because such models assume far too simplistic behavior on the part of the actors. He advocates a middle approach, which he calls "behavioral game theory": "start with a game or naturally occurring situation in which standard game theory makes a bold prediction based on one or two crucial principles; if behavior differs from the prediction, think of plausible explanations for what is

---

[7] Morton (1993) suggests that the greater convergence is due to subjects who were motivated to win independent of their payoffs. This modification is discussed in more detail in Chapter 4.

observed; and extend formal game theory to incorporate these explanations" (1997, pp. 167–8). Camerer states that his goal "is to be able to take a description of a strategic situation and predict actual behavior at least as well as current theories do. Better descriptive principles should also improve the prescriptive value of game theory, since players who desire to play rationally need to know how others are likely to play" (p. 168).

Behavioral Game Theory Applied. How do the steps Camerer advocates work? Camerer presents three examples of types of game theoretic situations with clear distinct predictions (the first step) as well as experimental evidence suggesting that the highly rational game theoretic solution fails (the second step). The third step is for theorist to provide new theoretical explanations for the contrary results and to incorporate these in devising a modified game theoretic model. One of Camerer's examples is a simple bargaining model, the ultimatum game, in which one player makes an offer on how to divide a pie and the other player decides whether to accept or reject the offer. (Chapter 2 discussed the alternating offer bargaining models of Rubinstein over the division of a fixed sum or pie; the ultimatum game is a one-period version of the Rubinstein bargaining model.) Game theory predicts that the first player will take almost all of the pie, leaving a negligible amount to the second player. Yet, experimental subjects rarely behave according to this prediction. In fact, the modal division is an even split of the pie. This suggests that players are motivated by concerns of fairness or altruism, concerns that are ignored in the highly rational game theoretic bargaining model. However, to merely assume that subjects are altruistic is too simplistic an answer. Subjects' behavior in a different bargaining game, the dictator game, shows that there are limits to altruism and that the strategic nature of the game does matter. In dictator games, the first player makes a proposal on how to divide the pie, and the second player has no choice but to accept the first player's division. In these games the first player usually divides the pie less evenly (leaving less for the second player) but still does not take all the pie as predicted by highly rational game theory (see Roth 1995 for a review of this literature).

As observed in Chapter 2, the Baron–Ferejohn legislative bargaining model is a variant of these simpler bargaining models in economics. McKelvey (1991) and Diermeier and Morton (1998) present experimental results on the Baron–Ferejohn model. They also find that players propose divisions more equal than theoretically predicted. In the three-player legislative bargaining game experiments of Diermeier and Morton, a player is chosen to make a proposal on how to divide a fixed sum; this proposal is then voted on by the three players (the actual bargaining game is more complicated in that the players are given different voting weights and the bargaining process can continue for a number of periods if a proposal is rejected). Theoretically, the proposer should choose a coalition partner, offer that partner a less-than-equal share of the sum, and exclude the noncoalition partner. The game between the coalition partners is like an ultimatum game, while the game between the proposer and the excluded player is similar to a dictator game. With behavior that is comparable to that seen in the ultimatum and dictator game experiments, proposers in the Baron–Ferejohn experiments typically choose to allocate relatively equally with a coalition partner but often exclude the third player.

Thus, an alternative theory is needed, one that (a) recognizes that the traditional game theoretic explanation fails to explain the divisions but (b) allows for strategic behavior as in traditional game theory, since the divisions do differ depending upon the strategic situation (divisions in the dictator game are more unequal than divisions in the ultimatum game). According to Camerer, the third step in devising behavioral game theory "is to incorporate findings like these into a theory that is more general but still reasonably parsimonious" (1997, p. 168). Camerer discusses a model proposed by Rabin (1993) that explains these results by adding "fairness" assumptions about individual choices to the traditional game theoretic model. In Rabin's model, players place an additional value on payoffs that are considered "kind" and subtract value from payoffs that are viewed as "mean," although these additional values become less important as the payoffs increase in monetary value. If the payoff allocations are unfair owing to chance, however, then the payoff is not interpreted as either mean or kind. Thus, the explanation of the lower shares given by proposers in the dictator game is that the position of dictator was chosen by chance and the proposal does not require consent by the other player. In the ultimatum game, the proposer cannot dictate choices without the consent of the other player, so fairness concerns matter.

Camerer's behavioral game theory differs from the boundedly rational game theoretic models discussed previously in at least two respects: (i) the role played by empirical (largely experimental) research in refining and modifying game theory; and (ii) the emphasis on devising a game theoretic approach to explain behavior accurately in simple one-shot games, rather than explaining how highly rational choice behavior may evolve or arise from repeated play by boundedly rational actors of the same game. Incorporating prospect theory (or other explanations for overconfidence in risky situations) into a game theoretic model is one approach mentioned by Camerer. (Prospect theory is addressed in Chapter 5.) In political science, Carrubba (1996) has incorporated prospect theory into a formal game theoretic model of legislative committees. Other examples of behavioral game theory are game theoretic models that allow for actors to make errors and to learn, as in the quantal response equilibrium concept of McKelvey and Palfrey (1995, 1998), which will be examined in the next chapter. Quantal response equilibrium has been used in political science by Signorino (1998) to model international conflict, which is also discussed in the next chapter.

Psychological Models. Psychologically based models look at individual choices and emphasize the process through which the decisions are made.[8] As Simon (1976) notes, most economics-based models confine their attention to substantive rationality whereas psychologists have emphasized procedural rationality. That is, economists focus on the rationality of the substantive nature of the decision, whereas psychologists are more interested in the rationality of the process of making the decision. Of course, our previous discussion shows how the work on bounded rationality in game theoretic models is breaking down this distinction between psychological and economic approaches. Nevertheless, in political science the distinction largely remains. Moreover, psychological models tend to be decision theoretic rather than game theoretic; that is, the actors make decisions as if their parameters or constraints are exogenous even when such parameters or constraints are the outcomes of other actors' choices. As in models of bounded rationality, the motivation behind psychological models is to incorporate explicitly the impact of cognitive limits on individual choices. These models generally examine decision making as adaptive and view individuals as using heuristics or "rules of thumb" to make decisions in complex situations that would (in a rational choice framework) involve complicated calculations. As a consequence, these models result in individuals making choices that have systematic biases.

The work of Milton Lodge and his various coauthors offers an interesting illustration of psychological decision theoretic models applied to political

---

[8] For presentations of this approach, see the work of Abelson and Levi (1985), Dawes (1988), Einhorn and Hogarth (1987), Hogarth and Reder (1987), and Payne, Bettman, and Johnson (1992).

science questions (see e.g. Lodge, McGraw, and Stroh 1989; Lodge and Stroh 1993; Lodge, Steenbergen, and Brau 1995). In this work, Lodge and his colleagues present a number of alternative models of how voters evaluate candidates, models that are based on research from psychology. In Lodge et al. (1995), for example, the authors characterize voters' information processing with the aid of an "on-line" model. Their model is not presented in the same way that the formal models discussed here are presented; the authors instead use flow charts to represent the process model they assume, which is put in equation form in their empirical estimation. These models skirt the boundary between formal models with explicit assumptions and nonformal models with hypotheses presented in diagram form. Another case of a formal model using a psychological approach is Zaller and Feldman (1992). The authors present a set of axioms concerning individual preferences and the way in which individuals respond to surveys; from this, the authors make deductions concerning the responses that will be received. Although the model is not mathematical, the authors use deductive logic and make explicit assumptions from which predictions are derived.

Computational decision theoretic models similar to the process psychology models just described have been developed by cognitive scientists. Computer simulations are designed to represent the cognitive theory of the process of decision making. These models have been applied to political science questions – most notably in the field of foreign policy, where computational cognitive models have been used to understand and describe the policy decision making process. See Taber and Timpone (1996) for a review of the literature.

3.3.2   Other Nonrational Choice–Based Formal Models

Other nonrational choice–based formal models in political science examine choices at higher levels of aggregation. In the field of international relations, some researchers (following the work of Richardson 1939) posit that country power relationships are given by a system of differential equations; see, for instance, Kadera (forthcoming). Rashevsky's (1947) work in using differential equations to study social classes has successors in differential equation models that have been applied in other areas of political science. For example, Brown (1993) uses a differential equation approach to analyze the 1964 U.S. presidential election at the party level.

These models are classified as nonrational choice because they do not make assumptions about the decision making process or about the choices of an individual or group of individuals; instead, they make assumptions about the process of interaction between groups of individuals. That is, the microfoundations of individual choice processes underlying the assumptions of the models are not specified. For example, Brown (1993) assumes that the following differential equations describe the change in support for the Democratic and Republican parties between elections:

$$\frac{dD}{dt} = \left[(1 + jD + yD^2)\left(q\left(\tfrac{D}{R}\right) + wDR + uD\right) + vN\right](1 - D)D,$$

$$\frac{dR}{dt} = \left[(1 + pR + sR^2)\left(f\left(\tfrac{R}{D}\right) + aDR + eR\right) + gN\right](1 - R)R,$$

where D and R denote support for the Democratic and Republican parties, t time, and N the proportion of the eligible population that is not voting (the remaining terms denote parameters of the model). Each term in the equations represents assumptions that Brown makes about the change in party support over time. These assumptions are based on empirical evidence and nonformal theories on voter choices: $q\left(\tfrac{D}{R}\right)$ and $f\left(\tfrac{R}{D}\right)$ represent the influence on party support of voters' sensitivity to the relative dominance of the parties; wDR and aDR are designed to capture interactive effects, where voters of one party are affected by the partisanship of voters of the other party; uD and eR measure overall growth rates in party support; $(1 + jD + yD^2)$ and $(1 + pR + sR^2)$ are terms to capture momentum effects; vN and gN are terms to represent mobilization of new voters; and $(1 - D)D$ and $(1 - R)R$ specify the upper and lower bounds on party support. These assumptions and the equation form are not derived from an explicit model of individual voter or party decision making. Brown solves these two equations simultaneously using computer simulations for given parameters, since it is not possible to solve the model analytically for D and R.

3.4   A Typology of Formal Models

Formal models in political and social sciences display a wide variety of assumptions about individual and group behavior. Many formal models in political science are rational choice–based, featuring actors who are assumed to make choices in order to achieve a given goal (or set of goals). A modeler

Table 3.1. *Formal models and assumptions of rationality*

Assumptions About Choice Behavior	Types of Formal Models		
	Individual Behavior Models	Game Theoretic Models	Aggregate Behavior Models
Strong Rationality	Expected Utility Theory	Standard Game Theory	
Almost Rational (e.g. Fairness, Framing, etc.)	Non-linear Expected Utility Theory, Prospect Theory	Behavioral Game Theory	
Non-Rational (e.g. Choice with Cognitive Limitations or Choice Behavior ignored)	Psychological Process Models (Individual level Dynamic Models and Markov Models)	Boundedly Rational, Fictitious Play, Evolutionary, Finite Automata	Aggregate Level Dynamic Differential Equations, Aggregate Level Markov Models

who assumes that actors make rational choices recognizes that their actual thoughts and choice processes may not involve the complex calculations required by rational choice models, but she will generally argue that the actors choose "as if" they do. Game theoretic models are used to analyze situations in which the decisions are strategic – that is, the choices of one individual are likely to be a function of the choices of another individual.

Rational choice–based models are popular and somewhat controversial, but there are many other formal models that use almost rational, boundedly rational, or psychology process models of individual decision making. Behavioral game theory comprises game theoretic models that have been modified to explain noteworthy empirical failures of highly rational game theoretic approaches. Some formal models make assumptions about overall interactions between individuals and groups without specifying explicitly the underlying decision-making process of the relevant agents. Table 3.1 presents the types of formal models used in political science classified by their assumptions about rationality of the actors. Formal models also use a multiplicity of mathematical tools and techniques. This chapter concludes with a discussion of these techniques.

3.5   Mathematical Techniques

We have mentioned – without specifying how they work – several mathematical techniques used in devising and solving formal models in political science. Many of the models discussed use calculus, linear algebra, and optimization theory; others use more sophisticated mathematical techniques. In most cases, we have attempted to provide nontechnical explanations when the examples are discussed. Although a detailed explanation of these tools is beyond the scope of the book, some readers may wish to know more about the variety of tools and their uses. Some of these techniques have already been discussed with respect to game theory and rational choice–based models in political science, and we gave some examples (Brown 1993; Kadera forthcoming) of the use of differential equations in formal models in political science. Such models can be distinguished by whether they assume a deterministic or stochastic process. In many cases (as in Brown and Kadera), complex differential equation models can only be solved numerically using computer simulations. (See Maki and Thompson 1972 for a discussion of differential equation models.)

Formal modelers also use a variety of models from probability theory. For example, probabilistic voting and quantal response game theoretic models are based on the work of Luce (1959) and McFadden (1974), which is explored in Chapter 4. Markov chain models have been used in political science; these models, too, are based on a concept from probability theory (see Taylor and Karlin 1984 for a more detailed explanation of Markov chains). In a Markov chain model, there is a "process" and a set of objects called "states." There is also a set of transition probabilities that define the probability that the process moves from one state to another (i.e., p_{ij} may be defined as the probability that the process moves from state i to state j). Given certain specific premises about the transition probabilities and the process, there are a number of mathematical theorems about Markov chains that can then be used to solve a model whose assumptions follow the same premises. Converse (1969) and Trevor (1995) analyze party identification using a Markov chain model. Markov chains are used to analyze repeated games with finite automata (discussed in Section 3.3.1) as well as probabilistic voting models, which are discussed in Chapter 6. Markov chains are also used in some stochastic game theoretic models.

Graph theory is another mathematical tool that has been used in social sciences. Most are aware of the meaning and use of graphs in mathematics and calculus. Typically, a graph is seen as the "picture" of a function of one or more real variables. In graph or network theory, however, the term *graph* has a different meaning: a collection of points and a collection of lines connecting certain pairs of the points. As with Markov chains, there is an extensive theory of graphs that has been used in social network theory and could be used as a basis for formal models in the social sciences. (For additional information on graph theory and applications to sociology, see Buckley and Harary 1990; Gould 1991, 1993; Macy 1991.)

PART III

Empirical Evaluation of Formal Models

CHAPTER 4

Fundamentals of Empirical Evaluation

Now that I have examined what formal models are and are not, I present in this chapter an overview of the fundamentals of empirically evaluating formal models. The basic question in such evaluation is: How does the structure of a formal model translate into the mathematical structure of an empirical or statistical model? Before addressing this question, I appraise the types of empirical evaluations of formal models.

4.1 Types of Empirical Evaluations of Formal Models

Empirical evaluation of formal models may be organized as follows:

1. evaluation of assumptions;
2. evaluation of predictions;
3. evaluation of alternative models.

As shown in Chapter 2, assumptions are an integral part of formal models, and many are not verified. Even so, empirical support for assumptions can be important for evaluating theory. I explore the meaning of evaluating assumptions in the next chapter. Evaluating predictions and alternative models are the two means of assessing a formal model, given its assumptions, with respect to the real world.

4.1.1 *Evaluating Predictions*

Imagine that the impossible is possible – that a formal model exists in which all of the assumptions have empirical support. Is it necessary then to evaluate predictions of the model at all? If the predictions have been derived appropriately, using deductive logic, can the researchers simply conclude that the predictions are true because the assumptions are known to be true? Even in such a perfect situation, it is still necessary to analyze predictions of models. A researcher may be in error in believing that the assumptions are true, or he may have erred in his deductive logic. As argued in Chapter 2, one of the chief advantages of formal models is that inconsistent or flawed logic is easier to detect than in nonformal models. A model is not evaluated if its predictions are not analyzed, regardless of how true the assumptions of the model are believed to be.

There are many different predictions made by formal models. I divide these predictions into four categories:

- point or equilibrium predictions;
- multi- or disequilibrium predictions;
- comparative static predictions;
- process or dynamic path predictions.

Point or equilibrium predictions are predictions a model makes about a variable (or variables) when the model's variables are said to be in "equilibrium" (a concept I address shortly). Empirical analysis of the point predictions of spatial voting models is considered in Chapter 6. However, sometimes a model predicts more than one equilibrium or no equilibrium or even disequilibrium (in which case the prediction is no equilibrium). Chapter 6 examines the empirical study of voting models with multiple equilibria using laboratory experiments.

Models provide predictions about the relationship between variables, which are typically called comparative static predictions. *Comparative statics* is the analysis of how the equilibrium value of an endogenous variable in the model (the dependent variable) changes with a change in the value of an exogenous variable in the model (the independent variable). Chapter 7 presents examples of comparative static analyses of models of voting on Supreme Court nominees. Finally, process or dynamic path predictions involve the comparison of real-world dynamic processes with a model's predicted dynamic path. Chapter 7 also discusses how models of political business cycles have been considered empirically using both laboratory and real-world data.

Equilibria in Games. So far I have not been very precise about what I mean by "equilibrium." Equilibrium definitions depend upon the type of model investigated and the assumptions made about individual or group behavior.

For example, as noted in Chapter 2, noncooperative game theory researchers often determine whether Nash equilibria exist. An outcome is said to be a *Nash equilibrium* when each player's strategy choice is a best reply to the strategy choices of the other players. That is, each player's strategy maximizes his or her expected payoffs from the game, given the strategy choices of the other players in the game. Unfortunately (or fortunately, depending on your point of view), many game theoretic models have multiple Nash equilibria. This has led to refinements of the Nash equilibrium concept that make additional assumptions about individual choice behavior. This will be discussed further when I address the empirical evaluation of multiple equilibria in Chapter 6.

Although recent game theory work in political science emphasizes noncooperative game theory, much game theoretic research in political science – particularly the early work – takes a cooperative approach (as discussed in Chapter 3). An equilibrium concept often used in cooperative game theory is the *core*, which requires that no set of actors or players in the game be able to deviate and take a joint action that makes all of them better off. One empirical problem with equilibria from cooperative game theory is that these concepts are typically ordinal rather than cardinal, which leads to some inability to interpret empirical data (see McKelvey 1991 for a discussion of this issue).

Equilibria in Other Models. Equilibria are also relevant in non–game theoretic models. For example, the theory of competitive equilibrium used in economics is not game theoretic. In the traditional economic theory of competition, firms, consumers, and factors of production all make decisions taking the actions of others as given and unaffected by their own decisions. Firms, consumers, and the factors of production observe parameters (e.g., prices of consumer goods, wages, etc.) and then optimize given those parameters. The parameters are functions of the combined decisions of the agents, and equilibrium occurs when all the actors are choosing optimally given the parameters. Osborne and Rubinstein discuss how game theory differs from the theory of competitive equilibrium.

Game theoretic reasoning takes into account the attempts by each decision-maker to obtain, prior to making his decision, information about the other players' behavior, while competitive reasoning assumes that each agent is interested only in some environmental parameters (such as prices), even though these parameters are determined by the actions of all agents.

To illustrate the difference between the theories, consider an environment in which the level of some activity (like fishing) of each agent depends on the level of pollution, which in turn depends on the levels of the agents' activities. In a competitive analysis of this situation we look for a level of pollution consistent with the actions that the agents take when each of them regards this level as given. By contrast, in a game theoretic analysis of the situation we require that each agent's action be optimal given the agent's expectation of the pollution created by the combination of his action and all the other agents' actions. (1994, pp. 3–4)

In general terms, equilibria in non–game theoretic models are derived by solving the models for analytical solutions to the equations that are used to describe the model. These solutions may or may not be stable. When a solution is stable, it is considered to be an equilibrium solution.[1] Note that rational choice–based models are not always game theoretic. That is, the actors are assumed to make choices given the parameters of the model; these parameters may be functions of the choices of other actors, which actors are free to ignore. Thus the model is decision theoretic rather than game theoretic as in the competitive equilibria of economics. Modelers find the equilibrium solutions to these models by solving for the optimal decisions of the actors, given the models' assumptions about (a) the relationships of actor decisions and (b) the actors' preferences over outcomes. (See Gates and Humes 1997 for examples of game theoretic and decision theoretic models in political science.) Finally, there exist game theoretic and decision theoretic models that are "almost rational choice"–based (as in behavioral game theory) or "nonrational choice"–based (as in evolutionary game theory, discussed in Chapter 3).

As mentioned in Chapter 2, some formal modelers work with computational models that have not been solved analytically. These modelers derive equilibrium predictions for given numerical values of the parameters of the model, which are then sometimes compared with the real world. The numerical predictions depend both on the model's assumptions and the assumptions of the computer simulation design (i.e., the numerics used for the simulations in setting parameters and initial conditions in dynamic models).

4.1.2   Evaluating Alternative Models

Advantage of Alternative Models. There are usually several formal models that can explain or address a given empirical phenomenon. Ideally, comparing alternative models tells us more than analyzing the assumptions or

---

[1] More precise characterization of the concepts of solution and stability depend on the type of formal model considered. For example, an equilibrium solution in differential equation models is a solution that is independent of time, whereas a steady-state solution is one that is valid for long intervals of time and is independent of initial conditions. Many differential equation models, like game theoretic models, do not have unique equilibria.

predictions of just one model. When a researcher evaluates one model's assumptions or predictions, the alternative is simply that they do not hold; there is no alternative theory if the model is rejected. This sort of analysis is useful, but it takes a researcher only part of the way to empirical discovery. Typically researchers end up revising the existing theory or model and then analyzing the revised version. The empirical results rejecting the model must therefore lead to more theorizing, which is then empirically evaluated.

In contrast, when researchers compare models they are evaluating one theoretical formulation against another. A study of alternative models should reveal more than the study of a single model, but a comparative analysis of alternative models is usually more difficult. First, a researcher must consider whether (say) two models are truly contrasting explanations. Each model incorporates a set of assumptions from which results have been derived. Are these assumptions inconsistent with each other? If the assumptions are inconsistent and the solutions to the models have distinct implications, a researcher can then examine the predictions of the models to test between them. A researcher can also analyze the differences in assumptions, but such evaluation cannot prove that one model's predictions are supported over the other. In Chapter 8 I present two example analyses of competing spatial voting models: one a comparison of predictions, the other of assumptions. Evaluating alternative models by considering their difference in assumptions does not always yield a definitive answer, since researchers know that all formal models make some false assumptions. Researchers should also look at differences in the models' predictions. Sometimes such studies are conclusive and a researcher can reject one model in favor of another. Often, however, results are not conclusive.

How Do We Tell When a Model Is an Alternative? If the assumptions are not inconsistent, does it make sense then to compare the two models' predictions? Suppose two models make very different predictions about the same phenomena. Would not evaluating the predictions of these models resolve the issue? Not necessarily. It may be that the two models are simply special cases of a third, more general model. By focusing on the competition between the two more restrictive models, empirical analysis of the issue may be flawed. In Chapter 8 I present an example (from the literature on campaign contributions) of two apparent alternative models that can be shown to be cases of a more general model, which is then evaluated. Again, formal models with explicitly stated assumptions allow researchers to recognize such cases. When two predictions are presented as conjectures of nonformal models without explicitly stated assumptions, it is impossible to know that the assumptions are not inconsistent and that the different predictions can be explained by a more general model.

Almost always, some assumptions are consistent across models and others not; likewise, two models with inconsistent assumptions may generate like and unlike predictions. Thus, most alternative models are both complements and substitutes. This makes evaluating models complex and not as easy or clean as researchers would "theoretically" prefer. Thus, researchers often need to make judgment calls that should be justified by further empirical analysis. Researchers need to determine the essential differences between models and what should therefore be studied. Chapter 8 presents two example analyses of principal–agent models that have differences as well as similarities.

In some cases the alternative that a formal model is compared with is a nonformal model. In this situation it is difficult to understand what a comparison between the competing predictions implies for our understanding of the phenomena. If the alternative theory has no specified underlying assumptions then what does it mean when the competing prediction is shown to be supported over the formally derived one? In my view, making empirical comparisons between a formal and a nonformal model is similar to testing the formal model against a more specified alternative hypothesis, but it is not an evaluation of competing theory. If the formal model is unsuccessful in an empirical comparison with an nonformally derived hypothesis then we must return to the theoretical drawing board, much as when a formal model is analyzed in isolation. The competing nonformal theory may help point us in a certain theoretical direction and thus be more useful than a less precise alternative hypothesis, but the competition cannot be viewed as theoretically satisfying until researchers formulate a precise and explicit model that has been supported by empirical analysis. Chapter 8 presents two example tests of formal models versus nonformal theorizing – one from the literature on international relations and one from the literature on Congressional bill sponsorship.

4.2   The Model, the Truth, and Randomness

While I classify the empirical evaluation of formal models into three categories, it is important to recognize that these are not independent "tests" of a model. That is, each type of evaluation plays a different and important role in model evaluation and is fundamentally related to the other types of evaluation. Comparing a model with alternatives is a crucial step in the evaluation of a model, and it implicitly involves evaluating the predictions and assumptions of the model as compared with other theories. Evaluating predictions, which is usually the main focus of empirical analysis of formal models, is not independent of assumption evaluation. The empirical analyses of the predictions of a model begin with decisions on how the formal model is translated into an empirical model for evaluation (the researchers' view of the relationship between the assumptions of the formal model and the real world). Thus, evaluating assumptions is the first step in relating the predictions of a formal model to the real world. Finally, this evaluation depends critically on the extent that predictions of the model hinge on the verifiability of the assumptions! These types of evaluation are not separate and distinct; they are interrelated and vital parts of a general evaluation process.

In the next chapter I discuss assumption evaluation in more detail: how it can be done, its limits, and some examples. But first, consider the researcher's decision given an existing formal model with a set of assumptions. How does the researcher conduct an empirical evaluation of the predictions of that model? Take, for example, the Banks and Kiewiet model of candidate competition discussed in Chapter 2. How should the researcher view the relationship between the formal model and the data that he plans to use in his analysis? The researcher must answer two questions as follows.

1. Should the formal model be viewed as a *complete* data generating process (Complete DGP) or as a *partial* data generating process (Partial DGP) for the data of interest? In other words, is the maintained assumption in the empirical evaluation that the formal model *is* the DGP or is it not? The answer to this question determines the extent to which the empirical model must match the formal model.
2. What is the nature of the variables in the formal model? That is, formal models are of two types: either *entirely* deterministic or *deterministic with unobservables* and/or stochastic elements. These two different types of formal models imply different types of empirical analyses and resulting empirical models.

The researcher's tasks depend upon answers to these two questions. I shall explore each of these questions in more detail.

When should a model be considered a Complete DGP? In Chapter 2 I noted that models are designed to answer particular questions and showed how the details that are emphasized or ignored depend upon the questions of interest. In modeling a bridge, for example, the artistic aspects of the bridge facade may be irrelevant to some questions about how the bridge works yet relevant for other purposes. Models must by definition make some false assumptions. One very common assumption is the ceteris paribus assumption (discussed in Chapter 2): there are aspects of the real world that might affect the analysis but are assumed constant or fixed for the analysis in question. For example, in the simple model of the relationship between income and turnout (Section 2.3.1), the model ignores the impact of other elections on the likelihood that a voter will vote in a single election. When the model was solved, this aspect of the real world was ignored. The empirical predictions that were made about the relationship between income and voting are only relevant for the case where there is a single election. Since the model has not been "solved" for the case of multiple elections, we can only conjecture about the effects multiple elections will have on turnout and on the relationship between income and turnout. One conjecture might be that a larger number of elections increases the benefits from voting and therefore the likelihood that the voter will turn out in the multiple election. The other election may have a bigger potential effect on the individual's income or perhaps a different or offsetting effect on the individual's income. Alternatively, the cost of voting may rise both because the general turnout level is increased (a relationship ignored in the simple model) and/or because the voter perceives participation as more costly owing to an increase in some exogenous decision-making cost. The model as it exists makes no assumptions or predictions about how multiple elections will ultimately affect turnout.

Now suppose that the same model's predictions about turnout are to be empirically evaluated. The data set the researcher would like to use combines data on voters across jurisdictions such that some voters are voting in only one election, others two, and others still more elections. The researcher has three choices: (1) re-solve the model for the case with multiple elections and assume that the model is a Complete DGP; (2) assume that the model is a Complete DGP and ignore the fact that the number of elections varies across voters; or (3) assume that the model is a Partial DGP, recognize that the variation in number of elections may have an effect on turnout, and attempt to control for this in the empirical analysis.

4.2.1   Option 1: Re-solving the Model

Choosing option 1 is an extremely tempting choice. Why should we even attempt to empirically evaluate a model that we know omits what may be very important factors? Choosing option 1 makes considerable sense when the theory of interest is what I called "pure theory" in earlier chapters. As discussed previously, "applied theory" means taking pure theoretical models and putting them in a context that facilitates empirical evaluation. Thus, choosing option 1 is sometimes a necessary step.

But we must accept the fact that all models make some false or inaccurate assumptions, so a researcher cannot repeatedly re-solve the model before conducting empirical analysis. Hence option 1 must, *at some point,* be abandoned. In fact, I think it can be dangerous to insist that an applied theoretical model be re-solved continually with more and more general formulations but without any empirical analysis. That is, a theorist who continues to work with a model that has received scant (or no) empirical evaluation may unwittingly ignore or perpetuate fundamental problems with basics of the model. This is the danger when theorists speak only to theorists using applied theory.

Demanding that theory be continually re-solved (to account for conjectured effects) before empirical analysis is conducted can also be dangerous for empirical research. Suppose a researcher has a choice of empirically evaluating a formal model that has precise and false assumptions versus empirically evaluating a set of nonformal conjectures that the researcher has about the data. If the empiricist rejects the formal model as a basis for analysis simply because of its restrictiveness and instead relies on the nonformal conjectures, there are limits to what can be learned from the data. As argued in Chapter 2, empirical analysis based on nonformal models can only tell us whether the conjectures are supported or not. This can be a starting point in theory, but ultimately we must work with a formally derived theory for data to help us build a better theoretical understanding of the real world.

Fortunately, most who attempt to empirically evaluate formal models in political science recognize the dangers of choosing option 1. As a result, most researchers choose option 3 (Partial DGP) or argue that choosing option 2 (Complete DGP) has merit. Sometimes a researcher chooses option 3, demonstrates that variables once suspected to be problematic are actually insignificant, and then uses this outcome to justify option 2. In other words, the researcher argues that the "problematic" variables are not significant effects on the dependent variable or that they are not biasing the empirical analysis of the model because they are not correlated with the independent variables. In this case the researcher presents the empirical analysis in terms of a model that is a Complete DGP with unobservable and/or stochastic elements. Most empirical analyses of formal models choose option 3 (Partial

DGP), although option 2 (Complete DGP) has been used in a number of notable cases. Next I discuss some reasons why assuming a Complete DGP may have value even though the researcher knows that – owing to the nature of its assumptions – the model cannot be a Complete DGP. I then discuss choosing option 3 (Partial DGP).

4.2.2   *Option 2: Complete DGP*

Using Naturally Occurring Data. A researcher who chooses option 2 (Complete DGP) is likely to be strongly criticized for ignoring a variable that could systematically affect the dependent variable (turnout) and might be correlated with the independent variable (measures of income), leading to bias in the estimated relationship between income and turnout. Researchers choosing option 2 are particularly likely to be criticized if they are using naturally occurring data, which are likely to cause measurement error when the researcher cannot control for many factors outside of the simple model.

Nevertheless, as a first "cut" at the data's relationship to the model, I believe that a researcher should choose option 2 before the other options. In fact, I suspect most researchers do conduct simple empirical analyses of data, implicitly taking option 2 as a start to empirical analysis. For example, in Schmidt, Kenny, and Morton (1996; discussed in Chapter 8), the researchers suspect that senators seeking re-election are more likely to choose policy positions closer to the position of their political party in their states than to the median voter in their states.[2] The authors use data for senator positions across states and a number of years to evaluate their prediction empirically. They first show, using tables and figures, the simple relationship between (a) the frequency of running for re-election and winning and (b) the distance of the senators' policy positions from both their state parties' positions and their state median voters' positions; this relationship supports their prediction. Then they present an analysis of the data – assuming the underlying formal model to be a Partial DGP – in two logistic regressions, inserting variables they suspect might also affect a senator's re-election probabilities (e.g., the senator's age and his party's control of the Congress).

As discussed in what follows, if the model is deterministic, makes stark unique point predictions, and is viewed as a Complete DGP, then any "errant"

---

[2] Although they do not present a formal model in their analysis, the hypothesis is a test of the convergence prediction of the Hotelling–Downsian model versus the divergence prediction of other formal models of elections.

observation is evidence that the model fails. Thus, unless a model has a stochastic component, option 2 is an extremely strong test for a formal model
to satisfy – particularly if a researcher focuses on point prediction success or
failure as distinct from comparative static or dynamic path predictions (see
Chapters 6 and 7 for more detailed discussion). Precisely because it is such
a strong test, option 2 is a useful beginning for the empirical analysis of a
model. Yet this also means that the results of the evaluation should not be
used to reject the model, since few models (and perhaps none that would be
very useful) would pass such a strong test without *any* errant observations.
The number of errant observations (and the distance they may be from our
predictions) give us crucial guidance in empirically evaluating this type of
model, but they are not reasons to reject the model unequivocally.

Using Experimental Data. Choosing option 2 when the data is experimental – when the researcher can control, through design, many of the factors
that are "outside" or ignored by the model – is also an important first step
in empirical evaluation of the model. This is called a "theory" or controlled
test of the model. Roth calls this "speaking to theorists," which he notes
"includes experiments designed to test the predictions of well articulated
formal theories, and to observe unpredicted regularities, in a controlled environment that allows these observations to be unambiguously interpreted in
relationship to the theory. Such experiments are intended to feed back into
the theoretical literature – i.e., they are part of a dialogue between experi-
menters and theorists"[3] (1995, p. 22).

  As discussed previously, Morton (1993) tests the Calvert model of policy-
motivated candidates using laboratory experiments. The empirical analysis
shows how the process of assuming the model is a Complete DGP can work.
The formal model presents explicit predicted (divergent) positions for the
two candidates when they do not know the policy position most preferred by
the median voter, and it predicts that the two candidates will converge at the
median voter's most preferred position when the candidates do know the median voter's preferences (a comparative static prediction). The experimental

---

[3] One way that some modelers explore the deductive logic of their models is by using computer simulations, as in the computational models discussed in Chapter 2. Simulations are
not the same as experimental analysis of models, since their role is primarily to help generate
predictions for given parameter specifications used in solving models rather than to provide
empirical evidence. Simulations are aids in solving rather than empirically analyzing models; the computer is acting as an extension of the modeler's brain. However, simulations can
be coupled with experimental analysis of models, as noted in Chapter 2.

evidence shows that when candidates have policy motivations and there is uncertainty, there is more divergence than otherwise. The empirical study thus shows support for the prediction that uncertainty leads to candidate divergence in positions. Yet the subjects in the experiment chose positions less divergent than predicted (an equilibrium point prediction). That is, the model predicts precise positions and the subjects chose positions that are significantly closer than predicted (although still divergent enough to support the prediction that uncertainty about voter preferences, coupled with policy preferences of the candidates, causes divergence). So the empirical results both support the comparative static prediction of the theory and reject the point prediction of the theory.

While seemingly inconsistent, the results provide important information about how a better model can be developed. That is, the new theory should keep the comparative static prediction that policy motivations cause divergence and that the degree of divergence is affected by the degree to which candidates are uncertain about the location of the median voter's ideal point. But the new theory should explain why the candidates converge more than predicted if they are motivated purely by policy preferences; it should explain why the point prediction fails. The experimental results, taking the theory as a Complete DGP, provide useful and significant information for devising a better explanation of candidate divergence in policy positions.

For another example of the usefulness of empirical analysis on theories assuming the model is a Complete DGP, consider again the experiments on the ultimatum and dictator bargaining games discussed in Chapter 3. Under the assumption that the theory is a Complete DGP, data analysis showing that the stark formal model fails to predict presents theorists with important new information on actual choices in the modeled situation. That the theory works better in dictator games than in ultimatum games is a meaningful result for future theories of the bargaining process. Because of early analysis of bargaining games under this approach, such modifications in existing theory as Rabin's fairness concept (discussed in Chapter 3) are possible. This type of empirical evidence is the crux of devising behavioral game theory (as discussed by Camerer 1997 and mentioned also in Chapter 3).

Digression: Experiments versus Naturally Occurring Data and Control. As previously noted, experiments allow a researcher to use the experimental design to control for variables or factors outside a formal model and so perform useful "theory" tests of the model. However, in the experimental environment it is important that the design not be "hard-wired" – in other words, that the subjects in the experiment *not* be told what decisions or choices they should make. Even though the researcher's model may assume that individuals choose noncooperative strategies, if the researcher told subjects what choices to make then the experiment is no more than a simulation. Thus, controlled tests in the laboratory should always allow for freedom of decision of the subjects in the experiments.[4]

These types of experiments, then, are empirical analyses of a formal model's ability to predict behavior in an environment as close as possible to the model's assumed environment. These theory-driven experiments are high in internal validity; that is, they are valid in terms of the design's internal consistency. They are controlled experimental analysis or "theory" tests (see Davis and Holt 1993). However, in a number of cases these types of experiments have been criticized as not having "external validity." Some researchers argue that, because the experimental design closely mirrors the unreal world of the model, it must have no significant relevance to the naturally occurring environment. These researchers argue that such theory-driven experiments, despite their internal validity, are not strong enough empirical tests of models. Experiments where the abstractions and misrepresentations of the model are not completely controlled – which Davis and Holt (1993) call experimental "stress" tests of models, to distinguish from "theory" tests – tell researchers something entirely different from the controlled experiments. They tell researchers the extent to which the model can help them understand what they observe in casual experience when some of the assumptions of the model no longer hold.

It is important to recognize that a researcher who designs the experiment as a "stress" test may still analyze the data as if the model were a Complete DGP. There are two separate issues: experimental design and how the model is viewed for empirical evaluation. That is, sometimes an experiment is designed as a "theory" test and the empirical analysis is conducted assuming the model is a Complete DGP, as in the example of Morton (1993). The empirical analysis shows that the theory has flaws, and later analysis may assume that the model is a Partial DGP. In an experiment designed as a "stress" test, the empirical analysis is also conducted assuming the model

---

[4] See Hoffman, Marsden, and Whinston (1986, 1990) for discussions of the links between experiments, simulations, and statistical analyses.

is a Complete DGP in order to see if the theory is still supported, much as nonexperimental data as a first cut can be analyzed as a Complete DGP.

My attitude is that both types of experimental designs (theory and stress) are valuable – but in distinct ways. If a model can satisfy both less controlled (stress tests) and controlled experiments (theory tests), the model has empirical support of an extremely high order. It helps researchers understand what they see in the naturally occurring world, and the logic of the model is substantiated. Similarly, a model that fails both types of analyses can tell researchers little about reality. Nevertheless, it is incorrect to conclude that such a model is worthless. The failure of the model can help theorists learn how to construct models of reality in better ways.

Suppose that a model's predictions are supported by controlled experiments but not by less controlled experiments. In this case, the logic of the model receives justification: the controlled experiments show that the model's hypotheses do follow *if* the real world looks like the model. But the less controlled experiments tell us that there are important ways in which the real world does not look like the model, aspects of the real world that need to be considered if theorists wish to make useful predictions. This kind of result will help lead theorists to explore relaxing the assumptions of the model and to construct better, more accurate abstractions from reality. In contrast, if a model is substantiated in the less controlled environment but not in controlled experiments then it is hard to see how useful the model is as a starting point for understanding the real world, since the model's internal logic is not supported empirically.

An Example of Theory and Stress Tests in Experiments: The Condorcet Jury Theorem. Consider a political science example of an experimental analysis of a model in which control is varied. Some of the more interesting and recently popular theoretical models describe majority voting under incomplete information. That is, suppose that all the voters in the electorate have common preferences over an outcome. For example, a jury needs to decide whether there is reasonable evidence that an individual is guilty of a crime, and all agree that making an accurate decision is desirable. Likewise, all may agree that electing an honest candidate is desirable, but voters do not know the level of honesty of the candidates before them. Assume that each individual receives some piece of evidence on the true state of the world and that the evidence is drawn from a known distribution. If all the information were truthfully revealed, the group would be able to make the correct decision. But suppose the individuals make their choice via majority rule. Will the majority-rule outcome match the one individuals make under complete information? Some theoretical results suggest it is highly probable that voters will not make the same choice and that the voting process will not be successful at aggregating information. The proposition that majority rule *will* successfully aggregate information is based on the work of Condorcet (1785) and is typically called the Condorcet jury theorem. Austen-Smith and Banks (1996) show that information aggregation may not occur.

How can this model be analyzed experimentally? One way to evaluate the Condorcet jury theorem empirically is to set up a laboratory experiment in which the true state of the world is a function of whether a black ball is drawn from an urn containing a fixed distribution of black and white balls. Each subject is given a "signal" about the true state of the world, which is also a random draw from an urn containing mixed colors of balls (and where the distribution of the balls is a function of the true state of the world). Note that each subject's signal is revealed privately and that the state-of-the-world draw is not revealed. After all subjects have been signalled, they vote on the two alternative states of the world. Their payoff is higher if their vote as a whole is correct (see Ladha, Miller, and Oppenheimer 1996).

This experimental design closely resembles the theoretical model and has a significant amount of control. What would a less controlled design resemble? One way to construct a less controlled design would be to make the ability of the subjects to distinguish the signal more subject-dependent. That is, instead of using an easily observed draw of a ball as the individual signals, a researcher could use more elaborate auditory or visual signals such as those used in psychological experiments.[5] This is slightly more realistic in that individuals may differ in their abilities to distinguish signals in the naturally occurring environment. The extent of information aggregation observed in the less controlled environment can provide additional information about the empirical reliability of the Condorcet jury theorem. Note that loosening control is more useful if researchers find information aggregation does occur through majority voting than if results in controlled experiments show that such aggregation does not occur.

Control, Experiments, and Partial DGPs. Interestingly, the standard reasoning on whether to use less controlled empirical analysis seems

---

[5] For a general review of experimentation in political science and of how psychological experiments are used, see McGraw (1996).

to depend partly on whether the analysis is conducted using real-world data versus data generated in the laboratory. When using real-world data, the assumption is typically that the more controlled the analysis with additional variables the better the analysis. This is implicitly assumed in most texts on methods in political science. If the analysis is evaluating a formal model, there is a tendency in the discipline to force a researcher to view the model as a Partial DGP (as just discussed), controlling for conjectures about variables or factors outside the model that might matter in the empirical evaluation. Researchers who attempt to take the model as a Complete DGP, ignoring what others suppose are important variables outside of the model, are unlikely to have their research published unless they can prove that the variables they ignore are insignificant.

In contrast, highly controlled experiments in experimental analysis are criticized for not having "external validity." Less control is seen as increasing the reliability of the experiments in terms of their validity for the external world. As a consequence, experimentalists are also pressured to assume that their models are Partial DGPs. That is, a researcher who introduces less control in a "stress" test will face the same pressure to use statistics and additional variables in the empirical data analysis as a researcher working with nonexperimental data.

Thus, methodologists often call for more control in standard empirical work on naturally occurring data and for less control when generating laboratory data; in both cases, researchers may be forced to assume their model is a Partial DGP. In my view, the need for more or less control depends upon the results from earlier analysis and the question that the researcher is interested in examining. I argue in the next section that researchers must be extremely careful when adding control variables to empirical analysis of formal models with naturally occurring data, since such additions can in fact significantly lessen the ability of the analysis to provide evidence on the empirical value of the formal model.

Deterministic Models and Complete DGP: The Zero-Likelihood Problem. The second important question for a researcher – which is combined with the decision about whether the model is to be viewed as a Complete or Partial DGP – is how to view the model's variables: as deterministic or not. Some deterministic formal models have already been discussed in Chapters 2 and 3. Consider a simple one-period version of the Baron–Ferejohn legislative bargaining game discussed in both chapters. That is, suppose that there are three parties in the legislature (all with less than 50% of the votes) and that one is chosen to propose a division of portfolios between the parties, which is voted by simple majority rule in the legislature. If the proposal is turned down then the parties will all receive a status quo allocation of portfolios. In equilibrium the party chosen to make a proposal will choose a coalition partner with the lower (of the other two parties) status quo allocation of portfolios and propose to that party just that amount of portfolios (assuming that an indifferent coalition partner will vote in favor of the proposal) and zero to the third party. The predictions of this model are stark and clear. If it is viewed as a complete data generating process, then any observation contrary to the predictions of the model is evidence against the model.

It is well known (see e.g. the discussion in Signorino 1998) that deterministic game theoretical analyses like the Baron–Ferejohn model are especially problematic for much of the statistical analysis used in political science as a result of the so-called zero-likelihood problem. That is, most statistical analysis used in political science involves finding a set of parameters in the empirical model that are the most likely to generate the observed outcomes. The procedure is to maximize a likelihood function that is the product of the probabilities of the observed outcomes for the values of the independent variables and the parameters of the empirical model (see King 1989). The statistical analysis then requires that the researcher assign a probability distribution over the outcomes of the dependent variable for the parameters and independent variables in the analysis. But the prediction of the deterministic game theoretic model with a unique equilibrium is that the equilibrium outcome will occur with certainty (probability equal to 1) and that nonequilibrium outcomes will certainly not occur (probability equal to 0).[6] However, if even a single outcome is not predicted by the model then the likelihood equation to be estimated (because it is a product of the probabilities) will equal zero, regardless of the parameters specified or the values of the independent variables. The statistical estimation is thus impossible.

Since it is hard to imagine that any data generating process would yield these kinds of absolute results except in very rare cases, it seems almost foolhardy for a researcher to approach data from this point of view (i.e. using a deterministic model and assuming that it is a Complete DGP). Moreover,

[6] Note that, if the equilibrium prediction is that the players will use mixed strategies such that all outcomes have a positive probability, then this problem does not arise. This issue is addressed in the following subsection.

if we could not employ our sophisticated statistical analysis then what use is it to view the model as deterministic and a Complete DGP? Does it ever make sense to take this approach when evaluating a formal model? In fact, there are two good reasons to take a deterministic model and empirically evaluate it under the assumption that it is a Complete DGP. The first reason is that the deterministic model's predictions might actually resemble a stochastic or random process. In some deterministic time-series processes that are nonlinear, the formal model's predictions are chaotic or widely variable over time and may look like stochastic time-series processes.[7] Thus, not all deterministic models make predictions as stark and absolute as the Baron–Ferejohn model.

Second, as argued before, it is desirable to evaluate a deterministic model as a Complete DGP in order to provide the theorist with better feedback on the success or failure of the model. To some social scientists, empirical research that assumes that a deterministic model is the DGP may seem uninteresting and of little value. Yet this empirical evaluation is a crucial link in building formal models that can significantly increase our understanding of naturally occurring data. If the empirical evidence supports the theory then the theory has received confirmation. Although empirical research supporting the theory is nice, usually the results also show limitations of the theory and, most critically, where these limitations lie. That is, results may be contrary to the theory in some ways but supportive in others, and this information can help the theorist build better theory. This is true even when the model is deterministic.

Deterministic/Stochastic and Complete DGP. Not all formal models are deterministic. Deterministic game theoretic models with unique mixed strategy equilibria in which all the possible outcomes are assigned a probability can be estimated using the sophisticated maximum likelihood estimation procedures described previously. However, this is a rare case. In some cases the randomness inherent in a model makes an empirical analysis almost impossible. Take for example models that are "cheap talk" games in which communication is costless (see Morrow 1994, pp. 250–6). In these models there are almost always babbling equilibria, equilibria in which the

---

[7] For example, dynamic games can be in equilibrium (a Nash equilibrium) while the state variable follows a chaotic trajectory, as in some dynamic public goods problems. Richards (1992) discusses deterministic models with chaotic trajectories and presents a method of testing time-series data for the presence of chaos in a deterministic process within what appear to be stochastic processes.

communication is totally unrelated to the information that the actors may have. But there are sometimes other equilibria in which actors are communicating. Suppose that a researcher wants to empirically estimate the model. The researcher could simply attribute "bad" observations to the babbling equilibria, but doing so would eliminate the possibility of evaluating the model. The problem of multiple equilibria and empirical evaluation is addressed in Chapter 6.

Adapting Deterministic Models with Unobservable Preferences. In other cases, deterministic models with unobservable and/or stochastic elements can be empirically evaluated. However, the analysis can be difficult to evaluate because the stochastic or unobservable element may make the empirical study tautological. One explanation for the contrary results in Morton (1993) is that the candidates have "mixed motives"; that is, they care about winning and about policy, but the utility they receive from winning is unobservable. When candidates have mixed motives their expected utility is a weighted average of the expected utility they would receive from winning alone and the expected utility they would receive from the policy chosen by the winning candidate. Thus, the existence of mixed motives can lead to less policy divergence between two candidates than the purely policy-motivated model would predict. However, unless the weight parameter is specified explicitly, adding the assumption of mixed motives amounts to a tautology; it can proffer a possible explanation of the lack of complete predicted divergence, but it cannot be said that the empirical evidence supports that explanation since it is not evaluated.

The analysis in Morton (1993) takes the following approach: If it is assumed that all error in meeting the equilibrium point prediction is due to mixed motives, what weight on being elected is implied by the empirical research? The model becomes a maintained hypothesis and the data is used only to calibrate the parameters in the model. There is no empirical evaluation of the formal model where candidates have mixed motives; the point is analysis of the implications of the model if it is true. Of course, some of the parameter estimates may be so suspect that one could discount the model on that account, especially if there is independent evidence on the size of the parameters estimated. Generally, however, for the mixed-motive explanation of the predicted divergence to be supported through empirical analysis, the researcher would need to make explicit assumptions (about the weight parameter) that can be considered empirically.

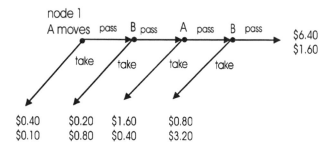

Figure 4.1. Centipede game.

The concept that the payoffs of players in games may be subject to unobservable factors that can explain the inability of the deterministic solution to fit the data is evidenced in a number of different formal game theoretic models. Two models of the centipede game provide an illustration of these types of formal models and how they have been empirically estimated using experimental data as Complete DGPs.[8] The version of the centipede game used in the experiments is illustrated in Figure 4.1.[9] The game has two players, A and B, and – as in alternating bargaining models – the players take turns making choices. At the first node of the game (labeled node 1), player A chooses "take" or "pass." If she chooses take, she stops the game and receives $0.40 while player B receives $0.10. If player A chooses pass then the game continues and player B has the next move at the second node. Then player B chooses whether to take (stop the game) or pass (continue the game). If player B chooses take, the game stops at node 2 and player A receives $0.20 and player B receives $0.80. If player B chooses pass, the game continues and player A has the next move at the third node. Player A, again, chooses take (stop the game) or pass (continue the game). If player A chooses take, the game stops at node 3 and player A receives $1.60 and player B receives $0.40. If player A chooses pass, the game continues and player B has the last move at the fourth node. At node 4 player B also chooses between take and pass. At node 4, if player B takes then A receives $0.80 and player B receives $3.20, but if player B passes then A receives $6.40 and B receives $1.60.

---

[8] See Fey, McKelvey, and Palfrey (1996) and McKelvey and Palfrey (1992, 1995, 1998). The centipede game was first discussed by Rosenthal (1982), whose version of the game has 100 "legs"; hence the name centipede.

[9] Two versions of the game were the subject of experimental investigation (one with four legs and the other six legs), but I will restrict my discussion to the four-leg version.

Standard game theory, assuming that players choose in order to maximize their payoffs, predicts that the game will end at the first move and that player A will choose to take, receiving $0.40 and with B receiving $0.10. Why should this happen when continuing to play the game could increase the payments significantly? The game is solved using the concept of backwards induction; that is, beginning at the last move of the game, node 4. What should player B do at the last move? Player B will choose to take ($3.20 > $1.60). Now, consider player A's choice at node 3. Player A, anticipating that player B will choose take at node 4, will choose take at node 3 ($1.60 > $0.80). What will player B do at node 2? Player B, expecting that player A will choose take at node 3, will choose take at node 2 ($0.80 > $0.40). Now, what should player A do at node 1? Player A, anticipating player B will choose take at node 2, will choose take at node 1 ($0.40 > $0.20). Note that players A and B are each making choices to maximize their expected payoffs that are optimal responses given the strategy of the other player; the outcome is a Nash equilibrium of the game.[10] Not surprisingly, in experimental plays of this game, subjects rarely make the choices predicted by standard game theory. McKelvey and Palfrey (1992) report that only 8% of the games end at node 1 as predicted by standard game theory.

How then can we explain these results? One explanation may be that players are uncertain about the payoffs that other players receive in the game. As Morrow notes: "If we introduce some uncertainty into the players' knowledge of each other's payoffs, we can find equilibria of the centipede game where both players continue the game for many moves. We create a small probability that one player always has to continue the game in every move. This uncertainty breaks the backwards induction and creates incentives for normal players to continue the game" (1994, p. 158). Yet in the experiments the payoff schedules were clearly explained to the subjects, so any uncertainty for the subjects must arise from a factor that is uncontrolled or unobservable to the researcher.

McKelvey and Palfrey (1992) propose that the subjects' choices may be explained by altruistic motives. That is, suppose the game is re-examined assuming that there is a known probability that either player might be altruistic and willing to choose pass even though her payment would thereby decline. (Technically, an altruist is defined by McKelvey and Palfrey as a

---

[10] Taking at the first move of the game and taking at each subsequent move is the subgame perfect equilibrium to the game, but not the only Nash equilibrium. I address this issue in more detail in Chapter 6.

player who chooses to pass at every node.) In that case, player A's choice at node 3, even if she is purely selfish, is no longer straightforward. Because she believes there is a positive probability that player B will pass at node 4 (i.e., that player B is an altruist), player A might choose to pass at node 3. Similar expectations about the chance that A is an altruist might induce player B to pass at node 2, and so on. Actually, just a small probability that players are altruistic may be sufficient to explain the experimental results, since players may try to build their reputation as altruists even if they are not. McKelvey and Palfrey fit the game theoretic model with altruism (and with the additional assumption that players' beliefs about the distribution of altruists in the population are heterogeneous) to the experimental data. They estimate that the distribution of altruists in the subject population is approximately 20%.

However, McKelvey and Palfrey (1998) note that adding a parameter for altruism to explain the results of the experimental centipede game is less than satisfactory owing to the lack of generality of the approach. They argue as follows:

> While this explanation of the data does account pretty well for most of the salient features of that particular data set, it is clearly ad hoc. The explanation involves the invention, or assumption, of a "deviant type" who systematically violates Nash behavior in exactly the direction observed in the data. A preferable explanation would be able to account for this data without resorting to such "adhocery." (p. 11)

McKelvey and Palfrey call for an approach that "has the desirable feature of being applicable to arbitrary games without necessitating the invention of systematically deviant types, tailored to the peculiarities of specific games."

Quantal Response Equilibrium. McKelvey and Palfrey (1998) offer a formal game theoretic model that they argue can explain the results in the centipede game and has the desirable feature of being applicable to many games. In standard noncooperative game theory, players in Nash equilibria are assumed to make choices that are best responses to the choices of the other players. This assumption does not allow for players to make any errors. McKelvey and Palfrey propose an alternative equilibrium notion in which players make what are called *quantal responses.* A quantal response is the "smoothed-out" best response assuming that (a) players are more likely to choose better strategies than worse strategies but (b) do not play a best response with probability 1.

The quantal response idea originates from the statistical literature used to estimate discrete choices, where the individual's utility from choices may have a random component (the random utility model) and where the individual's choices are made in order to maximize the true utility, which is unobservable to the econometrician. That is, the individual has an observed utility from an action, $u(a)$, where a is the action. The true utility that the individual receives from the action, however, is given by $u(a)^* = u(a) + \varepsilon$, where ε is a random variable. For example, as discussed in Chapter 2, Canon (1993) estimates his empirical model of amateur entry (a limited dependent variable) using two such statistical models, logit and event count (see Mc-Fadden 1974).

The game theoretic logit form of quantal response is similar, but the interpretation is slightly different. In the game theoretic version, the observed utility is the payoffs the player receives in the game. But the player's choice to maximize that payoff has a random component that is unobserved by other players. Player choices therefore have a stochastic element, and players do not always "best respond" according to their expected payoffs. Assume that a player plays strategy s_i with probability $P(s_i)$ and that the expected payoff from strategy s_i is given by $\pi(s_i)$. The logit quantal response function is then

$$P(s_i) = \frac{e^{\lambda \pi(s_i)}}{\sum_i e^{\lambda \pi(s_i)}}.$$

Notice that the parameter λ measures the extent to which the player deviates from his optimal choice (the strategy with the highest expected payoff) of s^*. That is, if $\lambda = 0$ then the player randomizes uniformly between all of his strategies; as λ increases, $P(s^*)$ approaches 1. Thus, in quantal response models, the response choices of the game's actors are viewed by the researcher as probabilistic rather than deterministic. Actors are more likely to choose better responses than worse responses, but will not choose best responses with certainty.

Unlike the decision theoretic models, which assume that each individual's choice is independent, game theoretic models feature choices that are interdependent. Players recognize that their payoffs are a function of all the players' choices and thus of the errors or unobservables that affect such choices, including their own. A quantal response equilibrium (QRE) occurs when the quantal response functions are based on the equilibrium probability distribution of the players' strategies.

The QRE concept, because of its origins in the statistical literature, can easily be translated into statistically estimable equations and so avoids the zero-likelihood problem discussed previously. McKelvey and Palfrey (1995) demonstrate how the concept can be used to derive equilibrium predictions for simultaneous-move games. To apply the concept to sequential games, they use an "agent" approach where the assumption is that a player cannot predict her own play later in the game. Thus, when a player makes a choice earlier in the game, she does not know what she will do later; it is as if an assigned agent (whose preference disturbance is unknown) will make these choices.

McKelvey and Palfrey (1998) apply the agent logit QRE (AQRE) to the centipede game and derive the equilibrium conditions and statistical estima-tion equations for an empirical study of the experimental data.[11] McKel-vey and Palfrey define the probabilities of each player's strategy choices as follows:

$p_1 = $ prob{A chooses take at the first move};

$p_2 = $ prob{A chooses take at third move (if reached)};

$q_1 = $ prob{B chooses take at the second move (if reached)};

$q_2 = $ prob{B chooses take at the fourth move (if reached)}.

Let $U_{11}(T)$ and $U_{11}(P)$ be the estimated expected payoffs to A at the first move from taking and passing, respectively. Then, assuming that A is risk-neutral and maximizes expected value, A estimates these payoffs to be

$$U_{11}(T) = 0.4 + \varepsilon_{1T} \quad \text{and}$$

$$U_{11}(P) = 0.2q_1 + (1 - q_1)[1.6p_2 + (1 - p_2)(0.8q_2 + 6.4(1 - q_2))] + \varepsilon_{1P},$$

where ε_{1T} and ε_{1P} are independent random variables with a Weibull distri-bution with parameter λ.

The logit formula then implies that the probability that A will choose take at the first move is given by

$$p_1 = \frac{1}{1 + e^{\lambda[0.2q_1 + (1-q_1)[1.6p_2 + (1-p_2)(0.8q_2 + 6.4(1-q_2))] - 0.4]}}.$$

The other probabilities can be similarly derived:

$$q_1 = \frac{1}{1 + e^{\lambda[0.4p_2 + (1-p_2)[3.2q_2 + 1.6(1-q_2)] - 0.8]}};$$

---

[11] Essentially the agent logit QRE assumes that, at each move, an "agent" for the player makes the choice.

$$p_2 = \frac{1}{1 + e^{\lambda[0.8q_2 + 6.4(1-q_2) - 1.6]}};$$

$$q_2 = \frac{1}{1 + e^{\lambda[1.6 - 3.2]}}.$$

The system of four equations can be solved recursively: starting with q_2, then solving for p_2, then solving for q_1, and finally solving for p_1. This solution is unique. McKelvey and Palfrey estimate the model with the experimental data on the centipede game using maximum likelihood procedures (see Fey et al. 1996 for a discussion of the procedures). They find that the model fits better than an alternative model that they call the noisy Nash model (NNM), which assumes that – at any information set (node in the centipede game) – players adopt the Nash equilibrium strategy (best response) with probability γ and randomize uniformly over all the other available strategies with probability $(1 - \gamma)$. Here $\gamma = 1$ is equivalent to $\lambda = \infty$ and $\gamma = 0$ is equivalent to $\lambda = 0$. In the empirical estimation, the AQRE model performs much better than the NNM. However, the AQRE model does not perform as well as the altruism model of McKelvey and Palfrey (1992). The authors note a number of differences between the two models besides the altruism assumption. For instance, the altruism model allowed for heterogeneity across players in beliefs and time trends (it was a five-parameter model versus the one-parameter AQRE model).

McKelvey and Palfrey (1995, 1998) and Fey et al. (1996) consider other applications of QRE to experimental data and find that the QRE model explains other deviations from the predictions of standard game theory. Chen, Friedman, and Thisse (1997) have developed a similar model in order to study learning dynamics (where "learning" can be said to occur if λ decreases over time) and label the equilibria "boundedly rational Nash equilibria" (see also Anderson, Goeree, and Holt 1997). Most noteworthy, the QRE and altruism models are examples of formal models that are empirically evaluated under the assumption that the model is a Complete DGP. The empirical models are derived directly from the formal models' mathematical formulation. Quantum response equilibrium is an exciting new approach to analyzing game theoretic situations because it is applicable to many types of games and yields equations that can be straightforwardly estimated. However, it should be noted that the QRE concept, like many other equilibrium concepts in game theory, may give rise to multiple equilibria (particularly for simultaneous games in which – unlike the centipede game – actors make choices without knowing the choices of other actors).

This creates a problem for empirical estimation that is discussed in more detail in Chapter 6.

QRE Applied to Politics. It is exciting that the first application of QRE to nonexperimental data was by a political scientist (Signorino 1998). Moreover, Signorino presents an extremely cogent explanation of how QRE works and can be applied to nonexperimental data, especially to models of international relations. Signorino addresses three important questions.

1. How can QRE be applied to nonexperimental data?
2. What happens if standard logit empirical analysis (which ignores strategic behavior) is used to empirically evaluate theories in international relations when the underlying theory's DGP is generated by a QRE?
3. What happens when we use QRE to re-estimate a game theoretic model that has previously been evaluated with a non–game theoretic empirical model?

With respect to the second question, Signorino shows, using Monte Carlo analysis in a model of crisis bargaining, that if strategic behavior exists and the statistical model does not incorporate that behavior then the analysis will yield incorrect answers. This is a significant result with particular relevance for empirical work based on game theoretic models in which a Partial DGP is assumed with a random error term added but not incorporated explicitly in the model. (I discuss this issue more thoroughly in the next section.) With respect to the third question, Signorino re-estimates the international interaction model of Bueno de Mesquita and Lalman (1992) using QRE and argues that there is less support for the model's prediction than previously believed.

Of particular relevance to the analysis of this chapter is how Signorino answers the first question of how to apply the QRE approach to nonexperimental data. As we have noted, the focus in experimental use of QRE has been estimating the value of the parameter λ given the specified payoffs in the experiment. In nonexperimental data we typically do not have direct measures of the payoff or utility that an actor derives from an outcome. Usually we are interested in how a set of explanatory factors, through effects on the actors' utilities, lead to particular outcomes. How can the QRE approach be adapted to a form that allows a researcher to evaluate the explanatory factors? Signorino argues that a natural extension would be to specify the utilities or payoffs of the actors in the game as functions of explanatory variables and then to estimate the effects of the variables as well as the overall fit of the model. For example: in the centipede game, instead of using the experimental payoffs directly in the estimating equations, a researcher could posit the actors' utilities as a function of the set of explanatory factors whose effects can be estimated during the empirical analysis. These explanatory factors would have "attached" to each estimated parameters. Thus, the estimation can be used to evaluate both the model in general and the individual effects of each explanatory factor. However, the model would then be "unidentified" since neither λ nor the set β of parameters could be estimated individually. Signorino's solution to this problem: constrain λ to equal 1, which is the standard logit model.

What does constraining λ mean for the empirical estimation?

Since the model is unidentified we can only estimate the joint effect of λ and β. In the case of utilities that are linear in β, we can either reparameterize the statistical model in terms of $\beta^* = \lambda\beta$ and then estimate $\hat{\beta}^*$ or we can set $\hat{\lambda} = c$ for some arbitrary constant $c > 0$ and estimate $\hat{\beta}$. The two methods are equivalent.... There are two implications of this. First, although we set $\hat{\lambda} = 1$, from an estimation perspective we are not saying anything about the degree of bounded rationality of the decision makers. In other words, we are not assuming a level of rationality for the decision makers and then estimating $\hat{\beta}$. Second, multiplying all utilities by a constant c (e.g., by rescaling the data) is equivalent to using the original utilities and multiplying $\hat{\lambda}$ by c.... Although the values of the parameter estimates may differ, the joint effect of $\hat{\lambda}\hat{\beta}$ will be the same in both cases, so the substantive interpretation of the effects of the variables and the probabilities of actions and outcomes will be identical. (Signorino 1998, pp. 11–12)

Even so, the unidentifiability of λ and β does limit the empirical conclusions that can be reached through the evaluation. Yet this limitation is not unique to QRE and does not present a problem if the stakes are expected to be positively related to rationality (actors are expected to make more rational decisions for higher-stakes outcomes). Signorino summarizes as follows:

we can tell whether the predicted behavior is more or less rational, but we cannot tell whether that is due to an intrinsic characteristic of rationality in the decision makers (λ) or to the size of the stakes (as a result of the βs). For most questions of interest in international relations, this is not problematic, since in the LQRE [logit QRE], higher stakes produce behavior that is more rational (a la Nash). Moreover, all random utility models, including binomial logit and probit, face the same problem of identifying the effects and variance parameters, so this issue is not unique to using the LQRE solution concept in estimation. (1998, p. 12)

Thus, although there can be an identification problem in QRE estimation, it is not significantly different from the problem that exists in other statistical techniques. The important point is that QRE is one mechanism whereby a game theoretic model can incorporate randomness explicitly, avoid the zero-likelihood problem, and be viewed as a Complete DGP in empirical estimation.

The QRE method is attractive because it allows a researcher to introduce randomness directly into the formal model and then derive equations (the empirical model) that can be directly estimated using sophisticated statistical techniques. However, there are problems with the approach. That is, the more strategy choices that actors have and the more actors involved in the game, the more complex the empirical estimation becomes. The complexity can escalate quickly. For example, solving and estimating the QRE equilibrium in a multiactor complex voting game may well become impossible. Thus, in many game theoretic models in political science, it is not possible to directly incorporate a stochastic or random factor and assume that actors strategically respond to that factor.

Is Option 2 Always Best? In conclusion, as a first cut with the data, I believe that evaluating a formal model as a Complete DGP has significant value when using either experimental or naturally occurring data. In some cases, as with QRE, it may be possible to directly derive estimating equations that enable the use of sophisticated statistical analysis of the formal model. Typically, however, this sort of analysis is not possible. Nevertheless, by first examining data from this perspective, a researcher can discover which of the disjunctures between the formal model and the empirical world matter. The researcher knows that any formal model, as an abstraction, will have such disconnects, so this sort of preliminary analysis provides necessary information about which of these are important and the extent of their importance. This type of empirical analysis is invaluable for building better theory. *After taking the theory as a given and finding its flaws,* the researcher can begin to modify the theory to correct for the areas where the disjunctures are important.

Choosing option 2 is an important first step in conducting the empirical analysis of a model, but it can be dangerous if the researcher stops at this point. That is, if the analysis actually supports the model's predictions but researchers suspect that important explanatory variables have been omitted, then option 1 or option 3 must be used to show that the model's predictions are still supported. The researcher must also consider the performance of the model as compared with alternative models and the reasonableness of the assumptions. Since both the choice of variables and the way they are measured are themselves assumptions about the DGP, they need to be considered before concluding that the model is supported. Similarly, if the analysis shows that the model's predictions are not supported, then the researcher may erroneously conclude that the model is deficient when the true results are masked by omitted variables or measurement problems.

4.2.3   Option 3: Partial DGP

The Modal Approach to Empirical Estimation of Formal Models. In the foregoing discussion I have emphasized the value in empirical study of considering a formal model as a Complete DGP. However, in many analyses of formal models, particularly those using naturally occurring data, researchers do not make this assumption. In fact, I would say the modal approach is to view the formal model as at best a Partial DGP. Why is this so? As observed in Chapter 1, much empirical research in political science is based on nonformal models. When a researcher is using a nonformal model as the basis for an empirical model, the latter is a mixture of hypotheses or conjectures about the data and some added random variable. A researcher might also include an analysis of the data for insight into its underlying distribution and modify the assumptions about the random variable accordingly, or he might use complicated multiple equation methods if the causal relationship in the data is thought to be complex. But since the basis of the empirical analysis is a nonspecified model, the researcher need not consider the relationship of the underlying model to the DGP. It is also common to consider conjectures about the variables suggested by other researchers as "controls" for the particular hypotheses under study.

When a researcher accustomed to this empirical approach then works with a prediction from a formal model, the prediction is often treated the same as predictions of conjectures from nonformal models. Such a researcher may add an error term without considering how the error might relate to the formal model. The researcher may even add other variables (representing the results from earlier analyses or even other formal models) as controls without considering how these variables explicitly relate to the formal model being evaluated. The researcher may choose an estimation procedure (perhaps the standard procedure in current nonformal work on the research question) without carefully analyzing how that estimation procedure may entail assumptions more restrictive than those of the formal model. The result is a mismatch of evaluation of a formal model, some random error term that is not part of the model, some additional restrictions implied by the estimation procedure, and some other unstructured hypotheses that are also unrelated to the formal model.

Advantages of a Partial DGP. I do not want to sound overly critical of this approach and should note that I have conducted my fair share of this type of empirical analysis. In many cases it is simply not possible to consider a formal model as a Complete DGP, either because re-solving the model to control for all aspects of the real world omitted would needlessly delay empirical analysis or because the model is deterministic, cannot be easily altered to a stochastic version, and must incorporate random data. Although I believe that considering a model as a Complete DGP is a useful first step in any empirical analysis, considering it *only* as a Complete DGP may lead to premature rejection of the model in many cases. It is thus not surprising that the modal method of evaluating formal models is to view them as Partial DGPs.

Moreover, suppose the point of the research is to compare the predictions of alternative models, either two or more formal models or a nonformal with a formal model. In this case the researcher's goal is to conduct an empirical study in which the models are contrasted and compared, so the empirical study should consider multiple hypotheses or predictions. However, there are significant issues to be addressed when multiple models are analyzed in one empirical study (i.e., how the underlying formulations relate to each other, etc.); these issues are discussed in Chapter 8. As illustrated there, in some cases it is appropriate to use a single empirical estimation that combines the models' predictions. This is the approach taken by Brehm and Gates (1993) and Carpenter (1996) to test between a number of principal–agent models and by Westholm (1997) to test between two voting models. On the other hand, combining explanations in a general empirical model may not be possible (i.e., the restrictions required for such estimation may be problematic), in which case a researcher may estimate separate equations that fit each model and then test which yields a better statistical explanation. Examples of this technique include Kessler and Krehbiel's (1996) test of explanations of cosponsorship, Offerman's (1996) examination of public good games, and Schmidt et al.'s (1996) test of models of Senate re-election (also discussed in Chapter 8).

Pitfalls of a Partial DGP.

Problems with Control Variables. What are the potential problems with viewing a formal model as a Partial DGP? When adding control variables that are conjectured to have an effect but are outside of the formal model, the researcher needs to recognize that she is conducting an empirical evaluation of both the formal model and her conjecture. The empirical analysis is no longer an evaluation of the formal model only but rather a *combined* evaluation of the formal model plus the conjecture(s). Thus if the data supports the empirical model, it is premature to conclude that it supports the formal model without the conjecture. A researcher must explicitly recognize the relationship between the formal model, the conjectures, and the data analysis – and must interpret the results accordingly. Measuring variables that are assumed to be exogenous and outside the formal model can also be problematic in empirical analysis. In Chapter 7 I discuss how Segal et al. (1992) must make additional assumptions in their empirical model that are beyond those made in the underlying formal model in order to measure some of the variables in the empirical analysis.

Problems with Random Error Terms and Estimation Procedures. When adding a random component to a deterministic model, it is also essential that the researcher have a theory of the measurement error and be sure that that theory is not inconsistent with the formal model considered in the empirical analysis. Estimation procedures make assumptions about the measurement error in the variables. Thus it is crucial that a researcher explicitly analyze both the underlying assumptions of the estimation procedure and the extent to which these assumptions are either more restrictive or in conflict with the formal models' assumptions. Chapter 8 discusses how, in the empirical evaluation of alternative models, Brehm and Gates (1993) and Kessler and Krehbiel (1996) attempt to select estimation procedures that do not bias the results in favor of one model.

The analysis of Alvarez and Nagler (1995) is a good illustration of how the estimation procedure and the assumptions about the randomness matter. The authors conduct an empirical test of a probabilistic voting model of the 1992 presidential election. In devising their empirical analysis, they confront the problems that estimation procedures can cause for analyzing more than three-candidate or -party spatial voting models.

To estimate a model of the 1992 election using traditional techniques we could proceed in three ways: 1) ignore the Perot candidacy and estimate models of binomial choices between Clinton and Bush; 2) estimate an ordered probit model; or 3) estimate multinomial logit models including Perot as a choice. . . . The first technique ignores the preferences of almost 20% of the electorate. More importantly, throwing out the third candidate and estimating binary-choice models on the remaining candidates is a clear case of selecting on the dependent variable, which will generate inconsistent estimates (Manski and Lerman 1977). . . . The ordered probit model assumes that the choices can be ordered on a unidimensional continuum. Since we are explicitly considering that voters may perceive multiple dimensions – issues and the economy – this model would be inappropriate.

The third technique, multinomial logit, assumes that the random disturbance terms associated with each candidate for each voter are independent. This is equivalent to making the strong behavioral assumption of "Independence of Irrelevant Alternatives" (IIA) with regard to the random disturbances in the model. . . . The multinomial probit model we use allows us to avoid this assumption. (1995, p. 723)

Each of the three estimation techniques that Alvarez and Nagler chose *not* to use make more restrictive assumptions in estimation than are made in the formal probabilistic voting model. The underlying formal model has more than two candidates, is multidimensional, and does not restrict the random disturbances as in multinomial logit. (Estimating probabilistic voting models is discussed more expansively in Chapter 6.) Estimation procedures often mean that researchers make assumptions that specify an empirical model more restrictively than the formal model being tested.

4.2.4 *Summary*

Answers to our two questions – about the relationship between the formal and the empirical model (i.e., Complete vs. Partial DGP) and the nature of the formal model (i.e., deterministic vs. deterministic with unobservable or stochastic elements) – determines in large part how a researcher will conduct the empirical evaluation of a formal model. Table 4.1 summarizes how these answers translate into different tasks.

4.3   Other Implementation Issues

After a researcher determines the nature of her model (i.e., deterministic vs. deterministic with unobservable or stochastic elements) and her view of the relationship between the formal model and the DGP, there remain some other concerns particular to the empirical analysis of formal models. These concerns involve the question of how the empirical model should be linked to the formal model. In particular, how can qualitative empirical analyses and case studies be used in the empirical evaluation of formal models? How should the researcher deal with strategic behavior? What is the role of parameter estimation in empirical examinations of formal models? What level (aggregate or individual) should the analysis consider?

Table 4.1. *Methods of empirical evaluation*

		Type of Formal Model	
		Deterministic	Deterministic and Stochastic
Researcher's View of Formal Model's Relationship to DGP	Option #2: Complete DGP	Count the errant observations	Implement the formal model as an empirical model and use observations to calibrate parameters or compute statistical likelihood functions
	Option #3: Partial DGP	Specify plausible control variables and/or stochastic components and then implement the formal model plus the control variables and/or stochastic components; calibrate parameters or compute statistical likelihood functions	

4.3.1 *Using Qualitative Data and Case Studies*

Some formal models that deal with qualitative empirical evidence (rather than quantitative measures) can best be examined by comparative case studies. A comparative case study when assuming the model is a Complete DGP is very similar to the problem facing a researcher in experimental design when devising a "theory" test of the formal model. That is, the researcher must make a case selection that can control for as many as possible of the factors assumed to be exogenous to the model. However, the number of available cases may be limited and the ability of a researcher to make an unbiased selection may be constrained. This is well known as the "small n" problem. How best to deal with this issue using qualitative data is beyond the scope of this volume; I recommend King et al. (1994) as a good source.

Case studies are also used to illustrate how formal models' predictions or assumptions are satisfied. Oftentimes authors of papers with formal models (but no explicit empirical test) begin their presentation with a discussion of some observation(s) from the real world that the authors wish to explain, and usually the paper ends with an empirical reference. For example, Bednar (1998) presents a formal model of how an elected federal government may find it desirable to take credit for policy outcomes that in fact are due primarily to the expertise of a state or regional government. She then uses a number of cases as empirical examples that "fit" her theoretical conclusions, such as Herbert Hoover's involvement in flood relief during the 1920s. Fearon and Laitin (1996) conclude with a discussion of empirical illustrations of the predictions of their theory of ethnic relations. Baron (1996) presents empirical illustrations of his theoretical predictions of his formal model of public policy formation as well as a discussion of the empirical observation that led to the theory.

The empirical illustrations in these examples serve to show how the theory may explain the real world and are useful for putting the theory in context, but they do not constitute an in-depth empirical evaluation of the theory. Rather, this type of case-study analysis is a useful first step toward building a connection between a formal model and the empirical world. In no way are the illustrations a substitute for rigorous empirical analysis, but they do at least confront the theory with real-world data. They help us begin the process of thinking how best to formulate an empirical evaluation, and they help us begin to answer the question: What is it in the real world that the abstract and symbolic formal model explains and does not explain? I think that this type of empirical illustration is extremely useful and often illuminating.

An alternative view of the relationship between case-study analysis and formal models is to use the case studies to build theory rather than to test theory in a general sense (see e.g. Tetlock and Belkin 1996). Chapter 2 discussed how researchers begin model building with empirical puzzles. Sometimes the researcher explicitly takes the empirical puzzle as the prototype, so to speak, on which to build the formal model – an explicit "fitting" of the model to the empirical case. Researchers who use this approach usually begin with a model that has been used in other contexts. The first part of the evaluation process is a careful in-depth determination of whether the models' assumptions and predictions apply to the particular case. The second step is then to derive empirical implications from the fitting of the model that can be used for empirical analysis (beyond the initial case study) of data from earlier periods or other cases. Bates and colleagues (1998) call this approach "analytic narratives" and advocate it as a useful way of

Table 4.2. *Challenger's payoff matrix*

	$a_2 = 0$	$a_2 = 1$
$a_1 = 0$	Π^1_{00}, Π^2_{00}	Π^1_{01}, Π^2_{01}
$a_1 = 1$	Π^1_{10}, Π^2_{10}	Π^1_{11}, Π^2_{11}

combining formal models with in-depth case studies – as in the field of comparative politics.

4.3.2   Dealing with Strategic Behavior

One problem with Banks and Kiewiet's and Canon's empirical studies of challengers (discussed in Chapter 2) is that they ignore the implications of the challengers' strategic behavior. That is, the decision of one challenger to enter is jointly determined by the decision of other challengers to enter, and vice versa. If the estimation procedure assumes that these decisions are independent then the empirical results are flawed. How can an empirical model be devised that allows for strategic interaction?

Consider the following adaptation of a simple two-player game, as presented for empirical estimation by Bresnahan and Reiss (1991) and Reiss (1996) but changed here to a more political context. Assume (as in Banks and Kiewiet 1989) that there are two potential challengers for an incumbent's elected office. The challengers, $i = 1, 2$, must choose whether to run against the incumbent or wait until the next term, when it is known the incumbent will retire and they can run in the open-seat race. Let $a_i = 1$ represent the event that challenger i enters the primary and let $a_i - 0$ represent the event that challenger i does not enter. The challengers' actions and payoffs are summarized in Table 4.2, where $\Pi^i_{a_1, a_2}$ is the challenger i's expected probability of achieving victory in the general election for actions a_1 and a_2.

Assume that the challengers enter simultaneously and maximize expected utility (see Chapter 5 for a discussion). What is the Nash equilibrium in this model? Recall that, in a Nash equilibrium, each challenger chooses an optimal strategy given the choice made by the other challenger. Thus, the Nash equilibrium strategies for each challenger can be summarized as follows (where the asterisk denotes an equilibrium strategy):

$$a_1^* = \begin{cases} 1 & \text{if } (1 - a_2)(\Pi_{10}^1 - \Pi_{00}^1) + a_2(\Pi_{11}^1 - \Pi_{01}^1) \geq 0, \\ 0 & \text{if } (1 - a_2)(\Pi_{10}^1 - \Pi_{00}^1) + a_2(\Pi_{11}^1 - \Pi_{01}^1) < 0; \end{cases}$$

$$a_2^* = \begin{cases} 1 & \text{if } (1 - a_1)(\Pi_{01}^2 - \Pi_{00}^2) + a_1(\Pi_{11}^2 - \Pi_{10}^2) \geq 0, \\ 0 & \text{if } (1 - a_1)(\Pi_{01}^2 - \Pi_{00}^2) + a_1(\Pi_{11}^2 - \Pi_{10}^2) < 0. \end{cases}$$

That is, if challenger 1 chooses to enter, then challenger 2 will receive either Π_{10}^2 or Π_{11}^2. It is optimal for challenger 2 to enter also if $\Pi_{11}^2 - \Pi_{10}^2 \geq 0$ (we assume that, if indifferent, the challenger enters) but not otherwise. Alternatively, if challenger 1 chooses not to enter then it is optimal for challenger 2 to enter if $\Pi_{01}^2 - \Pi_{00}^2 \geq 0$ but not otherwise. Similar analysis explains challenger 1's optimal choices. Set $\pi_1 = (1 - a_2)(\Pi_{10}^1 - \Pi_{00}^1) + a_2(\Pi_{11}^1 - \Pi_{01}^1)$ and $\pi_2 = (1 - a_1)(\Pi_{01}^2 - \Pi_{00}^2) + a_1(\Pi_{11}^2 - \Pi_{10}^2)$.

Notice that the strategic nature of the entry decisions means that each challenger's expected utility is dependent on the actions of the other challenger. Thus, the joint distribution of the challengers' expected utility must be specified in order to compute the probability that both challengers will enter, only one challenger will enter, or neither will enter. Following Reiss's analysis, assume that the expected probability differences π_1 and π_2 are linear functions of a set of observable exogenous variables X_i, estimable parameters θ, and unobserved variables ε^i. This yields the following dummy endogenous variable system:

$$\pi_1 = X_1\theta_1 + a_2 X_1 \theta_1 + \eta_1,$$

$$\pi_2 = X_2\theta_3 + a_1 X_2 \theta_4 + \eta_2.$$

This is a similar estimating equation system to that proposed and used by Heckman (1978).

This example shows one way in which a formal model with strategic behavior can be translated into an empirically estimable model with explicitly incorporated random error. As Reiss (1996) notes, the estimable model changes if the assumption of simultaneous moves by the challengers is changed to an assumption of sequential moves. This approach is not the only way that an estimable model incorporating strategic behavior can be derived from a game theoretic model; as already noted, quantal response equilibrium is another option. The big difference between this method and QRE is that in QRE the strategic behavior of the model's actors incorporates

the errors that other actors may make, whereas in this approach the interdependence of unobservables is not explicitly considered in deriving the
equilibrium predictions of responses. However, in some cases QRE equilibria can be difficult to calculate and so it may be necessary *not* to incorporate
explicitly the interdependence of unobservables for purposes of empirical
estimation.

4.3.3 *Parameter Estimation and Variable Measurement*

Researchers typically focus on evaluating formal models by examining either the truthfulness of the assumptions or the empirical likelihood of the
predictions. But a formal model has parameters that must be given numerical
values in order to make numerical predictions based on the model. Parameter estimation is important since a model can hardly be expected to predict
accurately if the parameters have been heedlessly selected. Hence, when
weighing the predictions based on a model, it is crucial to consider how accurately the parameters have been chosen. Often researchers use the same
data to estimate the parameters as to evaluate the hypotheses derived from
the model. This may introduce some systematic biases in the empirical estimation, which need to be accounted for. We have discussed like implications
of specifying a value for λ in Signorino's empirical work. The methods of
parameter estimation are of course beyond the scope of this book but they are
particularly important in dynamic modeling, where initial parameter specifications can greatly affect the results.

Parameter estimation can also be important in evaluating alternative for
mulations. In some cases one model may have more estimable parameters
than another, which allows for more flexibility in fitting the data. However,
some may argue that this makes the theory less falsifiable. Westholm (1997;
discussed in Chapter 8) makes this point in his comparison of the proximity
theory of voting with the directional theory of voting. He argues that the directional theory has an additional parameter (a region of acceptability) that
is estimated from the data, rendering the theory less falsifiable than the more
basic proximity theory. For another example, the altruism model of McKelvey and Palfrey (1992) has five parameters whereas the AQRE model has
only one. Since it is thus less falsifiable, from this perspective the altruism
model's better fit does not necessarily imply that it is a better theory. Hence
evaluating two theories solely on the basis of which fits the data better is not
always an appropriate test.

Naturally, along with parameter estimation, it is important that researchers consider carefully how the variables used in the empirical analysis appropriately "fit" the hypothesized variables. Many formal voting models make predictions about closeness of candidates' positions to the median voters in their constituencies. How should positions be measured? In particular, how can we measure the positions of challengers, who may not have records on issues that can be operationalized? How can the ideal point of the median voter in a constituency be determined? What is the constituency? If the model holds for multiple dimensions how many dimensions should be operationalized and measured? Schmidt et al. (1996; discussed in more detail in Chapter 8) use positions of past senators and data on state political party distributions and demographics to estimate median voter positions in their test of the Hotelling–Downsian convergence prediction with respect to Senate elections.

Similarly, in their study of the theoretical predictions about the relationship between ideology of members of Congress and their cosponsorship decisions, Kessler and Krehbiel (1996) measure the period of time in which a legislator decides whether to cosponsor a bill. The authors segment the period from the time the bill is first proposed to the time it is voted on (or Congress adjourns) into early, middle, and late periods. However, different bills have different lengths of time from when a bill is first proposed to its eventual acceptance or rejection. Kessler and Krehbiel need to make explicit assumptions about how they measure this variable, which may affect the analysis.

These issues have been well considered in empirical political science and are the subject of much noteworthy work by methodologists. I do not have the space to cover the techniques that have been developed for dealing with many of these problems. However, it is important in empirical tests of formal models for researchers to recognize that choices in measuring variables can introduce new restrictive assumptions in the empirical model that may not exist in the formal model. Thus empirical analysis of the formal model is only an evaluation of the model *as operationalized*. We *cannot* conclude whether the formal model, under different choices about how to operationalize the variables in the data analysis, would be supported.

4.3.4   *Individual versus Aggregate Data*

Generally there are several levels at which formal models make predictions: individual and various levels of aggregation. Since many formal models are based on assumptions of individual behavior, some researchers consider the individual level to be the most appropriate level for empirical analysis. If individuals do not behave as predicted, then how can the aggregate data have any meaning? Analyzing aggregate predictions is considered not as powerful a test of the individual behavior assumed or predicted by the model. This point of view is illustrated in Canon's comment on Banks and Kiewiet's empirical use of the fact that more challengers are elected to Congress by defeating incumbents than in open-seat races: "individual-level data are needed to test an individual-level theory" (Canon 1993, p. 1128). In some cases it is true that individual-level data are more useful than aggregate data, but this is not always the case.

An implicit assumption that individual-level empirical analysis is superior to aggregate-level analysis may lead to inappropriate and meaningless empirical study and to wrong conclusions. For example, consider Gerber's (1996b) model of the initiative process. Many states and localities allow voters to propose and vote on public policy measures directly. Gerber considers how the initiative process may constrain the policy choices of a legislature to more closely reflect the preferences of the state's median voter. She derives the comparative static prediction that laws passed in states with the initiative process are likely to be closer to the ideal preferences of the median voter in that state. The theoretical prediction relies upon a number of specific assumptions about voters' preferences, initiative proposers' preferences, and legislator preferences. In particular, the prediction is based on the assumption that, if a legislature passes a bill sufficiently divergent from the state's median voter's preferences *and* if proposing an initiative has a low cost, an initiative will be proposed to supplant the legislative bill. Thus, the bills passed in the states that allow voter initiatives are more constrained than otherwise.

What is the best way to study empirically the predictions of Gerber's theory? One alternative would be to examine more directly voting and initiative proposer behavior. Are initiatives proposed that are closer to the median voter's ideal point than the legislatures' proposals? Perhaps the occurrences of successful initiatives should be tallied on the assumption that states in which the process is used more often are more likely to enact policy closer to the median voter's ideal point. Perhaps we should investigate whether, as predicted, voters vote on initiatives as if they care about policy. All of these examinations are problematic, however. As Gerber points out, it is not actual initiatives that constrain legislative behavior but the *threat* that the process could be used to alter legislative choices. It is not voter choices but rather their potential threat that causes the prediction. Thus, analyzing individual behavior tells us very little about the empirical success of the theory.[12]

The best analysis of the theoretical predictions in this case is at the aggregate level: to examine whether the resulting legislation (even if not passed via the initiative process) is closer to the ideal point of the median voter in a state whose voters can use the initiative process. Gerber conducts such an analysis by examining the difference between voter preferences on abortion legislation and actual legislation in a cross-state comparison. She finds that states with the initiative process have abortion laws that are significantly closer to those preferred by the state's median voter than those in states without the initiative process. A focus on individual behavior as the only way to evaluate formal models would have missed the impact of the (threat of) initiative on laws passed.

4.4   The Value of Multiple Evaluations

This chapter has reviewed the basics of empirically evaluating formal models. Empirical analysis of formal models can take three perspectives: evaluating assumptions, predictions, or alternative models. Before beginning the evaluation, however, a researcher must first determine both the nature of the model (deterministic or not) and the maintained relationship between the model and the real world. Her analysis will depend upon her answers to these questions, as discussed in this chapter.

Much of the focus of the discussion has been on the limits researchers face in translating formal models into empirical models. These limits have one crucial implication for the empirical analysis of formal models: *Multiple empirical evaluation, with a large variety of specifications and assumptions in the empirical model, is essential to the empirical evaluation of theory.* For example, Alesina et al. (1993; discussed in Chapter 7) estimate three different empirical models based on the formal model they provide. All three empirical models are based on the formal model but differ in their degree of "closeness" – although none is exactly the same (i.e., even the closest model adds control variables and makes more restrictive assumptions than the underlying formal model). However, the variation in empirical specification allows the researcher to carefully evaluate which parts of the theoretical predictions are supported and how changing various options in the empirical

[12] In general, this is true of any game solved by "subgame perfection" as in Gerber's model.

model affects the analysis. For the same reason, I believe that experimentalists should conduct both theory and stress tests in evaluating formal models. Even when a researcher takes a formal model as a Complete DGP, he can rarely use the resulting empirical analysis to conclusively demonstrate either that the model is or is not supported. Since our ability to use formal models as Complete DGPs is severely limited and since much of our empirical analysis necessarily involves assuming the formal model is a Partial DGP, it follows that a single empirical study is highly unlikely to make conclusive statements about the value of a formal model.

For similar reasons I advocate using both naturally occurring and experimental data, whenever possible, to evaluate theory. In some cases, experiments are more advantageous (as in much of assumption evaluation, discussed in the next chapter); in others, naturally occurring data has greater advantages. Using multiple methodologies allows us to be more confident in either accepting or rejecting a theoretical argument.

Multiple evaluations are important, yet they do not preclude the possibility of devising a single "critical" test of a theory, as in the physical sciences. In the social sciences, with a formal model viewed as a Complete DGP, any errant observation is like a "critical test." At what point do we decide that enough of these observations are sufficient? Is just one sufficient to disprove the model? If the formal model is viewed as a Partial DGP then errant observations cannot take the same bite out of theory. Though I believe it is possible for single evaluations to serve as critical tests, I also believe that such cases are rare.

I now turn to a more detailed examination of the types of empirical evaluations. The issues considered so far with respect to the relationship between the formal model and the real world will arise again as we traverse the examples and illustrations of the next four chapters.

CHAPTER 5

Evaluating Assumptions

5.1   Justifying Assumptions

In Chapter 4 I argued that many assumptions in formal models are of necessity either false or not verified. They are definitely not all facts. Therefore,
should researchers bother with evaluating assumptions at all? What role
does empirical analysis play in exploring the nature of assumptions? Before answering this question, I first address how assumptions are typically
justified in formal models.

5.1.1   *Justifying Unverified Assumptions*

Modelers generally use one of two kinds of justifications when making an
assumption: (1) the assumption is "probably" true; or (2) the assumption is
false or suspected to be false, but if the assumption were "relaxed" then the
model's predictions would not change qualitatively.

The first type of justification argues that the assumption is indeed a logically realistic aspect of the world. For example, in almost all formal models
of turnout it is assumed that the consumption benefits received (or lost) by
a voter from the act of voting are separable from the utility or satisfaction
received (or lost) by that voter from the election outcome. Mathematically,
this is obvious in the standard presentation of the calculus of voting:

$$\Delta P \cdot B + D \geq C,$$

where ΔP is the effect of an individual's vote on the probability that her
preferred candidate wins, B is the utility difference (benefits) that the voter
would receive if her preferred candidate wins over an alternative candidate,

D is the voter's consumption benefits from the act of voting, and C is the voter's utility cost of voting. Because D and C are assumed to be added to or subtracted from $\Delta P \cdot B$, the equation is an explicit assumption that the utility benefits and costs of the act of voting are separable and independent of the utility benefits from the election outcome.

Occasionally this assumption is justified explicitly by arguing that, since the act of voting takes place at a different time than the consumption of the benefits from the election outcome, it is safe to contend that the income spent on the two are viewed as distinct and the two are separable (see e.g. Morton 1987 and Slutsky 1975). Most often, this assumption is not explicitly justified. Nevertheless, I know of no empirical investigation that evaluates whether this assumption is actually true.

Does this mean that formal modelers are cavalier about reality? Not necessarily. Empirical analysis of this assumption would add to scientific knowledge and would be useful. But how useful? It would involve somehow measuring voter utility from the act of voting and utility from electoral outcomes, varying both and determining if a change in the decision to vote affects the relationship between voter utility from different electoral outcomes. The point is that empirically proving this assumption would be extremely difficult and uninteresting to most researchers working on turnout issues. Given the limited resources available for empirical research, a choice has been made to almost universally accept this assumption in models of turnout even though researchers have no empirical proof that it is true. However, this does not mean that the assumption will always be accepted and never evaluated. At some point, a researcher may find a cost-effective way of analyzing this assumption, which will mean either that the existing models that use this assumption are justified in doing so or that they are not and the assumption is false. This might arise if the cost of empirical evaluation goes down or if a researcher perceives that the benefit of testing is increased by new work that could show the assumption to be more important than previously thought.

5.1.2   *Justifying False Assumptions*

What happens when an assumption is known to be false; how do modelers justify these assumptions? As we have noted, modelers freely admit making assumptions that are false. Assumptions that are known to be false are typically justified with the argument that relaxing them is not likely to change the qualitative results (predictions) of the theoretical analysis. Consider Richardson's (1939) arms race model, in which it is assumed that the higher a nation's level of armaments, the more incentive it has to decrease its level of armaments owing to the burden of defense. The Richardson differential equation represents this by the term $-ax$, where a is a parameter that is assumed constant and x is the level of armaments. This assumption is clearly false (see Lucier 1979 for a discussion of the effects of changing the values of the parameters in these models). Yet Richardson, as he argued in his seminal work, made this assumption in an attempt to derive a workable model of arms races, recognizing that he was simplifying a complex process. In McCarty and Rothenberg's (1996) model of campaign contributions, the authors assume a single legislator (and only two interest groups) and claim their arguments can be extended to a greater number of participants. Similarly, many models of Congress ignore the bicameral nature of the institution or the multidimensionality of some issues.

Often these false assumptions are called "restrictive" and so generalizing them is said to be "relaxing" the assumptions. When traditionally trained, empirically oriented political scientists express criticism of models whose assumptions could be (or are known to be) false, the usual response of formal modelers is to ignore such criticisms. Modelers argue that – unless a critic can show that theoretical results arising from a restrictive assumption would *change* if the assumption were relaxed – the criticism is meaningless. That is, theorists typically contend that when an assumption is demonstrated to be false, the next step is to explore how the theoretical results change when the assumption is relaxed. Does relaxing the assumption change the results significantly? If not, then the criticism is not as strong. This is what formal modelers assert when they state that "only theory can replace theory." *Criticizing a model for having restrictive or false assumptions is vacuous unless the resulting theoretical analysis can show that the models' results hinge acutely on the restrictive and false nature of those assumptions.*

Therefore, criticism of restrictive or false assumptions in formal models should carefully consider how relaxing the assumptions changes the model's predictions. But that does not mean that the analysis ends with theorizing. If relaxing the assumption does change the results, it is important to conduct subsequent empirical analysis of the new results. This consideration yields revised theory that must be evaluated – along with evaluating (if possible and cost effective) the new assumptions.

5.1.3   Why Evaluate Assumptions?

If the criticism of false assumptions should be met by examining the theoretical implications of relaxing those assumptions, does this mean that the empirical evaluation of assumptions is not a worthwhile exercise? No, empirically analyzing assumptions not known to be false can be quite useful and can help improve our understanding of the real world. If empirical work shows a previously unevaluated assumption to be false then the burden on theory is increased; that is, it becomes even more important to consider whether relaxing the assumption changes the theory's qualitative results. *Researchers discover the limits of theory when they evaluate nonverified assumptions, and such analysis can be quite valuable in the quest to understand political situations more fully.*

5.1.4   Is Assumption Evaluation Possible?

Despite the usefulness of assumption testing, many assumptions cannot be empirically evaluated in isolation, especially with naturally occurring data. That is, in only a few cases can we separate the effects of one particular assumption from others and so determine if that assumption is empirically verified. The examples presented in the next section incorporate assumptions about individual choice that have been analyzed using laboratory experiments, where the researcher has considerable control over other factors. But many assumptions of formal models cannot be evaluated in this fashion, and even in experimental work there remain underlying and untested assumptions (e.g., a common understanding of language) that are required for the empirical analysis. Thus, almost all assumption evaluation entails assessing a host of assumptions together, just as empirical evaluation of a formal model (like a Partial DGP) entails appraising that model jointly with its auxiliary assumptions about randomness and conjectures about the control variables. This is one reason why theorists are reluctant to discard an assumption even when evaluation may demonstrate its falseness. At one extreme, some theorists believe that – owing to the near impossibility of focusing on particular assumptions – assumption evaluation is not even a meaningful enterprise. Hence, *it is central that empirical results from assumption evaluation be recognized as qualified and limited in their applicability, because they themselves are often subject to untested and unevaluated underlying assumptions.* In summary, assumption evaluation is useful and necessary for building better theory (it is meaningful), but at the same time we should not discard or accept theories based on assumption evaluation alone.

5.2   Examples of Assumption Evaluation

In rational choice or other models of individual behavior, many assumptions are made about the nature of individual preferences or choice processes. Thus, assessing these assumptions implies appraising the implicit individual model of choice. In this chapter I discuss two examples of evaluations of assumptions on individual preferences that are implicit in many formal models in political science: (1) analyses of the independence axiom of expected utility theory; and (2) analyses of assumptions of separability of preferences.

First, to illustrate how assessments of assumptions about individual behavior have been conducted in the past and to recount the role that such evaluation has played, I discuss expected utility theory, some of the experiments that have tested the theory, the resulting theoretical explorations, and further empirical studies. An exploration of the assumptions of expected utility theory is important for scholars in political science independent of its usefulness as an example of assumption evaluation. Expected utility theory underlies the assumptions of rational choice in almost all game theoretic models in political science when there is imperfect or incomplete information. For example, Gilligan and Krehbiel's (1989) model of the role of information in legislative decision making is based on the axioms of expected utility theory. Similarly, Calvert's (1985) model of candidate competition assumes that candidates maximize expected utility. A large literature in political science is based on the axioms of expected utility theory, so the empirical relevance of these axioms has import for the usefulness of this literature.

After the discussion of expected utility theory, I examine the evaluation of another common assumption in political science formal models: separability. Much empirical and theoretical research on voter preferences and choices assumes that voters' preferences over issues are "separable." Yet there is new experimental evidence that separability may not hold. In fact, empirical observations implying that voter preferences can be manipulated by "framing" may just be the consequence of the survey questionnaire and nonseparable preferences. These issues are explored in detail in the second example.

5.2.1   Expected Utility Theory

The Axioms of Expected Utility Theory. The most analyzed assumptions of individual choice behavior are probably the axioms underlying von Neumann and Morgenstern's (1944) expected utility theory. Expected utility theory explains how individuals make decisions in risky situations. Von Neumann and Morgenstern formulated expected utility theory as an adjunct to their theory of games; they needed to analyze games in which information is imperfect and individuals must make decisions when outcomes are not known with certainty but have known probabilities. But what happens when individuals do *not* know the probabilities of the outcomes? Savage's (1954) response to such decision making under uncertainty was to formulate "subjective" expected utility based on the earlier work of von Neumann and Morgenstern, Ramsey (1931), and de Finetti (1937).

The approach used by von Neumann and Morgenstern in devising expected utility theory – and by Savage in developing subjective expected utility theory – is to posit a set of axioms from which a function that evaluates the preferences of an individual over outcomes can be derived. This function is called an expected utility function (in Savage's theory it is a subjective expected utility function). The set of axioms in expected utility theory are assumptions about an individual's preferences over risky outcomes. First assume that there is a set of outcomes X and that there is a set of probability distributions $P = (p, q, \ldots)$ that is defined over X. In other words, each $p \in P$ is a risky alternative that yields outcome $x \in X$ with probability $p(x)$ such that $\sum_{\text{all } x} p(x) = 1$. Also assume that P is convex. That is, if $p, q \in P$ and $0 \leq \lambda \leq 1$ then $\lambda p + (1 - \lambda)q$ is in P. Finally, define $\succ$ as an individual's preference relation over the set of risky outcomes; we interpret $p \succ q$ as denoting that p is preferred to q.

The standard preference-ordering axioms that are used to derive the expected utility function are as follows (applied to all $p, q, r \in P$).[1]

Axiom A1 (Order). The preference relation $\succ$ on P is asymmetric and negatively transitive. That is, if $p \succ q$ then: (a) either $p \succ r$ or $r \succ q$; and (b) $q \succ p$ is not true.

---

[1] See Fishburn (1982) for a full exposition of expected utility theory. Note that von Neumann and Morgenstern do not have independence as a separate axiom but that it follows from other assumptions made in the derivation.

Axiom A2 (Independence). If $p \succ q$ and $0 \leq \lambda \leq 1$, then $\lambda p + (1 - \lambda)r \succ \lambda q + (1 - \lambda)r$.

Axiom A3 (Continuity). If $p \succ q$ and $q \succ r$, then $\alpha p + (1 - \alpha)r \succ q$ and $q \succ \beta p + (1 - \beta)r$ for some α and β in $(0, 1)$.

The importance of these axioms is that together they hold for P and $\succ$ if and only if there is a real-valued function u on P such that, for all $p, q \in P$ and all $0 \leq \lambda \leq 1$: $p \succ q$ if and only if $u(p) > u(q)$. Most noteworthy, this real-valued function, called the *expected utility function,* has the property of linearity: $u(\lambda p + (1 - \lambda)q) = \lambda u(p) + (1 - \lambda)u(q)$. The linearity property allows researchers to express the utility of a risky alternative as the expectation of the utilities of the possible outcomes in that alternative; that is, researchers can use the expression $u(p) = \sum_{\text{all } x} p(x)u(x)$. This expression is used by most political scientists in modeling the utility of individuals' choices when there is imperfect information over outcomes and in many game theoretic models.

The Independence Axiom. The independence axiom plays a foundational role for the linearity property. As Machina notes:

> It is the independence axiom which gives the theory its empirical content by imposing a restriction on the *functional form* of the preference function. It implies that the preference function may be represented as the expectation with respect to the given distribution of a fixed utility function defined over the set of possible outcomes (i.e. ultimate wealth levels). In other words, the preference function is constrained to be a linear functional over a set of distribution functions, or, as commonly phrased, "linear in the probabilities." (1982, p. 278)

Graphically, choices in a risky situation can be represented as shown in Figure 5.1 for a system devised and used by Marschak (1950) and Machina (1982). Assume that there are three gambles, X_L, X_M, X_H, where the subscripts denote low, medium, and high, respectively. Assume then that $X_H \succ X_M$, $X_M \succ X_L$, and $X_H \succ X_L$. Assume there is a compound lottery in which each of the three gambles occurs with the objective probabilities of p_L, p_M, and p_H. The values of p_L are measured along the horizontal axis and the values of p_H are measured along the vertical axis (note that $p_M = 1 - p_H - p_L$). Then the diagonal from $(0, 1)$ to $(1, 0)$ marks the different combinations of p_H and p_L where $p_M = 0$. The diagonal lines $I_1, I_2, \ldots, I_9$, which have positive slope on the graph, are *indifference curves* for the individual. That is, along each indifference curve the individual is indifferent

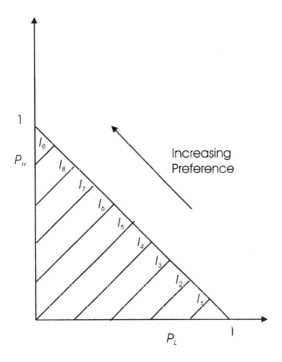

Figure 5.1. Marschak/Machina triangle.

between the compound lotteries given by the different values of p_L, p_M, and p_H. Note that utility increases with higher values of p_H, the probability of receiving X_H; that is, the utility from combinations on I_7 is greater than the utility from combinations on I_6, and so on. Notice also that the indifference curves are parallel straight lines, which is implied by the axiom of indifference.

Evaluating the Independence Axiom. The independence axiom is significant, then, as a basic assumption underlying expected utility theory. However, almost from the inception of the theory, evidence mounted suggesting that individual preferences violated the independence assumption; see in particular the work of Allais (1953, 1979), Kahneman and Tversky (1979), MacCrimmon (1965), MacCrimmon and Larson (1979), and Morrison (1967). This problem has been labeled the *Allais paradox* after the initial results of violations provided in the seminal work of Allais (1953).

Table 5.1. *Lottery outcomes*

	S Lotteries:			R Lotteries:	
Payoffs:	$3,000	$0		$4,000	$0
S1 **Probabilities:**	1	0	*R1* **Probabilities:**	0.8	0.2
S2 **Probabilities:**	0.25	0.75	*R2* **Probabilities:**	0.2	0.8

To see how the independence axiom might be violated, consider the following choice of four lotteries: $S1$, $S2$, $R1$, and $R2$. Lotteries $S1$ and $S2$ are over the two outcomes of receiving $3,000 and $0; lotteries $R1$ and $R2$ are over the two outcomes of receiving $4,000 and $0. Table 5.1 presents the probabilities of the different outcomes below the monetary values for the four lotteries.

Note that $S1$ and $S2$ are "safer" options than the respectively riskier options of $R1$ and $R2$. Notice further that $R2$ is a lottery over $R1$ and $0. That is, assume that the probability of receiving the lottery $R1$ is 0.25 and the probability of getting $0 is 0.75. Then $R2$ is the lottery of receiving $4,000 with a probability of $0.25 \times 0.8 = 0.2$ and of receiving $0 with a probability of $(0.25 \times 0.2) + 0.75 = 0.8$. Likewise, $S2$ can be shown to be a lottery over $S1$ and $0, where the probability of receiving $S1$ is 0.25 and the probability of receiving $0 is 0.75. Hence, the independence axiom implies that if $R1$ is preferred to $S1$ then $R2$ is preferred to $S2$.

In a set of famous experiments, Kahneman and Tversky (1979) show that subjects often make choices that violate the independence axiom in experiments using the hypothetical payoffs of this example.[2] In the experiments,

---

[2] These experiments, as often in psychology, assume that the subjects are motivated to give honest answers to the questions and that payment for participation is not (as it is in most experiments conducted by economists) tied to the choices made. In this case, tying the subject payments to the choices would result in a very costly experiment! Experiments with real payments (using lower amounts) have been conducted in which violations were also observed; see Camerer (1995) for a review.

80% of the subjects preferred $S1$ to $R1$ but 65% of the subjects also preferred $R2$ to $S2$. Thus, the experimental results suggest that subjects prefer the safe alternative when the probability of getting the safe alternative is extremely high (100%) but prefer the risky alternative when the probabilities of the two lotteries are close. It should be noted that other violations have been relatively easy to demonstrate (see the previously listed citations) and, in a well-known verbal encounter, Savage himself violated independence when answering a question presented to him by Allais about a choice between lotteries.

Responding to the Evidence: Questioning the Relevance. How have researchers responded to the Allais paradox? Some researchers have argued that expected utility is useful despite the experimental evidence. Essentially, they argue that the evidence that the independence axiom is violated does not apply. The reasons cited are typically of three forms.

1. *The violations are "mistakes" that individuals are unlikely to make if the violations are explained. Hence, the experimental evidence is that the subjects have trouble computing compound lotteries, rather than that their preferences violate Independence.* For example, Davis and Holt (1993) cite evidence suggesting that if the lotteries are presented more transparently then violations do not occur as often. Savage made a similar argument to excuse his own mistake in answering Allais's question. This view is supported by some experimental evidence that subjects change their minds when their "errors" are presented to them. However, it is difficult to separate out subjects making changes to please an experimenter from these results; see the analyses of MacCrimmon (1965) and Slovic and Tversky (1974).

2. *The violations only occur in situations where the outcomes are of very low or very high risks or payoffs, so expected utility can still be used safely in analyzing most situations of interest.* For example, evidence reported by Conlisk (1989) supports this view.

3. *In market or game experiments, subjects do not show independence reversals that are observed in individual experiments.* Some researchers contend that what is important is how expected utility explains "aggregate" choices and that evidence of failure in individual choices does not imply that these errors are significant in explaining choices in market or strategic situations. Many economic models based on expected utility do

explain market behavior well. Why this may be so when independence is violated in individual decision-making experiments has been explored experimentally by Plott (1986) and Smith (1991). Generally, researchers argue that individuals in market situations "learn" to behave rationally as errors due to systematic biases lead to systematic losses.

These justifications for continued use of expected utility theory in the face of disconfirming experimental evidence are examples of researchers arguing that the independence axiom *is* realistic in the relevant decisions analyzed. That is, the justification is that the evidence does not apply to the decisions that are analyzed with expected utility. It is a justification that acknowledges the evidence but argues that, despite the evidence of problems, expected utility theory is still a good predictor of behavior in relevant situations. In this view, accepting experimental tests of the independence axiom as a demonstration of the assumption's falseness must be coupled with additional *unevaluated* assumptions about learning, the size of risks or payoffs, and the process of translating behavior in individual decision-making contexts into behavior in group or market situations. Evaluating these individual assumptions is not possible even in controlled experiments, so the empirical evidence of violations must not be accepted uncritically.

Responding to the Evidence: Alternative Theories. However, claiming that expected utility is still useful despite the experimental evidence has not been the only reaction to the observed violations of independence. A number of researchers in both economics and psychology have found the experimental evidence convincing and have proposed alternative models (of choice in risky situations) in which the independence axiom is relaxed. Some of these models provide a set of axioms from which alternative utility functions are derived, as in Kahneman and Tversky's (1979) prospect theory, Chew's (1983) weighted expected utility theory, and Fishburn's (1982) skew-symmetric bilinear (SSB) theory. These alternative theories feature axioms that relax (or do not include) independence. The new set of axioms are used to derive generalized expected utility functions that are nonlinear in probabilities, thus accounting for the experimental failures.

Weighted Expected Utility Theory. How do these theories work? I will briefly review two of these alternatives: weighted expected utility theory

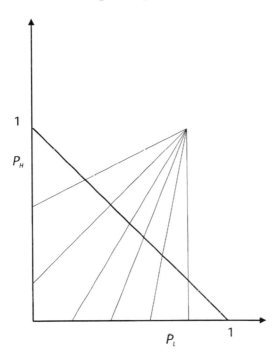

Figure 5.2. Indifference curves that fan in.

and prospect theory. Consider first weighted expected utility theory. The violations of the independence axiom imply that individuals' risk-aversion tendencies vary with the choices presented. Weighted expected utility assumes a weakened form of indifference that accounts for these observations. In "weak" indifference, if p is preferred to q then, for all λ between 0 and 1, there exists a unique μ between 0 and 1 such that $\lambda p + (1 - \lambda) r$ is preferred to $\mu q + (1 - \mu) r$ for all r. Notice that, in contrast, the independence axiom assumes that $\lambda = \mu$. Graphically, weighted expected utility implies indifference curves that are straight lines, as in von Neumann–Morgenstern expected utility. These lines meet at a point outside the triangle, fanning either in or out; that is, they are not parallel. An example of indifference curves that fan in is shown in Figure 5.2.

This relaxation of independence results in a weighted expected utility function of the form

$$u(p) = \frac{\sum_{\text{all } x} p(x) w(x) u(x)}{\sum_{\text{all } x} p(x) w(x)},$$

where $w(x)$ is the weighting function. Weighted expected utility can account for experimental violations of the independence axiom because it no longer has the property of linearity.

Prospect Theory. Prospect theory, proposed by Kahneman and Tversky (1979) as an alternative to expected utility theory, is more widely known among political scientists than the alternatives mentioned previously. In prospect theory, people value changes from a reference point other than their "wealth positions," as in most versions of expected utility. Moreover, the theory assumes that individuals weight probabilities nonlinearly when evaluating gambles. Kahneman and Tversky show that a derived value function (their version of an individual's preference in a situation of risk) is steeper around the reference point for losses than for gains (which they call "loss aversion") and that risk attitudes "reflect" around the reference point. That is, individuals are risk-averse for gains but risk-seeking for losses. As a result, the indifference curves are nonlinear and are most nonlinear near 0 and 1. Prospect theory's value function of a gamble between x and y is given by the following relationship (assuming the reference point is current wealth):

$$\pi(p(x)) v(x) + \pi(p(y)) v(y) \quad \text{when } x < 0 < y \qquad \text{and}$$
$$(1 - \pi(p(y))) v(x) + \pi(p(y)) v(y) \quad \text{when } 0 < x < y \text{ or } y < x < 0,$$

where $\pi(p(x))$ is the weighting function and $v(x)$ is the value of x. (For a more detailed analysis of weighted expected utility theory, prospect theory, and other theories and variations of these, see Camerer 1995.)

Assessing the New Theories. Alternative formulations have been devised for decisions under risk without using the strict independence axiom, and assessing the assumption has led to new theory. But the new theory leads to new questions, too. First, when incorporated in other formal models, do the new theories result in different qualitative predictions than those generated when expected utility is assumed? If the predictions are the same, then the justification for using expected utility in the face of the experimental deviations receives greater support. Machina (1982, 1989) shows that, in some economic models, using utility versions that relax the independence axiom yields qualitative predictions like those of the same models using von Neumann–Morgenstern expected utility theory. Carrubba (1996) considers how incorporating prospect theory in a formal model of legislative committees may yield different results from formal models of committees using expected utility. He finds that closed rules may be always preferable when prospect theory holds as a model of individual decision-making, whereas this is not true with standard expected utility theory.[3]

A second question, which has been investigated more extensively, is: Do the new theories predict individual behavior better than expected utility? Furthermore, how do we choose between the myriad alternatives that seem to have developed? There have been several noteworthy efforts to experimentally test the predictive capability of the alternative models versus expected utility in examining individual decision making. Camerer provides a careful review of this literature. He notes in his review that the "few attempts to fit models for individual subjects suggest that more general theories *fit* better than EU (since they have more degrees of freedom) but are no better in *predicting* new choices. More studies of this sort are crucial for establishing whether the new theories can actually make better predictions than EU" (1995, p. 642, italics in the original; EU denotes expected utility theory, EV denotes expected value). Despite this conclusion, Camerer does argue against using expected utility when it is possible to use a more generalized form. He contends that "the continued use of EU can only be justified in two fairly narrow ways: first, EU is not so badly violated in choosing over gambles with the same set of possible outcomes . . . , or with probabilities well above 0 and below 1 – though it is still statistically rejectable. Second, EU might be preferred in an application where parsimony is *very* highly valued compared to predictive accuracy (but even then, EV is often just as good)" (p. 642).

Political Science and the Alternative Theories. Political science empirical research on expected utility theory and its alternatives has focused on the comparison of prospect theory with expected utility in individual political decision choices. For example, Quattrone and Tversky (1988) present subjects with a number of hypothetical political choices designed to see if individual choices show violations of expected utility, comparing their results with predictions from prospect theory. The authors find support for prospect theory in the choices the subjects make in these

---

[3] Chew (1983), Fishburn (1982), and Machina (1982) consider applications of generalized models of expected utility to social choice and social welfare theory. However, this work has not been extended to more applied questions in political science.

hypothetical political situations. Others have considered prospect theory's individual choice predictions as explanations of the choices of actors in case studies in international relations (Boettcher 1995 argues the application gives only limited support for prospect theory) and comparative politics (Weyland 1996 contends that prospect theory explains the observed choices of actors in Latin American politics better than expected utility theory).

Summary. In my view, the empirical evidence of violations of independence is important for understanding the limits of expected utility theory. The testing of the independence axiom has led us to understand more fully the extent to which expected utility theory is an appropriate description of individual behavior. The experimental evidence shows that in some cases – when the outcomes are the same across the risky alternatives compared, or when the outcome probabilities are not close to either 0 or 1 – expected utility or even expected value can be a good approximation of behavior. However, we do not know (beyond the work of Carrubba) whether aggregate political outcomes are theoretically predicted to be different when we change our model of individual behavior and allow for a more general formulation of individual choice. And we do not know if other alternatives to expected utility (such as weighted expected utility) can also explain individual political choices. Testing the independence axiom should lead to more theoretical and empirical work as a consequence.

It should not be a surprise that most of the evidence on expected utility and on alternative models of individual decision making is experimental. One of the great advantages of laboratory settings is the experimenter's ability to use monetary incentives to manipulate and control the preferences of subjects over various choices. By making payment for participation contingent on the choices that subjects make, it is possible to measure the relationship between preference and choice – something extremely difficult to infer from real-world choice behavior. The history of experiments on preferences over risky situations illustrates how useful the laboratory can be in evaluating the reliability of assumptions about preferences.

Most political scientists are aware of the experimental results, conducted by psychologists, that discredit expected utility theory. But few are knowledgeable about the theoretical developments in economics that have taken place as a consequence or the subsequent experiments testing the competing theories by many social scientists across fields. The research in economics and psychology on testing expected utility theory, as well as the theoretical work on alternative models of individual choice that has arisen from that research, could well be important for political science, although there have been few inroads in terms of applications. It is potentially important because expected utility plays a big role in many formal models, game and decision theoretic, that are used to understand political situations.

Why have the alternatives to expected utility theory developed in economics had so little impact on formal models in political science? Political scientists tend to react to the experimental results on expected utility as evidence against all models that come from a rational perspective, rather than exploring the alternative choice models that are variations of expected utility. And those rational choice–based modelers who are unconvinced by the experimental evidence that expected utility is problematic for their scenarios are naturally not keen on adapting new approaches that they (like e.g. Davis and Holt 1993) deem unnecessary. As a result, these developments in economics have not been incorporated in political science, and the almost rational models of individual choice (like weighted expected utility theory) that have arisen in economics are little known.

5.2.2   *Separability of Preferences*

I now turn to an example of assumption testing that can also have an impact on much existing empirical political science research. One assumption that is standard in many formal models of voting is that the preferences of voters are "separable." This is also an implicit assumption in many empirical studies of public opinion that are based on nonformal models. Mathematically, *separability* is an assumption about the shape of an individual's utility function over various government policies. Suppose that voters care about policy choices over two issues, $\mathbf{x} = (x_1, x_2)$. If voters have a "weakly" separable utility function over these issues, then $U(\mathbf{x}) = F[g_1(x_1), g_2(x_2)]$. This function is *weakly separable* because the utility derived from each issue, $g_i(x_i)$ for $i = 1, 2$, is independent of the utility derived from the other issue. Define the $g_i(x_i)$ as subutility functions. Utility functions are nonseparable when this independence is not maintained, that is, when the utility from x_i is dependent on the values of x_j. For example, suppose that $F[g_1(x_1), g_2(x_2)] = -a(x_1 - b)^2 - (x_2 - c)^2$. In this case, $g_1(x_1) = -a(x_1 - b)^2$ and $g_2(x_2) = -(x_2 - c)^2$. An example of a nonseparable function is $F[x_1, x_2] = -a(x_1 - b)^2 - (x_2 - c)^2 + x_1 x_2$.

Separability means that an individual's preferences over one issue are not affected by the level of the other issue. Suppose, for example, that we are talking about the issues of abortion and tax policy. Separability implies that the individual's preferences over abortion policy are independent of the government's tax structure. It is actually easy to entertain the notion that this might *not* be true, as follows. Suppose an individual favors restrictions on abortion if the government uses the tax system to redistribute income from the rich to the poor but is willing to accept a less restrictive abortion policy if the government does not engage in much redistribution. In this case, government policy in one area affects the individual's preferences in another; the preferences are not separable.

Theoretical Implications of Separability. In order to understand why separability matters theoretically, consider majority voting. Assume first that the preferences over two issues, x_1 and x_2, are separable. Assume that only one of these issues is to be voted over. As is well known, when all voters' preferences over an issue are single-peaked, majority voting will result in the outcome most preferred by the voter whose ideal point (most preferred policy position) is at the median of the distribution of voter ideal points. Thus, if $g_1(x_1)$ yields single-peaked preferences for each voter, a majority rule voting equilibrium exists in this dimension. (For more detail, see Enelow and Hinich 1984 and Hinich and Munger 1997.) It is also well known that if voting is over more than one dimension, the requirements on the distribution of preferences are much stronger than single-peakedness in order to achieve a majority rule equilibrium; these requirements are not likely ever to be satisfied in the real world (see Plott 1967). Preference-induced equilibria, as they are called, are unlikely when voting is over more than one issue at the same time. Separability does not save us from this possibility.

Now suppose that we restrict voting to a single dimension and that voter preferences are separable. If voter preferences are single-peaked and voting is restricted to one issue at a time, then we can find what is known as a structure-induced equilibrium (see Shepsle 1979 and Slutsky 1977). Why is separability important for this result? After all, even if utility were nonseparable, it seems we could still solve for an individual's preferences on one issue (given that the other issues are held fixed) and then look at majority voting over that issue by using the derived preference function to represent the voter's preferences.[4] It turns out that – even if the underlying utility function over all the issues voted on is "nicely behaved" (i.e. quasi-concave) – if it is nonseparable in the issues then it is quite possible that the derived

---

[4] Technically this is called a mixed indirect utility function; sometimes it's labeled a public sector preference function.

preference functions are not single-peaked and that a majority-rule equilibrium does not exist even when we restrict voting to a single dimension at a time (see Diba and Feldman 1984 for a demonstration of this result). Assuming separability and single-peakedness of each of the subutility functions can yield a structure-induced equilibrium, a concept that has received considerable attention and has been widely used in models of majority voting. The assumption of separability is important because a structure-induced equilibrium may not occur without it.[5]

Empirical Implications of Separability. Lacy (1995) examines how relaxing the separability assumption theoretically alters the results of many accepted models of voting and public opinion. In particular, he argues that nonseparability may explain some empirical results that have been used to call into question rational choice–based models of voter choices and preferences. For example, he contends that some effects – previously attributed to "framing" effects in the wording of questions – can be explained by nonseparable preferences. In surveys, some political scientists have observed that the order in which questions are asked can affect the answers given. That is, if we ask an individual her preferences on abortion policy and then ask her preferences on redistribution through taxation, the responses may differ if the order is reversed. Some maintain that this effect is an instance of psychological priming or framing.

Lacy contends that a possible cause of the empirical differences is that the preferences over the issues are nonseparable. In surveys we force respondents to choose from a limited number of options. Suppose that we first ask an individual's opinion on redistribution. His actual preferred position may not correspond to any of the possible choices. Thus, the individual is forced to choose the position on redistribution that is *closest to* his first preference. Assume this means that the respondent chooses a more redistributive policy than his most preferred choice, given his current view of government abortion policy. Now he is asked his opinion on abortion policy. The respondent, taking as given that government policy is more redistributive than he most prefers given current abortion policy, may be more willing to accept a less restrictive abortion policy than he normally would were his preferences nonseparable. Suppose now that the question ordering is reversed. The respondent may likewise be forced to choose a more restrictive abortion policy than he prefers, and this may result in a preference for less redistribution in

---

[5] See Dion 1992 for a recent analysis of the robustness of structure-induced equilibria.

the subsequent question. What appears to be a framing effect may actually be a consequence of nonseparable preferences – not preferences that can be altered by framing or priming.

Lacy has conducted some preliminary survey experiments on the extent that nonseparability exists in voter preferences by examining the order effects isolated from framing. That is, he provides the subjects with "framing" before beginning the survey and then varies the order of questions to see if effects still occur. This early work supports the supposition that some question ordering effects are explained by nonseparable preferences. Notice that Lacy's work is also a test of two competing models of voter preferences, one from rational choice and the other from psychology.

Relaxing separability has both negative and positive implications for understanding political outcomes. On the negative side, nonseparability lessens the ability of majority voting models to yield predictable equilibria; while on the positive side, nonseparability can explain voter choices that have previously been labeled examples of nonrationality. Interestingly, in contrast to the assumption testing of expected utility theory, in this case the alternative theorizing about relaxing separability came before the actual testing of the assumption.

5.3   Assumptions, Complexity, and Pure Theory

I would like to close this chapter by noting how important it is that assumption evaluation not result in models that lose their predictive capacity. In Chapter 2 I pointed out that we often choose a formal model's assumptions so that we can make clear predictions. I discussed how, in designing a model of the Brooklyn Bridge, the factors that are emphasized are those that we wish to analyze and the factors that are ignored or more falsely represented are factors that we expect not to matter significantly for the analysis at hand. (Some of the artistic extra features of the towers are irrelevant to understanding the water flow through the bridge.) The same holds true in social science models. If we try to include everything in our models, they can become unwieldy and not as useful in making predictions.

In Chapter 2 I addressed how policy motives of candidates may lead to platform divergence and how entry of new candidates may have the same effect. If a model allows for both factors then it is less easy to distinguish which factor causes divergence when the model is empirically evaluated. As a consequence, it is sometimes best to work with an extreme version of a model, perhaps assuming no entry and candidates with policy motives – even though we know the assumptions of the model are false and the results may hinge crucially on the assumptions – in order to determine the prediction for that particular set of assumptions. Then the prediction can be compared empirically to a prediction for a different set of assumptions. We must be careful that our quest for "real" assumptions does not lead us to models that are so complex that they do not yield any predictions.

Finally, pure theory (also discussed in Chapter 2) often means models with assumptions that are extremely unreal *by design,* such as Einstein's Swiss tram cars running at the speed of light. My emphasis on assumption evaluation should not be interpreted to mean that only models that are the most "real" are useful. I cannot sufficiently reiterate that, without pure theory and the almost completely unreal early formal models of social science, our current applied models would not be possible. Moreover, continued purely theoretical research of this kind is fundamental to theoretical progress. Unrealness in these formal models should be allowed and even (to some extent) encouraged, since these mind-experiments can ultimately lead to understanding and better models of the real world.

5.4   Implications of the Examples

The foregoing examples provide a number of insights into how assumption testing is best done and what can be gained. These implications may be summarized as follows.

1. *Assumptions in descriptive models should be evaluated if possible. However, we should recognize that the results of the evaluation are qualified by additional underlying assumptions necessary for the empirical analysis.* The assumptions of models designed for descriptive purposes should be evaluated. Of course, not all models' assumptions should be or can be tested. Some models are not designed to be descriptive accounts of the real world but are instead mind-experiments, as discussed in Chapter 1. But if a formal model is designed as a descriptive account of the real world, then its assumptions should be evaluated against the real world if possible. However, when evaluating assumptions we must recognize that that evaluation generally carries a number of its own underlying assumptions and so the empirical evaluation of any assumption is qualified and limited. Thus, evaluation of assumptions is not a substitute for evaluation of a theory but only part of the overall evaluation process.

2. *We can classify the evaluation of an assumption as follows.*

- A determination that an assumption is likely to be *false.* If so, there are two possibilities.
  (i) If "relaxed," the qualitative results of the model still follow. The research of Machina (1982, 1989), for example, considers how relaxing the independence axiom yields the same qualitative results in economics models that use expected utility theory.
  (ii) The results of the model depend crucially on the false assumption, and further empirical and theoretical work is necessary to fully consider how relaxing the assumptions changes our theoretical and empirical understanding. The work of Lacy on separability can have this effect since we know that a number of spatial voting models' results do depend on assumptions of separability.
- A determination that an assumption is likely to be *true* for the situation modeled. We know that the axioms of expected utility theory are reasonable approximations of individual preferences in situations where the probability of an outcome is not very close to either 0 or 1 or when risky situations are compared in which the outcomes are the same across situations. It may be that the research of Lacy and others to follow will show that separability can be used to understand some political science choices; this is as yet unclear.

3. *Assumption evaluation should lead to further theorizing.* Assessing basic assumptions in formal models that have not been verified is definitely important. But proving an assumption false with an empirical study is only the first step. The next step must be theoretical: exploring the implications of a more general or alternative assumption within the formal model. How significant is the false assumption for the results? Empirical evidence on the falseness of the assumptions only starts us on the process of understanding the limitations of a model. When we discover that a model's assumptions are likely to be false, a necessary theoretical exercise is to explore the importance of that assumption for the predictions of the model. We are not changing the model or adapting it to fit the data, but rather establishing the boundaries of a given model's abilities to explain. Typically, as in expected utility theory, the response has been to generalize the assumptions of the model and to see if the model's predictions still hold. We are not restricting theory but making it more general.

This entire exercise in developing better theories is not possible if our starting point is a nonformal model. Since we cannot evaluate the assumptions of a nonformal model, we cannot consider how the model's predictions are a function of the assumptions. When a nonformal model is shown to be empirically unsupported it is true that there is not much to do beyond making that model more restrictive. Once a formal model is generalized, however, we cannot assume that the exercise is over. The new theory, with new assumptions and perhaps new predictions, must be empirically evaluated.

4. *Experiments are useful for assumption evaluation.* Experimental work can be a useful vehicle for evaluating assumptions of individual behavior or preferences. Tests of both the independence axiom and the separability assumption used laboratory approaches. The control that is possible in the laboratory allows us to uniquely focus on the main variable that we cannot control, individual behavior and choices. Thus, these assumptions are ideally assessed in the laboratory.

5. *Implicit assumptions of nonformal models should be evaluated.* Sometimes nonformal models make implicit assumptions that should be evaluated, just as the explicit assumptions of formal models should be evaluated. Lacy's work shows that the nonformal theorizing that uses evidence of question order effects to argue that framing of questions influences preferences and choices *implicitly* assumes that the preferences are separable. If we formally model preferences as nonseparable, then the question order effects may not be due to framing at all but simply a consequence of the nonseparability of preferences. Nonformal models' implicit assumptions are as likely to be false or nonverifiable as formal models' explicit assumptions. Assumption evaluation is relevant to any model.

6. Finally, *our quest for "realness" in assumptions should not lead us to build models so complex that they cannot yield predictions, nor should it keep us from engaging in pure theory mind-experiments that may require exceedingly unreal assumptions.* Again, formal models' predictions can be much less clear if our models are too complex. Too strong a focus on realness of assumptions can limit our ability to think through many of the purely theoretical possibilities that should be considered in the building of better explanatory theory.

CHAPTER 6

Evaluating Predictions: Equilibria, Disequilibria, and Multiequilibria

In solving formal models, we seek to find equilibrium outcomes. As mentioned in Chapter 4, the equilibrium concept a formal modeler uses often depends on the formal modeling technique. In general, equilibria are outcomes that are stable points. Depending on the modeling technique and the assumptions used, models can have unique equilibrium predictions or multiple equilibria predictions; sometimes, no equilibria are predicted. The type of equilibrium prediction a model makes is also a function of whether the model is deterministic or deterministic and stochastic. Each situation provides different opportunities and problems for the empirical assessment of the models.

6.1   Evaluating Equilibrium Point Predictions

6.1.1   *The Paradox of Point Predictions*

Point Predictions Are an Easy Empirical Target. Point predictions are predictions of a unique particular outcome, like the policy position convergence prediction of the traditional Hotelling–Downsian two-party or two-candidate spatial model of electoral competition. A point prediction is the equilibrium outcome of a model, which by definition must ignore details and have false assumptions. Of course, in the real world the ignored details exist and not all the assumptions hold. More significant for equilibrium point predictions is that we rarely are able to measure the real world at the state of "rest" that equilibrium analysis implies. This means that point predictions are less likely to be observed in less controlled empirical analyses than in controlled empirical tests. Most formal modelers expect

164

that outcomes will likely diverge from point predictions in empirical analysis. When a formal model with a point prediction is viewed as a Complete DGP, an empirical assessment of the point prediction is highly unlikely to be supported. When the formal model is viewed as a Partial DGP, point predictions perform better, but the very fact that the model is viewed as a Partial DGP leads to a questioning of the relevance of the point prediction. The easiest way to attack a formal model as not empirically relevant is to show that the point predictions are not supported, given that they rarely are (as discussed in Chapter 4). As a result, formal modelers sometimes appear little disturbed when more empirically oriented political scientists argue that not observing point predictions in the "real" world means a model is suspect.

Desirability of Unique Point Predictions.

Formal Models Seek Unique Point Predictions. Not only do formal modelers often seem uninterested in empirical attacks on point predictions, almost perversely they actually often desire to derive unique equilibrium point predictions and discard or criticize models that do not provide them. From a theoretical perspective, unique equilibrium point predictions are sometimes seen as the ultimate goal. For example, in the late 1970s some theorists found multidimensional spatial voting models uninteresting because of their inability to provide equilibrium point predictions.[1] More telling is the focus of game theorists throughout the 1980s. That is, much of the history of game theory during this period is the quest for "equilibrium refinements," criteria by which a modeler can argue that one or a few equilibria are more likely than others. As discussed in Morrow (1994, chaps. 5–7), such concepts as subgame perfection are methods by which game theorists attempt to be more precise about equilibrium predictions. Typically these refinements work by placing additional "rationality" constraints on Nash equilibria.

Some equilibrium refinements are considered relatively innocuous, greatly simplify the theoretical solution, and are used without further justification. For example, many game theoretic models are solved only for "symmetric" equilibria, where players of the same type are assumed for

---

[1] Some believe that the perceived "negative" results of disequilibrium led to rejections of theoretical work in this area by editors and referees of theoretical journals, although this rumor is difficult to prove.

technical simplicity to choose the same strategy even though many asymmetric equilibria may exist.[2]

Game theoretic modelers also generally focus only on pure strategy equilibria even when they suspect that mixed strategy equilibria might exist. Pure strategies are choices a player would make with certainty, whereas mixed strategies exist when players have a probability distribution over the possible choices they can make. In a pure strategy Nash equilibrium, players choose the best response pure strategies to the optimal pure strategies of the other players; in a mixed strategy Nash equilibrium, players are "mixing" optimally over their pure strategies given the other players' optimal mixed strategies. (See Morrow 1994, pp. 81–8, for an explanation of pure and mixed strategies.) Yet many times game theorists ignore mixed strategies. One reason is the lack of a general agreement among game theorists on the descriptive meaning of playing mixed strategies.

Osborne and Rubinstein (1994, pp. 37–44) discuss five different perspectives of mixed strategy equilibria:

1. the naive view, where players are assumed to directly choose to randomize their choices over strategies;
2. the steady-state interpretation of the game (recall the discussion in Chapter 4 of equilibria as a steady state of an environment in which players act repeatedly), where players formulate mixed strategies based on beliefs about the frequency of actions in similar games in the general population or over time;
3. the "bigger game" approach, where mixed strategies are really pure strategies in an extended game that is not explicitly modeled;
4. the "altered game" approach, where mixed strategies are pure strategies in a perturbed version of the game (see also Harsanyi 1973); and
5. the "belief" approach, where mixed strategies are really a profile of beliefs about the actions each player will take and each player takes a single action but the equilibrium is defined in terms of the beliefs.

Each of these interpretations can have slightly different implications when a mixed strategy equilibrium is used for empirical evaluation. Generally, applied game theorists prefer concentrating on pure strategy equilibria rather

---

[2] For instance, in describing his model of electoral competition, Palfrey notes: "To simplify the proofs, we will only investigate properties of 'symmetric' equilibria. In other words, we will investigate stable behavior in which only two *identical* voters will make identical voting decisions. Therefore, a voter views the strategy of each other voter as the *same* function σ" (1989, p. 74).

than justifying mixed strategies as reasonable descriptions of individual behavior. However, this is not always the case. Alt, Calvert, and Humes (1988)
find the mixed strategy prediction to be an accurate description of the behavior of a hegemon in an international bargaining situation.

Subgame perfection is an example of a popular equilibrium refinement
used to narrow multiple Nash equilibria; it is the requirement that an equilibrium be a Nash equilibrium in all subgames of a game.[3] Recall the centipede game presented in Chapter 4 (see Figure 4.1). In this game, "taking"
at the first move for both players characterizes the Nash equilibria strategies.
But Nash equilibria could also involve taking at the first move but "passing"
at a subsequent move. That is, since taking at the first move means that the
game ends at the first move, it follows that *any* choices at the subsequent
moves are "best responses" – all that is required for a Nash equilibrium.
Thus, there are many Nash equilibria. However, if the game actually did
reach a later node, passing would not be a Nash equilibrium in the part of
the game that is left (a subgame), since both players would prefer to take
rather than pass. Hence, the only subgame perfect Nash equilibrium in the
centipede game is taking at every node. The essential argument is that a
strategy that involves passing, even at a node the player will never reach, is
not rational.

Subgame perfection places a stronger degree of rationality on player
choices than required by a Nash equilibrium. The subgame perfect concept reduces the number of Nash equilibria in the centipede game to one
(taking at every node). Other equilibrium concepts that have become popular in political science (such as sequential equilibrium, perfect equilibrium,
etc.) are similarly designed to reduce the number of equilibria possible by
arguing that rational players would choose these equilibrium strategies over
other alternatives.

Why Are Point Predictions Useful?   Why are formal modelers so
enamored of unique point predictions when they can be so problematic for
empirical evaluation of their models? There are two reasons. First, it is
more difficult (although not impossible, as I discuss shortly) to think about
the empirical implications of models with multiple equilibria. Thus, formal modelers are attracted to unique point predictions because they provide

---

[3] Very loosely, a *subgame* begins at any point in a game where the players have complete information about previous moves in the game. See Morrow (1994, p. 128) for a formal definition.

precise statements about what – according to the model – can be expected in the real world.

Second, and perhaps more significant, comparative static and dynamic path predictions (which are easier to demonstrate empirically than point predictions, as discussed in the next chapter) are easier to make if we begin with unique point predictions. Hence there is a near inverse relation between the likely empirical viability of comparative static and dynamic path predictions and equilibrium point predictions. That is, the more likely an equilibrium prediction will be a single point and thus easier to refute empirically, the more likely that comparative static and dynamic path predictions will exist that can be empirically supported. Comparative static and dynamic path predictions, as predictors of relationships, are seen by many as more empirically useful than point or other equilibrium predictions. Relationship predictions forecast how variables will change in relation to each other or over time, which tells us more than what will occur under very specific conditions at a single point in time. An important aim in our research is to discover how empirical relationships in politics work across time and other factors, so relationship predictions, which help us increase this knowledge, are viewed as more useful than equilibrium predictions.

Should We Be Concerned about the Empirical Viability of Point Predictions? Yet many formal modelers are concerned with the verifiability of point predictions. The most famous paradoxes in formal modeling involve point predictions that are not observed, such as complete convergence of candidates or parties in policy positions (the Hotelling–Downsian prediction). These paradoxes are the subject of much theoretical and empirical investigation attempting to understand why the point predictions are not verified. The theoretical investigations return to the models and explore how differences in assumptions may lead to different, more empirically relevant, point predictions.

Oftentimes the theoretical exercise leads to multiple explanations, and empirical research is then used to attempt to distinguish between the explanations. A case in point is the paradox of not voting, that is, the paradox that predicts that turnout in elections should be much smaller than empirically observed. This false prediction has led to a large number of alternative explanations (incorporating consumption benefits, the role of groups, etc.) for why we observe turnout as well as a substantial empirical literature on the viability of these various explanations. (See Aldrich 1993 and Morton 1991 for reviews.) This is a body of literature, both theoretical *and* empirical, that might not exist if the original false theory had not first been explored empirically. A very false point prediction has led to a huge amount of theoretical and empirical examination of turnout. There are other examples of false point predictions leading to theoretical and empirical literatures that increased our understanding of politics. The prediction of platform convergence, for example, has led to a sizeable theoretical literature that explains platform divergence by relaxing assumptions in the Hotelling–Downsian model and also to empirical investigation of convergence predictions (see e.g. Schmidt et al. 1996 and the discussion in Chapter 8).

6.1.2   *Effective Evaluation of Point Predictions*

Given that point predictions are likely to be (a) proven false in most empirical investigations when a model is viewed as a Complete DGP and (b) suspect, even if supported, when a model is viewed as a Partial DGP, how then should we assess point predictions? There are two ways to evaluate point predictions effectively. The first method is to make explicit assumptions about the nature of the random effects on the point predictions that may have prevented those predictions from being observed empirically. A quantal response equilibrium (see Chapter 4) can be used for introducing randomness in a deterministic model, allowing for empirical evaluation of the model's predictions. The second method of evaluating point predictions is to use controlled laboratory experiments to eliminate as many as possible of the random effects that occur in the natural environment. I shall examine each method in detail, presenting examples of how these methods have been used in political science.

Incorporating Randomness in the Model. When we anticipate that we cannot statistically (or through experimental design) control for the effects we believe will falsify a point prediction, explicitly making assumptions about the expected randomness allows us to evaluate the point prediction. However, as noted in Chapter 4, evaluating the point prediction is also assessing the assumption about the nature of the randomness, so we do not have a truly independent test of the point prediction.

There are many different ways that randomness can be added to a deterministic formal model, and each can have a different effect on the predictions of the model. Thus, we should consider several ways of adding randomness before rejecting a deterministic formal model on the basis of empirical evaluation, especially since some techniques do not always yield useful or clear results for empirical evaluation. With QRE we saw that adding randomness led to an identification problem. An interesting case to consider is how randomness has been added to models of majority voting to yield "probabilistic voting" models. Probabilistic voting is particularly noteworthy because much of the motivation for adding randomness is to translate spatial voting models into more empirically viable formal models. Spatial voting theory is the example that Bartels and Brady (1993) present to illustrate how sophisticated methods and formal models might be effectively combined (see Chapter 1).

The Theoretical Reason for Probabilistic Voting. Spatial voting models (typically called probabilistic voting models) are examples of formal models that explicitly incorporate randomness. The original impetus for adding random factors to spatial voting models was not to help in the empirical testing of point predictions, although the motive was empirical. Probabilistic voting was originally devised to explain how equilibria may occur in majority voting models of candidate competition in multidimensional issue space. Early theoretical research showed that, when the issue space moved beyond the single dimension of the Hotelling–Downsian model of candidate or party competition, disequilibrium results were predicted. Researchers began to add randomness to voting in order to solve the disequilibrium problem. The motivation for adding randomness was empirical, since it seemed obvious that candidate competition was stable and not chaotic as the disequilibrium results predicted. Furthermore, researchers argued that randomness in voting is realistic and that adding randomness increased the models' empirical validity. Note also that researchers wanted predictions from the theory that could be empirically evaluated.

In order to understand how randomness alleviates the disequilibrium problem, consider first how with*out* randomness two-candidate or two-party competition can lead to disequilibria. Assume two candidates or parties who choose policy positions to maximize the probability of election. It is well known that, if voter preferences are symmetric and single-peaked, we can show that the candidates will locate at the policy position most preferred by the electorate's median voter – when the policy space is unidimensional. What happens when policy is multidimensional? Imagine that the policy

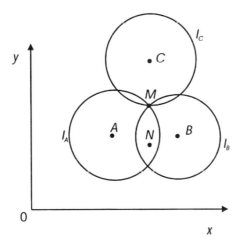

Figure 6.1. Lack of equilibrium in two-dimensional issue space.

space is two-dimensional, with x and y as the two issues.[4] Each voter has preferences over the issues that are symmetric about a single ideal point. Graphically, we can draw a voter's preferences as for voter C in Figure 2.2. The point C is voter C's ideal position. Voter C's utility decreases mono-tonically as policies move away from this point. We can graph voter C's utility by drawing indifference curves to represent policy positions that are equidistant from point C, such as the circle I_C. Voter C is indifferent with regard to all policy combinations on I_C. Policy combinations inside I_C pro-vide voter C with higher levels of utility and policy combinations outside I_C provide voter C with lower utility. We can imagine that for every point in xy space there is a corresponding indifference circle.

Now assume there are three voters A, B, C whose ideal points are given by points A, B, C in Figure 6.1, as well as two candidates $1, 2$, who are choosing points in xy space in order to maximize the probability of achiev-ing election. Suppose that candidate 1 has chosen the policy combination given by point M. By assumption, point M is on an indifference circle for each voter: I_A, I_B, I_C for voters A, B, and C. Notice that there are now

---

[4] For further details on models of candidate competition, both deterministic and probabilistic, see Calvert (1986), Enelow and Hinich (1984), Hinich and Munger (1997), and Mueller (1989, pp. 196–216).

points within the three lenses formed by the intersecting indifference curves that will defeat M. For example, point N is closer than M to points A and B and thus would defeat M in a pairwise vote. Hence, candidate 2 might choose to locate at N. But if candidate 2 chooses N, we can similarly find points that candidate 1 could choose that would be closer than N to two of the voters, who would then defeat N. As demonstrated by Davis, DeGroot, and Hinich (1972) and Plott (1967), under certain symmetry assumptions about voter preferences it is possible to derive a unique equilibrium position for both candidates in multidimensional issue space; this is analogous to the median voter theorem in unidimensional issue space. However, the symmetry conditions are highly unlikely to be satisfied (as they are in the example of Figure 6.1).

When the symmetry conditions are not satisfied, one can show that a candidate can always increase her probability of winning to 100% simply by changing her position, given the position of her opponent. Even small moves in position can have this effect. Since voting decisions are deterministic, the probability that a voter will vote for a candidate in a two-candidate race is either 1, 0, or 0.5 (when the voter is indifferent between two candidates). What if candidates are uncertain about voters' preferences or willingness to vote? Can we then find an equilibrium in multidimensional issue space? If voter preferences are less certain, then the probability of winning for a candidate does not change to 1 or 0 with small moves in policy positions and an equilibrium is possible.

The Empirical Reason for Probabilistic Voting. The theoretical problem of achieving equilibrium in multidimensional issue space in two-candidate competition was one catalyst for the turn to probabilistic voting, but it was not the only one. As Coughlin argues, the other motivation for turning to probabilistic voting was likewise primarily empirical.

Spatial voting theorists have become interested in the implications of candidate uncertainty about voters' choices primarily because there are good empirical reasons for believing that actual candidates often *are* uncertain about the choices that voters are going to make on election day. First, candidates tend to rely on polls for information about how voters will vote, but "information from public opinion surveys is not error-free and is best represented as statistical" . . . . Second, even when economists and political scientists have developed sophisticated statistical models of voters' choices and have used appropriate data sets to estimate them, there has consistently been a residual amount of unexplained variance . . . . (1990, p. 145 [italics in original])

Abstention and Uncertainty. Unquestionably, adding some uncertainty in spatial voting models is an attractive idea. The difficulty is: What should be the source of the uncertainty? One obvious option is to allow for voter abstention and candidate uncertainty over turnout choices. This is the direction chosen by Hinich, Ledyard, and Ordeshook (1972). The authors assume that voters may choose not to vote for two reasons that have been suggested in the empirical and theoretical literature: abstention due to indifference and abstention due to alienation. Abstention due to *indifference* captures the idea that, when candidates choose positions close to each other, the benefit of voting is not so great and voters should abstain. The benefit from voting for a given candidate depends on the difference in candidate positions, since only then does a vote have the potential of affecting policy outcomes. If candidates are at positions close to each other, then voting can make little difference in the policies that are ultimately enacted. Abstention due to *alienation* describes the case when candidates' positions are so far from a voter's preferred positions that the voter's likelihood of voting is decreased. That is, voters see both candidates as undesirable (see Enelow and Hinich 1984 for a technical presentation).

Adding uncertainty to a formal model cannot be done successfully unless the researchers make sure that the logic and the consistency of the model is not threatened. Unfortunately, Hinich et al.'s (1972) abstention functions were inconsistent with other assumptions they had made about voter preferences. That is, the abstention functions implied that voters would make choices contrary to assumptions that had already been made elsewhere in the model about the relationship between voter preferences and vote choices. Abstention due to alienation is particularly problematic if we also make standard assumptions about voter preferences and rationality. That is, if voters' utility functions from policy are concave then, for a given difference in candidate positions, the benefit from voting should actually increase as candidates move far from voters' ideal policy positions.[5] It seems that accounting for randomness implies that the researcher must relax assumptions of rational voter choices elsewhere in the formulation of turnout in order to derive functions for probability of voting that have desirable properties.

Alternatives. How can the situation be resolved? One approach is to assume that voter decisions are deterministic but that candidates are

[5] See Slutsky (1975) for an exposition of the problems of Hinich et al. and an alternative approach to incorporating abstention.

uncertain about the decisions. Essentially, the uncertainty is due not to turnout but to uncertainty in candidates' minds over preferences in the electorate. This is the approach taken in the work of Coughlin and Nitzan (1981), Enelow and Hinich (1984), Erikson and Romero (1990), Hinich (1977), and Samuelson (1984). In Coughlin and Nitzan (1981) and in other probabilistic voting models, candidates are assumed to form their expectations according to a model drawn from mathematical psychology, the "binary Luce" model (see Becker, DeGroot, and Marschak 1964; Luce 1959; Luce and Suppes 1965). In Enelow and Hinich (1984), Hinich (1977), and Londregan and Romer (1993), the assumption is that there are nonpolicy reasons (which could be candidate characteristics) that make voters' decisions hard to predict. Another alternative is simply to assume that voter preferences over policy are subject to random shocks – that is, make voter decisions probabilistic as in Alesina (1987), Alesina, Londregan, and Rosenthal (1993), and Alesina and Rosenthal (1996). This literature is discussed in the next chapter.

Returning to the question of abstention as an explanation for randomness in voting, Ledyard (1984) models abstention as a rational choice in the context of a two-candidate spatial voting model in which candidates know the distribution of voter preferences (but not the preferences of individual voters). Making turnout fully rational, however, raises another issue: the paradox of not voting. It is widely held that, since the probability of a single vote affecting the outcome in most large elections is negligible, the expected benefits of voting as an investment in future policy outcomes is likely to be less than the positive cost of voting (see Riker and Ordeshook 1968). In order to make turnout rational and possibly positive, Ledyard assumes that voters recognize there are cross-effects to abstention. That is, it may be rational not to vote according to expected utility calculations if a voter perceives that the probability of her vote affecting the outcome is negligible. However, if all voters make the same calculation then clearly a single vote could have a significant impact. Ledyard endogenizes the probability of being decisive and demonstrates that majority-voting two-candidate equilibria are possible.

In another approach to using turnout as the random factor in voting, Morton (1987, 1991) and Filer et al. (1993) present a probabilistic model of voting in which turnout decisions are made at a "group" level, at which the probability of being decisive is likely to be large enough to justify rational turnout. The group is then assumed to enforce the decisions on its members. The cost of voting is subject to random effects, leading to probabilistic voting. Unfortunately, in both the Ledyard approach and the group approach, in equilibrium the candidates converge and then rationally no one votes. In order to explain turnout, these models must assume the existence of forces that prevent candidates from converging in equilibrium, perhaps owing to policy preferences (see Morton 1991).

The myriad ways in which probabilistic voting has been modeled demonstrate that: (1) incorporating randomness is not straightforward, since it is necessary to make sure that a model's logic and consistency are not violated; and (2) the manner in which randomness is incorporated is likely to affect a model's predictions. As noted before, the first problem may mean that assumptions made in the original model need to be relaxed in order to incorporate uncertainty. Almost all of the approaches (except for Ledyard's) resulted in some relaxation of rationality – either in the candidates' minds or in the voter decision process.

Uncertainty and Predictions. What of a model's predictions? How are they affected by adding randomness? The principal point prediction of the Hotelling–Downsian model is that candidates converge in equilibrium under precise symmetry conditions; when these conditions do not hold, disequilibria are predicted. Probabilistic voting models are able to find convergent equilibria even if the symmetry conditions do not hold. The particular point predictions (i.e., the convergent positions of the candidates) are different under voter uncertainty, and equilibria may not always exist. Hinich's (1977) paper on probabilistic voting is subtitled: "The Median Voter Result Is an Artifact." The point predictions of candidate locations depend on the specific assumptions (about voters and candidates) that are used to derive the probability of winning functions. Moreover, assumptions about candidate motivations that would not make a difference in deterministic voting can affect the candidate equilibria in probabilistic voting. Feldmann (1997) shows that, when voting is probabilistic, different equilibria emerge depending upon whether candidates are assumed to be maximizing plurality or the probability of winning. If additional assumptions are made such as adding candidates with policy preferences (as in the papers by Alesina and coauthors; see also Calvert 1985; Londregan and Romer 1993; Morton 1991), divergent candidate positions can be found in probabilistic voting equilibria, a result that does not hold with deterministic voting.

Only recently have researchers begun to examine probabilistic voting with more than two candidates. I am aware of only two papers that attempt to derive probabilistic voting equilibria for this case (Lin, Enelow, and Dorussen 1996; Nixon et al. 1995); the results are inconclusive. It is well known that, in deterministic voting situations in unidimensional issue space, the results on candidate locations are complicated by more than two candidates or parties (see Shepsle 1991 for a review of the theoretical literature). When equilibria do occur in the multicandidate or multiparty situation, they are likely to be characterized by divergence and the lumping of the parties together at divergent positions. The theoretical literature on multicandidate competition also generally assumes that voters vote sincerely for their first preferences. In summary, the predictions of candidate locations in probabilistic voting are likely to depend on the nature of the randomness assumed, the number of candidates or parties assumed, and other assumptions of the model – none of which makes a difference in candidate location if voting is deterministic.

What about predictions concerning voter decisions? Probabilistic voting models do make predictions about voter decisions that can be evaluated. But again, the way in which randomness is incorporated in a model affects its predictions. If the source of uncertainty is nonpolicy characteristics of candidates, for example, voter choices are likely to be different than if the origin of uncertainty is turnout variability (due, perhaps, to random effects on the cost of voting). In other words: if the root of uncertainty is nonpolicy, then some voters may vote for a candidate whose policy position is not the closest to them because of perceived nonpolicy advantages of candidates further from their ideal points; but if the source of the uncertainty is variations in the cost of voting, we would not expect this type of voting. Probabilistic voting models which assume that voter decisions are deterministic but that candidates or parties have incomplete information about voter decisions make *different* predictions than probabilistic voting models which assume that voter decisions are actually affected by random factors. That is, candidate information about voter decisions may vary with the type of voter, and therefore the probabilistic nature of the model may be affected by voter type.

The comparative static predictions are also likely to vary with the way in which randomness is added to the model. For example, the Ledyard and group models predict that turnout will be a function of candidate location decisions and the closeness of the election; whereas models that assume voting is random (or that voting is deterministic but candidates have incomplete information about voter preferences) do not predict such a relationship.

Models in which the uncertainty arises owing to nonpolicy characteristics also imply different comparative static predictions about the relationship between these characteristics, voter decisions, and candidate locations.

The Empirical Research. A number of empirical studies have attempted to test the predictions of probabilistic voting models. Enelow and Hinich (1984) apply their model to the 1976 and 1980 presidential elections. Erikson and Romero (1990) conduct a similar analysis for the 1988 election. In both cases, the authors use information from voter preferences to infer candidate locations in policy space and the nonpolicy characteristics. They assess whether the model accurately predicts voter decisions when voters care both about the nonpolicy characteristics and policy positions of the candidates; the researchers find support for their predictions. It should be noted that specifying the policy dimensions and the nonpolicy characteristics empirically in these cases requires assumptions about the dimensions that are available and the number and type of characteristics that can matter. Thus, evaluations of the models are tests of the predictions and these other assumptions combined.

Empirical evaluations of probabilistic voting models have also examined elections in other countries. For example, Nixon and colleagues (1995) apply their model to an analysis of voting in Israel, and Alvarez, Bowler, and Nagler (1996) study the application of spatial voting models to elections in Great Britain. Nixon et al. follow the approach of Coughlin in assuming that the probabilistic nature of voter decisions arises because parties lack complete information and so estimate voter decisions; Alvarez et al. assume that voting decisions are actually probabilistic, that is, affected by random error. It is not clear whether these assumptions' differences lead to significant differences in the predictions of the two models in the cases examined.

One complication in the empirical applications of these models is that many of the elections examined have involved more than two parties or candidates. Most of the theoretical results on probabilistic voting are truly applicable only to two-candidate races in which sincere voting is the same as strategic voting. Sincere voting is voting for a candidate that a voter most prefers, regardless of the election's expected outcome, whereas strategic voting is voting for a candidate who maximizes the voter's expected utility given expectations about the likely outcome. Strategic and sincere voting are equivalent in two-candidate elections, but not in elections with more than two candidates. Little theoretical work has been done with strategic probabilistic voting on more than two candidates or parties. Since in these cases voters may make nonsincere voting decisions (i.e., vote strategically for a candidate or party who is not their first preference but who may be more likely to win), modeling voter choice and incorporating randomness are *both* complicated. One cannot just assume that all voting for a less preferred candidate is due to the randomly determined factor. In some cases, strategic voting has been empirically handled by adding ad hoc party specific parameters in the empirical estimation. With this technique, the formal model is treated as a Partial DGP with an added variable. It is desirable to re-solve the model with explicit assumptions about the nature of randomness and to derive predictions about the extent that strategic voting is predicted, thus creating a model that can be more effectively viewed as a Complete DGP in empirical evaluation.

Comparative static predictions of probabilistic voting models have also been assessed. As discussed in the next chapter, Alesina et al. (1993) evaluate their probabilistic voting model using time-series data on U.S. elections. Their model is used to make predictions about outcomes of presidential and Congressional elections, so their focus is on the viability of these predictions. Again, the empirical work tests both the model's predictions (that voters moderate votes between the presidency and Congress) and the way in which randomness has been incorporated. Similarly, Filer et al. (1993) evaluate the predictions concerning turnout in their group probabilistic voting model. In the next chapter I discuss an application (Segal et al. 1992) of probabilistic voting to Congressional voting on Supreme Court nominees.

The example of probabilistic voting shows that incorporating randomness in a formal model must be approached carefully. First, the randomness must be consistent with the logic of the rest of the model. Adding uncertainty in an ad hoc fashion can lead to a model that makes predictions that are inconsistent and therefore meaningless for empirical analysis. Secondly, the model's predictions may be affected by the randomness, and the empirical tests should take this into account. The empirical analysis should consider the way in which randomness has been incorporated into the model and the ways in which it has *not* but could have been. Finally, empirical support for (or rejection of) the model must be carefully interpreted in terms of all the assumptions, including the assumptions about randomness in the model. Rejection or acceptance of a model's prediction will imply some acceptance or rejection of the assumptions of randomness, and the extent that the randomness matters for this evaluation must be scrupulously weighed.

Laboratory Experiments. The second effective way to evaluate point predictions is in the laboratory, where the environment can be controlled closely to mitigate those details of the real world that the model ignores. These are the "theory" tests discussed in Chapter 4. If a point prediction fails in the laboratory, then (as discussed in that chapter) we expect it is less likely to hold in the naturally occurring environment – even at the "rest" implied by an equilibrium.

The equilibrium predictions of majority voting models have also been evaluated experimentally in both theory and stress tests. McKelvey and Ordeshook review much of the literature on spatial voting experiments (most of it work of their own and with various coauthors), including experimental evidence on voting models in which a unique point prediction occurs (1990, pp. 99–120). In the experimental design, many of the problems encountered in this section are no longer troublesome. For example, by restricting the competition to just two candidates, we need not be concerned with issues of sincere versus strategic voting. We can also isolate the effects of candidate behavior by viewing voters as artificial actors who always vote for the candidate whose position is closest to theirs; this enables testing of the model's predictions on candidate behavior (convergence predictions, for example).

Are Experiments Real? Despite the advantages, we do face some problems with using the laboratory for testing theoretical point predictions. That is, to what extent are the experiments simply "demonstrations" rather than "real" tests of predictions of the theory? In Chapter 4 it was noted that, although experimental design can control many variables, it cannot control the experimental subjects' behavior. In the laboratory experiments we describe in this book the subjects are real humans and are given real choices. In most of the experiments we discuss, payments depend on these choices and subjects are paid real money for their participation. We set up the experiment to influence these choices in certain ways and we have theoretically derived expectations about these choices, given the influences. Good experimental design does not "hard-wire" the subjects' choices, else the experiment is a mere simulation. While these are theory tests and thus highly controlled to maintain internal validity, they are not simply demonstrations of the model.

That such experiments are more than simulations leads to another problem for the laboratory evaluation of predictions. Even controlled laboratory experiments may not yield enough control to effectively evaluate the theory.

That is, predictions based upon many game theoretic models can be problematic for empirical assessment in the laboratory. Under the assumptions of rationality used in game theoretic equilibria, we expect zero errors in decision making. Thus, observations that do not match the equilibrium predictions reject the predictions and the theory both. Some argue that this makes statistical analysis of theoretical predictions impossible even when using data from controlled laboratory experiments. Why is it not satisfactory to just add in random errors on the part of the subjects? In game theory we make explicit assumptions about individuals' expectations about other individuals' behavior. Thus, we need to consider how these expectations may be altered when we incorporate random errors (see Hey and Orme 1994). Again the zero-likelihood problem arises (see Chapter 4), and it is no surprise that the methods (discussed in that chapter) of dealing with this problem, such as QRE, have been applied primarily to experimental data. At what point do we say that subjects are making errors rather than not behaving as predicted?

What Do Theory Experiments Tell Us? Even if we account for the problem of errors in our empirical examination of the experimental data, our analysis still leaves a number of unanswered questions. If we evaluate the Hotelling–Downsian candidate convergence prediction, then the empirical assessment is really a "goodness of fit" test of the theory, with the alternative hypothesis simply that convergence is no more likely than any other candidate location. For two reasons, experimental success of the point prediction is only the first step in showing that the theory has merit: (1) we cannot be sure that the results can validly be extended to the naturally occurring environment; and (2) we have not tested the theory against a carefully specified alternative prediction – our alternative hypothesis is simply that the theoretical prediction does not hold. We can alleviate the second concern by constructing assessments of alternative models wherein our predictions can be tested against other predictions, a subject addressed in Chapter 8.

How do we alleviate the first concern? When we find that point predictions are successful in the laboratory, we should conduct further empirical investigation to alleviate the limitations of the analysis. We need to conduct stress tests of the predictions, as discussed in Chapter 4. That is, although one major advantage of using experiments to evaluate point predictions is the ability to control for factors that the researcher is less able to control for in data from the naturally occurring environment, it is useful to use experiments to gradually loosen that control in order to see how well the model predicts in new environments. McKelvey and Ordeshook (1990) report on a number of experiments in which subjects are given incomplete information: either voters uninformed about candidate positions or candidates and voters both uninformed about voter preferences. In contrast to using empirical analysis from the naturally occurring environment, where we suspect that voters or candidates may be uninformed, in the laboratory setting we can directly control the information that each has. We can compare the behavior of informed and uninformed voters without having to estimate voter information levels. Thus, we can find some answers to questions regarding the external validity of our results by step-by-step relaxation of the experimental controls.

Experimental success should thus lead to additional empirical and theoretical research. Experimental failure of point predictions should also result in significant subsequent research, both theoretical and empirical. One classic example is contained in the experimental literature on the free-rider problem and voluntary public good provision. When a good is provided by a collection of individuals with voluntary contributions, there is an incentive for each individual to not contribute and enjoy the good provided, paid for by the other individuals. As a consequence, the good may not be provided at all. The early experimental research showed that this free-rider problem is not as strong as theoretically predicted, and this research has resulted in much additional investigation – both theoretical and empirical (see Ledyard 1995 for a review).

In summary, evaluating point predictions of formal models is an extremely useful enterprise, and experiments can play a unique and important role in that empirical investigation since they allow us to focus on the role that each assumption plays. In the laboratory we are more able to reproduce the model (theory test) than in the real world and can thus assess the point prediction more closely. And, by successively relaxing the assumptions and letting the experimental environment gradually approximate the real world (stress test), we can explore how and when point predictions fail. As with evaluating assumptions, however, assessing point predictions in a carefully designed laboratory environment is just one step in what should be ongoing empirical and theoretical research, as new theory meets the challenge of empirical analysis.

6.2   What Does Disequilibrium Mean for Empirical Predictions?

Many formal models do not have unique equilibria but result in either disequilibria or multiple equilibria.[6] For our purposes, disequilibria is the case where no equilibrium exists in the model. Therefore, we can make no prediction about the likely outcome of the model. The predictions of deterministic voting models in multidimensional issue space are a prime example of disequilibria. These results, which became most evident in the late 1970s, led some political theorists to conclude that political science is truly the "dismal science" and that disequilibria is pervasive (see Riker 1980). Much ensuing work, both theoretical and empirical, has concentrated on determining whether political disequilibria truly are widespread and, if not, why not. (Wilson 1996 reviews this literature.)

Whether a model yields an equilibrium or not can depend upon the solution concept used to define equilibria and the assumptions that are made about the model. How does the existence of equilibria depend on the solution concept? For example, most game theoretic models with disequilibrium predictions in pure strategies can have equilibria in mixed strategies (see the discussion in Section 6.1). Thus, deterministic game theoretic models with only mixed strategy equilibria do not yield unique point predictions, but they do yield a predicted probability distribution over outcomes that can be empirically evaluated. There is no general agreement on how to consider the descriptive predictions of mixed strategies. However, mixed strategies can be seen as empirically "nice" since they can (if all outcomes are possible in the mixed strategy equilibrium) solve the zero-likelihood problem of unique equilibrium predictions.

How does changing assumptions affect the existence of equilibria? As discussed in Chapter 5, Slutsky (1977) and Shepsle (1979) show how restricting voting choices to one dimension at a time can lead to voting equilibria whereas voting over all issues simultaneously does not. Typically, in order to achieve equilibria, the assumptions must be made more restrictive as in Slutsky's and Shepsle's work. Since the disequilibrium predictions can be "theoretically" corrected either by changing our solution concept or by

---

[6] Note that sometimes we analyze models that have equilibria but we expect are not in equilibrium (i.e., we examine the adjustment process to equilibrium). This case is discussed in Chapter 7.

adding more restrictive assumptions, what is the worth of working with a model that has no equilibrium predictions?

Sometimes a modeler, working with a model that does not have an equilibrium, is not sure which additional assumption or solution concept will work and would like to try a number of different alternatives. Simulations are a mechanism by which we can take a model without equilibria, add assumptions about the parameters in the model, and solve the model using the computer for those parameters. The simulations provide predictions given the parameters that we add, so we can try a number of different parameters.

We can also assess models without equilibrium predictions by using experimental research. We can set up the experimental design to closely approximate the assumptions of the model (theory test). However, since we have no prediction about the outcome, the resulting empirical evaluation is not the same as an evaluation of a point prediction or other type of prediction. The empirical evaluation is not an evaluation of the model. For example, suppose we observe a single outcome. This could mean that the model is missing an important detail or assumption about individual behavior, or that the solution concept we are using (which yields no predictions) is bereft, or that the outcome just randomly occurred in the manner observed. Because we have no priors on the distribution of randomness, we cannot rule out this type of occurrence as supporting the disequilibrium prediction. The empirical evaluation is useful in that it might point us in a new direction in terms of building better theory, but its usefulness otherwise is extremely limited.

6.3 Multiple Equilibria Predictions

6.3.1 *Examples of Formal Models with Multiple Equilibria*

Many formal models have multiple equilibria. For example, noncooperative game theoretic models often have multiple equilibria. I shall now discuss three types of game theoretic models with multiple equilibria: games of coordination, repeated games, and signaling games.

Games of Coordination.

Battle of the Sexes. Consider the simple battle of the sexes game, which I will present in its traditional "sexist" form. That is, a heterosexual

Table 6.1. *Payoffs in a battle of the sexes game*

		Wife's Choices	
		Boxing	Ballet
Husband's Choices	Boxing	10, 5	0, 0
	Ballet	0, 0	5, 10

couple has two choices over what to do in the evening, go to a ballet or to
a boxing match. The wife would prefer the ballet, the husband the boxing match. However, both would prefer going together to either event than
going alone. We can represent this game in terms of the following payoff
matrix. The first number in each cell represents the husband's payoff and
the second number represents the wife's payoff. This game has two Nash
equilibria, one in which both go to the boxing match and the other in which
both go to the ballet. That is, if the husband is going to the ballet, the wife's
optimal choice is to go to the ballet and vice versa. If the wife is going to
the boxing match, the husband's optimal choice is to go to the boxing match
and vice versa. We call this a game of cooperation, since the players' utility is greater when they cooperate than when they do not; however, there
exist more than one cooperative solution. (For a more detailed discussion
of game theory, see Morrow 1994.) Table 6.1 presents an example payoff
matrix for this game.

The message of research in the spatial voting literature of the late 1970s
was that disequilibria was pervasive and political science was the dismal science, but the message of the new, more applied spatial voting literature of
the early 1990s is quite the opposite. The recent literature finds that multiple
equilibria are extremely common, and the "coordination" problem in politics
has been brought into the spotlight. Cox (1997) argues that understanding the
cooperation problems for political parties is central to understanding comparative electoral systems. Aldrich (1995) also emphasizes the importance
of coordination games in real-world political situations. Thus, a number of

Table 6.2. *Voter payoff matrix*

	Candidate Types		
Voter Types	**x**	**y**	**z**
1	1	α	0
2	α	1	0
3	0	0	1

noted researchers see the battle of the sexes game's coordination problem as illustrative of a general problem in many political science formal models.

A Political Science Example. The majority voting model of Myerson and Weber (1993) presents an example of how coordination is important in a political science context. Myerson and Weber's model is an expansion of the Hotelling–Downsian model to more than two candidates. They find that in many cases it is possible to have a number of different majority-voting equilibria. One instance is particularly interesting. Suppose that there are three candidates in a race (x, y, and z) with three types of voters (1, 2, and 3). Assume further that voter utilities over these three candidates are given by Table 6.2, where $0 < \alpha < 1$.[7] That is, voters of types 1 and 2 most prefer candidates x and y, respectively, with y and x their second choices, respectively. Voters of type 3 most prefer candidate z and are indifferent between candidates x and y. Let us assume further that 30% of the voters are of type 1, 30% are of type 2, and 40% are of type 3.

Notice that, in this example, if the candidates were to face each other in separate pairwise electoral contests then candidate z is a Condorcet loser;

---

[7] In contrast to the Hotelling–Downsian approach, here we assume that voters have utility functions directly over candidates rather than policy. The implicit assumption is that candidates have chosen policy positions and that voters' preferences over candidates are induced from their policy preferences.

that is, z would be defeated by either x or y (see Condorcet 1785). This example is one in which the majority (60%) of voters' preferences are apparently divided between two candidates, while the minority (40%) of voters' first preference is the least preferred by the majority. Myerson and Weber suggest that this example is similar to the situation that occurred in the three-candidate U.S. presidential race between Roosevelt, Taft, and Wilson.

Myerson and Weber argue that how a voter perceives the relative likelihood of the assorted "close races" should matter in the voter's ballot choice. They assume the following.

- Near ties between two candidates are perceived to be much more likely than between three or more candidates.
- The voter's perceived probability that a particular ballot changes the outcome of the election between candidates is proportional to the difference in the votes cast for the two candidates. The authors define p_{jk} as the "pivot" probability that candidates j and k are in a close race for first place. These pivot probabilities are assumed to satisfy the following ordering condition: with three candidates j, k, h, if fewer votes are cast for j than for k then $p_{jh} \leq \varepsilon \cdot p_{kh}$, where $0 \leq \varepsilon < 1$.
- Voters make ballot choices in order to maximize their expected utility from policy (see Chapter 5).

Under these assumptions, voter i will choose a vote vector that maximizes

$$\sum_{j=1,2,3} \sum_{\substack{k=1,2,3 \\ k \neq j}} p_{jk}[u_i(\pi_j) - u_i(\pi_k)](v_j - v_k)$$

$$= \sum_{j=1,2,3} v_j \sum_{\substack{k=1,2,3 \\ k \neq j}} p_{jk}[u_i(\pi_j) - u_i(\pi_k)].$$

Myerson and Weber (1993) show that the pivot probabilities can be rescaled to sum to 1 and, as ε goes to 0, the rescaled pivot probabilities converge to a limit vector $\mathbf{q} = (q_{12}, q_{13}, q_{23})$, which also sums to 1.[8] They further demonstrate (Theorem 2) that $q_{jk} > 0$ only if one of the following conditions holds:

[8] Note q_{jk} is then the rescaled pivot probability that candidates j and k are in a close race for first place.

- candidates j and k are both in the set of likely winners; or
- either j or k is the unique likely winner and the other candidate has the second-highest predicted score.

Thus, if candidate j is expected to receive the third highest vote totals or to be the second highest vote receiver but the other two candidates are tied, then $q_{jk} = 0$ for all $k \neq j$. That is, voters perceive that candidate j has no chance of winning unless he is expected to be in first place alone, in a tie for first place, or in second place when there is an expected unique first place winner; hence voters will place a zero weight on the utility gained or lost from voting for that candidate as compared to another. Voters will place a positive weight on the utility gained or lost from voting for candidates that are expected to be in first place alone, in a tie for first place, or in second place when there is an expected unique first place winner, since in those cases they perceive that their votes may affect the election's outcome. Voters vote for the candidate for whom their expected utility gain is highest, given their expectations of the outcome. Myerson and Weber assume that, in equilibrium, these expectations are justified.

In the foregoing example, there are three possible voting equilibria. In the first voting equilibrium, voters of type 1 vote sincerely for candidate x, voters of type 2 vote strategically for candidate x, and voters of type 3 vote sincerely for candidate z. Observe that the election is expected to be a win for candidate x, candidate z is expected to be in second place, and candidate y is expected to be in third. Thus, it is rational for voters of types 1 and 3 to vote sincerely and for voters of type 2 to vote strategically in this equilibrium. The second voting equilibrium is one in which the roles of votes of type 1 and type 2 are reversed. That is, voters of type 1 vote strategically for their second choice of y and voters of type 2 vote sincerely for y, while voters of type 3 vote sincerely for z. Again the voting strategies are justified by the equilibrium. Finally there is a third equilibrium in which all three types of voters vote sincerely for their first choices. That is, voters of type 1 vote for x, voters of type 2 vote for y, and voters of type 3 vote for z. Hence the model predicts three possible pure strategy equilibria, two in which the majority voters "coordinate" on one of the majority candidates and one in which coordination does not occur and the Condorcet loser (minority candidate) wins.

Table 6.3. *Payoffs in a public goods game*

		Player B's Choices	
		Contribute	Not Contribute
Player A's Choices	Contribute	6, 6	4, 8
	Not Contribute	8, 4	5, 5

Public Goods and Repetition. In contrast to the battle of the sexes game, many games do not have a cooperative solution when played once but do have cooperative solutions if repeated. The following is a version of the classic "public good" game in which two individuals choose whether to contribute to the production of a good that, if provided, will be provided to both individuals.[9] The payoffs to the individuals from contributing and not contributing are functions of whether the other individual contributes or not. That is, assume that the cost of providing the public good is 4 units. If the public good is produced, each player receives 3 units and, if at least one player contributes, the public good will be provided. If both players choose to contribute the cost of production of the good is divided between them, but if only one player chooses to contribute then she pays the entire cost of production. The payoffs are summarized in Table 6.3.

It is easy to see that, in a one-shot play of this game, not contributing is the optimal strategy for both players (since a player who contributed would not be optimizing given the choice of the other). If A contributes then B's optimal choice is to not contribute, and vice versa. The only situation where each player's choice is optimal, given the choice of the other player, is where both have chosen not to contribute. This is the Nash equilibrium of the game.

However, if this game is repeated infinitely then for *both* players to contribute is an equilibrium, since repeated play can allow players to punish

---

[9] The term "public good" refers to characteristics of the good rather than the producer of the good. A pure public good is a good that is not divisible or rivalrous, whereas a pure private good is divisible and rivalrous. An example of a pure public good is a hurricane protection levee in New Orleans, an example of a pure private good is a good steak.

noncooperators and this makes cooperation an optimal response. For instance, suppose that player A adopts the strategy of contributing as long as Player B contributes, but if Player B does not contribute once then player A does not contribute forever after (this is called the "grim trigger" strategy). It can be shown that, if the game is to be played infinitely, then for player B to adopt the same strategy will be optimal and cooperation will be an equilibrium. However, this is not the only equilibrium: not contributing forever is also an equilibrium.[10] In general, when a game is repeated, it is likely that the number of possible equilibrium outcomes increases dramatically. This result is called the "folk theorem" because it has no particular author and is therefore considered part of game theory "folklore."

Public good games have been considered in a number of different contexts in political science, most notably as models of legislative vote trading. For example, Bernholz (1978) claims that legislative vote trading is best viewed as an infinitely repeated public good game and thus argues for the possibility of cooperative vote-trading outcomes in legislatures.[11] Another example of an iterated version of a one-shot game with folk theorem results that has been used in political science is the Bianco and Bates (1990) iterated version of Holmstrom's (1982) production by teams game. These models are discussed in more detail in Chapter 8 (on empirical evaluation of alternative models).

Incomplete Information and Beliefs. A third type of multiple equilibria occurs in incomplete information games such as signaling games. In the two games presented previously, each player knows with certainty the payoffs that the other player receives from the various outcomes of the game. However, there are a number of political situations where that is not likely to be the case. For example, in probabilistic voting models, where candidates are uncertain about the preferences of voters, voter payoffs from the candidates are unknown to the candidates. Alternatively, suppose that a legislature must decide how much decision-making power over a policy outcome to delegate to a regulatory agency. The agency could be of two types, either low- or high-ability. The legislature cannot observe the agency's type

---

[10] For a more precise explanation, see Fudenberg and Tirole (1991, chap. 5) and Morrow (1994, pp. 268–78).

[11] See Mueller (1989, chap. 5) for a review of the literature on vote trading in one-shot and infinitely repeated public good games.

directly. However, the agency chooses whether to engage in acquiring expertise about the policy outcome (e.g., sending out field agents to investigate a particular industry), which the legislature *can* observe. The legislature decides how much authority (a lot or a little) to delegate to the agency once the legislature observes whether the agency engages in the research. The legislature would like to delegate a lot to the agency if it is a high-ability agency. The agency benefits from acquiring expertise if it is a high-ability agency, but acquiring expertise is costly if the agency is a low-ability agency. Whether the agency chooses to acquire expertise serves as a signal to the legislature of the agency's abilities. A *separating* equilibrium exists when the different types of agencies choose different signals so that the legislature can determine the agency's type by its signal. A *pooling* equilibrium exists when the different types of agencies choose the same signal and the legislature cannot determine the agency's type. A *semiseparating* equilibrium exists when the agencies neither pool nor separate (see Morrow 1994, chap. 8, for more detail).

Technically this game (and all incomplete information games) cannot be solved, since the legislature does not know the agency's type and so the payoffs of the various outcomes are unknown to the legislature. However, we can use a method devised by Harsanyi (1967–68) to transform the game into one of imperfect information by assuming that "nature" first chooses the type of agency according to a probability distribution of types known to both players. Figure 6.2 illustrates the extensive form of this game (a player who chooses at a decision node that is connected by a dotted line does not know which of the connected nodes he is choosing from).[12] The first number at each outcome represents what the agency will receive at that outcome; the second number represents what the legislature will receive. Nature chooses a high-ability agency $\frac{2}{3}$ of the time and a low-ability agency $\frac{1}{3}$ of the time.

There are two pooling equilibria to this game and no separating equilibria. In one of the pooling equilibria, both types of regulatory agencies choose to acquire expertise; in the other, both choose not to acquire expertise. In both equilibria, the legislature chooses to delegate because – given that the agencies "pool" – the legislature cannot update its beliefs about the type of agency. As long as the legislature believes there is a greater than $\frac{1}{2}$ probability that the agency is of high ability, delegation is the preferred strategy.

---

[12] This example is based on a game presented in Davis and Holt (1993, pp. 399–405).

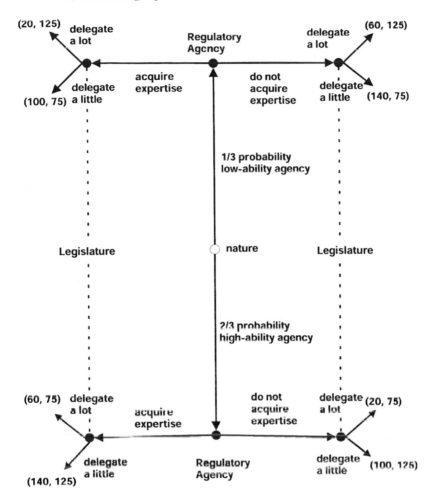

Figure 6.2. A signaling game with multiple equilibria.

The first pooling equilibrium, where both types of agencies acquire expertise, is sustained by agencies believing that an agency that does not acquire expertise will be punished with no delegation. The second pooling equilibrium, where both types of agencies do not acquire expertise, is sustained by the agency believing that if it acquires expertise the legislature will think it is a low-ability type pretending to be a high-ability type and punish it with no delegation. Hence both pooling equilibria are possible, depending upon the beliefs of the agency.[13]

Games of incomplete information like this signaling game have become popular in political science because they provide a unique way to formalize communication in such political situations as the relationship between committees and the floor of Congress (Gilligan and Krehbiel 1987) and between interest groups and legislators (Austen-Smith and Wright 1992).

6.3.2   Theoretically Reducing the Number of Equilibria

Focal Points. I have emphasized three sources of multiple equilibria in game theoretic models: games with multiple cooperative equilibria, repetition of games without cooperative equilibria in the one-shot case, and signaling games. One solution to the multiple equilibria problem is to contend that equilibria are selected as focal points, as first argued by Schelling (1960). But how do we determine which equilibria are likely to be focal? Without some outside criteria, we can only conjecture as to which equilibrium will be more likely. In some cases, the multiple equilibria can be ranked by normative criterion such as Pareto optimality: if an equilibrium is an outcome where at least one player is better off and no player is worse off in comparison to another equilibrium, then it is Pareto superior to that equilibrium. For example, in the infinitely repeated public goods game, the cooperative equilibrium where both players contribute is clearly superior to the equilibrium where both players do not contribute. So you might argue that this equilibrium is focal, or more likely, since it is obviously better for everyone. Similar arguments are sometimes made to restrict the analysis of formal model equilibria to those that are most "informative" in signaling games. (See Austen-Smith and Wright 1992 and the discussion that follows.)

Equilibrium Refinements. Another solution to the multiple equilibria problem is to seek equilibrium refinements by considering the constraints of rationality (as discussed before with respect to subgame perfection) and/or to restrict analysis to symmetric equilibria and/or pure strategies. We could apply the "intuitive criterion" equilibrium refinement of Cho and Kreps (1987)

---

[13] These equilibria are sequential Nash equilibria; see Kreps and Wilson (1982). ´

to the signaling game just considered and rule out the second pooling equilibrium, where both types of agencies choose not to acquire expertise. That is, in this equilibrium it is unreasonable for the legislature to believe that a deviation (a regulatory agency choosing to acquire expertise) means that the agency is a low-ability type, since the low-ability agency cannot gain from deviating (acquiring expertise) whereas the high-ability agency could gain. The low-ability agency's payoff cannot increase by deviating, but the high-ability agency's payoff can increase by deviating. Thus, the legislature's response to deviation should not be "no delegation." Given that, a high-ability agency should deviate by acquiring expertise and we no longer have an equilibrium. Note that this does not mean there now exists a separating equilibrium. Rather, given that the high-ability regulatory agency will acquire expertise and that this is rewarded with delegation, low-ability agencies will also acquire expertise and so we have the first pooling equilibrium. The intuitive criterion rules out one of the pooling equilibria and so narrows the possibilities. Like subgame perfection, it allows the modeler to make a more precise prediction of a game's equilibrium.

Problems with Focal Points and Equilibrium Refinements. However, using equilibrium refinements or focal points is not as simple as this sounds. Experimental evidence suggests that these procedures sometimes fail to predict behavior. For example, Van Huyck, Battalio, and Beil (1990) show that, in some cooperative games, groups coordinate on equilibria that are not Pareto optimal; hence we cannot conclude that Pareto optimality is always a focal point in coordination games. Refinements such as subgame perfection and Cho and Kreps's intuitive criterion have also been shown to fail experimentally in some types of games. Diermeier and Morton (1998) show that subgame perfection is a poor predictor of behavior in the Baron–Ferejohn legislative bargaining game. In the experiments, subjects' behavior is better characterized by Nash equilibria ruled out by subgame perfection. The nonsubgame perfect equilibria depend on players believing noncredible threats that the other players will make choices in later stages of the game that would not be rational at that point of the game. Brandts and Holt (1992) report evidence that, in a game similar to the signaling game just presented, subjects may in some cases choose strategies corresponding to the pooling equilibria ruled out by the intuitive criterion. In contrast, Camerer and Weigelt (1988) and Banks, Camerer, and Porter (1988) present evidence supporting intuitive equilibria and other subtle refinements. The experimental evidence on equilibrium refinements is still developing, but it is clear that support for a refinement often depends on the type of game and other parameters and specifications that are independent of the refinement. Thus, using these refinements to rule out a priori an equilibrium as a possible prediction of a formal model is dependent on the type of game analyzed and should be done cautiously.

One-Shot Games and Infinity. In the public goods game of Section 6.3.1, we saw that repeating the game generates multiple equilibria. One solution to the multiple equilibrium problem in this case is to focus on equilibria in the "one-shot" game, contending that such a formulation is sufficient. Many game theoretic models used in political science are presented as one-shot games. Although the understanding is that the game is probably repeated, the repeated game is not always solved. In many cases this seems suspect. For example, most models of electoral competition (e.g. Palfrey 1984; Calvert 1985) are modeled as one-shot games even when it is clear that the "game" may be played repeatedly. Since repeated games may have more equilibria than one-shot games, how should we deal with the empirical testing of these one-shot models?

An important issue is whether it is appropriate to consider the game as infinitely or finitely repeated. It is only when the public good game above is infinitely repeated that the number of equilibria expand; if the game is finite, then the only equilibrium is for both players not to contribute. To see how this is true, consider the last period of the finitely repeated public good game. Since both players know the game will not be repeated, there is no benefit from using a strategy that would be contingent on future play, and not contributing is the optimal strategy for both players. What happens in the next-to-last period? Both players know what will happen in the last period, so a punishment strategy is not viable in the next-to-last period, either. For each previous period we can show that both players will choose not to contribute, given that punishment strategies unravel in the last period.[14]

---

[14] It is possible that, with incomplete information about player preferences (e.g., assuming some players are altruists and always contribute), the finitely repeated public good game can yield equilibria of both players contributing. However, in the final stage, not contributing is the only equilibrium strategy (except for the pure altruists), so contributions decline as the game approaches its end. This prediction is also supported in experiments (see Ledyard 1995).

A similar result occurs in models of electoral competition when candidates have policy preferences. In Calvert's (1985) model, candidates care about policy but are constrained to enact the policy positions that they advocate prior to election. Thus, his model predicts that candidates who become more certain about the location of voter ideal points will converge to the position most preferred by the median voter, despite their individual policy preferences. Wittman (1990) analyzes the literature on electoral competition in which candidates are not so constrained. If the electoral competition is one-shot, the winner will always enact her ideal policy position if elected. However, if the electoral competition is infinitely repeated then equilibria are possible in which candidates' positions will converge toward the median voter's ideal position.[15] Nevertheless, if the competition is finitely repeated, in the last period the winner will again choose her own ideal position and so will not converge. Therefore, when candidates have policy preferences, convergence depends on the game being infinitely repeated.

How Relevant Are One-Shot Games? Which scenario is more relevant? Osborne and Rubinstein (1994, p. 135) argue that what matters is how the players *perceive* the repeated game, not whether it is actually finitely or infinitely repeated. The implication is that if electoral competition is perceived as an infinitely repeated game then we should consider the equilibria that occur under the infinitely repeated game. Of course, in electoral competition this perception depends on whether we view the competition as between parties or candidates. Many might argue that parties are perceived to have closer to infinite lives than candidates. Alesina and Spear (1988) present an interesting overlapping generations model – with finitely lived candidates and infinitely lived parties – in which candidates' transfers through the party system can lead candidates to choose more convergent positions.

Not all repeated games' equilibria depend as significantly on whether the game is finitely or infinitely repeated. This difference occurs only in such special cases as the public goods game or electoral competition (see Osborne and Rubinstein 1994, pp. 155–61). It is possible that the finitely repeated game can also have a large number of equilibria when the payoffs from defecting are not as high as in the public good game described earlier. Nevertheless, since public good games and games resembling electoral competition

---

[15] The extent of convergence depends on assumptions of the model concerning candidate knowledge of voter preferences, etc.

are prevalent in political situations, the distinction as to whether the game is best viewed as finitely or infinitely repeated is important for understanding whether analyzing the one-shot game is sufficient for understanding the relevance of theoretical predictions for the real world. If the game is perceived by its participants as finite then, in many cases, analyzing the one-shot game is sufficient for making predictions that are applicable to political situations.

This discussion suggests that using results from one-shot games may be problematic when tested against the real world in situations best viewed as infinitely repeated; one solution is to use the laboratory to test the predictions. In the laboratory we can manipulate the repetition of the game and measure the extent to which the game's expected length affects outcomes. As Ledyard (1995) notes, repeated public good games in the laboratory show a decreasing contribution rate as the repeated game approaches the final period. However, we face a different problem when we use laboratory experiments to test the predictions of one-shot games. That is, many experimentalists test one-shot games by administering the one-shot game repeatedly, randomizing the subjects' payoffs and cohorts or pairings between each period. The randomization is used to prevent the subjects from viewing the one-shot games as part of a supergame. Repeating the one-shot game is desirable – both to increase the data that can be generated and to control for "learning" that may occur in the initial administering of the game. To recapitulate, empirical analysis of game theoretic results from one-shot games should carefully consider (a) the extent that the empirical world is characterized by one-shot or repeated play and, if repetition exists, (b) the degree to which participants view the repetition as infinitely or finitely repeated.

Classifying Equilibria into Regimes. Sometimes a formal model enables the researcher to narrow the expected equilibria by classification into equilibrium "regimes." For example, in the signaling game, the particular equilibrium that occurs depends on the beliefs of the players. If there were a way to measure these beliefs then we could classify the data by regime and then consider each regime individually. Chapter 7 presents Moraski and Shipan's (1998) model of Supreme Court nominations, which predicts that different equilibria will occur under different conditions on the relative locations of the ideal points of the president, the Senate, and the existing members of the Supreme Court. The authors are able to classify the data according to regime and then evaluate the empirical predictions of the formal model with respect to the theoretically predicted regime. Often, however, a researcher may be able to classify equilibria but the variables that organize the equilibria are not easily observed. Such is the case in many game theoretic models under incomplete information (e.g. the signaling game). Section 6.3.4 presents an example (Austen-Smith and Wright's 1994 empirical study of lobbying) where it is not possible to organize the data by regime; in this case, the researchers must evaluate the data as possibly generated by distinctly different equilibria.

Using Computer Simulations. Computer simulations may also serve to help reduce the number of expected equilibria. If we take a formal model and make assumptions about the parameters of the model, we can then generate the expected solutions for those parameters. The simulations are like equilibrium refinements: they tell us the solutions or predictions of the model given additional assumptions. (The limitations of computational models for empirical analysis are detailed in Chapter 2.) The simulations' predictions can then be compared to the empirical data. Kadera (forthcoming) uses predictions from simulations for empirical evaluation in this manner.

6.3.3   *Multiple Equilibria: Types of Empirical Evaluation*

We have discussed five ways that multiple equilibria can be reduced for empirical analysis: focal points, refinements, viewing a game as one-shot or finitely repeated, classifying the equilibria in regimes, and using computer simulations. However, when we are not confident that certain equilibria are focal, that our refinement makes sense in the formal model considered, that equilibria in the one-shot game are reasonable for empirical analysis, that we can classify the equilibria in regimes by observable variables, or that our computer simulations capture all the possibilities that we can observe, our empirical analysis must then confront a formal model with multiple equilibria. How should the empirical analysis be conducted if we do not have a clear single prediction?

A simple way to evaluate formal models with multiple equilibria is to determine behavior that should occur in *none* of the equilibria and to examine the extent to which this unpredicted behavior does occur. One way to evaluate the Myerson and Weber model's predictions is to examine whether there are voting strategies that would not be chosen in any of the equilibria.

Voting behavior that would violate any equilibrium in the model would be type-2 voters choosing either x or y and type-1 or type-3 voters choosing z. In other words, evidence that individuals vote for their least preferred candidates suggests that the model is problematic and that voters are not maximizing expected utility as assumed. This negative result would be strong evidence against the model, but a positive result is less conclusive.

In some cases the existence of multiple equilibria prevents any real empirical evaluation of the formal model because all possible observations are potentially explained. For example, as noted in Chapter 4, cheap-talk games (where communication occurs but is not costly as in the signaling game) always exhibit "babbling" equilibria in which players ignore the communication. Thus, any errant observations of communication can be simply assigned as outcomes from these babbling equilibria. It is not possible to rule out communication choices as nonequilibrium strategies. Yet, in many formal models with multiple equilibria we can rule out *some* behavior as not supported in any equilibrium and thereby derive hypotheses that can be used as a basis for empirical analysis. In the next section I consider how Austen-Smith and Wright (1994) derive hypotheses about the types of behavior that multiple equilibria predict and empirically evaluate these hypotheses. The authors view their formal model as a Partial DGP and evaluate an empirical model that combines their hypotheses with other control variables and a random error term.

A second way to assess formal models with multiple equilibria is to consider what factors might lead to the choice of one equilibrium over another. This is not an assessment of the model per se but more an assessment of our conjectures about focal points or about equilibrium refinements proposed by theorists. Much of the experimental analysis of formal models with multiple equilibria, like the Brandts and Holt (1992) study of signaling games, takes this approach. Section 6.3.4 also includes two examples of how researchers may use empirical evaluation to choose between equilibrium predictions; in both these analyses (Forsythe et al. 1993; Offerman 1996), the model is viewed as a Complete DGP. Finally, a third way to evaluate formal models with multiple equilibria is to examine the comparative statics or dynamic paths or processes that may occur in one equilibrium or more or across equilibria. Austen-Smith and Wright's predictions are also a type of comparative static prediction, as I shall discuss. For more detail on comparative statics and dynamic path predictions, see Chapter 7.

6.3.4   *Multiple Equilibria: Examples of Empirical Evaluation*

Counteractive Lobbying.

The Theory. Austen-Smith and Wright (1994) provide empirical analysis on predictions of their signaling model of legislative lobbying (Austen-Smith and Wright 1992). In the theoretical model, lobbying is represented as a game of strategic information transmission. The model assumes that there are two interest groups with opposing preferences over a unidimensional issue and a legislator who will make a voting choice (the legislator chooses between two actions, a and b). The legislator is uncertain about the electorate's preferences over the issues but would prefer to vote according to those preferences. The interest groups may have information over voter preferences, which they may or may not choose to reveal to the legislator.

The signaling game has multiple equilibria, including ones where no information is conveyed. Austen-Smith and Wright first restrict their empirical analysis by choosing to consider the most informative equilibria as focal points. In that case, as with other models of incomplete information, the equilibria that occur depend on the prior beliefs that the players have about the state of the world. Assume that p is the common prior belief that action a is appropriate and that $p < \frac{1}{2}$. Then there are three types of equilibria that can occur: (1) equilibria when p is sufficiently low and no groups lobby; (2) equilibria where only one group lobbies, that which prefers the legislator take the opposite choice from his uninformed choice (i.e., the group that prefers action b); and (3) equilibria where both groups lobby. The three types of equilibria depend also on the cost of auditing interest-group information. In fact, given a cost of auditing and a common prior belief, the model predicts a particular type of equilibrium for each combination.

The Empirical Predictions. Austen-Smith and Wright (1994) examine their comparative static predictions using an empirical model tested against the lobbying activities in the battle over Robert Bork's nomination to the U.S. Supreme Court. How should the authors translate the formal model into an empirical model for estimation? Ideally, the researchers could use data on the two variables, the common prior beliefs and the cost of auditing, and compare the lobbying observed given these values with the theoretical predictions for that combination. This is known as the "regime" approach, discussed in Chapter 7. However, Austen-Smith and Wright do not have data on these two variables. Thus, they must investigate predictions that can be made for data when it is not possible to classify a priori the data by equilibrium regime. In effect, they have data that could be generated by a number of different equilibria and they cannot distinguish between the observations by the type of equilibrium.

Austen-Smith and Wright (1994, pp. 31–3) derive three predictions from the model that can be used in this context:[16]

1. "Ceteris paribus, when a legislator is lobbied by groups from just one side of an issue, the only groups that lobby are those opposed to the legislator's ex ante position."
2. "The decision of a group to lobby an 'unfriendly' legislator is independent of the lobbying decisions of opposing groups."
3. "Conditional on a 'friendly' legislator being lobbied by an opposing group, a group's decision to lobby that legislator is purely counteractive."

Note that Austen-Smith and Wright use the term "counteractive lobbying" to describe the lobbying that occurs in the third prediction (although it is modeled as a simultaneous decision, not a sequential one). The simultaneity assumed does not necessarily mean that the groups make their decisions at exactly the same time; the key is that their decisions are made in ignorance of the other groups' decisions. That is, the third prediction is that a group will lobby a friendly legislator only when that friendly legislator is being lobbied by an unfriendly group.

These general predictions are also comparative static predictions. They are predictions of how the Nash equilibria in the lobbying game will change in response to changes in exogenous factors in the model. In this case, the exogenous factor is the "friendliness" of the legislator (prior level of bias toward one side of the issue) and the endogenous factor is the type of lobbying that will occur. In the Nash equilibria, although the groups make their decisions simultaneously, their decisions are optimal – given the decisions of the other actors in the model – and incorporate expectations or beliefs about those decisions.

---

[16] This is, of course, an incomplete representation of the model, which makes a number of other predictions. See Austen-Smith and Wright (1992) for complete details.

The Empirical Model. In this case, the theoretical model does not yield directly estimable equations. Instead, the authors devise a two-equation empirical model that is estimated using two-stage least squares.

$$L_{Pi} = \beta_{0P} + \beta_{1P}\text{PRO}_i + \beta_{2P}C_i + \beta_{3P}V_i + \beta_{4P}O_{Pi}$$
$$+\gamma_{1P}L_{Ai} + \gamma_{2P}\text{PRO}_i \times L_{Ai} + \varepsilon_{Pi},$$

$$L_{Ai} = \beta_{0A} + \beta_{1A}\text{ANTI}_i + \beta_{2A}C_i + \beta_{3A}V_i + \beta_{4A}O_{Ai}$$
$$+\gamma_{1A}L_{Pi} + \gamma_{2A}\text{ANTI}_i \times L_{Pi} + \varepsilon_{Ai},$$

"where L_{Pi} is the number of pro-Bork groups that lobbied senator i; L_{Ai} is the number of anti-Bork groups that lobbied senator i; C_i equals 1 if i is a member of the Judiciary Committee, and 0 otherwise; V_i is a voting score for senator i during first half of 1987 (higher scores meaning more liberal); O_{Pi} is the number of pro-Bork groups with strong organizations in senator i's state; O_{Ai} is the number of anti-Bork groups with strong organizations in senator i's state; PRO_i equals 1 if senator i's prior belief implies i votes for confirmation in the absence of any additional information, and 0 otherwise; ANTI_i equals 1 if senator i's prior belief implies i votes against confirmation in the absence of any additional information, and 0 otherwise; and $\varepsilon_{Pi}, \varepsilon_{Ai}$ are stochastic terms for the pro-Bork and anti-Bork lobbying equations, respectively" (1994, pp. 35–6).

Austen-Smith and Wright (p. 36) represent the hypotheses derived from the formal model in the form of the following predictions about the coefficients in the model:

Hypothesis 1: $\beta_{1P} < 0$ and $\beta_{1A} < 0$;
Hypothesis 2: $\gamma_{1P} = \gamma_{1A} = 0$;
Hypothesis 3: $\gamma_{2P} > 0$ and $\gamma_{2A} > 0$.

Hypothesis 1 predicts that, ceteris paribus, senators who are expected ex ante to support (or conversely, oppose) the nomination will be lobbied by fewer pro-Bork (anti-Bork) groups that senators expected to oppose (support) the nomination. Hypothesis 2 predicts that the number of pro-Bork (anti-Bork) groups that lobbied does not depend on the number of anti-Bork (pro-Bork) groups that lobbied. Hypothesis 3 predicts that the greater the number of anti-Bork (pro-Bork) groups that lobbied a senator who ex ante was expected to support (oppose) the nomination, the greater the number of pro-Bork (anti-Bork) groups that lobbied.

Though the researchers focus on these three hypotheses, they note the theory also predicts that $\beta_{2j} > 0$ and $\beta_{4j} > 0$ for $j = P, A$.

There are a number of important differences between the empirical model and the formal theoretical model. First, the researchers have introduced a control variable, V_i, "as a general control for other influences on lobbying that may not be captured by our theoretical model or our conception of lobbying" (p. 36). Second, the empirical model is a stochastic model whereas the formal model is deterministic. The error term is introduced to control for measurement errors and random effects on group decisions that are unmodeled. These variables are entered linearly, and the authors assume that $E[\varepsilon_{Pi}, \varepsilon_{Ai}] \neq 0$. These differences illustrate some of the points made in Chapter 4: the necessity for control and the introduction of randomness in empirical evaluation of the formal model. Thus, the formal model is viewed as a Partial DGP in their empirical estimation. In the estimation of the empirical model, Austen-Smith and Wright find general support for their hypotheses, with significant effects and expected signs of coefficients predicted to be nonzero and with nonsignificance of coefficients predicted equivalent to zero (except for β_{1P}, which had the predicted sign but was not significant).[17]

It is useful to reflect on the choice of evaluating comparative static predictions versus assessing assumptions (the model does not make dynamic path predictions). Some of the assumptions are blatantly false, and it makes little sense to test these. The assumption that interest groups provide information in lobbying is supported by empirical qualitative studies of lobbying cited by the authors. Austen-Smith and Wright (1994) note that their comparative static prediction of counteractive lobbying is contrary to that of previous nonformal studies of lobbying, which argue that lobbyists rarely lobby those a priori opposed to their interest group's position. In contrast, Austen-Smith and Wright contend that lobbying a friendly legislator occurs in response to the opposition's lobbying of that legislator. Thus, their empirical study is also an example of evaluating a formal model against nonformal theorizing.

The Empirical Results. The estimation does yield evidence on the empirical viability of the empirical model. The model explains 72% (resp. 78%) of the variance in the lobbying decisions by groups supporting (opposing) Bork. Austen-Smith and Wright (1996) compare the relative sizes

---

[17] Baumgartner and Leech (1996a,b) criticize Austen-Smith and Wright's study for its static formulation and use of a single legislative choice for an empirical test. See also the response by Austen-Smith and Wright (1996).

of the coefficients in the model; they find that the counteractive coefficients are third and second in relative size – behind the control variable in both cases (supporting and opposing) and behind membership on the judiciary committee in the first case. The control variable is the largest predictor, so is the model then inaccurate? No, because the model does provide useful information about the relationship between preferences of legislators and the likelihood of being lobbied. The example illustrates the usefulness of comparative static predictions in understanding the theoretical value of the model. If we focus solely on the overall predictive capacity of the empirical model and ignore the explanatory power and significance of the comparative static predictions, we thereby ignore the fact that the model provides a relationship prediction that is supported.

Nevertheless, since our assessment is of the model as a Partial DGP, the empirical evaluation is a test of these predictions coupled with the assumptions about randomness and control variables that are also part of the empirical model. Another issue that limits support for the theory from the empirical analysis is that researchers focus only on one particular vote by Congress. Ideally, empirical predictions would be evaluated with other legislative–interest group interactions.

QRE and Multiple Equilibria. Austen-Smith and Wright's analysis uses the formal model as a Partial DGP in devising their empirical model. One problem with this approach is that it is generally not obvious how to derive estimating equations directly from a theoretical model so that it can be used as a Complete DGP when multiple equilibria exist. For example, the QRE concept of equilibrium, like many other game theoretic equilibrium concepts, can make multiple equilibrium predictions. How should we use the maximum likelihood procedure in this context? This was the problem faced by Offerman (1996) in his empirical assessment of QRE as a predictor of behavior in a set of public goods experiments similar to the public goods game discussed in Section 6.3.1. In one of the experimental treatments, seven subjects were simultaneously given the option of contributing (or not) to the production of a public good, and each subject bore a cost only if she contributed. If three or more subjects contributed, then the public good was provided and all (contributors or not) received the payoff value of the public good (which was a function of the number of contributors). Thus, subjects faced the classic free-rider problem.

In Offerman's game, QRE gives rise to multiple equilibria. He first restricts his analysis to symmetric equilibria, where each individual contributes with a probability p_c and expects each other member of the group to contribute with the same probability. He argues that the assumption of symmetry is reasonable since the subjects receive information only about the aggregate contribution levels in their groups. Offerman then derives the symmetric equilibrium value of p_c:

$$p_c = \frac{1}{1 + \exp\{\lambda[c - (f(s) - c)\binom{n-1}{x-1}p_x^{s-1}(1 - p_x)^{n-s}]\}},$$

where c is the cost of contributing, $f(s)$ is the value of the public good, n is the number of members in the group, and s is the number of contributors. Solving this equation yields one, two, or three solutions depending on the value of λ. As λ approaches ∞, the solution converges to a symmetric mixed strategy Nash equilibrium.

Offerman divides the solutions into three intervals based on the values of p_c: high unique values of p_c on the interval $\lambda \in [0, 0.0456]$, middle values on the interval $\lambda \in [0.0446, 0.0456]$, and low on $\lambda \in [0.0446, \infty]$. He then determines the maximum likelihood estimate of λ for each interval and chooses the one with the highest likelihood for generating the data as predicted by QRE. Offerman estimates a value of $\lambda = 0.0454$ and a log likelihood of 627.7, which is statistically significant at the 1% level. Offerman also compares his analysis with an alternative formal model of behavior in the public goods game, discussed in Chapter 8 (Offerman, Sonnemans, and Schram 1996 use a similar procedure).

Multicandidate Competition and Focal Points. Offerman's analysis does not specify a prior about which equilibrium he expects to occur. Another alternative would be to find variables that can lead to one or at least two of the equilibria being more likely than the others. In Forsythe et al. (1993; forthcoming) and in Myerson, Rietz, and Weber (1993), the authors assess the voting model in Myerson and Weber (1993) under the assumption that the two equilibria that require coordination are less likely to occur than the one in which all voters vote sincerely. However, if majority voters have access to coordination devices then coordination equilibria are more likely than those that result in victory for the Condorcet loser. These authors argue, in other words, that voters can use campaign contributions and/or pre-election polls as coordination devices to enable the majority voters to avoid the third equilibrium in which the minority candidate wins. It is argued that coordination devices such as campaign contributions or poll results serve as focal points.

Myerson et al. (1993) evaluate their hypothesis in laboratory elections. In some cases they allow voters to purchase campaign ads that run (candidate names flash on the computer screen) before each election. The reasoning is that the majority candidate who receives the most ads will then be the winner in the election as the majority voters coordinate on that candidate. In other laboratory elections, Forsythe and colleagues run pre-election polls that are also assumed to serve as coordination devices for the majority voters. They compare these election results with results from a baseline experiment in which voters are not allowed such coordination devices. The researchers find evidence that, as predicted, the ability of majority voters to coordinate does significantly reduce the probability of the Condorcet loser candidate winning. This is similar to the argument that Pareto optimality is a focal point. However, the crucial aspect of the experiment is that the authors test whether their conjecture about focal points is true rather than use it as an a priori equilibrium refinement. Notice that in these empirical analyses the researchers take the formal model as a Partial DGP, conjecturing that variables outside the model serve as coordination mechanisms rather than explicitly incorporating these mechanisms within the models and re-solving the theory for explicit predictions.

6.4   Implications of the Examples

The examples and analysis in this chapter have highlighted many of the issues in evaluating equilibrium point predictions, models without equilibria, and those with multiple equilibria. The examples provide us with some guidelines on these issues, which are summarized in this section (see also Table 6.4).

1 *Equilibrium point predictions are unlikely to be observed in naturally occurring data.* There are two solutions to this problem, as follows.

- *Adding randomness* to the model. Adding randomness is not straightforward, and a number of important questions must be addressed.
  - (a) A modeler must specify exactly how the randomness affects the results of the model. As we saw in the discussion of probabilistic voting, if randomness is added to the model by assuming that voters' preferences are deterministic but candidates cannot measure

Table 6.4. *Empirical evaluation of equilibrium predictions*

	Types of Equilibrium Predictions		
	Equilibrium Point Predictions	Disequilibrium Predictions	Multiple Equilibria Predictions
Direct Empirical Evaluation	❖ Can directly evaluate. ❖ But likely to fail to receive empirical support	Model has no predictions that can be directly evaluated	❖ Derive predictions that are true across equilibria ❖ Evaluate focal point predictions about which equilibria will occur ❖ If statistically possible determine which equilibrium has the highest likelihood occurring
Methods to Improve Empirical Evaluation	❖ Add random factors so that model can be viewed as Complete DGP with naturally occurring data (solve zero-likelihood problem) ❖ Use controlled laboratory experiments (theory tests, and then stress tests)	Attempt to derive equilibrium predictions by: ❖ Adding assumptions ❖ Changing the solution concept ❖ Using simulations to generate predictions (thus solving model for particular parameters) ❖ Using laboratory experiments to suggest likely outcomes	Reduce the number of equilibria by: ❖ Restricting to pure strategies and/or symmetric equilibria ❖ Using equilibrium refinements ❖ Focusing on focal points ❖ Using one-shot games ❖ Classifying equilibria in observable regimes ❖ Using simulations to predict which equilibria are most likely (thus solving model for particular parameters)

these preferences, then the effect on predictions of turnout and voter choices are different than if the randomness is added by assuming a random effect on the cost of voting.

(b) A modeler must make sure that the assumptions of randomness are not inconsistent with the other assumptions of the model. We saw that an early attempt to make voting choices random (Hinich et al. 1972) made assumptions about voter preferences that were inconsistent with the assumptions about voter preferences made elsewhere in the model.

(c) A modeler also must ensure that randomness is not added tautolog-
ically. That is, randomness should not be added in such a way that
all observations are explained as not satisfying the theoretically predicted results *because* of the randomness.

- *Using controlled laboratory experiments* to evaluate the model. Controlled experiments likewise raise a number of other concerns.

  (a) Laboratory experiments should not be designed so that they are
"hard-wired"; that is, individuals in the experiments should not be
told how to make choices. In the experiments that we discuss (by
McKelvey and Ordeshook, Offerman, Forsythe et al., and Myerson
et al.), the subjects were given choices that mirrored choices suggested by the theory.

  (b) The experiments can be strong tests of the basic theory. However,
it is necessary to gradually lessen the control of the experimental
environment to test whether the theory continues to predict well as
the assumptions of the model are relaxed in the experimental design.
McKelvey and Ordeshook gradually lessened the information that
the voters had on candidates (and that candidates had on voter preferences) to test whether the spatial voting model's predictions were
supported in a less than controlled experimental environment. An
advantage of the laboratory is that we can relax our control gradually, one assumption at a time.

2. *Many formal models make multiple equilibrium predictions, and these
present problems of their own for empirical estimation.*

- A modeler can consider options that reduce the number of equilibria before conducting the empirical analysis. However, when choosing options
a researcher should also provide a justification that the choice is reasonable. Options include:

  (a) restricting the analysis to symmetric and/or pure strategy equilibria;
  (b) focusing on equilibria that the researcher believes are "focal points";
  (c) in a repeated game, determining that equilibria of the one-shot game
are likely to be the only equilibria suitable for descriptive explanation;
  (d) using equilibrium refinements such as subgame perfection or the intuitive criterion;
  (e) classifying the data into equilibrium regimes using observable variables;

(f) using computer simulations to narrow the equilibria by specifying values of the parameters that are relevant for the empirical analysis.

- If the model's multiple equilibria cannot be reduced, the researcher needs to determine predictions of events that will never occur in any of the equilibria. If these events occur then there are strong reasons to question the model's predictions. In the tests of the Myerson and Weber model, some voting behavior is clearly not expected in any of the equilibria. The researcher may be able to make predictions that are true across equilibria and so can serve for empirical assessment, as in Austen-Smith and Wright (1994).

- If the model can be directly estimated as an empirical model (viewed as a Complete DGP) as with QRE, then the researcher can evaluate the different intervals of equilibria to determine which has the highest likelihood of generating the observed data and then test for the statistical significance of the maximum likelihood estimation.

- Otherwise, empirical analysis of models with multiple equilibria can often be more of a diagnostic analysis rather than an empirical evaluation. The empirical analysis can be an evaluation of a hypothesis about which equilibria are expected under what circumstances. For example, Forsythe et al. and Myerson et al. expect that polls and campaign contributions can serve as focal points for the selection of equilibria in the Myerson and Weber voting model, and their empirical analysis supports that hypothesis.

3. *Disequilibrium cases.* Models without equilibria can make no empirical predictions. Models may lack equilibria because of the assumptions of the model or the solution concept used; as with structure-induced equilibria in spatial voting models, changing assumptions can yield equilibria in a model that previously did not have one. Computer simulations or laboratory experiments may be able to yield empirical predictions for given values of the parameters of the model. Thus, the first question should concern the reasonableness of changing the model to a model that does predict equilibria.

CHAPTER 7

Evaluating Relationship Predictions

In Chapter 6 I discussed the difficulties of evaluating equilibrium predictions. Nevertheless, evaluating these predictions is a useful and important step in overall model evaluation, just as analysis of the model's assumptions is vital. However, most of political science is focused on understanding the relationships between variables. Empirically oriented political scientists often approach a research paper with the question: "What is the dependent variable? What is this paper trying to explain?" The implication is that knowledge of the dependent variable implies discovering the independent variables (explanatory or causal factors) on which the dependent variable depends. Formal modelers are interested in the same question; they, too, wish to discover relationships. Relationship predictions are generally of two types: either they predict relationships between variables at one moment in time in equilibrium (comparative static predictions) or they predict relationships between variables over time or between time and a variable (dynamic path or process predictions). Relationship predictions may also be a combination of the two. This chapter presents examples of each type.

I also illustrate two other important uses of these empirical evaluations: to increase our understanding (1) of empirical cases beyond the focus of the original theory and (2) of the implications of proposed policy changes. Researchers often have different perspectives on the applicability of their models across data sets. That is, sometimes a researcher is interested generally in how members of Congress vote, but uses a particular type of vote (such as Supreme Court nominations) in her empirical analysis. Other times a researcher is interested in the nomination process, and uses a set of data on nominations that are measurable. At what point is a model considered an explanation only of a particular situation and not of a political process that is generalizable to a number of similar processes? Extending the empirical focus is important for determining the limits of a model. Sometimes a model that "fits" the data best is not the best model.

In discussing the examples, I focus on how the formal models' predictions are translated into empirical models. The translation often requires the addition of control variables for factors assumed constant or fixed in the formal model and of random error terms when the formal models are viewed as Partial DGPs. Typically the assumption is that the random error is due to measurement error in the data. This can explain some deviations from the formal models' predictions, but does not explain others (as demonstrated with reference to Moraski and Shipan's model of Supreme Court nominations in Section 7.1.2). Moreover, just choosing the data and deciding how to measure the data can involve additional restrictions on the underlying formal model.

7.1   Evaluating Comparative Static Predictions

Many empirical analyses of formal models assess comparative static predictions. For example, Filer et al. (1993) predict a particular causal relationship – between the position of a voter on the distribution of income and the voter's turnout decision – that is subsequently tested by examining the empirical evidence in presidential election voting across counties in the United States. Rather than testing the theoretical prediction of how a particular voter with a particular income may choose to vote, they examine whether the theoretically predicted pattern is substantiated empirically.

Two examples will be presented in order to illustrate how comparative static predictions of formal models can be tested empirically. The examples are from the formal and empirical literature on voting over Supreme Court nominations in the U.S. Congress. The first is an application of probabilistic voting to explain the roll-call votes (Segal et al. 1992). This example illustrates some of the problems that researchers face when they incorporate "control" variables into an existing formal model and view the model as a Partial DGP for the empirical analysis. That is, the model assumes that a senator's constituents' preferences are exogenously determined. But when researchers need to measure this variable, they must make explicit assumptions about the theoretical determinants of a senator's constituents' preferences. Thus, in evaluating the empirical model, they are evaluating not only the formal model that began the analysis but also the additional assumptions made about the theoretical determination of constituent preferences.

The second example presents research that builds on the first and addresses the strategic game between the president and the Congress when a new Supreme Court justice is chosen (Moraski and Shipan 1998). In this example, a different issue arises in translating the formal model to an empirical model. Specifically, the type of nominee that a president will select will depend upon the policy positions of the president, the Senate, and existing members of the Supreme Court. There are three possible configurations or equilibrium regimes. Presidents are constrained in their choices by the equilibrium regime that exists; thus, the model makes different predictions depending on the regime. As discussed in Chapter 6, researchers can sometimes classify the data into regimes and then estimate the model accordingly. The authors construct an empirical model that allows them to evaluate each prediction and the overall formal model.

7.1.1   Roll-Call Voting over Supreme Court Nominations: Probabilistic Voting Applied

A Model of Senatorial Voting. The previous chapter discussed how some models of voting in elections incorporate randomness by assuming probabilistic voting. Probabilistic voting has also been used in models of roll-call voting in legislatures. In particular, Segal, Cameron, and Cover (1992) apply a probabilistic voting model (an extension of Cameron, Cover, and Segal 1990) to explain voting in Congress over Supreme Court nominations. In the model, senators are assumed to vote sincerely if the "utility" they expect to receive from the nominee's selection is greater than a "reservation" value of utility specific to each senator and nominee. The assumption of sincere voting in this model is based on previous empirical research. The authors assume further that utility received by a senator is a function of observables and unobservables and thus voting is probabilistic. The implication is that senators vote deterministically, but we cannot measure all the impacts on individual senators' utilities and so empirically observed voting is probabilistic.

Segal et al. (1992) derive the following description of the voting of senator i over Supreme Court nominee j:

$$\text{vote for } j = \begin{cases} \text{yea} & \text{if } V_{ij}(n_{ij}, s_{ij}, \beta) - \bar{u}_{ij} \leq e_{ij}, \\ \text{nay} & \text{if } V_{ij}(n_{ij}, s_{ij}, \beta) - \bar{u}_{ij} > e_{ij}, \end{cases}$$

where $V_{ij}(\cdot)$ is senator i's observable utility from nominee j, which is positively related to n_{ij} (relevant characteristics of nominee j for senator i

"including contextual features of the nomination such as presidential control of the Senate") and negatively related to s_{ij} (the Euclidean distance between senator i's ideal point for judicial ideology on a 0–1 scale and nominee j's judicial ideology on the same scale); β is a vector of parameters; $\bar{u}_{ij}$ is a reservation utility level that may vary across senators and nominations; and e_{ij} is the random component of senator i's utility from nominee j. The authors assume that $V_{ij}(\cdot)$ is linear in parameters and that each e_{ij} is independently and identically distributed (IID) in accordance with the Weibull distribution, so that logit analysis can be used to estimate the model. Note that the model is decision theoretic rather than game theoretic (see Chapter 3). That is, each senator makes an independent voting decision based on his utility from judicial ideology and the quality dimension.

Predictions of the Model. The model makes the following comparative static predictions: (1) the closer the nominee's judicial ideology is to the senator's ideal point for judicial ideology, the more likely it is that the senator will vote for the nominee; and (2) the higher the quality of the nominee on the characteristic dimension, the more likely the senator will vote for the nominee.

As Segal et al. note, a senator's ideal point for judicial ideology may be a function of both her own ideological preferences and those of her constituents. To the extent that a senator votes her own ideological preferences more than her constituents', she is said to be "shirking." Segal et al. show that there are six possible configurations that can occur when the senator's ideal point for judicial ideology diverges from her constituents' preferences. In cases 1 and 2, the nominee's ideology position is either between the senator's most preferred point and the constituents' most preferred point or, if both ideal points are on the same side as the nominee's position, the senator's most preferred position is closer to the nominee's position. These cases yield ambiguous predictions for the effect of shirking on the senator's vote, but they argue that shirking can be expected to make the senator more likely to vote for the nominee in cases 1 and 2. In case 3, the constituent's ideal position is on the same side as the senator's most preferred point, with the constituents' ideal point closer to the nominee's position. The authors show that, in this case, shirking will lower the probability that the senator will vote for the nominee. Thus, Segal et al.'s empirical analysis of shirking is twofold: they test comparative static predictions of the effects of shirking

and simultaneously test whether shirking actually occurs. That is, the goals
of the empirical analysis are (1) to determine if shirking occurs (i.e., is a
shirking variable significant?) and, if it does occur, (2) to determine if it has
the predicted sign (the comparative static prediction).

Measurement Issues and Implications for the Theory. The formal model
directly yields estimating equations for the empirical model, but there are a
number of complex measurement issues that Segal et al. must deal with in
specifying the variables in their empirical model (e.g., ideology measures for
the judicial nominee, the senator, and the constituents). These measurement
issues necessitate making additional explicit assumptions in order to conduct the empirical analysis. Specifically, the formal model that Segal et al.
present of senatorial voting is incomplete. It "black boxes" the determination
of senators' constituents' preferences by treating this term as exogenously
determined. But in order to empirically estimate the formal model, the researchers need an estimate of senator preferences that can be used to derive
their measure of shirking. This means getting into the black box and explicitly modeling the determination of senators' constituents' preferences.

Segal et al. first need a measure of the ideology in the senator's state.
They use states' votes for the Democratic nominee in presidential election
years 1964, 1972, and 1984, which the authors contend were the most ideological elections (and ones for which there were no third-party candidates).
However, using this measure as a senator's constituents' preferences implies
a particular model of electoral competition. In other words, is the senator's
relevant constituency *all* the voters in the state (so that he should choose a
position preferred by the state's median voter, as in the Hotelling–Downsian
model discussed in Chapter 2), or is it only the voters of the senator's own
party (as suggested by other theories of electoral competition; see Chapter 8)? Because the formal model treats constituent preferences as exogenous, it provides no guidance on this decision. Hence the researchers use a
dummy variable for the senator's party (set to 1 for a Democrat and to 0 for a
Republican) and also a dummy variable if the senator is a Democrat from the
South (considered to be more conservative in general than the rest of the nation) as predictors of the senator's constituency's preferences. To measure
shirking they estimate three regression equations, with ideological scores
measured by the Americans for Democratic Action (ADA) as the dependent
variable and with the closest presidential election vote and their partisanship

measures as independent variables. They use the predictions from the regressions as their measure of constituent preferences, and the residuals are assumed to be measures of shirking.

It is important to note that their measure of shirking thus depends on the reasonableness of their assumptions that (a) a senator's relevant constituency is her party constituency rather than the state as a whole and (b) a state's partisanship variables are linearly related to its presidential vote totals on the ideological scale. Shirking is used as a descriptive term for a senator's making choices that are not in line with constituency preferences. If electoral competition is truly best described by the Hotelling–Downsian model, then introducing the partisan variables leads to an inaccurate measurement of shirking, since "shirking" should also include decisions that are a function of the senator's partisanship. The assumption of a linear relationship between presidential vote totals and the partisanship variables may also introduce error and thus also affect evaluation of the model's predictions. Hence the empirical evidence either supports or rejects their model, given the way in which the authors have defined shirking and given the implicit theory of electoral competition underlying their measure. The empirical analysis is not an evaluation of just the model but rather of the model with these additional assumptions about shirking and constituent preferences.

Segal et al. recognize that their measure of shirking may have error due to the nature of these assumptions. They argue that evidence that their shirking measure changes over the electoral cycle and correlates with previous electoral margins (suggesting that shirking is electorally punished) implies that their measures can be reasonably assumed to represent actual shirking. Adding the partisan variables may be likely to reduce the shirking variable and reduce the ability of the general model to predict. Thus, one could argue that the choice they have made places a stronger test on their model. This means that, if their empirical model is not supported empirically, one cannot necessarily conclude that the original formal model is not supported.

The researchers must also devise measures of the judicial nominee's position in the policy space. This also involves adding assumptions to the model. In particular, Segal et al. (1992, apx. A) make assumptions about the relationship between the senator's policy position and the nominee's position. The point is that – even though the relationship between the formal model and the empirical model appears clear-cut and the authors can directly derive estimating equations – simple data measurement issues introduce additional assumptions for the empirical model.

The Empirical Results and Substantive Implications. Given these measurement issues, Segal et al.'s empirical model is estimated using logit on the confirmation votes from 1955 to 1988. The dependent variable is the senators' votes. Independent variables are the distance between the nominee's ideology and the constituents' ideology, a qualifications measure, the interaction of distance and qualifications, a measure for shirking for cases 1 and 2, a measure for shirking for case 3, and other variables designed to capture the effects of such relevant characteristics as presidential strength, whether a senator is in the same party as the president, and measures of interest-group lobbying for and against a nominee. Segal et al.'s empirical analysis uses pooled cross-sectional data to measure the comparative static or relationship predictions within years and over time. All of the variables are significant and have the predicted signs. Hence, the analysis yields support for the authors' theoretical comparative static predictions *and* provides evidence of "shirking" as they have defined it. Segal et al. also note that the model's point predictions (predictions of votes) are correct 97% of the time.

The focus so far has been on the relationship between the formal model and the empirical model and its estimation, but Segal et al.'s analysis is significant primarily because it adds substantively to our understanding of how Supreme Court nominees are selected. In particular, the authors find that senatorial shirking does affect voting on Supreme Court nominees, which suggests that there is evidence of nonrepresentational behavior. They also find that factors which they contend measure general characteristics of the nominee (e.g., the strength and popularity of the president and the mobilization of interest groups) are significant predictors of senatorial voting for nominees.

7.1.2 Presidents and Supreme Court Nominees: The Regime Approach

A Game Theoretic Model of Presidential Nominations. The model of Segal et al. (1992) treats presidential nominees to the Supreme Court as exogenous. Yet if senators are likely to vote for or against nominees according to their policy preferences, why shouldn't the president likewise make nominations in order to further his own policy preferences? That is, presidential nominations should also be a function of the spatial location of the president's ideological preferences. Moraski and Shipan (1998) examine a game theoretic model of the presidential nomination process. They endogenize a number of the variables that Segal et al. consider exogenous. However, they also take some of Segal et al.'s results as exogenous and build upon that work. Thus their analysis shows how the two models together can add to our understanding of the Supreme Court nomination process.

Moraski and Shipan assume (as in Segal et al.) that the policy space is unidimensional. They assume that presidents have symmetric utility functions over the ideological space that are single-peaked at an ideal point P. The justices of the Supreme Court are also assumed to have single-peaked symmetric utility functions over the same ideological space. A president who makes a nomination faces a court consisting of only eight justices. The authors assume that, if the president's nominee is defeated, the Supreme Court will make decisions given the existing eight justices. They also assume that the Court's decision-making procedure is majority rule, so that the expected outcome of Supreme Court decisions is the median ideal point in the Court. Suppose the eight existing judges are aligned in the policy space such that justice i's position is to the right of justice $i - 1$ and to the left of justice $i + 1$, and define J_i as justice i's ideal point in the policy space. Then, if a justice is not added to the court, the court's median position will be any point between J_4 and J_5. Moraski and Shipan assume the actors believe that, in the absence of the appointment of a new member, the Court will choose policy outcomes equal to $J = (J_4 + J_5)/2$. Rather than model senatorial voting explicitly (as in Segal et al.), Moraski and Shipan black-box the Senate and assume that it can be represented by a single-peaked symmetric utility function with an ideal point equal to S. We will denote the policy position of the judicial nominee as N.

Moraski and Shipan argue that the president selects a nominee and the Senate approves or not based on how close the new Court median will be to their respective ideal points. However, the existing judges constrain the ability to alter the Court's actions significantly. That is: appointing a justice who is to the left of J_4 will be certain to shift the Court median only as far as to J_4: appointing a justice to the right of J_5 can move the Court median only as far as to J_5; and appointing of a justice in between the two points would lead to that justice as the new median voter. Moreover, the president is also constrained by the Senate's preferences. Define $I_s = 2S - J$. Moraski and Shipan show "that there are three distinct theoretical regimes: one in which N is a function of P, one in which N is a function of I_s (which in turn is a function of S and J), and finally, one in which N is a function of *J*" (1998, p. 12). They solve their model using the concept of subgame perfection (discussed in Chapter 6).

The Empirical Model with Regimes. Moraski and Shipan are able to classify their model into measurable equilibrium regimes (in contrast to Austen-Smith and Wright as discussed in Chapter 6). Having classified the data, they can then empirically evaluate the model's comparative static predictions across the three regimes and so assess how the policy position of the nominee changes with changes in these variables. But in order to do so, the researchers must construct an empirical model that captures how the equilibrium changes with the regime. They do this by constructing dummy variables (set equal to 1 if the regime exists and to 0 otherwise), which interact with the variables that are expected to explain the nominee's position in the relevant regime. Moraski and Shipan conclude as follows. "The argument that different variables are important in different regimes must be reflected in our empirical approach. The theoretical analysis suggests that the proper specification of the empirical model is:

$$N = \beta_0 + \beta_1 \times D_1 \times P + \beta_2 \times D_2 \times I_s + \beta_3 \times D_3 \times J + e,$$

where D_1, D_2, and D_3 are dummy variables indicating the nature of the regime. . . . As the theoretical model and the empirical specification . . . make clear, the nominee's position is affected by *either* the president *or* the Senate's indifference point *or* the Court's median" (1998, p. 13 [italics in original]). The theory actually predicts that β_1, β_2, and $\beta_3 = 1$ and that $\beta_0 = 0$.

Moraski and Shipan's theory gives precise predicted values for the breakpoints between the regimes. This is not always the case, and the researcher may not be able to specify a priori which regime applies. A researcher can use an empirical estimation technique that allows for the breakpoints to be endogenously determined in order to maximize the likelihood of prediction (see Lee and Porter 1984).

Moraski and Shipan view the formal model as a Partial DGP and add the random variable e to capture the effects of measurement error in the variables. They do not assume that the actors themselves make errors, which would mean that the strategic nature of the game might be different (as discussed in Chapter 4). For example, if the Senate sometimes votes in error then the president may incorporate that error and propose different types of nominees. Without re-solving the model to incorporate that error, we can only conjecture about the predictions of the theory when the actors make errors themselves.

Dependent Variable: Nominee Position or Success? Moraski and Shipan use data from Supreme Court nominations between 1949 and 1994. The perfect information theory predicts that all nominees will be approved by the Senate. For the period investigated, there were 28 nominations to the Supreme Court, of which only three were rejected. Although the overall success of presidential nominees is supportive of the theory, the three rejections are just that – rejections of the theory. The formal model, translated as a Partial DGP with measurement error to the empirical model just described, should still predict only successful nominees. How do the researchers deal with this issue? Should they estimate their empirical model on successful nominees only, arguing that the model can explain only their positions? Or should they estimate the model on all nominees, arguing that the prediction of the model is about the president's choice given the parameters of the model and so the defeated nominees should be included (since they, too, are data on the type of nominee selected)?

The question concerns which type of prediction of the formal model is the focus of the empirical evaluation. If the prediction is that all nominees are successful, then the empirical model as formulated fails to explain the observations; the measurement error in positions cannot account for the failures. It is useful to consider why these three nominations failed. In one case, a scandal occurred between the nomination and the Senate vote (Clarence Thomas was almost a casualty for this reason), in another case the candidate was woefully unqualified, and in a third case public opinion appeared to drastically change between the nomination (of Bork) and the Senate vote. We could conjecture how the perfect information model might be altered to explain these observations, but at some point we are "fitting" the data to the formal model. Even though some nominees were defeated, the success of the overwhelming majority is supportive of the model's prediction. The empirical estimation conducted by Moraski and Shipan is designed to evaluate their prediction of the policy position of the president's nominee. As a consequence, it is appropriate to include the policy positions of the rejected nominees also (as they do in their estimation). Moraski and Shipan find that the empirical model is supported by the data and that the regime variables are significant, except in regime 2.

Moraski and Shipan also estimate an empirical model with control variables that others have argued are important factors in Supreme Court nominations, such as presidential popularity, nominee qualifications, and so on. The authors find that these variables are, in general, insignificant. This is not surprising since these factors are probably more important in determining the success of the nominee than the policy position of the nominee.

Other Translation Issues. Like Segal and colleagues, Moraski and Shipan face a number of measurement issues in determining which regimes apply to which nominations. Two are particularly relevant to the relationship between the formal and empirical models: (1) how to define the ideological dimension, and (2) how to classify the data by regime. The first issue arises because measures of judicial ideology (compiled by Segal and Cover 1989 and reported by Epstein et al. 1996) were developed by focusing on the civil liberties and civil rights tendencies of the nominees, whereas measures of the Senate and presidential ideal points are determined based on an overall liberal–conservative dimension. Although they recognize this is a potential problem, the researchers argue that evidence of correlation between the two measures – and especially the lack of available alternative measures – prevents a solution. They also conduct a number of different empirical estimations using alternative measures of the Senate and presidential ideal points. In this case the overall predictive success of the model, across measures, supports their choices. The second issue is partly a consequence of the small amount of data and measurement error. Moraski and Shipan have only 28 observations: 18 in regime 1, 3 in regime 2, and 7 in regime 3. As the authors illustrate, assigning data to the regimes is not straightforward. In particular, the three observations in regime 2 could easily have been classified as in either regime 1 or regime 3. This suggests that the lack of the model's predictive success in regime 2 may reflect incorrect assignments. One method that could check for regime assignment is to estimate a switching regime regression (see Lee and Porter 1984) and then compare with the hypothesized switches.

7.1.3 Comparison of the Two Studies

The two formal models address different aspects of voting on Supreme Court nominees. Segal et al. consider the nominee's position as exogenously determined. Senators are more likely to vote for a nominee whose position is closer to their ideal point. They consider the underlying determination of senators' ideal points in terms of their constituents and shirking. Moraski and Shipan, in contrast, take senatorial ideal points as exogenous and endogenize the position of the nominee. Segal et al. use a decision theoretic model, whereas Moraski and Shipan examine a strategic, game theoretic model. Both models demonstrate the importance of policy position on nominee success and selection.

Each study constitutes a piece of the puzzle, yet there are inconsistencies between the models. Segal et al. find that such factors as qualifications and presidential popularity are important in explaining the votes for a nominee, whereas Moraski and Shipan find these factors to be unimportant predictors of the nominee's position. A president who knows that these other factors matter in the success of a nominee could then choose a nominee closer to his own ideal point, but Moraski and Shipan do not find such an effect. The two models also differ in their predictions about the effects of a judicial nominee's position on senator voting. In Moraski and Shipan, the probability that a senator will vote for a nominee is deterministic and does not change beyond a certain policy position. That is, since these authors assume that the senators focus on the overall policy position of the Court rather than the nominee and that the nominee can affect the court's position only within a given range, it is possible that a senator is as likely to vote for nominees significantly far from her ideal point as for those whose positions are at her ideal point. Future research questions of interest include (1) the extent to which senatorial voting is related to the nominee's position versus the Court's position if the nominee is selected and (2) a re-evaluation of the effects of such control variables as presidential popularity.

7.1.4   A Digression: Model Fitting and Explanatory Power

The examples of Segal et al. and Moraski and Shipan illustrate the complexities involved when devising a model for a particular research question. Segal et al. propose their model as a general model of roll-call voting in the Congress that is applied to Supreme Court nominations. Under reasoning similar to that of Austen-Smith and Wright's use of the Bork nomination to analyze interest-group lobbying of Congress (see Chapter 6), Segal et al. use the votes on judicial nominees because of their ability to measure the policy position of the nominee. That is, they can measure directly the expected policy outcome of the voting and then empirically assess the spatial voting model in that context. With other roll-call votes it is more difficult (more subjective) to make these types of evaluations. Yet because Segal et al.'s model is applied only to a particular type of voting, we need further empirical support before we can conclude that the model does have the general applicability to roll-call voting claimed by the researchers – just as evaluation of Austen-Smith and Wright's lobbying model needs to be extended to other lobbying situations in order to validate their general claims.

Moraski and Shipan, in contrast, make fewer claims about their model of the constraints and politics of Supreme Court nominations generalizing to other types of presidential nominations to Congress. As a consequence, "fitting" the model by adding assumptions or parameters to explain the three failed nominees is potentially problematic since the model almost ceases to be a model in this case and becomes instead a description of reality. However, Moraski and Shipan's model could also be considered in a more general context and hence be used to analyze other nomination processes. If the model is evaluated in this context then the explanations added to account for the failures of some nominees can be better assessed. It would be possible to determine if there are aspects of Supreme Court nominations that are distinct from other nominations (a point of view that seems to be suggested in Moraski and Shipan and other literature on these nominations). Alternatively, Moraski and Shipan note that, in the nineteenth century, judicial nominees were much more likely to be defeated. Extending the empirical analysis back in time (if the data can be found) is a method of evaluating such added assumptions or parameters. The point is that adding parameters or assumptions that explain the few failures in Moraski and Shipan's model can prove useful only if subsequent empirical evaluation of the new model is conducted. Otherwise, the model loses its explanatory power. The model is a better model if these added assumptions or parameters are supported beyond the data set that suggests them.

The three groups of researchers examining the Supreme Court nomination process (Austen-Smith and Wright 1994; Moraski and Shipan 1998; Segal et al. 1992) view their formal models as Partial DGPs in order to devise empirical models. The question of whether to view the formal model as a Partial or a Complete DGP is a recurring one when evaluating empirical models devised from formal models in light of a given data set. Recall the discussion (in Chapter 4) of McKelvey and Palfrey's two alternative methods of generalizing the theoretical explanations of behavior in the centipede game. They argue that their first approach (adding altruistic motives to the model) is too specific to the particular game and not as generalizable to other situations as their second approach (adding error to the model), even though the first model fits the data better than the second model. The goal of an empirical model that is based on a formal model – whether viewed as a Complete or a Partial DGP – is not simply a good fit to one particular data set. Rather, *the goal is to build models that can be generalized to explain many data sets.*

7.2   Evaluating Process or Dynamic Path Predictions

Many formal models are dynamic, that is, time is explicitly incorporated in the model. I have already discussed repeated games and how repetition of a one-shot game can lead to different outcomes than observed in the one-shot game. One-shot games can also be dynamic – when modeled in extensive form (using a game tree, as in Chapter 4's centipede game). The game may specify the order in which events occur, and equilibrium predictions are about a particular dynamic path among the possible choices that individuals can make. For example, in the complete information version of the centipede game, the subgame perfect equilibrium predicts the game will end at the first move. The altruistic or QRE versions predict that the game will continue longer. Thus, the predicted dynamics of the game depend upon the way in which the game is solved. As explained in Chapter 3, there are a number of non–game theoretic dynamic models in political science that use differential equations to model aggregate behavior over time (see e.g. Kadera forthcoming) as well as game theoretic models that use differential equations (e.g. Mebane 1997). These models make predictions about which paths will occur.

One question that has precipitated a large literature in both political science and economics is the extent to which political competition affects economic activity. Do political choices in one period affect economic activity in another and/or vice versa? This literature is quite broad. Here we shall focus on the empirical examination of two particular dynamic formal models of the relationship between politics and economics. The first example is a probabilistic voting model of macroeconomic unemployment and inflationary policies that cycle in response to electoral factors; this model is tested on the path of twentieth-century U.S. political and economic variables. The formal model combines two theories about the macroeconomic relationship between the economy and politics (rational partisan theory and rational retrospective theory), and the researchers devise three empirical models to evaluate the predictions of the formal model. The formal model is viewed as a Partial DGP, but the empirical models vary in their restrictiveness and relationship to the theory (the more restrictive, the closer the empirical model is to the formal model). Thus, this example illustrates how a dynamic formal model can be empirically evaluated and also how alternative empirical specifications can be used in the evaluation.

The second example is a neoclassical growth model with two candidates who choose consumption levels that determine future economic growth. It is evaluated using laboratory experiments and demonstrates how an experimental methodology can be utilized. The example illustrates some of the issues involved in designing an experiment to assess a complex formal model as well as how theory and stress tests can be used to evaluate a formal model's predictive power.

7.2.1 A Political Macroeconomic Model: A Dynamic Formal Model as a Partial DGP

The Literature and the Empirical Question. Most of the literature on political business cycles takes a macroeconomic approach. The macroeconomic literature has five main explanations for the relationship between political outcomes and the economy:

1. *political business cycle theory* (e.g. Nordhaus 1975) – incumbents engage in pre-electoral inflation surprises to cause bursts of economic growth and increase the probability of re-election;
2. *partisan theory* (e.g. Hibbs 1977, 1987) – political parties have different economic policy preferences and thus (a) the economy growth and inflation rates will differ depending on which party is in power and (b) these differences will persist;
3. *rational partisan theory* (e.g. Alesina 1988) – political parties have different economic policy preferences and, because of uncertainty about which party will win an election, elections can cause unexpected inflation or deflation that in turn may cause electorally induced business cycles;
4. *naive retrospective theory* (e.g. Fair 1988) – voters vote for or against incumbents based both on their partisan preferences and the current state of the economy as a predictor of the incumbent's competence in managing the economy;

5. *rational retrospective theory* (e.g. Rogoff 1990; Rogoff and Sibert 1988) –
   voters vote for or against incumbents based both on their partisan preferences and the current state of the economy, but they rationally estimate
   how much the current state of the economy reflects the incumbent's competence or is just "good luck."

All of these theories make predictions about the relationship between political and economic outcomes over time. Alesina, Londregan, and Rosenthal (1993) present a formal model combining rational partisan theory and
rational retrospective theory. They begin their research by noting (p. 12) five
empirical regularities that should be explained by any theory of the relationship over time between political and economic outcomes.

1. "Presidential elections are strongly influenced by the business cycle."
2. "Congressional vote shares are less sensitive to economic conditions . . . ."
3. "There is a midterm electoral cycle where the party holding the White
   House loses plurality in midterm congressional elections . . . ."
4. "Since World War II, in the first half of the Republican administrations,
   economic growth tends to decelerate, reaching its minimum during the
   second year of each term, while the economy grows more rapidly than average during the first half of Democratic administrations. In the last two
   years of each term, there are no significant differences between growth
   rates for Democratic and Republican administrations . . . ."
5. "The rate of economic growth is not systematically higher than average
   in election years . . . ."

Alesina and colleagues (1993) argue that their formal model can explain
these empirical regularities. They view the formal model as a Partial DGP
and use it as the basis of an empirical model for evaluating time-series data
on the U.S. economy. I explore how the formal model works, examine its
predictions, and discuss how the authors translate the model to an empirical
model.

The Formal Model. In the formal model examined here (based on contem-
poraneous but later-published work of Alesina and Rosenthal 1995, 1996),
the economy's output in each period is a function of the natural rate of growth,
unexpected inflation, and a random term. Unexpected inflation causes output to be higher because, following Fischer (1977), workers are assumed to
have signed fixed nominal wage contracts and the unexpected inflation results in a lower real wage, which in turn induces an increase in employment

(more workers are hired since they are cheaper) and output (as a consequence of the higher employment). If inflation is unexpectedly lower then the opposite occurs: real wages rise, employment and output fall. The random term has two components that cannot be distinguished by voters: (i) a transitory shock representing unanticipated economic events (such as the oil shocks of the 1970s); and (ii) an administration competence level that differs by political party and has inertia (evolves according to a first-order moving average, or MA(1), process).

Specifically, the authors assume:

$$g_t = \bar{g} + \gamma (\pi_t - \pi_t^e) + \varepsilon_t,$$

$$\varepsilon_t = \zeta_t + \eta_t,$$

$$\eta_t = \begin{cases} \mu_t^R + \rho\mu_{t-1}^R & \text{if } R \text{ president at } t, \\ \mu_t^D + \rho\mu_{t-1}^D & \text{if } D \text{ president at } t, \end{cases}$$

$$E(\mu_t^R) = E(\mu_t^D) = 0,$$

$$\text{Var}(\mu_t^R) = \text{Var}(\mu_t^D) = \sigma_\mu^2,$$

where g_t is the rate of growth of output in period t, $\bar{g}$ is the "natural" rate of growth, π_t is the rate of inflation in period t, and $\pi_t^e = E(\pi_t \mid I_{t-1})$ is the rational expectation of the inflation rate based on the information available at period $t - 1$. The error term ε_t comprises a transitory shock ζ_t, which is IID with mean 0 and variance σ_ζ^2, and an administrative competence η_t. Note that the researchers assume that the error term's two components cannot be separately observed by voters or by econometricians.

Two political parties are assumed to compete for control of the government. The parties have policy preferences, that is, they have distinct preferences over the rate of inflation and the rate of growth of output. The assumption is that there is a trade-off between inflation and unemployment and that the parties differ in their preferences over this trade-off.[1] The model also incorporates some institutional features that are abstractions of the U.S. governmental system. That is, the president is elected for two periods using majority rule and the entire legislature is elected each period by proportional rule. One period thus equals two years. Voters are assumed to vote probabilistically: voters' ideal points over inflation are drawn from a uniform distribution that is a function of a random variable drawn independently each period (voters have common and fixed preferences over output levels).

---

[1] Morton (1996) argues that these assumptions may be internally inconsistent.

The researchers assume:

$$W^j = \sum_{t=0}^{\infty} \beta^t \left[-\frac{1}{2}(\pi_t - \bar{\pi}^j)^2 + b^j g_t \right],$$

$$0 < \beta < 1,$$

$$\bar{\pi}^D > \bar{\pi}^R \geq 0,$$

$$b^D > b^R > 0, \quad b^i = b > 0,$$

$$\bar{\pi}^i \sim U[\mathbf{a}, 1 + \mathbf{a}],$$

$$\mathbf{a} \sim U[-w, w],$$

where the index j equals either D, R, or i for voter i, W^j is j's preference function, and β and b^j are parameters.

There are two ways in which politics affects economic growth in the theory: (1) the "surprise" difference in inflation that occurs with presidential elections (rational partisan theory) and (2) changes in competence with administration changes (rational retrospective theory).[2] Consider the surprise change in inflation. Why do "surprise" changes in inflation occur? The parties have policy preferences over inflation and there is uncertainty due to probabilistic voting, so in equilibrium the parties choose divergent inflation rates. Alesina et al. (1993) assume that Democrats prefer higher inflation rates than Republicans. Voters rationally calculate the time-consistent expected inflation rate as a function of the election's expected outcome, given the parties' known utility functions.[3] The nominal wage contracts are signed before the election, given the expected inflation rate. Because each party has a positive probability of winning the presidency, the expected inflation rate is actually *between* the preferred values of the two parties. As a result, if a Democrat is elected president then inflation is higher than expected; if a Republican is elected then inflation is lower than expected. Hence the theory predicts that the period after a presidential election will show a higher rate of growth (due to the unexpected increase in inflation) if a Democrat is elected and a lower rate of growth (due to the unexpected decrease in inflation) if a Republican is elected. Alesina et al. call this "rational partisan theory"

[2] Alesina and colleagues' empirical work may be viewed as investigating two competing theories of politically induced business cycles, competence theory (based on the work of Rogoff and Sibert 1988) versus rational partisan theory (based on Alesina 1988).

[3] Anticipating that both parties have an incentive to choose a higher inflation rate in order to increase output by surprise, voters also rationally calculate time-consistent inflation policies for both parties. See Brophy-Baermann and Conybeare (1994) for an application of a similar model to governmental choice of time-consistent policies of optimal retaliation to terrorism (with an empirical test of the dynamic path predictions).

since voters anticipate rationally the expected inflation rate. The surprise is a consequence of the election's measure of unpredictably.

Solving this complex model is not straightforward. Like many majority voting models, there are multiple equilibria and there is a coordination problem for voters. Alesina and Rosenthal (1995, 1996) use the refinement of coalition-proof Nash equilibria (Bernheim, Peleg, and Whinston 1987) to reduce the number of equilibria (see the discussion in Chapter 6). As Alesina et al. observe: "The basic idea is that equilibrium strategies should be robust to 'credible' defections of coalitions, as well as of individuals; that is, no 'credible' coalition of voters would want to modify the electoral outcome by changing their votes" (1993, p. 17). Alesina and Rosenthal show that, for a large set of parameter values, the model has a unique equilibrium where presidential elections are uncertain. The uncertainty in the presidential elections results in rational partisan business cycles and the observed midterm electoral cycle. Thus, the authors claim their formal model yields predictions that are consistent with their list (quoted earlier) of five empirical regularities to be explained.

Translating the Formal Model into Empirical Models. Alesina et al. (1993) estimate a four-equation system on U.S. data for 1915–88. The equations determine the growth rate of the economy, the midterm popular vote for the House of Representatives, the popular vote for president, and the popular vote for the House in presidential election years. The equations are estimated separately and then in two different restricted systems (the more restrictive system assumes a version of the empirical model that more closely matches the theoretical specification). Thus, the researchers estimate three different empirical models. The first empirical model is the "system restricted model," where the most restricted equations are estimated simultaneously; the second empirical model is the "equation restricted model," where each equation is estimated in its restricted form simultaneously with the other equations in their unrestricted form; and the third empirical model is the "unrestricted model," where all equations are estimated in their unrestricted forms.

Are There Competency Shocks? The authors check first for evidence of competency shocks to the economy. They estimate the following growth equation, which is the same across empirical models:

$$g_t = \gamma_0 + \gamma_1 pe_t + \gamma_2 mm_t + \zeta_t + \mu_t^j + \rho\mu_{t-1}^j,$$

where pe_t is a "partisan effect" variable that is set to 1 in the second year of a Republican administration, -1 in the second year of a Democratic administration, and 0 otherwise; mm_t is the rate of military mobilization in year t; and j equals D for a Democratic president or R for a Republican president.

The growth equation illustrates a number of important ways in which the empirical model differs from the underlying formal model. The partisan effect variable captures the prediction of a change in economic growth due to unexpected inflation rates as a consequence of electoral uncertainty. The formulation of this dummy variable assumes that the partisan effect is symmetric, which is more restrictive than the formal model's assumption (i.e., it implies that the ideal points of the parties are symmetric, requiring a particular distribution of power between parties and branches of government). The theory predicts that the surprise will be greater for the party with the lower a priori probability of winning election. The theory also assumes that Congressional elections will result in inflation surprises, which Alesina et al. ignore – arguing that such effects have been shown to be empirically insignificant. They chose the second year as when they expect to observe the impact on output of the unexpected change in inflation, a choice based on empirical results on the lags in the real effects of monetary policy. Alesina et al. expect that military action is likely to have a significant impact on economic growth and so they add a control variable to the growth equation. Thus the empirical model – while more restrictive than the formal model – also adds variables that the formal model assumes are constant (the ceteris paribus assumption).

Before estimating the other equations in their empirical model, Alesina et al. first determine whether there is evidence of competency effects. That is, does the party in power really matter for the growth rate of the economy? They define θ as the covariance between the two parties' competency shocks. The theoretical model implies that $\theta = 0$. As discussed in their work's appendix, a predicted value of θ cannot be derived from the estimated growth equation because the equation is underidentified. But the researchers can test the relationship between $\rho\sigma_\mu^2$ and $\rho\theta$, which tests both the MA(1) model and the competency-based model. Alesina et al. find support for the MA(1) model over the competency model. Hence they argue there are no party-specific competency shocks and their growth equation of choice is the MA(1) model, which is the same across empirical models:[4]

$$g_t = \gamma_0 + \gamma_1 pe_t + \gamma_2 mm_t + \rho\mu_{t-1} + \mu_t.$$

[4] An alternative would be to look for president-specific competency shocks. However, the data are probably insufficient for such an analysis.

The System Restricted Empirical Model. There are two versions
for the other three equations in the empirical models, the restricted and the
unrestricted version. The restricted versions of the three other equations are:

$$v_t^p = \psi_0 + \psi_1 r_t + \psi_2 v_{t-2}^{hm} + \psi_4 \hat{g}_t + \psi_5 \mu_t + \varphi_t^p,$$
$$v_t^{hp} = \lambda_0 + \lambda_2 v_{t-2}^{hm} + \lambda_6 \varphi_t^p + \varphi_t^{hp},$$
$$v_t^{hm} = \kappa_0 + \kappa_2 v_{t-2}^{hp} + \varphi_t^{hm},$$

where v_t^k is the share of the vote for the party of the incumbent president in
the kth election at time t (k equals p for the president's vote share, hp for
the vote share in the House of Representatives at the time of the presidential election, and hm for the vote share in the House of Representatives for
the midterm election); r_t is set to 1 if the incumbent is a Republican and to
0 otherwise; $\hat{g}_t$ is predicted growth rate at time t from the growth equation;
and φ_t^k are disturbance terms orthogonal to the growth shocks and measures
for the kth vote share.

Consider the system restricted empirical model (where all four restricted
equations are estimated simultaneously) and its relationship to the underlying formal model. The incumbent's presidential vote share is a function
of his party, the vote share his party received in the last House midterm
election, the expected growth rate, and the incumbent's competency disturbance. The vote shares for the House elections are functions of the previous
House election vote shares. The theoretical model predicts that there exists
a cutpoint in inflation rates that divides the electorate's preferences in the
election. Voters with ideal points less than the cutpoint vote for the Republican candidate while voters with ideal points greater than the cutpoint vote
for the Democratic candidate. In this model the cutpoint may be different
from the median voter ideal point, so a party may receive more than half of
the vote; the variable r_t is designed to capture that effect.

The theoretical model predicts that the partisan effect on the cutpoint will
not change over time because voters have fixed preferences and parties have
fixed positions. But Alesina et al. recognize that this may not be true for
the long period of time studied in their empirical investigation. They do
not expect this ceteris paribus assumption to hold when applying the formal
model to the data. Thus they posit that the incumbent's presidential vote
share is a function of the share of his party's vote for the House in the previous midterm election, and that the House election vote shares likewise vary
over time. The researchers reason as follows:

This variable can be proxying for several effects. First, the locations of the parties
relative to the distribution of the voters may adjust slowly in time, whereas they are

assumed to be constant in the theoretical model. Second, the independent preference shocks in the theoretical model are likely to be serially correlated in practice. Third, incumbency advantage in the House may directly improve chances of winning the presidency. None of these mechanisms is included (for reasons of tractability) in our theoretical model, but our results suggest they are empirically relevant. (1993, p. 20)

These terms are included because Alesina et al. believe that partisan preferences are not constant over time, whereas the growth and competency terms are included to test whether voters are rationally or naively retrospective. Since the estimation of the growth equation showed that there is no competency effect, Alesina et al. argue that if voters are rationally retrospective then $\psi_4 = \psi_5 = 0$, if naively retrospective then $\psi_4 = \psi_5 > 0$. The authors estimate the four restricted equations simultaneously in the restricted system empirical model using Rothenberg's (1973) optimum distance technique.

The Less Restricted Empirical Models.   The unrestricted equations also attempt to account for factors that are left out of the formal model but conjectured by Alesina et al. to matter empirically. In particular, they include mm_t in the vote equations to capture "rally 'round the flag" effects of military mobilization. In the restricted empirical model the growth shock affects share of the votes in the House indirectly through its effect on the share of the vote for president, as in the formal model. In the unrestricted equations these variables are directly included in the House vote share equations. The unrestricted equations are as follows:

$$v_t^p = \psi_0 + \psi_1 r_t + \psi_2 v_{t-2}^{hm} + \psi_3 mm_t + \psi_4 \hat{g}_t + \psi_5 \mu_t + \varphi_t^p,$$
$$v_t^{hp} = \lambda_0 + \lambda_2 v_{t-2}^{hm} + \lambda_3 mm_t + \lambda_4 \hat{g}_t + \lambda_5 \mu_t + \lambda_6 \varphi_t^p + \varphi_t^{hp},$$
$$v_t^{hm} = \kappa_0 + \kappa_2 v_{t-2}^{hp} + \kappa_3 mm_t + \kappa_4 \hat{g}_t + \kappa_5 \mu_t + \varphi_t^{hm}.$$

Alesina et al. estimate two empirical models that are less restrictive than the restricted system empirical model. In the restricted equation model the restricted version of each equation is estimated with the other equations as unrestricted; in the unrestricted model, all equations are estimated in the unrestricted form.

The Empirical Results.   Most noteworthy, Alesina et al. find support for the restricted system model, which is closest to the underlying formal model. The growth variables are insignificant in the unrestricted House vote share equations and there are no significant rally-'round-the-flag effects. Theoretical predictions such as midterm electoral loss and significant partisan effects on economic growth are supported. The authors conclude that their analysis "indicates that growth rates during the second year of Republican administrations with no changes in the level of the armed forces will average under 2%, while during the corresponding year of a Democratic administration, the economy will typically grow by almost 5%" (1993, pp. 21–2). However, there are some empirical results that do not support the theoretical predictions. The authors do find empirical support for their hypothesis that $\psi_4 = \psi_5 > 0$, which they argue is evidence of naive retrospective voting. They also find evidence of a Presidential incumbency advantage that the formal model does not predict.

Although the underlying formal model of Alesina et al. is complicated, it still simplifies significantly many aspects of politics and economics. Yet despite these simplifications, the researchers are able to devise an empirical model that comes very close to the underlying formal model. That they find support for the empirical model versus less restrictive versions is impressive. Their research presents a useful example of how multiple specifications can be used to effectively evaluate a model. Moreover, the empirical model shows how a model's predicted path may be empirically estimated.

7.2.2 A Neoclassical Economic Growth Model and Political Competition: Theory versus Stress Tests

Most modelers (including Alesina et al.) of the effects of politics on the economy take a macroeconomic approach. Boylan and McKelvey (1995) take a different approach. They examine the consequences of elections on economic growth in the context of a standard neoclassical growth model from microeconomic theory. Boylan and associates (1991) assess the neoclassical model using laboratory experiments. This example illustrates how a laboratory experiment can be used to evaluate a dynamic path prediction.

The Theory. Assume that an economy is given by a simple one-sector neoclassical growth model. In each period, output (the country's gross national product) can be either consumed or saved (invested), and output in the next period is a function of the physical capital stock that has accumulated over time (which depends on how much output in previous periods has been saved). It can be shown that, for each period, the following fundamental equation of growth theory holds:

$$c_t + k_{t+1} = f(k_t) + (1 - \lambda)k_t,$$

where c_t is the per-capita consumption at date t; k_t is the per-capita capital stock at the beginning of date t; $f(\cdot)$ is the production function of output y_t (which is assumed to be twice continuously differentiable, with a positive first derivative and a negative second derivative); and λ is the rate of depreciation of the capital stock. Any path that satisfies this equation (and for which $k_0 > 0$, $k_t \geq 0$, and $c_t \geq 0$) is called a *feasible consumption–investment path*. It can be shown that there is a corresponding consumption path and that a consumption–investment path is determined completely by the corresponding consumption path.

Suppose we wish to consider what happens when we incorporate two candidates and a set of voters with utility over consumption paths. First we assume that voter i's utility is given by

$$U_i(c) = \sum_{0 < l < \infty} \delta_i^t u_i(c_t),$$

where δ_i is voter i's discount factor (assumed to be less than 1) and $u_i(c_t)$ is a standard concave utility function over consumption in period t. Assume that two candidates compete for four-period terms and that the winner will choose consumption levels for each period during her term.

Boylan and McKelvey (1995) show that if the two candidates can commit to multiperiod consumption paths and there is heterogeneity in voter preferences, then no majority voting equilibrium exists. Thus, commitment implies randomness in consumption over time. However, if candidates cannot commit to a consumption path for the term and can only choose consumption paths one period at a time, then there exists a majority voting equilibrium in which consumption follows the optimal path of the median voter. Intuitively, commitment to a multiperiod consumption path is a multidimensional voting game, whereas choosing consumption one period at a time restricts the political competition to one dimension at a time, as in a structure-induced equilibrium. Hence we should note that, with commitment, economic policy will be quite random independent of any macroeconomic effects of politics on inflation (as in Alesina et al.).

Designing an Experiment to Evaluate the Theory. Boylan and colleagues (1991) conduct an experimental analysis based on the formal model of Boylan and McKelvey (not published until 1995). They conduct two experimental tests, one a theory test and the other a stress test (see the discussion in Chapter 4). In the theory test, researchers consider whether the models' dynamic path is supported; this is a controlled test of the theory's prediction that consumption will follow the median voter's optimal path. In the stress test, the authors incorporate more realistic features of political competition, such as voters and candidates with limited information about voter utility functions and polls of voters (between each period of an incumbent's term) on their approval or disapproval of his progress. They wish to see if these factors will cause politically induced business cycles. A politically induced business cycle could occur in theory if a candidate overinvests early in his term to provide extra consumption in the last period before the election. The theory predicts that candidates will not induce political business cycles since they cannot commit to future consumption patterns. Instead, the theory predicts that the candidates will follow the consumption–investment path most preferred by the median voter.

The Theory Test. In the theory test (version-B experiments), the researchers conducted six experiments. Each was a series of elections where two candidates compete for four-period terms. Before each election, both candidates make a campaign promise of consumption and investment levels in each of the four periods of the upcoming term. Voters then vote, and the candidate receiving the majority of the votes is elected (candidates are rewarded based on the votes they receive). The candidates are not allowed to commit to their proposed policies. Thus, the theory predicts that the candidates will choose the optimal consumption path of the median voter. Note, however, that since the candidates can only make promises, there is an implicit assumption that they "commit" to the first period's promise although the design does not actually force such a commitment. In this sense the researchers do not exactly match the theory

Once elected, the incumbent in each period observes the total real income, y_t, which is given by the following production function: $f(k_t) = a(1 - e^{-bk_t})$, where a and b (as well as other parameters in the model) are constants. Two different production functions are used – production function 1 potentially reaches higher income levels than production function 2. The incumbent chooses how to divide the income between nonnegative values of investment i_t and consumption c_t. Investment increases the capital stock and, as a consequence, the real income available for future periods. After the fourth period there is a new election. Given the complexity of the production function, the researchers need to present consequences of the choices in a straightforward manner. They do this by providing all the subjects with a contour graph that shows – for different investment levels – what the next-period budget will be, given the existing capital stock. Hence voters know how the choice made in one period affects the choice available in the next period from a simple-to-read graph. Voters receive payoffs each period according to the utility function $U_i(c) = \sum_{0 < 1 < \infty} \delta_i^t d_i c_t^{e_i}$, where the parameters are constants. Note that the utility function varies across voters.

One principal difficulty in designing a theory test of this model type is that the theory models time as infinite and no experiment can effectively capture that constraint. Voters do discount the value of consumption in future periods, as given by the discount rate. The discount rate is analogous to a randomly determined end to the game. Thus the researchers induce a common discount by randomizing when the game ends. After each period, a random number is drawn between 0 and 1. If it is greater than 0.97, then the experiment is ended; if it is less than or equal to 0.97 then the experiment continues and the payoffs cumulate. However, experiments still in session at 40 periods were terminated. This 40-period limit was unknown to the subjects.

The Stress Test.   The researchers conducted ten stress-test experiments. The stress test (version-A experiments) differs from the theory test in four ways:

First, the voters and candidates are not told the functional form of the voter utility functions. They are only told that the utility functions are increasing with consumption, but not that they increase at a decreasing rate. Second, the candidates do not make a promise for a consumption path over the entire four-period term of office. Rather they make a consumption–investment promise only for the last period of the term of office about their approval or disapproval of the incumbent's performance while in office. . . . Fourth, the discounting is done somewhat differently. . . . Rather than having a fixed discount rate over the course of the experiment, we have a discount rate that declines in time. (Boylan et al. 1991, p. 42)

Analyzing the Experimental Data.   The theory predicts that candidates will choose consumption–investment paths over time that are preferred by the median voter. This path should not exhibit business cycles. Thus, the first question addressed by the researchers is to what extent the data follows the predicted path. Viewing the model as a Complete DGP, there exist (not surprisingly) cases where candidates do not make choices on the optimal path. Boylan et al. focus on the comparison between the paths chosen in the theory test with those chosen in the stress test. With the exception of one of the treatments (which exhibited some cyclical behavior), candidates in the theory test do closely follow the predicted path. In the stress test, however, there are a number of politically induced business cycles. These cycles occur because of the lower-information environment of the stress test and are not due to macroeconomic political effects (as in Alesina et al.). Moreover, in the stress test the candidates tend to overinvest. The researchers contend that this is because they make promises about the last period's consumption that cannot be met on the optimal path. Thus the candidates overinvest in general and so induce a business cycle, resulting in higher consumption levels at the end of their terms.

Because Boylan et al. view the formal model as a Complete DGP in their empirical analysis, they focus on what the results suggest for future research on the political economic process. That is, since the formal model's precise predictions are expected to fail in the empirical study, the findings – that in almost all the theory treatments the predicted path is followed and that, in comparison to the stress treatments, political business cycles are rare – provides us with insight into possible causes of electorally induced business cycles. The empirical analysis is a first step in working toward an understanding of the dynamic process rather than a definitive evaluation of the theory. In this case, the empirical analysis is designed to feed back into the theoretical enterprise.

7.3   Extending the Empirical Focus

The study of evaluating relationships in this chapter (and of equilibrium predictions in the preceding one) has featured examples of assessments of models using the empirical cases for which they were originally designed. But one aim of empirical analysis of a formal model might be to discover the limits of the theory by evaluating it using data that the theory was not originally designed to consider. (This point was noted in discussing the empirical focus of Austen-Smith and Wright, Segal et al., and Moraski and Shipan.) A significant portion of the formal work in political science has focused on the effects of institutional rules and structures specific to the U.S. Congress. This formal literature has provided much useful insight, but in order to understand the limits of the theory it is important that we expand the empirical analysis beyond the U.S. Congress. One way of doing this is to examine how the formal literature on Congress empirically explains behavior and outcomes in legislatures at lower levels of government; for example, we can consider state and local legislative bodies. Another approach is to apply the analysis to legislatures in other countries, as in Huber's (1992) application of the predictions of formal models of Congress to the French National Assembly.

Such a study, like loosening control in the experimental environment, can be a stronger assessment of the theory than when it is applied only to those areas for which it was originally designed. However, there are a number of issues to consider in such an expansion of the empirical analysis of a formal model. First, we need to evaluate to what extent the model's assumptions should be altered to account for the new empirical reality. This evaluation need not imply that the empirical analysis is improper if they are *not* satisfied: we know that the assumptions of a model are at some level never all satisfied, so the point is not how realistic the model is in the new application but rather that we need to make explicit what the fit is between assumptions of the model and the empirical world investigated.

Huber discusses three differences between U.S. Congressional and French politics: (1) in Congress the political actors are the individual legislators, whereas in parliamentary systems the party and the government are the actors; (2) in parliamentary systems the government is dependent on the confidence of the parliament; and (3) committees in the French system are not as powerful as in Congress, and the French government plays more the role that is played by committees in Congress.

Second, we need to consider to what extent the predictions of the theory are different in the different empirical environment. In investigating how the assumptions of the formal models of Congress may or may not apply to the French National Assembly, Huber recognizes that the predictions of the formal models must be changed to reflect the differences between the two institutions. Principally, the role played by committees is now played by the government in the four hypotheses that he derives from the formal literature on Congress and tests on the French case. The four hypotheses tested by Huber are as follows.

1. "The probability that the government will use restrictive procedures on a bill increases as the number of issue dimensions pertaining to the bill increases."
2. "The probability that the government will use restrictive procedures on a bill increases when the bill is distributive in nature."

3. "As the government's status becomes weaker or more heterogeneous, the probability that restrictive procedures will be invoked on a bill increases."
4. "Restrictive procedures are used to hasten action on the floor of the National Assembly." (1992, pp. 678–80)

The first three hypotheses derive from the work of Denzau, Riker, and Shepsle (1985), Krehbiel (1991), and Shepsle and Weingast (1984); the fourth is based on the work of Baron and Ferejohn (1989a,b).

It is important to note that Huber does not present these formal models that are the basis of his theoretical predictions. As I argue in Section 2.4, it is rare that a researcher can effectively present a complete formal model and the complete empirical evaluation of that model. Many of the examples in this book are cases where the formal model is presented in a separate research article from the empirical evaluation. Consider these examples: Austen-Smith and Wright's (1994) estimation of predictions from Austen-Smith and Wright's (1992) formal model; Alesina et al.'s (1993) estimation of the predictions of Alesina and Rosenthal's (1995, 1996) formal model; and Boylan et al.'s (1991) estimation of the predictions of Boylan and McKelvey's (1995) formal model. In other cases, like Huber, the formal model was presented by other researchers.

Finally, the new empirical case must be evaluated in terms of other important factors that might affect the predictions arising from knowledge of that particular case. Huber suggests two additional hypotheses that ensue from the empirical literature on French politics.

5. "The government will invoke restrictive procedures on bills to protect its majority from embarrassing votes and debates."
6. "The government will use restrictive procedures to prevent changes by the National Assembly to the government's draft of a bill; or, the probability that the government will invoke restrictive procedures on a bill increases as the preferences of the government and the National Assembly diverge." (1992, p. 680)

Huber assesses these six hypotheses using French data on amendment and procedural activity for 356 government bills between March 21, 1978 and the end of the legislative session in December 1989. He finds some support for his hypotheses derived from the formal models of Congress. Hypothesis 2 in particular receives strong support, suggesting that there are important similarities in the types of French and U.S. bills on which restrictive procedures are used.

7.4   Policy Implications of Formal Models

I remarked previously that formal models can help us forecast or predict the implications of possible policy changes and that simulations based on formal models (such as those conducted by Gilmour and Rothstein 1994 on the effects of term limits) can be quite serviceable for policy predictions. Many of the theoretical questions that we ask with formal models have normative aspects. Thus, our empirical analysis of a formal model's predictions are sometimes focused toward providing answers to normative questions.

Proposed policy changes can often be fruitfully examined using laboratory experiments. Gerber, Morton, and Rietz (1998) present an experimental analysis of the anticipated effects of cumulative voting systems for minority representation. Cumulative voting is a procedure that has been advocated by a number of minority activists, such as Lani Guinier, to increase minority representation in legislative bodies. Cumulative voting differs from what Gerber et al. label "straight" voting as follows. Suppose *two* legislators are to be elected from a single district. Under straight voting each voter is given two votes, of which she can allocate at most one to each of any two candidates. Under cumulative voting, the voter can allocate either two votes to one candidate or one to each of two candidates. Cumulative voting has been hypothesized to allow minority voters to cumulate their votes and increase the probability of a minority candidate achieving election. Gerber et al. show that cumulative voting can increase minority representation.

Cumulative voting, while not nearly as widespread in the United States as straight voting, has been used in some cases. Hence another way to evaluate the impact of cumulative voting is to empirically examine these cases. Adams (1996) examines Illinois state legislative elections where cumulative voting was used from 1870 to 1982. The Illinois case is particularly interesting because it allows an examination of cumulative voting under multi-member districts within an existing two-party system. An important policy question is: How would changing our voting rules affect our party system in the United States? The Illinois case is also useful because it provides us with comparative data from years after 1982, when the system was changed to single-member districts.

Adams begins his analysis by summarizing the theoretical results on multimember versus single-member districts. These results, he argues, imply that candidates in multimember district elections are likely to be dispersed away from the position most preferred by the median voter, whereas candidates in single-member district elections are likely to be close to the position most preferred by the median voter.[5] To empirically evaluate these predictions using data on the Illinois state legislature, Adams devises an empirical model with specific assumptions that are more restrictive than the theoretical models. For example, he assumes (i) that voters are myopic and vote in each election without anticipating future effects and (ii) that candidates choose positions that are fixed during the election process and make policy choices if elected that reflect these positions. Using these assumptions, Adams shows that the theory predicts that the distribution of the policy positions of party's nominees will have a higher variance under multimember districts than under single-member districts.

Using data from the Illinois Political Action Committee (which rates policy positions of legislators in that state on a liberal–conservative scale), Adams investigates the variance under the multimember district system versus the variance under the single-member district system. He finds that the two parties are more diverse ideologically under the multimember district system than when the legislature is elected using single-member districts. The results are interesting because they illustrate that changing the electoral system to multimember districts can have consequences for the internal ideological variance within our political parties. The results illustrate how empirical analysis based on formal models can help us anticipate the effects of proposed policy changes.

7.5   Implications of the Examples

Relationship predictions can be quite useful in the empirical study of formal models. Comparative static predictions are the expected changes of variables' equilibrium values that occur when another variable changes. These comparative static predictions are relationship predictions that can be tested empirically, as we saw in the work of Segal et al., Moraski and Shipan, Huber, and Adams. Dynamic path or process predictions are predictions

---

[5] Shepsle (1991) reviews this literature; see also Cox (1990a,b).

about how a variable or set of variables will change over time. These predictions can be tested as in Boylan et al. and Alesina et al. and so increase our empirical understanding. Our examination of the examples suggest the following conclusions concerning formal-model relationship predictions and their value to empirical study.

1. *Comparative static and dynamic path predictions, when evaluated, each yield two types of information.* That is, support for these predictions provides support for the formal model *and* tells us about the strength of the relationship. Segal et al. first test whether shirking occurs and second if shirking occurs as predicted by the formal model. Alesina et al. test whether partisan-driven macroeconomic cycles occur and whether they occur as predicted by the formal model. Thus, tests of relationship predictions of formal models can provide much useful empirical knowledge.

2. *In empirical analysis of formal models, it is important always to specify carefully how the empirical model's assumptions compare with the assumptions underlying the theoretical formulation.* These issues are particularly significant when dealing with estimation of formal models using naturally occurring data. Operationalizing the predictions requires assumptions that need to be considered explicitly in evaluating the empirical results.

- The empirical model is often more restrictive than the underlying formal model because of choices made in the way the model is specified (Alesina et al. assuming that the effect of unexpected inflation is symmetric across parties) or in data measurements (Segal et al. assuming that a senator's relevant constituency is given by his party identity).
- Adding control variables and random error terms to the applied formal model, thus viewing the formal model as a Partial DGP, means that the empirical evaluation is of a different model than the underlying formal model.

3. *Relationship predictions can be evaluated experimentally using theory tests and stress tests.* Theory tests can be designed to mirror the theoretical formulation and evaluate the predictions of the formal model when given its best chance to be viewed as a Complete DGP. However, stress tests are important to demonstrate whether the model's predictions continue to hold when the design allows for disconnects between the theory and the experiment. The experimental tests in Boylan et al. allowed researchers to consider how consumption paths changed over time – under both a controlled environment and a less controlled environment. The laboratory provides a

unique opportunity to test how choices may change as subjects make choices over time. The settings for these tests can at first closely mirror the formal model and then gradually loosen that model's assumptions to more closely approximate the real world. Testing dynamic path or process predictions in the laboratory can be quite valuable in helping us understand real-world dynamics.

4. *Relationship predictions derived from a formal model can and should be used to understand empirical relationships in settings not originally considered as the basis for the model.* Huber takes the predictions of formal models used to analyze the U.S. Congress as a basis for empirical research on the French National Assembly. Of course, it is crucial that the application not be cavalier – that the researcher carefully evaluate how well the formal model's design and assumptions empirically fit the new case. However, if an applied formal model fits only its original empirical application, the model is less useful in helping to build understanding of politics.

5. *Relationship predictions from formal models can be used to consider anticipated policy changes.* The investigations of Gerber et al. and Adams of differences in voting procedures provide important information about how an advocated policy change may affect electoral politics.

In this chapter and the preceding one I have considered how evaluating predictions of formal models helps us to assess their empirical usefulness. However, ideally we would like to compare our theoretical predictions against alternative theoretical predictions. The task of comparing formal models with each other and with nonformal models is taken up in the next chapter.

CHAPTER 8

Evaluating Alternative Models

At first glance, evaluating alternative models appears to be a higher level of empirical analysis than simply assessing the assumptions or predictions of a given formal model. After all, an evaluation of alternative models provides us with a theoretical substitute for the rejected model, something that an assessment of a single formal model does not provide. First, however, we need to determine if the alternative models truly are contrasting explanations with sets of assumptions that are inconsistent with each other. Sometimes testing alternative models provides less insight than devising a more expansive theoretical formal model and evaluating the predictions of that model. Thus, the decision to assess a formal model against an alternative model or models is not always the best choice and should be carefully evaluated.

In other cases the models are contrasting, with sets of assumptions that are inconsistent with each other and distinct predictions. Yet in most situations models have more complex relationships – are both substitutes and complements – and testing between them is more difficult and less likely to yield conclusive results. Finally, some alternatives to formal models are "nonformal" models. How should empirical analysis be constructed with both formal and nonformal explanations tested together? Before dealing with these issues, I first present an example of an empirical analysis that shows how two seemingly alternative models may actually be special cases of a general model.

8.1 Alternatives or Not?

The formal literature on the motives of campaign contributors presents two standard views. One perspective sees campaign contributions as "position-induced," in which contributions are given in order to help preferred elected officials achieve victory. That is, a contributor gives to candidates in order to see candidates elected who are most likely to make policy decisions that he prefers. In policy-induced models of campaign contributions, candidates choose positions in policy space, interest groups give campaign contributions to the candidates whose positions they most prefer, and the contributions are then used somehow by the candidates to induce voters to vote for them.[1] The other strand in the literature is that contributions are given as a quid pro quo for "services" from or "access" to elected officials – that is, they are "service-induced." The connection with policy, if there is one, is typically unclear.[2] Thus it appears that we have two alternative models of why campaign contributions are provided.

McCarty and Rothenberg (1996) argue that interest groups give campaign contributions for both reasons. Rather than posit that these two explanations are at odds, these authors consider how theoretically both purposes might interact in determining the campaign contributions of an interest group. In their formal model they assume two interest groups and an incumbent legislator.[3] They assume that interest groups give contributions for two reasons: to elect representatives that they prefer on a policy dimension and in order to receive access after election. They model the electorally motivated contributions as occurring prior to the election and model contributions for access as occurring after the election. They also assume that access-motivated contributions are independent of the policy position that motivates electoral contributions. They note that their previous empirical work supports the assumption that contributions for access occur after the election.[4] Furthermore, they assume that the interest groups have incomplete information about each other's value for access and thus solve for a perfect Bayesian–Nash equilibrium. Note that they use this concept to reduce the number of equilibria, as discussed in Chapter 6 (see Morrow 1994 for more detail on this equilibrium concept).

In solving for the equilibrium expected total contributions for an interest group to the incumbent (denoted as $E(y_{ij})$, with y_{ij} the total campaign contributions of group i for candidate j), McCarty and Rothenberg show

---

[1] How contributions actually motivate voters is the weakest point in these models, as discussed in Chapter 1. See also Morton and Cameron (1992).

[2] See Baron and Mo (1993) for an attempt to incorporate both policy and service in a model of campaign contributions.

[3] They note that expanding the number of interest groups will not change the qualitative results of the model.

[4] The contribution and access levels after the election are assumed to be determined via a noncooperative bargaining game between the interest groups and the incumbent.

that their model's assumptions result in the predicted relationships summarized by their equation (11):

$$E(y_{ij}) = E(x_i^a \mid \lambda) + E(x_i^e \mid C, \lambda, g_i),$$

where $E(\cdot)$ is the expected value of the relevant variable; x_i^a is the access contribution of group i, which is increasing in λ (a parameter of the distribution of types of interest groups with higher values of λ means that the interest groups are more likely to place a greater weight on contributing to the incumbent); x_i^e is the electoral contribution from group i, which is decreasing in C (the electoral conditions that are orthogonal to campaign spending) and increasing in g_i (group i's utility from policy from re-electing the incumbent, which can be positive or negative).

McCarty and Rothenberg find that the predicted effect of λ on $E(x_i^e)$ is ambiguous. Intuitively, this is because as λ increases there are two effects on campaign contributions that work at cross-purposes. An increase in λ may lead to more contributions since access to the incumbent has a higher value; however, an increase in λ may also lead to free riding of some interest groups on the contributions of high–access demand types.

The theoretical contribution of equation (11) is that the factors responsible for access-induced campaign contributions are also determinants of electorally induced campaign contributions. That is, changes in conditions that affect access contributions also affect the contributions that are motivated for electoral reasons. Moreover, the effect is interactive. If an incumbent has a sufficiently high probability of re-election – independent of any interest group's campaign contribution – we expect that the only contributions the incumbent receives will be access-motivated. Note that this effect occurs even though McCarty and Rothenberg have assumed that the access services are independent of policy positions.

One nice aspect of McCarty and Rothenberg's equation (11) is that it can be easily translated (with the addition of a random term) into an estimable equation in an empirical model; hence the formal model is viewed as a Partial DGP. The authors assume that the randomness is due to measurement problems in the data for the empirical analysis and not to randomness in the model's actors, who choose deterministically and are able to measure all terms exactly. Thus they do not re-solve the model for a QRE, for example. That is, we can rewrite equation (11) as follows:

$$y_{ij} = \beta_1 \mathbf{X}_{ij} + \beta_2 \mathbf{E}_j + \beta_3 \mathbf{E}_j \mathbf{X}_{ij} + \varepsilon_{ij},$$

where $\mathbf{X}_{ij}$ is the set of variables related to interest group i's expected demand for access (a set of instruments for λ and g_i), $\mathbf{E}_j$ is the set of variables related to the electoral conditions facing incumbent j, and ε_{ij} is a random variable.

The hypotheses McCarty and Rothenberg evaluate with their empirical model are the predictions that (1) the interaction terms are significant and consequential and thus that electoral and access contributions are related rather than independent; and (2) short-run electoral conditions largely explain the contribution patterns. The first hypothesis is a comparative static prediction that the total campaign contributions are affected significantly by the interaction of access and electoral motivations. The second hypothesis is an assumption of the model that short-run factors are important in explaining campaign contributions. The authors assess the model using data on large PAC contributions to members of Congress during the 1993–94 electoral cycle (they use a Tobit model for estimation).

McCarty and Rothenberg find that a large amount of the variability in contributions is explained by the interaction terms. As they note:

findings concerning seniority for corporate and trade PACs echo the results for committee membership. More junior members who were in trouble received substantially less in the way of financial resources than their more senior colleagues (to whom access is presumably more valuable for the groups). Indeed, a typical freshman seeking re-election receives about the same from corporate and trade PACs regardless of whether they occupy a safe seat or one that is a toss-up. By contrast, a member of Congress with twice the average level of seniority (18 as compared to 9 years) gets about a 70 percent larger corporate PAC contribution and about a 20 percent greater trade PAC donation when a seat is a toss-up rather than safe. (1996, p. 21)

Hence, they find support for their comparative static prediction.

This example illustrates the negative and positive sides of investigating comparative static predictions. As McCarty and Rothenberg admit, "our means of investigating our model's worth do not involve classical hypothesis testing. Rather, nonsignificant findings for the interaction terms specified – or substantially inconsequential if statistically significant results – would lead us to reject our view of the contribution process" (1996, n. 21). The point is that they do not provide an alternative model that would support the alternative hypothesis to their proposed hypothesis. As with all evaluations of predictions of models – whether point, comparative static, or dynamic – inconclusive results suggest further theorizing rather than providing support for an already existing alternative model.

However, their work also shows the limits of a view that there are competing interest-group motivations for providing campaign contributions. That is, an alternative empirical tactic might have been to take the existing theoretical literature with the different assumptions about interest-group motivations and test between these two approaches as in competing models. Of course, such an empirical strategy would have hidden the possibility that the motivations are interactive. This example highlights an interesting case: where devising a new formal model that incorporates both theoretical assumptions is more useful than assuming the two original models are in conflict and attempting to test between them. The comparative static assessment, though not classical, is more informative than a classical hypothesis test based on alternative models.

8.2   Contrasting Explanations

Testing between alternative models is not problematic when it is clear that the models have sets of assumptions that are inconsistent with each other and make distinct predictions. However, the comparison is not simple. The problems lie in the construction of the empirical model or models to be used for the comparison process. Ideally, we would take each formal model as a Complete DGP, evaluate each model with a given data set, and compare the models' abilities to explain the data. The formal model that performs the best would be considered superior. But even this ideal process is unlikely to yield definitive answers. That is, the comparison would still hold only for the data set used. The researchers would then need to expand their analyses to further data sets.

In this section I furnish three examples of assessments of contrasting formal models. In the first example, a researcher views each formal model as a Complete DGP and compares the empirical success of the two models in a general sense for the data set used. The two models differ in their assumptions about the way in which players in a public goods game form expectations: in one model, the players form rational expectations; in the other, players ignore important strategic aspects of the game. The second and third examples are cases of researchers viewing each model as a Partial DGP.

8.2.1   *Comparing Models as Complete DGPs: QRE versus QRNB*

In Chapter 6 I discussed the empirical analysis of Offerman (1996). Offerman assesses the ability of QRE to explain data in a series of public good experiments, and he compares the results from the QRE estimation with an alternative model, Quantal Response Naive Bayesian Model (QRNB). QRNB is like QRE in that the players try to make choices that maximize their expected utility but fall prey to errors. The difference between QRE and QRNB is that, in QRNB, the players adapt their expectations nonstrategically, like "naive Bayesians." Offerman describes naive Bayesians as follows: "The adjective 'naive' refers to the property of the model that players neglect strategic aspects of the interaction. The model is general in the sense that it can be applied to any discrete choice game without the introduction of additional auxiliary assumptions. This model has been used by Brandts and Holt (1992) for signaling games and by Eichberger (1995) and Eichberger, Haller, and Milne (1993) for various two-player games" (1996, p. 51). The model is thus an example of behavioral game theory, as discussed in Chapter 3. In QRNB the players do update their expectations based on observed behavior of errors, but they do not recognize that the other players may be engaging in similar strategic calculations. The players make quantal responses and, as in QRE, these responses are functions of λ.

Specifically, in QRNB each player expects each other group member to contribute to the public good with probability θ and the individuals' priors are that θ has a uniform distribution. Denote s_k as the sum of a player's observations of other group members' former play. The posterior distribution on θ is a beta distribution. According to QRNB an individual will contribute with probability p_c^B as follows:

$$ p_c^B = \frac{1}{1 + e^{\lambda[c - (f(s) - c) \times g(s - 1 \mid s_k)]}}, $$

where c is the cost of contributing, $f(s)$ is the value of the public good, s is the number of contributors, and $g(y \mid s_k)$ is the density of the predictive distribution for a new observation y.

As with QRE, because the players make quantal responses, the formal model incorporates explicit assumptions about the randomness that may be observed in the data. QRNB can be viewed as a Complete DGP. Thus it is possible to compare the two formal models with the same data set. Offerman argues as follows.

A comparison of the likelihood of the data under both models can be interpreted as giving information about the likelihood of the expectations predicted by either model. Given that people give quantal responses, is it more likely that their expectations are generated by the QRE model or by the QRNB model? Second, it is useful to recognize that the *random* model is nested in a similar way in both models. According to the random model a decision maker chooses either alternative with probability

$\frac{1}{2}$. The restriction $\lambda = 0$ in either the QRE model or the QRNB model yields this random model. The exercise of comparing the likelihoods of the models may thus be interpreted as a search for the answer to the following question: under which model does the rationality parameter λ add most to the likelihood of the data, using the random model as the benchmark? (1996, p. 148)

Nevertheless, even in this case the comparison of the two models is not as straightforward as it sounds. In Chapter 6 we noted that there are multiple equilibria in the QRE model; QRNB, however, gives a unique equilibrium prediction. As discussed in Chapter 6, Offerman uses a procedure that evaluates the equilibrium predictions of QRE with the data and chooses the fit that gives QRE its best shot. Offerman then uses this best-shot version of QRE to compare with QRNB. He finds that QRNB is superior in that its predictions more nearly match the data in almost all of the experiments.

8.2.2   *Comparing Models as Partial DGPs*

Offerman's comparison of QRE and QRNB predictions shows how alternative models can be compared, assuming the models are Complete DGPs. Yet this ideal process is rarely used to evaluate competing formal models. Typically, a researcher takes each formal model as a Partial DGP and then compares the analysis of the two formal models. Oftentimes the researcher perceives this as the only choice, since there may be variables that are assumed constant in the formal models that are not constant in the data set and this will likely affect the analysis. Also, measurement error may exist that could bias the analysis toward one model over another. The estimation procedure, which makes assumptions about the distribution of the data, can further complicate the comparison. Thus, such issues as how the data are measured, what other variables should be included in the empirical analysis, and what estimation procedure is to be used can be important in comparing two or more models even when the models make clearly contrasting assumptions or predictions. All of these important factors place limits on our ability to use the comparison to either discard or accept a formal model.

This section presents two examples of this type of analysis from the spatial voting literature. One tests the Hotelling–Downsian median voter theorem versus a number of models that predict nonconvergence of candidate positions; the other tests between two models of how voters vote, directional theory versus proximity theory. The first is a test of alternative predictions, the second a test of alternative assumptions. These examples demonstrate many of the difficulties that can arise in measuring data, in determining what other variables to include, and in estimation procedures when comparing alternative models.

Convergence versus Divergence: Contrasting Predictions.

The Formal Models. As is well known and noted (perhaps ad nauseam) in earlier chapters, the traditional Hotelling–Downsian model of two-candidate competition predicts convergence at the ideal point of the voter who is at the median in the distribution of preferences.[5] A number of alternative models have been devised using different assumptions that yield the contrary prediction that candidates will diverge in position. For example:

1. Palfrey (1984) adds a third candidate and demonstrates that, with sincere voting and candidates who maximize votes, the two major candidates who choose positions first will diverge;
2. Bernhardt and Ingberman (1985) present a dynamic model in which incumbents are restricted in movement in the policy space by their previous positions and so, as voter preferences change over time, the candidates diverge;
3. Morton (1987) demonstrates that different (and perhaps more realistic) assumptions about the shape of voter preference functions can lead to divergence;
4. Austen-Smith (1987) and Cameron and Enelow (1992) show that asymmetric policy effects on voters or campaign contributors can lead to divergence,
5. Ingberman and Villani (1993) explain divergence as the consequence of multiple government institutions and risk averse parties;
6. Feddersen (1992) establishes that, with purely strategic voters and costly voting, policy-minded voters will choose two distinct positions.

The most popular approach, however, is to assume that candidates have policy motives (or are selected by party elites with policy preferences); then, with probabilistic voting, candidates diverge in position. For example, see Aldrich (1983), Aldrich and McGinnis (1989), Calvert (1985), and Wittman (1977, 1983, 1990). The important point is that all of these approaches involve different assumptions than those contained in the Hotelling–Downsian

---

[5] There are a number of specialized assumptions necessary for this conclusion. See Enelow and Hinich (1984) and Hinich and Munger (1997).

model, and all make a contrary prediction – that candidates diverge in policy positions.

The Empirical Models. Schmidt et al. (1996) test between the two predictions using 1962–90 data on senators' decisions to seek re-election and the likelihood of success. Their empirical analysis is similar to much of the traditional nonformal-model based empirical analysis in political science. Since a large number of formal models make the theoretical prediction of divergence, it does not make sense to think of the formal models as anything but Partial DGPs. Thus, while the empirical analysis can provide support (or not) for the divergence prediction as compared with the convergence prediction, it cannot be said to be supportive of any one particular formal model. The empirical analysis is useful, but it is not an evaluation of a model; rather, it is an evaluation of the predictions of a number of models as compared with the convergence prediction.

Schmidt et al. construct four sets of empirical models to evaluate the two predictions. Two sets of empirical models are logit estimates of a senator's decision to run for re-election (Running Logits) and the other two are logit estimates of a senator's chances for winning re-election (Winning Logits). The empirical models assume that voters vote retrospectively for senators based on their policy choices while in office. The Running and Winning Logits are further divided into two sets each: one set has as an independent variable the distance between the senator's policy position and the predicted position of her state's party (Distance to Party) while the other set has as an independent variable the distance between her policy position and the predicted position of her state's median voter's ideal point (Distance to Median). The empirical models also have a number of independent variables that are used to control for factors (e.g., senator's age and measures of party success in the Senate and the state) that are considered constant in the underlying theoretical models but may affect the empirical model's dependent variables. In the empirical analysis, the authors estimate divergent predicted party positions by state for each senator. These are estimated by running separate regressions for each state predicting ADA scores over time. States were omitted from the analysis if their two-party competition was not strong enough in the years examined to estimate the predicted party positions. The median voter positions were constructed by a weighted average (based on party dominance) of the predicted party positions.

The Empirical Results. In the Running Logits, the Distance to
Party variable is significant with a *t*-statistic of −3.25 while the Distance to
Median variable is insignificant with a *t*-statistic of 0.19, strong support for
the divergence prediction. In the Winning Logits, however, both variables
are significant (although Distance to Party has a higher *t*-statistic). A comparison of the two predictions in the Winning Logits overall success shows
that the divergent platform prediction explains approximately 50% of the
variation in the dependent variable whereas the convergence prediction explains approximately 18% of the variation.

In order to test more formally between the two alternative explanations,
the researchers use the J-test for nonnested models (proposed by Davidson
and MacKinnon 1981). Schmidt et al. explain the test as follows.

> To perform this test for the seeking re-election logits [Running Logits], first pre-
> dicted values are generated from the ... best specifications of the two competing
> models explaining the decision to run. Each of the logits is then re-estimated with
> the predicted values from the competing model as an additional regressor. When a
> variable representing the predicted values from the median voter model is included
> in the divergent platform model, its coefficient is insignificant with a *t*-statistic of
> 1.29, indicating that we cannot reject the null hypothesis that the divergent plat-
> form hypothesis is the correct model. When the predicted values from the divergent
> platform model are included in the median voter model, the coefficient is highly sig-
> nificant with a *t*-statistic of 4.03. We therefore reject the null hypothesis that the
> median voter model is the correct model. These two results suggest that the diver-
> gent platform hypothesis is superior to the median voter hypothesis for the purposes
> of explaining a senator's decision to run for office. It should be noted that our results
> are quite strong since the J-test often gives "significant" and inconsistently signed
> *t*-statistics. Similar results are obtained when the J-test is applied to explaining who
> wins re-election.[6] (1996, p. 564)

Limitations of the Analysis. Thus, the pure Hotelling–Downsian
approach is rejected. However, Schmidt et al. do not test between the number of competing formal models that can explain the divergence. Moreover,
these alternative models are themselves all revisions or extensions of the
original Hotelling–Downsian model. Hence, it is difficult to truly call this
an evaluation of competing models, even though one modeling approach
was deemed more empirically relevant than the other. The rejection of the

---

[6] A similar analysis by Francis et al. (1994) on the decisions of House members to run for the
Senate and to be selected as their party's nominee also supports divergence over convergence
in candidate positions.

Hotelling–Downsian approach is limited to the extreme version that predicts convergence.

While the results yield support for the alternative models in a general sense, they do not clarify which approach is more likely to explain the observed divergence. Suppose that we wish to distinguish between two of the prominent explanations of divergence, Palfrey's entry model and the Aldrich–Calvert–Wittman policy preferences approach. Which model is the right answer? How can we tell? There are two ways of evaluating the two models. One way is to weigh them theoretically. Which model is more general, less restrictive in its assumptions, closer to the "real world"? Even though we know that neither model can be perfect, we can evaluate the validity of each in a comparison; we can consider the logical consistency of the arguments of the two approaches. Both have significant theoretical problems. The policy-mindedness story does not explain the initial distribution of candidate or party policy preferences (they just happen to be on opposite sides of the median voter) or why the uncertainty exists that is necessary for the divergent outcome. The entry story does not explain why voters vote sincerely when strategic voting might be more rational or why the entrant, who always loses, bothers to enter at all. This sort of evaluation is difficult and highly idiosyncratic, depending upon researcher biases over initial assumptions.

Alternatively, we can evaluate the two models empirically. Both models predict platform divergence, but the causes of the divergence should mean that divergence will vary in different cases in the two models. If entry is a cause of divergence, then we should find more divergence when entry of third parties is more likely. For example, states vary in the ability of third parties and candidates to get on the ballot in local and state elections; hence, states with looser controls should have a two-party system that exhibits greater divergence than states with strong controls over entry. This effect is not likely to be observed if entry is not a cause. On the other hand, if policy-mindedness is a cause of platform divergence, then we should expect that the wider the divergence in the average preferences between parties, the greater the divergence of the two parties' platforms from each other. Since the entry model assumes that all parties care about winning the most votes, this relation should not be observed if entry is the major cause of divergence, in which case parties would converge regardless of policy preferences. A comparative state study of entry controls and the policy preferences of party members may yield some answers as to the relative value of the two proposed theoretical explanations.

Unfortunately, there is not enough of this type of empirical analysis. There is a tendency for formal modelers to focus on one explanation at a time rather than constructing the kind of cross-model tests advocated here. For example, the study just suggested has not, to my knowledge, been conducted.[7] We see much more comparative static investigation of one model's predictions than comparisons of two or more models' comparative static predictions.

Direction versus Proximity: Contrasting Assumptions.

The Directional Theory of Voting. A voting choice model that has been proposed as an alternative to the Hotelling–Downsian approach is the directional theory of voting, as presented in Rabinowitz and Macdonald (1989) and in Macdonald, Listhaug, and Rabinowitz (1991). In standard spatial voting models as described so far, voters' preferences are assumed to be based on the proximity of the parties' or candidates' positions on the issues to their own most preferred position. The closer a candidate's or party's position is to a voter's ideal point, the more that voter prefers that candidate or party. Typically the choices are presented as points on a continuous policy space. For example, the issue may be abortion policy. In most formulations of the Hotelling–Downsian model, the assumption would be that there are an infinite number of variations in the degree of legalization of abortion over which parties or candidates may vary. Macdonald et al. label these assumptions "proximity theory" of voter preference. Notice that here we discuss voter preferences rather than actual choices, which may be strategic in a Hotelling–Downsian model and so lead voters to choose candidates or parties who are not closest to them in the issue space. Moreover, some spatial voting models allow for asymmetric voter preference functions that in some cases would also imply voters preferring candidates who are farther than other candidates from their ideal points.

Macdonald et al. submit that voters do not evaluate candidates in continuous policy space. Rather, they posit that voters see issues as dichotomous.

---

[7] Gerber and Morton (1998) find that, in states with closed primary systems (greater party control over nominations), elected members of Congress diverge more from the median voter's position in their district. This finding supports the policy preference approach.

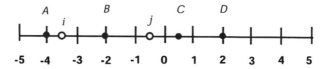

Figure 8.1. Directional theory compared with proximity theory.

For example, voters are argued to perceive abortion in terms of two extremes: widely legalized abortion versus highly restricted abortion. Voters evaluate candidates or parties based on the direction that the candidate or party chooses on an issue. Policy gradations are not factors in voter preferences, in this view. When surveys ask voters to place parties or candidates on a linear scale, Macdonald et al. contend that the values represent "intensity" of the parties' or candidates' direction rather than an actual policy position in voter minds. Voters evaluate parties and candidates on the basis of this direction and intensity. First, a voter chooses between parties or candidates based on whether the parties or candidates are perceived to choose policies in the voter's preferred direction; then, the voter chooses the party or candidate whose position is more intense in that direction (when two or more parties or candidates are perceived to choose policies in the direction preferred by the voter). The researchers operationalize this by arguing that the utility any one voter associates with each of a set of parties increases monotonically with the product of the voter and party positions. Note that in directional theory there is also an assumed region of acceptability for all voters such that voters penalize candidates or parties who are perceived to be too extreme.

Directional Theory Compared with Proximity Theory. Figure 8.1 illustrates how voters' preferences differ under the two models. Under proximity theory, all the points on the line segment between -5 and 5 represent possible positions on a unidimensional policy space. Assume that a voter places four parties (A, B, C, and D) at -4, -2, 0.5, and 2, respectively. If the voter places himself at point $i = -3.5$ then, according to proximity theory, his preference ordering is given by $A \succ B \succ C \succ D$ (where $M \succ N$ means that M is preferred to N). A voter who places herself at point $j = -0.5$ has the preference ordering $C \succ B \succ D \succ A$. Under directional theory, the line segment does not represent points on a continuous policy space but rather intensity positions. The point 0 is a level of zero intensity for either direction. Points less than 0 reflect intensity levels for policy at the left end of the scale, points above 0 reflect intensity levels for policy at the right end of the scale. We will assume that all these points are within the region of acceptability. A voter who places himself at point $i = -3.5$ has the same preference ordering as under proximity theory, $A \succ B \succ C \succ D$. However, a voter who places herself at a less extreme point such as $j' = 0.5$ has a preference ordering under directional theory that is significantly different from that under proximity theory – that is, $A \succ B \succ C \succ D$, which is the same as a voter who places herself at point i. The two models, then, make very different assumptions about voter preferences. Notice that these different assumptions concern the voter's intrapersonal comparisons over a set of parties or candidates.

The preference orderings can be expressed mathematically for multidimensional space as follows.

Directional model: rank-order$(U_{iA}, U_{iB}, \ldots, U_{iM}) =$
                     rank-order$(\mathbf{i} \cdot A - P_{iA}, \mathbf{i} \cdot B - P_{iB}, \ldots, \mathbf{i} \cdot M - P_{iM})$;

Proximity model: rank-order$(U_{iA}, U_{iB}, \ldots, U_{iM}) =$
                     rank-order$(-d_{iA}, -d_{iB}, \ldots, -d_{iM})$.

Here $\mathbf{i} \cdot \mathbf{K}$ is the scalar product of voter i's placement on the issue scales and party K's issue stands; P_{iK} is voter i's extremeness penalty on party K (the penalty is 0 if party K is within the region of acceptability); and d_{iK} is the distance between voter i's placement and party K's issue stand. Macdonald et al. argue that the models also make distinctive predictions about party and candidate locations and voting outcomes.

An Empirical Comparison.   Most empirical evaluations that have compared the two models feature the differences in assumptions concerning voter preferences. However, as noted by Westholm, the vast majority of these tests involve interpersonal rather than intrapersonal preference comparisons.

In the prototypical case, the evaluation scores for each party or candidate are analyzed separately, so that all the variation is contained between rather than within individuals. In some cases, pooled analyses combining evaluation scores for multiple parties or candidates are also reported. Yet since no attempt is made to isolate the intrapersonal element in these analyses, they become for all practical purposes just another interpersonal comparison. (1997, p. 868)

Westholm argues that a more appropriate comparison of the two models would examine the data on intrapersonal preferences. To see the difference,

Table 8.1. *Voter utilities* (minimum, 0; maximum, 100)

	Party A	Party B
Voter 1	70	60
Voter 2	40	50

consider the voter utilities (from Westholm) listed in Table 8.1. Assume that the maximum evaluation scale is 100 (minimum is 0). A comparison across columns for a given row is an intrapersonal comparison, whereas a comparison across rows for a given column is an interpersonal comparison. Westholm contends that the best way to compare the theories is to conduct the following analysis.

The theories predict that the rank order of the dependent variable *within* individuals should match the corresponding rank order of the independent one. Hence, all we have to do in order to assess the fit is to transform the data to intrapersonal ranks and then compute the correlation between them (Spearman's rho applied intrapersonally). (1997, p. 869 [italics in original])

The problem with empirically comparing the two assumptions of voter preferences is that the two models are highly correlated; in many cases, they make the same prediction. Using a 1989 Norwegian election study of voter evaluations of parties in the Sorting elections, Westholm finds that the intrapersonal rank-order correlation between party evaluation and proximity is 0.55 and 0.49 between party evaluation and the scalar product. Although the difference is statistically significant, it is clear that the measures are strongly intercorrelated.

Westholm asserts that the solution is to compare the models using interval-level measures, which requires more specific assumptions about the functional form than required by the theory. That is, the empirical model assumes that preferences are specifically linear rather than only monotonically increasing. Westholm estimates a number of variations on the following empirical model with the same Norwegian data:

$$Y_{ik} - \bar{Y}_i = b_p(X_{ik}^p - \bar{X}_i^p) + b_d(X_{ik}^d - \bar{X}_i^d) + u_{ik},$$

where Y_{ik} is voter i's evaluation of party k, $\bar{Y}_i$ is voter i's mean evaluation across all parties, X_{ik}^p is the score of voter i for party k on the proximity model, $\bar{X}_i^p$ is the mean for voter i across parties on the proximity model, X_{ik}^d is the score of voter i for party k on the directional model, $\bar{X}_i^d$ is the mean for voter i across parties on the directional model, and u_{ik} is the random term.

Westholm faces a number of measurement issues in conducting the empirical analysis. In particular, how should the distances in multidimensional issue space be calculated in the empirical analysis? The two alternatives, Euclidean distance and city-block distance, are both compatible with each theory.

$$\text{City-block distance:}\quad \sum_{k=1}^{n} |i_k - j_k|;$$

$$\text{Euclidean distance:}\quad \sqrt{\sum_{k=1}^{n} (i_k - j_k)^2}.$$

Westholm chooses the city-block measure for three reasons: (1) the implied information processing for individuals is less; (2) the transition from unidimensional to multidimensional issue spaces is parallel in the two theories; and (3) the empirical estimation from the city-block method is linear in unconstrained estimations (the estimation using the Euclidean measure is nonlinear). Thus, in order to conduct the empirical analysis, Westholm must make particular restrictive assumptions on the functional form of the voter preference functions. The empirical model is more restrictive in its assumptions about voter preferences than *either* underlying formal model. Such restrictions are often necessary, as Westholm persuasively argues, but it is important to recognize that they limit our ability to conclude that the resulting analysis is a definitive comparison of the two formal models. Moreover, we must be careful that the assumptions necessitated by empirical analysis do not bias the comparison in favor of one or more of the competing formal models.

Westholm finds support for the proximity assumptions over the directional assumptions. This is in contrast to the work by Macdonald et al., who test between the two models' preference assumptions using the same basic data but measured differently. That is, Macdonald et al. use an interpersonal comparison of voters, mean party placements rather than individual mean placements for interval measures, and Euclidean (or squared Euclidean) distance measures for proximity rather than the absolute-value distance measures of Westholm. Westholm's test between directional and proximity theory is just one of many such investigations, and the analysis here is certainly not a full review of these empirical tests. The interested reader should examine the empirical work of Macdonald and colleagues as well as a number of symposium papers in the January 1997 issue of *Journal of Theoretical Politics.*

It should also be noted that an evaluation of the two models' assumptions is not as straightforward as the comparison summarized in this section. First, if we estimate the region of acceptability as well as testing the two models, then the prior lack of specification means that observations that seem to violate assumptions of the directional model can be explained by manipulating the boundaries of the acceptability region and the size of the penalty. Even if we assume that the region is the same across all voters, there still is substantial flexibility, which makes the model's assumptions less precise and thus less refutable and comparable to the proximity theory.

Implications.   The analyses of Westholm and Macdonald et al. illustrate how differences in empirical models' assumptions can lead to drastically different conclusions about the relative merit of two formal models. The difference in results arises when we move from the formal model to its empirical interpretation. Because the models' assumptions differ in how voters make intrapersonal comparisons, it follows that we should test which models' assumptions fit observed intrapersonal comparisons. Moving to an empirical model also requires explicit and restrictive assumptions about how we estimate proximity, the intervals for measurement, and the region of acceptability and corresponding penalty values. In this case, some of these assumptions may make one model a better predictor than another. Westholm argues that absolute-value measures of proximity yield a better-fitting proximity model than Euclidean measures, so that using Euclidean measures stacks the deck in favor of directional theory. Similarly, estimations of the region of acceptability and the penalty values may affect the ability of directional theory to explain the data. Ideally, the empirical model should not be biased toward one model over another. If such biases exist, they should be acknowledged explicitly when evaluating the results.

8.3   Dimensions of Comparability

Not all alternative models are clearly part of a general model or completely contrasting explanations. In many cases the models that are being considered are somewhere in between the two, similar in some dimensions but contrasting in others. In the examples of the previous section, the models compared also had similarities. The key in testing between alternative models is to determine how they differ *and* the significance of the difference. If the difference between the alternative models is not significant empirically, then either (or neither) model is acceptable as an explanation. Ideally, true alternative models have differences that are significant empirically. Below we present two examples of evaluations of alternative models from the literature on bureaucracy to illustrate how essential differences between models can be identified and assessed. These examples also illustrate how it is important to devise an empirical model that is general enough such that one particular model is not advantaged over another.

8.3.1   *Principal–Agent Models and Bureaucrats*

Just as the archtypical public good game captures a ubiquitous feature of many political situations, the principal–agent problem is also pervasive. That is, agents may not always do what principals desire either because of moral hazard problems (i.e., agents shirk and perform at lower levels than preferred) or because of adverse selection problems (i.e., agents differ in their abilities to perform and principals have imperfect knowledge of particular agent types). One of the empirical questions of Schmidt et al.'s (1996) study of senator positions concerns the ability of voters as principals to use retrospective voting and control their agents (the senators). (Schmidt et al. 1996 also review the theoretical literature on principal–agency problems in elections.) Principal–agent models have also been applied to the study of the public bureaucracies. These models make somewhat conflicting predictions – as noted by Brehm and Gates (1993), who empirically test between these alternative models.

The Theories. Brehm and Gates (1993) examine empirically the predictions of three versions of principal–agent models: production by teams (Holmstrom 1982), an iterated version of production by teams (Bianco and Bates 1990), and the trust/honor game of Kreps (1990) and Miller (1992). The Holmstrom model is a one-shot model in which managers must supervise a set of agents whose productivity is a function of total effort. Holmstrom shows that, with complete information, a manager can use rewards and punishments to the group as a whole in order to achieve a Nash cooperative equilibrium. When information is incomplete, managers can use monitoring of the group as well as rewards and punishment to achieve cooperation.

Bianco and Bates iterate the Holmstrom model and allow for two manager types, "limited" managers (as in Holmstrom) and "enhanced" managers, who can set incentives for individuals rather than just groups. One complication of the Bianco and Bates model is that, because the game is repeated infinitely, cooperation is possible even without a leader.[8] However, they argue that cooperation is more likely when leaders use rewards and punishments (as in Holmstrom) and when leaders are enhanced rather than limited.

Kreps and Miller examine the contracting problem between principals and agents. Is it possible for a principal to design a contract that would alleviate the principal–agent problem in a game where the principal must "trust" that the agent will make a choice that benefits the principal even when some alternative is less costly for the agent? If the game is one-shot, Kreps and Miller argue that it is impossible to devise an enforceable and efficient contract that overcomes the principal–agent problem. If the game is repeated, then (as in Bianco and Bates) there are likely to be many equilibria, some of which will be cooperative. Kreps contends that, in selection over equilibria, focal points are important; Miller argues that cultural norms and conventions in organizations will determine the equilibria on which individuals will "focus." Thus, the Kreps–Miller model predicts (a) that shirking is related to adherence to a cultural norm for defection whereas nonshirking is related to a norm of cooperation and (b) that conformity among agents depends on the network of associations among the agents. Note that these networks can lead to either cooperation or defection. Furthermore, supervisory resources result in less shirking by agents when agents adhere to a cooperative cultural norm than otherwise.

Differences in Predictions. Comparing these three models empirically is not straightforward. As noted before, the models have multiple equilibria and make many similar predictions. The empirical analysis, as with Schmidt et al., cannot be evaluations of any of the particular formal models as a Complete DGP. Instead, the empirical comparison must focus on differences that do exist between the models and on the extent to which the empirical evidence supports one model versus another. There is a key distinction in these three models: those of Holmstrom and Bianco–Bates differ from the Kreps and Miller models in their emphasis on the role of leaders versus internal

---

[8] The agents acting alone can use strategies that induce each other to cooperate when the game is repeated infinitely and the discount rate is low. See the discussion of repetition in Chapter 6.

norms and on networks among agents in solving principal–agent problems. Brehm and Gates (1993) stress this difference in their empirical examination. They use a data set of observations of police officer work patterns (conducted in Washington, Boston, and Chicago in 1966) to test between the alternative models. The dependent variable in the empirical model is the degree of shirking by the police officers. In order to test between the theoretical predictions, the researchers use independent variables such as the degree of professionalism, dislike for duties of the job, dislike for other officers on the job, positive attitudes toward other officers, and satisfaction with superiors.

Specifying the Empirical Model. In devising the empirical model to test between the three principal–agent models, Brehm and Gates wish to use an empirical model whose assumptions about the nature of the relationship between independent and dependent variables do not bias the empirical estimation in favor of one of the models. Because of this possibility, they do not wish to use standard OLS estimation procedures. They explain the dilemma as follows.

Our most important reason is that the shape of the distribution of compliance implied by each model may vary significantly from the unimodal, symmetric normal distribution. Some principal–agency models lead to strong predictions about the possible shape of distribution of compliance for which some of the models predict very skewed outcomes: the Holmstrom and Bianco and Bates models assert that most subordinates comply given sufficient effort by the supervisor. One possible outcome of Miller's model implies that we could see two different camps of subordinate compliance, anchored at opposite extremes by competing organizational cultures. Of course, a rival hypothesis is that nothing a supervisor or a subordinate does really influences the subordinates' compliance. A general empirical model of compliance must be flexible enough to account for these variations in the shape of the distribution. (1993, pp. 566–7)

The beta distribution is flexible enough to allow for a general specification. Notice that, because the researchers are evaluating comparative differences from distinctly different formal models, their empirical estimation more nearly follows the trend in general empirical methodology of using the least restrictive estimation procedure possible. In contrast to empirical estimation – where hypotheses arise from nonformal models and the desire for an unrestricted estimation procedure is partly an attempt to "let the data speak for itself" – in this case the less restrictive empirical estimation procedure is desirable so that the different models can be compared without bias.

Therefore, Brehm and Gates estimate their empirical model using the beta distribution. They find some evidence that cultural norms and networks among agents explain the levels of shirking: professionalism negatively affects shirking, as does an officer's "liking" for his job.[9] The empirical analysis of Brehm and Gates shows how one can distinguish between models that make similar predictions as well as the importance of using an empirical estimation procedure that does not bias the analysis in favor of one of the models.

8.3.2   Bureaus and Budgetary Control

The research examined so far focuses on the abilities of lower-level managers to overcome principal–agent problems. A significant body of research in political science addresses the extent to which the federal bureaucracy (in particular, regulatory agencies) is controlled by the legislature and/or executive branch in a general sense. As Carpenter notes: "In the twentieth century, legislative and executive authority over an agency's budget – the proverbial 'power of the purse' – has emerged as one of the most forceful and frequently exercised tools of political control" (1996, p. 283). Although evidence exists that agencies do respond to budgetary control, Carpenter argues that there are a number of unanswered questions in the literature. In particular, he features three questions: (1) How does budgetary influence work within an agency? (2) Does the budget control lie more in presidential or legislative hands? (3) How efficient is the budget process as a tool of control? Carpenter's analysis of the first question involves a test of three competing models, whereas answers to the other two questions involve new empirical discovery, given a model of budget control. Thus, Carpenter tests competing models of budgetary control *and* provides new information through his analysis of how the branches of government interact and the efficiency of that interaction. In this section I highlight his analysis of the competing models.

The Empirical Models.   Carpenter identifies three theoretical models of the impact of budgetary influence within an agency. Carpenter begins with empirical models that he contends represent the theoretical assumptions of the three models. Thus, the empirical models are derived directly from known

---

[9] Brehm and Gates (1997) present a general theoretical model of the principal–agent problem that expands on this literature. With a more extensive data set, they then test their model's theoretical predictions.

assumptions of the three theories rather than explicitly from formal models. In all three of the empirical models, the underlying theoretical framework is viewed as a Partial DGP.

The first model, the *aggregate production* model, is based on the theoretical work of Bendor and Moe (1985). This formulation is used as the empirical model in much statistical study of budgetary control (see e.g. Wood and Anderson 1993; Wood and Waterman 1993):

$$Y_t = \alpha + \delta_1 BT_1 + \sum_{k=1}^{K} \beta_k \mathbf{X}_{kt} + \varepsilon_t,$$

"where Y_t is agency monitoring or enforcement behavior, BT_t is the agency's budget (in real dollars) for year t, $\mathbf{X}_{kt}$ is a set of K control variables (each of t observations), α, δ, and β_k are coefficient parameters to be estimated, and ε_t remains the equation disturbance term" (1996, p. 285). Carpenter maintains that this empirical model implicitly assumes that the level of the agency budget is a factor of production in a linear production function with constant returns to scale. Essentially, the focus in this theory is on the determination of the budget; the implicit assumption is that the agency's response is immediate.

The second model, the *serial updating* model, is based on the signaling model of Ferejohn and Shipan (1990):

$$Y_t = \alpha + \psi Y_{t-1} + \delta_2 \Delta BT_1 + \sum_{k=1}^{K} \beta_k \mathbf{X}_{kt} + \varepsilon_t,$$

"where Y_{t-1} is one-period lagged performance, $\Delta BT (= BT_t - BT_{t-1})$ is the yearly change in the agency's budget, ϕ and δ_2 require estimation" (1996, p. 286). The empirical model assumes that the change in the budget is the signal sent to the agency and that the agency updates its output level using a Bayesian updating procedure, where period t's output is a weighted average of the previous period and the budget signal. In this model, the agency responds under an implicit assumption of rational expectations.

The third model, proposed by Carpenter as an alternative to the other two, is called the *cascade processing* model:

$$Y_t = \alpha + \delta_3 \Gamma(m, \lambda) \kappa(L) \Delta BT_1 + \sum_{k=1}^{K} \beta_k \mathbf{X}_{kt} + \varepsilon_t,$$

where $\Gamma(m, \lambda)$ is the gamma function–density function (i.e., m = levels of hierarchy, where each level is a time-invariant linear system whose response time is independent of other levels, and λ is another parameter of the gamma with distribution assumed equal to 1) and $\kappa(L)$ is the distributed lag function (i.e., $\kappa(L)\Delta BT_1 = \Delta BT_1 + \Delta BT_{1-1} + \Delta BT_{1-2} + \cdots + \Delta BT_{1-k+1}$). Intuitively, the cascade processing model assumes (i) that agencies form expectations using an adaptive mechanism, rather than rational expectations; and (ii) that agencies are "engaged in the continuous-time processing of discrete-time signals" (p. 288). Hierarchy is included through a cascade formulation in which "the m levels of hierarchy are linked in sequential fashion such that the output of the highest level is the input to the second, the output of the second is the input to the third, and so on" (p. 288). Graphically, as the levels of hierarchy increase, the gamma function's shape dictates an increased agency response time to signals. Agencies in the serial model weight all past information equally, whereas agencies in the cascade model assign lower weights to older information.

The Empirical Estimation. In contrast to Schmidt et al., Carpenter estimates a single combined empirical model of the three models:

$$Y_t = \alpha\phi Y_{t-1} + \delta_1 BT_1 + \delta_2 \Delta BT_1$$

$$+\delta_3\Gamma(m,\lambda)\kappa(L)\Delta BT_1 + \sum_{k=1}^{K} \beta_k \mathbf{X}_{kt} + \varepsilon_t.$$

Carpenter uses data from the U.S. Food and Drug Administration (1938–90) and the Federal Communications Commission (1933–90) to evaluate the combined empirical model. Carpenter uses the simplest model of hierarchy (two levels), with $\lambda = 1$ and $m = 2$ in the analysis. As with Brehm and Gates, Carpenter wishes to use an estimation procedure that gives each theoretical specification its "best shot." He therefore uses the model construction approach on agenda criteria described in Granato (1991), explaining the procedure as follows.

I first enumerate all possible independent variables consistent with a prior causal model. Estimation of this initial model ensues, followed by application of a battery of diagnostic tests, principally the joint chi-squared statistic of Jarque and Bera (1980), which allows the researcher to test simultaneously for autocorrelation, heteroscedasticity, and nonnormal residuals. Once any violations of model assumptions have been corrected, model reduction follows, resulting in the elimination of all insignificant variables. I then diagnose and estimate this reduced model and report it alongside the initial version, along with some relevant diagnostic statistics. (1996, p. 290)

Using this procedure, Carpenter finds that the cascade processing model performs best of the three alternatives. His next step, then, is to calibrate the cascade model to determine the optimal specification in terms of hierarchy and to conduct auxiliary empirical analysis addressing the second and third questions unanswered by the literature. With respect to the question of Congressional versus executive control, Carpenter compares appropriations signals versus presidential budget proposal signals and finds significant support for stronger Congressional influence. He addresses the question of efficiency by examining whether the transformation of the Bureau of the Budget into the Office of Management and Budget led to more political control. Carpenter finds evidence of increased political control for the FDA but not for the FCC.

8.4 Generalizability of Empirical Comparisons of Alternative Models

The analyses by Brehm and Gates and by Carpenter each demonstrate that we can identify distinctions in formal models that are largely similar to representations of the relationships between principals and agents. Brehm and Gates examine moral hazard issues and Carpenter highlights responses to budget signals, but both analyses illustrate the complexities of comparing alternative formal models empirically.

Each of the examples presented takes a different approach in empirical analysis. The first three examples illustrate the potential pitfalls for comparisons of models using a particular estimation procedure. Offerman, since he views each model as a Complete DGP, can compare the models in terms of their ability to predict the likelihood of the observations. Yet the multiple equilibria problem in QRE makes the analysis not straightforward. In his analysis, the best-shot QRE was less successful than the QRNB. What if, instead, QRE's best shot had received more support than QRNB while other equilibrium estimations performed less well? Then it would have been much more difficult to conclusively argue that one of the formal models is supported over the other. The empirical comparison Offerman makes requires that he choose a specification of QRE for the empirical analysis. The empirical analysis adds restrictions. A similar potential problem can arise with the J-test (as noted in Schmidt et al.) since the J-test may also give less than conclusive results. The J-test compares the two empirical models given the other restrictive assumptions in the analysis of the data. This makes it difficult for the underlying formal models to be compared in a general manner. Finally, Westholm needed to make restrictive assumptions about voter preferences in order to construct his empirical comparison, and these assumptions may limit the generalizability of his analysis. What does that mean for the comparison?

Brehm and Gates and also Carpenter confront this issue by using empirical estimation procedures that (it is hoped) add the fewest restrictive assumptions. In particular, they wish to choose an estimation procedure that is as neutral with respect to the formal models as possible. Nevertheless, in choosing or measuring variables, the empirical analysis still restricts the comparison and in unknown ways may bias the results toward one approach. How generalizable are Brehm and Gates's conclusions to other public employees? How generalizable is Carpenter's analysis to other governmental agencies? I conclude that multiple evaluations of formal models are needed and would be extremely useful in answering these questions. Moreover, analyses such as those described here must be used cautiously as evidence for or against particular formal models, recognizing that each is an empirical evaluation of the formal models *as translated* using the empirical model or models and the estimation procedure. Even in Offerman's analysis, which comes closest to the ideal, choosing which QRE equilibria to compare limits the generalizability of the analysis, and his use of data from only one set of experiments also limits the conclusions.

8.5   Formal versus Nonformal Models Redux

So far I have examined the empirical investigation of alternative models when the alternatives are all formal models. However, a large body of existing theoretical knowledge in political science is built on nonformal theorizing. How do we evaluate a formal model against the theoretical results of nonformal theorizing? In some cases formal models' predictions are not contrary to nonformal theorizing. That is, formal models sometimes provide a formalization of a prediction that is already widely accepted in political science. For example, as discussed in Chapter 2, the theoretical prediction that differences in electoral laws can affect the number of political parties has been a well-known result since Duverger's (1953) empirical analysis and nonformal theorizing. Yet it is the subject of much subsequent formal theoretical study, as illustrated by Cox (1997).

When theory tells us something we already know, some may argue that the formal model is unnecessary and serves no purpose. This view ignores a number of important details. First, as argued in Chapter 2, a formal model provides us with both a prediction and a reason *why* the prediction occurs. Thus, the formal model adds to our knowledge even if the prediction is already well known and predicted by nonformal theorizing. Second, because the formal model has assumptions and may make other predictions (e.g., comparative static or dynamic predictions), the formal model can be evaluated further and thus is potentially more powerful since it can be more carefully scrutinized empirically. Hence, even if a formal model's predictions are already well known, the formalization can add much to our knowledge of politics. For example, I believe that Cox's (1997) theoretical and empirical work based on the formal model of Duverger's law has added significantly to our understanding.

In other cases, formal models provide predictions that are contrary to or distinct from those in the literature based on nonformal theorizing. As noted in Chapter 6, Austen-Smith and Wright's (1994) prediction of counteractive lobbying is contrary to the general nonformal wisdom. In this case, then, it is useful to assess the predictions of the formal model versus the predictions of the nonformal theorizing. The next section presents two examples of empirical analysis that compare the predictions of formal models on signaling with those of nonformal theorizing. The first example is drawn from the literature on international politics, the second from the formal literature on legislatures. The first example allows also a consideration of the difficulties in applying a game theoretic model to empirical data. In particular and as noted in Chapter 4, if the formal model is viewed as a Partial DGP assuming actors to make random errors, then the empirical model may erroneously lend support (or not) to the formal model.

8.5.1 *Crisis Bargaining*

The Gap in the Literature. A good example of testing a formal model against nonformal theorizing is presented in Fearon's (1994) analysis of crisis bargaining. As Fearon observes, an important question in international relations is the extent to which nations can use threats effectively to protect their interests. This question has been the subject of considerable empirical research based on nonformal modeling, yet there have been limited linkages between formal models and the extensive data generated. Fearon's discussion of the state of the literature is reminiscent of Chapter 1's remarks on the campaign contributions literature:

On the one hand, we have a growing theoretical literature that uses recent developments in game theory to study the evolution and dynamics of international disputes.... On the other hand, we have seen slow but steady improvements in the number and quality of data sets on international confrontations.... But with the notable exception of Bueno de Mesquita and Lalman (1992), there have been few efforts to test theoretical results empirically using these data sets.... there have been virtually no efforts to draw specific hypotheses about the effects of threats from the new game theoretic crisis models *and* to evaluate them empirically. (Fearon 1994, pp. 236–7 [italics in original])

Fearon notes that the "fault" for the gap lies both with empiricists and modelers:

First, as yet no crisis data set has been constructed with any game-theoretic model (or models) in mind. In consequence, distinctions that appear critical from the theoretical perspective provided by various models are not recognized in organizing crisis data, and evidence that might help evaluate them is not collected.... Second, modelers have probably not done enough to draw out hypotheses that can be tested using simple, plausible, and readily available measures. (1994, p. 237)

However, there is a data set that Fearon believes can be effectively used for game theoretic analysis: Huth and Russett's (1988) crisis data. The data is coded in a sequential form that fits easily into a formal model, and there are measures of the actors' military capabilities.

Furthermore, Huth and Russett (1988) and Huth (1988) have proposed a number of hypotheses on the extent that deterrent threats are most likely to succeed or fail, using nonformal rationalist arguments – concerning the impacts of the balance of military capabilities and the balance of interests on the credibility of a threat – as a foundation. Huth and Russett make the following predictions: (1) the greater the ratio of the defender's capabilities to the challenger's and/or (2) the stronger the defender's level of interest in the protégé, the more likely an immediate deterrent threat will succeed. Thus, Fearon can provide a game theoretic model for empirical use and can also compare the model's success with the nonformally derived predictions of Huth and Russett.

The Two Models' Predictions. The formal model that Fearon uses as the basis of his analysis is contained in Fearon (1992). In the model there are two actors: a challenger and a defender. The actors vary in the value they place on conflict. Neither actor knows for sure which type will be faced in the bargaining situation, but there is a known distribution of actor types. The game is thus one of incomplete information transformed to a game of imperfect information, as discussed in Chapter 4. Fearon shows that the game has a unique sequential equilibrium (an equilibrium refinement also discussed in that chapter). The equilibrium is a separating equilibrium in that different types of actors take different actions.

Fearon argues that his game theoretic analysis demonstrates that the nonformal theorizing, which overlooks the fact that states should strategically use and manipulate information, reaches incorrect or inaccurate predictions. He asserts:

> To the extent that relative capabilities and interests are observable before a crisis begins, rational challengers should take these into account. When the observable balance of interests favors the defender, only relatively resolved challengers will choose to threaten, implying that the defender's effort at immediate deterrence will be relatively unlikely to succeed (contrary to the standard hypothesis). When the observable balance of capabilities favors the defender, challenges will tend to occur on issues that are of initially doubtful interest to the defender. Hence a strong deterrent signal by the defender will be relatively likely to work in response, but due to the challenger's initial beliefs and choice of issue rather than (directly) due to the defender's superior military power. (1994, p. 238)

The Empirical Model. Fearon tests his predictions using Huth and Russett's data. He evaluates the two nonformal hypotheses separately by examining the data from a number of perspectives. Fearon's predictions about the relationship between the balance of capabilities distinguish between the timing of the capability measure. The key is that the balance of military capabilities does not directly determine whether deterrence works but instead does so indirectly – through effects on the relative resolution of the challengers and the challenger's degree of uncertainty about the defender's resolution. Thus it is important to distinguish between ex ante and ex post capability measures. Loosely stated, *ex ante* capabilities affect the decision to challenge and the success of immediate deterrence because challenges take place when there is uncertainty about the defender's resolution. In contrast, *ex post* measures of capabilities apply to information that the challenger learns about the defender (and thus also will be related to the success of deterrence).

In order to evaluate whether the ex ante–ex post distinction matters, Fearon examines the data from a number of different perspectives. One clear example of where the nonformal model's prediction is contrary to the formal model's is in the relationship between a defender's nuclear status and the success of immediate deterrence. The nonformal theory predicts that, since nuclear weapons are unlikely to be used, they will not matter in immediate deterrence (not a credible threat). In contrast, the formal theory suggests that they are a good predictor of the success of immediate deterrence because challengers are likely to challenge defenders who have nuclear power only on issues believed not to be significant to the defender. Immediate deterrence by the defender, then, signals to the challenger that its belief was incorrect. The challenger backs down and the immediate deterrence is successful.

Fearon re-estimates a logit equation of the effect of defender nuclear status on the success of immediate deterrence. Defender's nuclear status is more strongly correlated with immediate deterrence than are other variables that would be expected to matter on the basis of nonformal theorizing. Fearon's analysis is, of course, limited by the few data points available. Nevertheless, the empirical results suggest that the game theoretic model is supported in its prediction of the relationship between military capabilities and the success of immediate deterrence. With respect to the first nonformal hypothesis, Fearon concludes as follows.

Although the capacity to blunt a rapid offensive may make a general deterrence more likely to succeed, its apparent effect on immediate deterrence is not due to the specific military attributes of the balance. Rather, when the defender is relatively strong, challengers tend to threaten on issues on which a concerted response by the defender is quite uncertain; hence a costly signal in response is likely to work. (1994, p. 266)

Fearon also finds that, with respect to the second hypothesis, "[i]mmediate deterrence is significantly less likely to work when protégé and defender have an alliance, and the same appears true if defender and protégé are geographically close, although the level of statistical confidence is lower" (p. 259). This supports his contention that immediate deterrence is less effective when the balance of interests favors the defender. The results also support his analysis that balance of capabilities is significant but that the causal relationship is different from that supposed by the nonformal theorizing.

Digression: What If the Underlying Model Is QRE? Fearon's research shows that nonformal explanations of the effects of deterrence may be flawed because they fail to incorporate strategic concerns. Yet his empirical analysis views the formal model as a Partial DGP – using logit much the same way that Schmidt et al. do – adding control variables and a random error term.

The random error term in the model is presumed to represent measurement error while the control variables represent factors that the model assumed are constant or fixed. But suppose that instead the actors in the model make mistakes and that the error represents these mistakes rather than measurement problems? Mistakes are likely to lead to different sorts of strategies than predicted in the perfect sequential equilibrium. What does that mean for the use of a logit empirical model?

Signorino (1998) asks this question using a streamlined complete information version of Fearon's game. He shows that the simple logit empirical model may give incorrect predictions if the underlying DGP is really given by a QRE model. The analysis shows that there can be serious pitfalls from using simple logit to evaluate hypotheses if the underlying DGP is strategic and the actors make errors, since the logit may report positive or negative linear relationships between variables when the actual relationship is nonlinear. However, this does not mean that Fearon's results are necessarily in error, because (a) the underlying DGP may in fact *not* be given by a QRE model in which actors make errors and respond strategically to this possibility (the assumptions of QRE) and (b) it is unclear what the QRE predictions are in the incomplete information environment of Fearon's model. Nevertheless, Signorino's analysis shows the value of carefully considering the relationship between the formal model that is evaluated and the underlying DGP. If the disconnect between the two is presumed to be error by the actors and the formal model assumes that the actors are strategic, then this should be taken into account when assessing the model empirically. Otherwise, the empirical results may have little meaning.

8.5.2 Cosponsorship

The Theories. Another example of comparing a formal model's predictions with nonformal theorizing is Kessler and Krehbiel's (1996) analysis of cosponsorship. Kessler and Krehbiel point out that electoral connection theories founded on the nonformal theorizing of Mayhew (1974) imply that, for members of Congress, cosponsoring a bill with other members can be a low-cost way of establishing a position on an issue.[10] Thus, these theories predict (i) a close correspondence between the legislator's positions on the

---

[10] Of course, there is a large body of formal work – also based on Mayhew's informal theorizing – that assumes legislators choose positions on issues in order to achieve election (e.g., in the work of Alesina et al. and Segal et al. discussed in Chapter 7). However, these models have not hypothesized the implications of electoral connection for cosponsorship.

issues for re-election and the policies of the legislation that they cosponsor and (ii) that election motives should matter in cosponsorship. Kessler and Krehbiel suggest the electoral connection theories specifically predict that moderates should engage in higher rates of cosponsorship – if we add the assumptions that moderate bills are more likely to pass and that legislators with uncertain electoral prospects are more likely to cosponsor.

In contrast, formal signaling models of Congress (e.g. Gilligan and Krehbiel 1989) make different predictions. The signaling models view the audience for cosponsorship as internal (the legislature) rather than external (the re-election constituency). The signaling models view cosponsorship as a way of building support for proposals on which some members wish to convey information to other members. The information concerns the number of votes that a measure can secure in the legislature. Thus, cosponsorship for a bill will be independent of ideological position (i.e., cosponsoring signals a support level in Congress as a whole, not of the individual legislator), and early cosponsorship should be from extremists on both sides with cosponsorship from all positions later (the early signals contain different information than the later signals).

Empirical Comparison. Kessler and Krehbiel (1996) review the several previous empirical studies of cosponsorship and argue that these studies suffer from two problems: (1) they do not provide an explicit test of competing hypotheses; and (2) the empirical analysis is static even though the process of cosponsorship – using either the electoral connection or signaling approach – is implicitly dynamic. Their work, by testing between the two theories, does present a test of competing hypotheses. However, analyzing the dynamics introduces a number of questions about how the empirical model should be formulated. In particular, the data generated tell us about sponsorship decisions over time until the bill is passed; but how should non-cosponsorship decisions be treated, given that some of these decisions may not actually be made before a bill is passed or Congress ends? Kessler and Krehbiel specify a hazard function that maps the determinants of duration and time elapsed into the probability of the event occurring (given that it had not yet occurred). Notice that the models are thus viewed as Partial DGPs with measurement error.

Kessler and Krehbiel use data on 51 bills in the 103rd Congress with at least 50 cosponsors. They partitioned the bills' lifetimes into three periods – early, intermediate, and late. They then estimate two empirical models: a constrained model, which assumes that the effect of preference extremity is equal for liberals and conservatives; and an unconstrained model, which allows for the effect of preference extremity to vary with ideology.

Kessler and Krehbiel's study is a good example of the necessity of considering how the estimation procedure can affect the empirical research. That is, the researchers estimate the baseline hazard (the baseline probability of cosponsorship) as a nonparametric function of time and legislator preferences, rather than using a parametric functional form to estimate the baseline (or not estimating the baseline at all). The authors explain why they choose the nonparametric form as follows.

The questions posed by theoretical frameworks . . . are twofold. Although the question regarding the influence of preferences on the *decision* to cosponsor or not to cosponor can be answered with conventional proportional hazards models, the question regarding the influence of preferences on the *timing* of the decision to cosponsor cannot be answered with the conventional approach. Simply allowing preferences to shift the baseline hazard proportionality assumption may conflict with the predictions of timing generated by some of the theoretical models. If it does conflict, then hypothesis tests based on estimates from conventional models could not be used to distinguish among the theories. For example, a conventional proportional hazards model would not necessarily allow preference extremity to increase hazard rates by a greater amount early in a bill's life, if the early cosponsorship hazard for moderates were less than or equal to the late cosponsorship hazard for moderates. (1996, p. 559 [italics in original])

Kessler and Krehbiel find support for the signaling model. Specifically: early cosponsorship tends to be by extremists on both sides of an issue, and these distinctions diminish over time. Notably, the authors point out how their empirical study suggests future theoretical and empirical analysis. The existing signaling models are more simplistic than the true dynamic situation facing members of Congress, and a theoretical investigation may explain some of the results that the existing theory does not explain. They also note that their results suggest not that electoral connection theories are inappropriate for understanding legislative behavior in general but rather that their usefulness is limited for an analysis of cosponsorship. The point is that they do not argue that the less-supported theory should be rejected; instead they claim that, for the empirical application considered (cosponsorship), the theory is less applicable than the signaling model.

Summary. Formal models can work with and also build on the nonformal theorizing of political science, thereby increasing our understanding, just as the analyses of Fearon and of Kessler and Krehbiel reveal new evidence on crisis bargaining and legislative activities, respectively. Testing between a formal model and a hypothesis based on nonformal theorizing tells us more than simply testing nonformal theory alone. The formal model forces us to be precise about the underlying causal relationships that may be the source of our nonformal hypothesis. Fearon's work explored the strategic considerations ignored by the nonformal theory, and in Kessler and Krehbiel the researchers considered the dynamics of cosponsorship overlooked by the nonformal theory.

8.6   Implications of the Examples

The examples in this chapter have illustrated a number of important issues that need to be considered in testing between alternative models. These may be summarized as follows.

1. *Sometimes an apparent case of alternative models may actually be special cases of a more general model,* as McCarty and Rothenberg demonstrate in their empirical study of campaign contributions. When we set out to test between alternative models, it is important to consider whether the models truly are alternatives; are these models really inconsistent with each other? If not then we may be making an unproductive empirical comparison, especially if it leads to discarding a model that has merit. That is, if the two models are both special cases of a more general model, then subsequent empirical understanding may be hampered if the discarded other "case" (the alternative model) becomes more empirically relevant in a different situation. We also may miss interactions between the two alternative models.

2. *Statistically testing between alternative models is not straightforward.* When we conduct an empirical analysis based on a theoretical construct, our empirical tests generally take one of the hypotheses as given and then measure the extent that this supposition is false. Schmidt et al. were able to make the comparison in both directions with conclusive results, using nonnested tests of the alternative models. But it is rare that empirical comparisons such as these are conclusive, and we often see that empirical analysis lends support for both models, not suggesting a definitive answer. Because of the potential of multiple equilibria, it may not be possible to compare the alternative models in overall fit. As a consequence, tests of alternative models typically suggest more research (both theoretical and empirical) instead of providing conclusions to research agendas.

3. *Tests of alternative models may be tests of assumptions* (as in West-holm) *or tests of predictions* (as in Schmidt et al., Brehm and Gates, and Carpenter), *but neither approach is sufficient for evaluating alternative models.* Comparing the empirical viability of the assumptions of alternative models can be quite useful in determining whether one model is more empirically supported. However, since all models make some assumptions that are false or nonverifiable, such comparisons can only tell us part of the story. Hence, testing predictions of alternative models is as necessary as comparing the empirical support for the alternative models' assumptions.

4. *Not all alternative models' predictions are different, and we need to consider which differences are the key, testable ones.* In Brehm and Gates and in Carpenter, the researchers identify how the alternative models' predictions differ on certain dimensions but are alike in others. They then focus empirically on the distinctions between the alternative models.

5. Once again, specification of the empirical model must be carefully done. In particular, *it is important that the empirical model or estimation procedure not bias the analysis in favor of one formal model over another.* Westholm considers how different techniques of measuring the variables can lead to one model seeming more supported than another. Brehm and Gates use the beta distribution in order not to bias the results. Kessler and Krehbiel use a more general hazard model so that the estimation is not biased in favor of a particular theory.

6. *We can evaluate a formal model against an alternative hypothesis from nonformal theorizing.* As in Fearon and in Kessler and Krehbiel, formal models sometimes provide different predictions from those that arise from nonformal theorizing. Testing which prediction receives greater empirical support can indicate the limits of our nonformal theorizing. In some cases, nonformal theorizing is supported by formal work and our nonformal intuitions are substantiated. In other cases – such as those illustrated by the examples of this chapter – nonformal theorizing ignores effects that, when incorporated, can lead to different predictions.

PART IV

A Second Revolution

CHAPTER 9

The Present and the Future

In this chapter I recast the foregoing analysis (of example implications) in a set of guidelines for empirical analysis of formal models. But I do not wish to end my exploration with just a simple set of rules. As noted in Chapter 1, in political science today there is a gap – between much of the empirical based research and formal modeling – which this book is an attempt to bridge. In Chapter 1 I explored why this gap has developed. I believe that, by bridging the gap, political science could advance to a second revolution in which methods and models work together. In the next section I present my practical side, the guidelines for empirical analysis of formal models. Then I examine the empirical analysis of formal models as part of the big picture, my vision of the future of political science in the second revolution.

9.1   Guidelines for the Present

9.1.1   The Process of Empirical Analysis

My hope is that this study of the empirical analysis of formal models will lead to an increased use of formal models in empirical work and vice versa. I have stated that my aim is to provide a framework or blueprint for the empirical analysis of formal models. I present this framework in the form of a series of steps, although the steps analogy does not here imply that the empirical analysis should be undertaken only in this order.

Step 1: Understanding Assumptions. The first step in examining the empirical viability of a formal model is an explicit understanding of the assumptions. The following questions should be asked.

279

1. *Are the assumptions internally consistent?* If the assumptions are not internally consistent, then the model's deductive logic is flawed and the model should be reformulated. The strength of formal models is their ability to provide predictions that are derived from explicit assumptions. If the model is not a coherent and logically consistent framework then it should be discarded, regardless of its empirical viability.

2. *Are the assumptions true or verifiable?* As noted in Chapter 5, if we determine that an assumption is false then we must evaluate the extent to which the model's theoretical results hinge on the assumption. If the results hinge crucially on the assumption, then we need to consider alternative models with different assumptions and the empirical viability of their results.

Note that much of the exercise of understanding assumptions of a model requires further theorizing. Evaluating assumptions should not be just an empirical enterprise, because such evaluation is part of the overall theory building process. Evaluating assumptions cannot be the end of our empirical study but is properly placed as a first step. Laboratory experiments can play a unique role in evaluating the assumptions of formal models, particularly assumptions about individual behavior.

Assumption evaluation is *limited*. Any evaluation of an assumption carries with it additional assumptions related to the empirical analysis used, the way the data is measured, and so on. Thus our evaluation is only as good as the other assumptions inherent in that evaluation. We also know that, because the model is only a model, some of its assumptions must be false or nonverifiable. For these reasons, *we should never* (a) *discard a model purely because its assumptions fail* empirical evaluation *nor* (b) *think assumption evaluation is a substitute for empirical evaluation* of a formal model. We should also recognize that, *if we make our models too complex, we may lose our ability to derive useful predictions* for empirical evaluation. Finally, *purely theoretical models may* (and often should) *have extremely unreal assumptions.*

Step 2: Determining Predictions. The predictions of formal models are derived or deduced from the models' assumptions. Evaluation of the models involves assessing whether these solutions are accurate in the empirical world. Even if we are satisfied with a model's assumptions, we need to specify what these assumptions predict and how well these predictions are supported empirically. As with assumptions, there are a number of questions that need to be answered.

1. *If the model makes a unique equilibrium point prediction, how likely or unlikely is it that this point prediction will be satisfied?* In many cases the prediction is unlikely to be observed in the naturally occurring environment. There are two solutions.

(a) We can *add randomness* to the model. Then we need to make sure that the assumptions of randomness are consistent with the other assumptions of the model and carefully evaluate how the randomness affects our predictions. The randomness, if added to help test the models' predictions, should not be tautological.

(b) We can *use controlled laboratory experiments* to evaluate the model, conducting a theory test. But we should also lessen the controlled environment, conducting a stress test, using the advantage of the laboratory to gradually test which aspects of the real world affect our realization of the equilibrium predictions.

2. *If the model makes disequilibrium predictions, how can we change the model to achieve an equilibrium before evaluation?* A model without predictions cannot be evaluated since "anything" is a possible outcome. Models lack equilibria owing to the assumptions made or the solution concept used to solve the model. Hence, in order to derive a prediction of the model, we must either add assumptions or change our solution concept. One option may be to use simulations to "solve" the model for given sets of parameters. When using the simulations we derive predictions based also on the additional assumptions inherent in the simulations, which are more restrictive than those of the original model. Once we add assumptions or change the solution concept, we can then evaluate the predictions of the model. It can be useful to conduct laboratory experiments of the model. However, such experiments should be viewed not as evaluations of the model but as suggestions about what the model could be missing.

3. *If the model makes multiple equilibrium predictions, can we reduce the predictions to a unique equilibrium prediction using one of the following methods?*

(a) restricting the analysis to symmetric and/or pure strategy equilibria;

(b) focusing on equilibria that the researcher believes are "focal points";

(c) in a repeated game, determining that the equilibria in the one-shot game are likely to be the only equilibria;

(d) using equilibrium refinements such as subgame perfection or the intuitive criterion;

(e) classifying the data into equilibrium regimes using observable variables;
(f) using simulations to suggest which equilibria are more likely.

4. *Are there predicted relationships that are contrary to prior formal or nonformal theorizing or to our intuition?* Evaluating the equilibria predictions of a formal model is only the first step in exploring a model's predictions. Ultimately we want to understand the relationships between variables. Thus, comparative static and dynamic process or path predictions are crucial for assessing whether a formal model actually increases our understanding of reality.

5. *Are there predictions or implications of the formal model besides those observations that motivated its construction?* As discussed in Chapter 2, the formal model has typically been constructed to answer a given empirical puzzle. Yet if we "fit" a model to only the original empirical impetus, that model is limited in its generality. We need to consider how the model may explain other empirical realities – realities that we may not expect and that may be open to evaluation.

One of the values of formal models is that the process of solving an explicitly developed model allows us to more carefully consider how we expect the real world to work. In many cases we find that the model provides us with new understandings of relationships and predictions that can be assessed.

Step 3: Examining Alternative Formal or Nonformal Models. It is attractive to test between alternative formal or nonformal models, but doing so is hardly straightforward. We should consider the following questions.

1. *Are the models' assumptions and/or predictions different from those in a reasonable alternative model?* How do we define "reasonable"? A reasonable formal model is one that has been shown to be based on logically consistent assumptions that have some empirical justification. A reasonable nonformal model is one that has received some prior empirical support. Ideally, we should evaluate formal models against "strong" opponents; that is, we should not construct a straw man to topple over. The strength of the alternative test is greater, the more widely the alternative model (formal or nonformal) is accepted and supported.

2. *Once a reasonable alternative model is selected, we should make sure that the model is indeed a contrasting explanation. Are the alternative and the proposed models special cases of a general model? Are the assumptions of the two models truly logically inconsistent?* An empirical evaluation of

two models' predictions, even if they are contrasting, is not very informative if the models really are *not* contrasting in their underlying formulations. We may be only assessing which case of a general model occurs in the data set we have, not truly evaluating two alternative models. Thus, we could prematurely discard some aspect of a general model on the basis of available data, not because we have actually shown that one model is better than another.

3. *If there are dimensions over which the proposed model and its alternative are in disagreement, is there one that is key or primary?* We can test between formal models by assessing contrasting assumptions or predictions. Testing between assumptions is useful, but limited if only one (or neither) model's predictions are empirically supported. Testing between predictions tells us another piece of the story about the difference between models. We need to consider *both* ways in which the models can differ and evaluate as many differences as possible before making any conclusive statements about the empirical reliability of one model over the other.

Step 4: Choosing an Empirical Model. In choosing an empirical model we must be extremely careful that its assumptions do not change the predictions we have derived from the formal model. Here are some of the questions that should be addressed.

1. *How is the underlying formal model to be viewed in relationship to the empirical data?*

(a) Is the model to be viewed as a Complete or Partial DGP?
(b) Is the model deterministic or deterministic with stochastic or random elements?

As discussed in Chapter 4, the answers to these questions determine, to a large extent, the process of empirical evaluation of the formal model and the construction of the empirical model. I advocate first attempting to view the model as a Complete DGP, even though we know that the formal model (because it is a model) will have disconnects with the empirical world. Such an examination can yield useful insights not possible when we begin analysis viewing a model only as a Partial DGP. However, we should not discard a model completely simply because viewing the model as a Complete DGP results in errant observations. Viewing a model as a Partial DGP may in some cases be unavoidable – owing to factors the model ignores that must be controlled for – before we can effectively evaluate the model's predictions. In their formal model, Alesina et al. do not consider the effects of war on output or electoral outcomes. Yet they reasonably expect that military conflict may mask or complicate their empirical analysis unless they control for this in the empirical estimation.

2. *To the extent that the empirical model's assumptions are more restrictive, are the restrictions a "special" case of the more general formal model? Or are the empirical model's assumptions less restrictive and, if so, how and why?* Methodologists in political science have developed a norm of being careful about the restrictiveness of assumptions in empirical models and in seeking ways to estimate models that are as unrestrictive as possible. Yet in many of the examples discussed in this book we have seen that the empirical models are often, by necessity, more restrictive than the underlying formal model. These differences between the formal model and the empirical model should be made explicit and carefully considered when determining whether the formal model receives support from the estimation of the empirical model.

3. *Does the estimation procedure or the way the data is measured add more restrictive assumptions to the empirical model that increase the disconnections between the empirical and underlying formal model?* Estimation procedures make assumptions about error terms, distributions of variables, and so forth. As Alvarez and Nagler show, the estimation procedure in evaluating spatial voting models can have a big impact on the results of the analysis and hence on our conclusions from the empirical research. It is important that we truly understand the implicit assumptions made when we choose multinomial logit over ordinary least squares to estimate the empirical model.

4. *Does the estimation procedure or the way in which the data is measured bias a comparison of alternative models in favor of one particular model or models?* As discussed in Chapter 8, Westholm, Brehm and Gates, Carpenter, and Kessler and Krehbiel all attempt to find estimation and data measurement procedures that are theory-neutral.

5. *When assessing alternative models, should each model be evaluated individually and then compared or should a single empirical model be constructed?* Which approach to use depends largely on the reasonableness of using a single empirical model; that is, would a single empirical model make theoretical sense? Is one model nested in another? If it is not reasonable to use a single empirical model, then the researcher should evaluate each model individually and use an overall test (such as the Davidson–MacKinnon J-test) to test between the two or compare the likelihood that the data is explained

by the two models. However, such analyses have the potential of yielding inconclusive results. Thus, multiple evaluations are often necessary to reach more definitive conclusions.

6. *Can a formal model be tested on a different data set than the model was originally intended to explain? How should the new empirical model be devised?* Extending the empirical focus of a formal model to new political situations can be quite valuable in helping us understand both the new political situation and our own theoretical understanding. However, we must be careful about how the new situation alters our theoretical predictions and in choosing the empirical model used to evaluate our theoretical predictions.

7. *Can the empirical model be used to evaluate policy and make predictions from our theoretical and empirical study?* If we find support for our theoretically derived hypotheses, then our empirical analysis may be able to consider how proposed policy changes will result in different empirical outcomes.

Step 5: Evaluating the Analysis. If the model passes the "evaluation" are we finished? In my view, typically not. Acceptance of models is a corporate activity of science; it happens when a large number of scientists find the empirical analysis convincing. A single empirical test may provide this sort of convincing evidence when many researchers are convinced by the results of such a test. This is what makes a "critical" test. However, generally we need to provide further empirical analysis.

Moreover, even if a model is supported empirically, further theoretical work is still important. Since we know that the model has false and unverified assumptions (even if much of the model is supported empirically), we need to understand the limits that these assumptions place on the theory. Empirical support for a given theory does not, of course, show that the theory will succeed if confronted with data generated from a world vastly different from that theorized. This is particularly true for political science. For example, much of our theory concerns the effects of institutions that we observe and hypothesize. However, our imagination limits our ability to effectively perceive what institutions may arise in the future and what effects they may have on political outcomes. Hence, we ought not believe we have solved all our theoretical questions simply because existing data supports our theory.

When models do *not* pass empirical tests, there are a number of possible reactions that researchers can follow. One approach is to totally discard the model and go back to the drawing board. In some cases the model may be so discredited that this is the proper response, but this is rare. More often, researchers simply alter the model in an attempt to fit it to the results that the model does not adequately satisfy. In some cases, this is done by making the model more restrictive. That is, some formal modelers make arguments that their models do not apply to all the data, restricting the model's assumptions. This has been labeled as "post hoc" theorizing and considered by many a serious problem for formal modelers.

I believe that this response is due to a misunderstanding of how theoreticians can learn from empirical results. Most theorizing subsequent to a model's failure in the empirical world does not make a model more restrictive. In Chapter 5 I presented an example of how theorizing after empirical results that discredited expected utility led to more general formulations. I have also shown how the failure of the Hotelling–Downsian model to explain observed candidate divergence led to much additional theorizing to account for this failure. The additional theorizing generalized assumptions that had previously been restrictive (allowed for candidate entry, differences in candidate motives, and uncertainty). Instead of being more restrictive, the subsequent theorizing led to generalizations of the theory. This does not mean these revised models should not be tested. What it means is that seemingly post hoc theorizing is misconstrued when the modeler might be making the model more general, not more restrictive, in reaction to the empirical results.

9.1.2   The Steps Analogy

I like the steps analogy because it captures the idea that we cannot divorce one part of the process of formal model evaluation from any other part, and that all parts work toward a common goal. A formal model is not just its predictions or its assumptions, but rather their combination. Thus, evaluation of the model is of the entire creature, not just one part of it. However, I dislike the analogy because it implies that the evaluation of a formal model is a one-way process. Of course it is not, and even if a researcher tried it would be extremely difficult to actually follow the steps in order. For example, an assumption may seem very reasonable at first until a prediction fails, or a prediction's success may seem to support a model until the model is shown to hinge crucially on a false assumption that was previously viewed as acceptable. Yet the steps analogy does suggest an important feature of the empirical analysis of formal models: the process of investigation does lead somewhere; we do learn and reach new heights through the investigation. I hope the steps I have laid out are not like M. C. Escher's steps, which lead ever nowhere.

9.2   Revolutionary Political Science

Although I am not usually a "big think" person, I conclude this book with a vision of the future for political science in the second revolution. There can be no mistake that my dream political science is idiosyncratic, highly unlikely (if not impossible) to be realized, and possibly even offensive to some. I recognize that it takes an enormous amount of hubris to claim to know what is best for an entire discipline! Yet I fundamentally believe that the vision of political science suggested here would be an improvement over our current operating procedures.

9.2.1   *Laboratories Everywhere*

Any reader of this book understands by now that I believe the experimental method can play an important role in political science research. I hope that I have demonstrated, through my arguments and examples, why I believe this to be true. Experiments are often the best way to evaluate some assumptions about individual behavior in formal models; experiments can allow us to evaluate different political institutions holding actors' preferences constant; and experiments provide us with a valuable degree of control over factors outside of formal models – allowing both theory and stress tests that can effectively demonstrate the limits and values of formal models. Because of these advantages, the use of experiments has greatly expanded in political science. Nevertheless, the experimental method is still considered a novelty (at best) among most mainstream political scientists, and the data from such experiments is misunderstood. Very few political science departments have active experimentalists on the faculty, teach graduate students the experimental method, or have access to an experimental laboratory. In my view, for political science to reach its potential in the second revolution, the experimental method should take a more fundamental role in graduate training and research. Political science departments that see themselves at the forefront of the discipline need to recognize the crucial role that experiments can play, and those departments that wish to grow with the second revolution would be wise to encourage the experimental method.

9.2.2   *Rethinking the Fields of Political Science*

The current primary division of political science by geographical area can seriously impede the progress of the second revolution. It implies that the "place" we study is more important in determining the nature of the political activity there than *any other variable.* At first this section was entitled "The End of American Politics" but that was more extreme than I intend. I do agree that there are features of American politics (as well as of the politics of Eastern Europe, or the politics of Southeast Asia) that are distinctive. History and culture do matter. I think that qualitative research on the workings of Congress or the Russian parliament is extremely valuable. However, the focus on geographical areas as the primary division has meant that some view much formal work (on legislatures, electoral processes, etc.) as part of American politics rather than political science in general.

To a large extent we are increasingly using and applying the research of formal models to the politics of other geographical areas. Our meetings are less organized by the geographical areas we study than by what we study. But it is time to restructure our graduate programs and our hiring. It is extremely useful for *some* students to learn substantive historical and cultural factors about particular geographical areas in their graduate training, but we need to train many students who do *not* have any geographical area as a field of study and we need to be willing to hire such students as colleagues in our departments.

9.2.3   *Required Graduate Training in Formal Models and Methods*

Most graduate programs in political science now offer some training in formal modeling and sophisticated methods. Yet this training is rarely a *required* feature of our graduate programs. Many graduates of our Ph.D. programs cannot read many of the papers in our top journals. Thus we continue to train political scientists who will fail to achieve in the second revolution. Graduate students who do not have basic, fundamental knowledge of formal modeling cannot conduct empirical analysis of these models. Graduate students who are poorly trained in methods also will suffer. Graduate programs that present training in formal modeling or methods as optional are wasting minds. Not only do we fool ourselves when we tell students they can survive without this training, we also set up those students to fail.

9.2.4 *A New Undergraduate Political Science*

Although most of us attempt to convey to undergraduates the substantive knowledge about politics that current and past political science research has achieved, we do very little training that conveys how we actually perform political science research. Some programs require majors to take a "methods" or "research design" class, but many programs consider these classes as optional if offered at all. Classes in formal models are even more sparse in offerings and enrollments. A serious consequence of this disconnect is that many of our graduate students have extremely false views of the discipline of political science when they begin their graduate study. Moreover, the types of students who select graduate study in political science are influenced by the way we teach undergraduate political science. Students who like modeling choose economics or other disciplines that use models, even if their substantive interests are in politics. Here I speak from personal experience. Mathematically inclined students are less likely to go to graduate school in political science simply because they are not sure the discipline can use their skills and think that their skills might even be a detriment. We need to end the disconnect between our undergraduate programs and the discipline of political science.

I believe that the main reason this disconnection exists is because we fear the consequences for our departments if we make undergraduate training more mathematical. We fear that enrollment will decline and thus our departments' budgets and number of faculty will be severely affected. The problem with this perspective is that we fail to see the positive outcomes from a change in our undergraduate programs. That is, there are students who do not major in political science because they find the way it is now taught is boring. It is not intellectually interesting to them because they are exposed only to a particular type of political science. Thus we could *attract* students by making undergraduate training more like true political science. I do not mean to imply that we are currently too easy on our students; I do believe that there are many undergraduate political science courses besides modeling and empirical analysis that are intellectually challenging to students, and I think we can still teach these classes (albeit perhaps differently). But if this is the only type of undergraduate training we offer, then (a) we encourage our undergraduates in a false perspective of the discipline and (b) we lose potential students who would be attracted to modeling and empirical analysis.

How can we make this change? We need to offer courses to freshmen that use math, models, and empirical analysis in political science. This will mean more advertising to students who normally enroll in mathematics and mathematically oriented disciplines. We must make it clear from the beginning of students' undergraduate study what political science is like. Since it is true that we will find students who are turned off by this approach, we also need to rethink how we teach modeling and methods at the undergraduate level. In many of the "hard" sciences, introductory courses are accompanied by laboratory sections where students learn by doing. We can use laboratory sections also. How? Students can learn a lot about how spatial voting models work by participating in simple spatial voting games. Students can similarly learn a lot about how empirical methods work by using data themselves. We can make lab reports a required participatory exercise and a significant part of their grades. By constraining our teaching of political science to a standard classroom experience of discussion and lecture, we constrain our ability to reach the students. Making learning more participatory can make the experience more enjoyable for our students. We may find that teaching political science this way attracts not only different students but more students!

Finally, there is no reason why we cannot continue to teach interesting substantive topics to undergraduates while at the same time incorporating how models and methods work to help understand these issues. A course on minority politics can introduce students to how electoral rules affect outcomes. A course on foreign policy can introduce students to bargaining models and their empirical examination. A course on new democracies can discuss models of political careers. And a course on the media's role in politics can discuss the strategic concerns of candidates and interest groups in shaping messages. Many of these things we already incorporate in our teaching but without showing the students how models work. If we introduce students to models in the context of interesting questions, they are more likely to find the models themselves interesting.

9.2.5   *You're OK, I'm OK*

Most of the preceding discussion deals with how we teach political science to undergraduates and graduates. But for the second revolution in political science to be realized, we also need to conquer some of our divisions. This book focuses on the divisions between modelers and methodologists. I hope to provide a guide to bridging the gap between the two. However, having a guide is only one step. We also need to stop playing some of the games that divide the discipline and that limit our ability to achieve in the second revolution.

My Method Is Better than Your Method. Some methods are better suited for particular problems than others. As argued before, I believe that there are questions (e.g., in evaluating assumptions) that can best be answered using experiments. Nevertheless, sometimes a method is simply the wrong choice for a particular problem. Choosing binomial logit when the underlying problem requires multinomial logit can lead to errors in analysis. Ignoring strategic behavior when we expect that it exists is likely to result in incorrect answers. If a model has an analytical solution, then we should try to solve the model analytically if at all possible. We should try to view formal models as Complete DGPs when we can, or at least be aware of the constraints of viewing a model as a Partial DGP. If we can derive predictions about aggregate behavior or outcomes directly from individual choices, then we should. If a model makes predictions about individual behavior that can be measured, then we should try to evaluate these empirically. Whenever possible, we should try to evaluate our theories using large numbers of cases and precise quantitative methods.

It is wrong to claim that one method is the only method that can be used for all problems – or even that it is always "best" for a certain class of problems. Sometimes naturally occurring data can help us evaluate assumptions. Sometimes simple ordinary least squares is the best way to analyze a data set. Sometimes it is appropriate to assume that actors' behavior is less than rational and/or nonstrategic. Sometimes simulations provide us with answers when we cannot or do not know how to solve a model analytically. Sometimes it makes sense to evaluate a model of individual behavior by analyzing aggregate outcomes. Sometimes we need to analyze behavior at an aggregate level, black-boxing internal party decisions or the decision making process within a government. Sometimes we have only a few data points or cases to analyze, or our data must be qualitative. And I would argue that empirically analyzing a model as a Complete DGP is often impossible.

Yet we should intelligently continue to debate the appropriate application of methods or models in our research. We may disagree over which modeling technique or method is applicable; controversies and disputes will continue and *should* continue. Because new methods and models will arise and old ones will evolve, it is impossible to expect that we will completely agree on when it is appropriate to use many particular methods or models at any point in time. The key is not to discard a method or model or to advance one as "the" answer for a particular question prematurely. We must not let debates over methods and models keep us from learning from each other.

The Burden of Proof Game. I hope that this book will lead to more theoretically based empirical work and to more empirically evaluated theoretical work in the discipline. I recognize that this enterprise is exceedingly difficult. One challenge arises simply from the specialization that occurs naturally in academic research. Very few can maintain a high level of expertise in the statistical methods used in empirical research and the latest techniques in formal modeling. This is frustrating for the theorist who wants to evaluate her work using empirical analysis but finds that her statistical approaches are now considered out of date and suspect. It is similarly discouraging for the empiricist who may not have training in formal modeling approaches and hence does not understand the complex language and notation used in game theory or differential equation models. As a consequence, we end up in a game of "shift the burden." Theoreticians criticize empiricists for not using formal models in their empirical work. But from the perspective of many theorists, it is the empiricist's responsibility to determine how to take the formal model and evaluate it empirically – to connect the formal and empirical models. Empiricists, on the other hand, criticize formal modelers for not providing enough empirical support for their models. They argue that it is the theorist's responsibility to provide a formal model that can be used as an empirical model. Empiricists see formal modelers as failing to adequately specify the randomness that would facilitate empirical analysis and as failing to provide equations that can be estimated directly.

Where should we place the burden? Ideally, cooperative research between experts in both areas works best. But this requires a basis on which to cooperate, an understanding of what formal models are and how to evaluate them. I hope this book will provide a framework for the empirical analysis of formal models that can help alleviate these difficulties. If a common view of the mechanics of empirically evaluating formal theory can be accepted within the discipline, then I trust it will not prove difficult to conduct empirical estimation of formal models and see the work published.

I also feel that development of an accepted formula for empirical analysis of formal models should make it easier for theoretical research (without empirical work) to be condoned by the majority of political scientists. That is, it is probably an impossible task to incorporate a fully developed formal model as well as a carefully crafted empirical study within the traditional journal article. Moreover, some of the more interesting empirical studies I advocate involve comparing or combining formal models. Integrating that sort of analysis with the presentation of the theories would be even more difficult. What happens if political scientists believe that theory should be published only if accompanied by empirical work? To banish theory without empirical work implies banishing theory in a much larger sense than intended even by those who hold this belief. Theoreticians must be able to publish their work in the first place, or empirical applications will never follow. If there is a common understanding of what it means to empirically evaluate a formal model, then empirically focused political scientists should find it more interesting to read purely theoretical pieces with future empirical analysis in mind. Likewise, those who specialize primarily in theory development should find reading empirical work more engaging when it is clear how the empirical study relates to existing theory. Agreement concerning empirical evaluation of formal models should make theoretical papers more absorbing to empiricists and vice versa.

This means, however, that empiricists need to be more accepting of pure theory and that theorists need to be more accepting of empirical research based on nonformal modeling. I argued in Chapter 1 that pure theory is necessary for research in political science. It is not just a mental exercise but rather is an important part of the theoretical process that ultimately can lead to applied theory and formal models for empirical evaluation. I also believe that empirical research that is purely "searching for facts" can be invaluable for the discipline. It is a mistake to ban either type of research from our journals, books, or graduate training. *If we value and publish* only *directly testable theory or empirical research that has formal theory, the second revolution will fail.*

9.3   A Call for "Constructive Criticism"

In my view, political science is at the advent of a new revolution. But the revolution will not succeed unless we (1) train our undergraduate and graduate students in political science as it currently is practiced; (2) embrace and understand the methods and models available to us; and, most importantly, (3) continue to build bridges between methodologists and modelers. I hope that this book will help in the process of achieving these goals.

In writing this volume I have become aware of two fundamental realities: (1) most political scientists concur that this book is sorely needed, but (2) it is impossible to write a book on this subject that satisfies the perceived need. I expect that many will find my proposed approaches to bridging the gap too weak or too strong and that others will find some of my views on research too cynical or (more likely) too naive. This reality was brought home to me when some of the most critical readers of first drafts of these chapters were exceptionally eager for early copies of the same chapters for use in their graduate classes. Thus, I must accept the certainty that – although this book will provide a framework for bridging the gap between empiricists and theorists – it will doubtless not be "the" sole prescribed method of connection. Moreover, if the book were to provide such a final denouement then it would be a failure. That is, this book should lead to more dialogue on how we empirically evaluate formal models and an increased focus on the issue, allowing for many to contribute their perspectives and unique insights. I truly welcome readers to be aggressively critical of my proposed approach *while also* concentrating carefully on alternative methods or frameworks that could be used to combine our theoretical and empirical sides and so build a better political science.

References

Abelson, Robert P., and A. Levi (1985). "Decision Making and Decision Theory." In G. Lindzey and E. Aronson (Eds.), *Handbook of Social Psychology*, 3rd ed. New York: Random House.

Adams, Greg D. (1996). "Legislative Effects of Single-Member vs. Multi-Member Districts." *American Journal of Political Science* 40: 129–44.

Aldrich, John H. (1983). "A Downsian Model with Party Activism." *American Political Science Review* 77: 974–90.

Aldrich, John H. (1993). "Rational Choice and Turnout." *American Journal of Political Science* 20: 246–78.

Aldrich, John H. (1995). *Why Parties? The Origin and Transformation of Party Politics in America*. University of Chicago Press.

Aldrich, John H., and Michael D. McGinnis (1989). "A Model of Party Constraints on Optimal Candidate Positions." *Mathematical and Computer Modeling* 12: 437–50.

Aldrich, John H., and Forrest D. Nelson (1984). *Linear Probability, Logit, and Probit Models*. Beverly Hills, CA: Sage.

Alesina, Alberto (1987). "Macroeconomic Policy in a Two-Party System as a Repeated Game." *Quarterly Journal of Economics* 102: 651–78.

Alesina, Alberto (1988). "Credibility and Policy Convergence in a Two-Party System with Rational Voters." *American Economic Review* 78: 796–805.

Alesina, Alberto, John Londregan, and Howard Rosenthal (1993). "A Model of the Political Economy of the United States." *American Political Science Review* 87: 12–33.

Alesina, Alberto, and Howard Rosenthal (1995). *Partisan Politics, Divided Government, and the Economy*. Cambridge University Press.

Alesina, Alberto, and Howard Rosenthal (1996). "A Theory of Divided Government." *Econometrica* 64: 1311–42.

Alesina, Alberto, and Stephen E. Spear (1988). "An Overlapping Generations Model of Electoral Competition." *Journal of Public Economics* 37: 359–79.

Allais, Maurice (1953). "Le Comportement de l'homme Rationel Devant le Risque, Critique des Postulates et axiomes de l'ecole Americaine." *Econometrica* 21: 503–46.

Allais, Maurice (1979). "The So-called Allais Paradox and Rational Decisions under Uncertainty." In M. Allais and O. Hagen (Eds.), *The Expected Utility Hypothesis and the Allais Paradox*. Dordrecht: Reidel.

Alvarez, R. Michael (1997). *Information and Elections*. Ann Arbor: University of Michigan Press.

Alvarez, R. Michael, Shawn Bowler, and Jonathan Nagler (1996). "Issues, Economics and the Dynamics of Multiparty Elections: The British 1987 General Election." Working Paper no. 949, School of Social Science, California Institute of Technology, Pasadena.

Alvarez, R. Michael, and Jonathan Nagler (1995). "Economics, Issues and the Perot Candidacy: Voter Choice in the 1992 Presidential Election." *American Journal of Political Science* 39: 714–44.

Alt, James E., Randall L. Calvert and Brian D. Humes (1988). "Reputation and Hegemonic Stability: A Game-Theoretic Analysis." *American Political Science Review* 82: 423–44.

Anderson, Simon P., Jacob K. Goeree, and Charles A. Holt (1997). "Stochastic Game Theory: Adjustment to Equilibrium under Bounded Rationality." Working Paper, Department of Economics, University of Virginia, Charlottesville.

Ansolabehere, Stephen, Shanto Iyengar, Adam Simon, and N. Valentino (1994). "Do Negative Campaigns Demobilize the Electorate?" *American Political Science Review* 84: 829–38.

Ansolabehere, Stephen, and James M. Snyder, Jr. (1996). "Money, Elections, and Candidate Quality." Working Paper, Department of Political Science, Massachusetts Institute of Technology, Cambridge.

Arrow, Kenneth J. [1951] (1963). *Social Choice and Individual Values,* 2nd ed. New Haven, CT: Yale University Press.

Arrow, Kenneth J. (1968). "Mathematical Models in the Social Sciences." In May Brodbeck (Ed.), *Readings in the Philosophy of the Social Sciences,* pp. 635–68. New York: Macmillan.

Austen-Smith, David (1987). "Interest Groups, Campaign Contributions, and Probabilistic Voting." *Public Choice* 54: 123–39.

Austen-Smith, David (1991). "Rational Consumers and Irrational Voters: A Review Essay on *Black Hole Tariffs and Endogenous Policy Theory* by Stephen Magee, William Brock, and Leslie Young, Cambridge University Press 1989." *Economics and Politics* 3: 73–92.

Austen-Smith, David (1997). "Interest Groups: Money, Information, and Influence." In Dennis C. Mueller (Ed.), *Perspectives on Public Choice: A Handbook,* pp. 296–321. Cambridge University Press.

Austen-Smith, David, and Jeffrey Banks (1988). "Elections, Coalitions, and Legislative Outcomes." *American Political Science Review* 82: 405–22.

Austen-Smith, David, and Jeffrey Banks (1996). "Information Aggregation, Rationality, and the Condorcet Jury Theorem." *American Political Science Review* 90: 34–45.

Austen-Smith, David, and John R. Wright (1992). "Competitive Lobbying for a Legislator's Vote." *Social Choice and Welfare* 9: 229–57.

Austen-Smith, David, and John R. Wright (1994). "Counteractive Lobbying." *American Journal of Political Science* 38: 25–44.

Austen-Smith, David, and John R. Wright (1996). "Theory and Evidence for Counteractive Lobbying." *American Journal of Political Science* 40: 543–64.

Axelrod, Robert (1984). *The Evolution of Cooperation*. New York: Basic Books.

Banks, Jeffrey, Colin Camerer, and David Porter (1988). "An Experimental Analysis of Nash Refinements in Signalling Games." *Games and Economic Behavior* 2: 389–426.

Banks, Jeffrey, and D. Roderick Kiewiet (1989). "Explaining Patterns of Competition in Congressional Elections." *American Journal of Political Science* 33: 997–1015.

Banks, Jeffrey, and Rangarajan K. Sundaram (1993). "Adverse Selection and Moral Hazard in a Repeated Elections Model." In William A. Barnett, Melvin J. Hinich, and Norman Schofield (Eds.), *Political Economy: Institutions, Competition, and Representation*. Cambridge University Press.

Baron, David P. (1989). "A Noncooperative Theory of Legislative Coalitions." *American Journal of Political Science* 33: 1048–84.

Baron, David P. (1991a). "Majoritarian Incentives, Pork Barrel Programs, and Procedural Control." *American Journal of Political Science* 35: 57–90.

Baron, David P. (1991b). "A Spatial Theory of Government Formation in Parliamentary Systems." *American Political Science Review* 85: 137–65.

Baron, David P. (1996). "A Dynamic Theory of Collective Goods Programs." *American Political Science Review* 90: 316–30.

Baron, David P., and John A. Ferejohn (1989a). "Bargaining in Legislatures." *American Political Science Review* 89: 1181–1206.

Baron, David P., and John A. Ferejohn (1989b). "The Power to Propose." In Peter C. Ordeshook (Ed.), *Models of Strategic Choice in Politics*, pp. 343–66. Ann Arbor: University of Michigan Press.

Baron, David P., and Jongryn Mo (1993). "Campaign Contributions and Party–Candidate Competition in Services and Policies." In William A. Barnett, Melvin J. Hinich, and Norman Schofield (Eds.), *Political Economy: Institutions, Competition, and Representation*. Cambridge University Press.

Bartels, Larry M. (1985). "Alternative Misspecifications in Simultaneous-Equation Models." *Political Methodology* 11: 181–99.

Bartels, Larry M., and Henry E. Brady (1993). "The State of Quantitative Political Methodology." In Ada W. Finifter (Ed.), *Political Science: The State of the Discipline II*. Washington, DC.: American Political Science Association.

Basil, M., C. Schooner, and B. Reeves (1991). "Positive and Negative Political Advertising: Effectiveness of Ads and Perceptions of Candidates." In F. Biocca (Ed.), *Television and Political Advertising – Volume I: Psychological Processes, Communication and Society*. Hillsdale, NJ: Erlbaum.

Bates, Robert H., Avner Greif, Margaret Levi, Jean-Laurent Rosenthal, and Barry R. Weingast (1998). *Analytic Narratives*. Princeton, NJ: Princeton University Press.

Baumgartner, Frank R., and Beth L. Leech (1996a). "The Multiple Ambiguities of 'Counteractive Lobbying'." *American Journal of Political Science* 40: 521–42.

Baumgartner, Frank R., and Beth L. Leech (1996b). "Good Theories Deserve Good Data." *American Journal of Political Science* 40: 565–9.

Becker, Gordon M., Morris H. DeGroot, and Jacob Marschak (1964). "Measuring Utility by a Single-Response Sequential Method." *Behavioral Science* 9: 226–32.

Bednar, Jenna (1998). "The Credit Assignment Problem." Working Paper, Department of Political Science, University of Iowa, Iowa City.

Bendor, Jonathan, and Terry Moe (1985). "An Adaptive Model of Bureaucratic Politics." *American Political Science Review* 79: 755–74.

Bernhardt, M. D., and Daniel E. Ingberman (1985). "Candidate Reputations and the 'Incumbency Effect'." *Journal of Public Economics* 27: 47–67.

Bernheim, Douglas, B. Peleg, and Michael Whinston (1987). "Coalition Proof Nash Equilibria." *Journal of Economic Theory* 42: 1–12.

Bernholz, P. (1978). "On the Stability of Logrolling Outcomes in Stochastic Games." *Public Choice* 33: 65–82.

Bianco, William, and Robert Bates (1990). "Cooperation by Design: Leadership, Structure, and Collective Dilemmas." *American Political Science Review* 84: 133–48.

Binmore, Ken (1990). *Essays on the Foundations of Game Theory*. Cambridge, UK: Blackwell.

Black, Duncan (1948a). "On the Rationale of Group Decision Making." *Journal of Political Economy* 56: 23–34.

Black, Duncan (1948b). "The Decisions of a Committee Using a Special Majority." *Econometrica* 16: 245–61.

Black, Duncan (1958). *The Theory of Committees and Elections*. Cambridge University Press.

Boettcher, William A. III (1995). "Prospect Theory in International Relations." *Journal of Conflict Resolution* 39: 561–83.

Bohm, P. (1972). "Estimating Demand for Public Goods: An Experiment." *European Economic Review* 3: 111–30.

Bowen, Howard R. (1943). "The Interpretation of Voting in the Allocation of Economic Resources." *Quarterly Journal of Economics* 58: 27–48.

Boylan, Richard T., and M. A. El-Gamal (1993). "Fictitious Play: A Statistical Study of Multiple Economic Experiments." *Games and Economic Behavior* 5: 205–22.

Boylan, Richard, John O. Ledyard, Arthur Lupia, Richard D. McKelvey, and Peter C. Ordeshook (1991). "Political Competition in a Model of Economic Growth: An Experimental Study." In Thomas R. Palfrey (Ed.), *Laboratory Research in Political Economy*. Ann Arbor: University of Michigan Press.

Boylan, Richard T., and Richard D. McKelvey (1995). "Voting over Economic Plans." *American Economic Review* 85: 860–71.

Box-Steffensmeier, Janet M. (1996). "A Dynamic Analysis of the Role of War Chests in Campaign Spending." *American Journal of Political Science* 40: 352–71.

Brandts, Jordi, and Charles Holt (1992). "An Experimental Test of Equilibrium Dominance in Signalling Games." *American Economic Review* 82: 1350–65.

Brehm, John, and Scott Gates (1993). "Donut Shops and Speed Traps: Evaluating Models of Supervision on Police Behavior." *American Journal of Political Science* 37: 555–81.

Brehm, John, and Scott Gates (1997). *Working, Shirking, and Sabotage: Bureaucratic Response to a Democratic Public.* Ann Arbor: University of Michigan Press.

Bresnahan, Timothy F., and Peter C. Reiss (1991). "Empirical Models of Discrete Games." *Journal of Econometrics* 48: 57–81.

Brians, C. L., and M. P. Wattenberg (1996). "Campaign Issue Knowledge and Salience: Comparing Reception from TV Commercials, TV News and Newspapers." *American Journal of Political Science* 40: 145–71.

Brock, William A., and Stephen P. Magee (1978). "The Economics of Special-Interest Politics: The Case of the Tariff." *American Economic Review* 68: 246–50.

Brophy-Baermann, Bryan, and John A. C. Conybeare (1994). "Retaliating against Terrorism: Rational Expectations and the Optimality of Rules versus Discretion." *American Journal of Political Science* 38: 196–210.

Brown, Courtney (1993). "Nonlinear Transformation in a Landslide: Johnson and Goldwater in 1964." *American Journal of Political Science* 37: 582–609.

Buchanan, James M. (1954). "Individual Choice in Voting and the Market." *Journal of Political Economy* 62: 334–43.

Buchanan, James M., and Gordon Tullock (1962). *The Calculus of Consent: Logical Foundations of Constitutional Democracy.* Ann Arbor: University of Michigan Press.

Buckley, Fred, and Frank Harary (1990). *Distance in Graphs.* Redwood City, CA: Addison-Wesley.

Bueno de Mesquita, Bruce, and David Lalman (1992). *War and Reason.* New Haven, CT: Yale University Press.

Calvert, Randall (1985). "Robustness of the Multidimensional Voting Model: Candidates' Motivations, Uncertainty, and Convergence." *American Journal of Political Science* 29: 69–95.

Calvert, Randall (1986). *Models of Imperfect Information in Politics.* Chur: Harwood.

Calvert, Randall (1995). "Rational Actors, Equilibrium, and Social Institutions." In Jack Knight and Itai Sened (Eds.), *Explaining Social Institutions.* Ann Arbor: University of Michigan Press.

Camerer, Colin (1995). "Individual Decision Making." In John H. Kagel and Alvin E. Roth (Eds.), *The Handbook of Experimental Economics*, pp. 587–704. Princeton, NJ: Princeton University Press.

Camerer, Colin F. (1997). "Progress in Behavioral Game Theory." *Journal of Economic Perspectives* 11: 167–88.

Camerer, Colin, and Keith Weigelt (1988). "Experimental Tests of a Sequential Equilibrium Reputation Model." *Econometrica* 56: 1–36.

Cameron, Charles M., Albert D. Cover, and Jeffrey Segal (1990). "Senate Voting on Supreme Court Nominees: A Neoinstitutional Model." *American Political Science Review* 84: 525–34.

Cameron, Charles M., and James M. Enelow (1992). "Asymmetric Policy Effects, Campaign Contributions, and the Spatial Theory of Elections." *Mathematical and Computer Modelling* 16: 117–32.

Cameron, Charles M., David Epstein, and Sharyn O'Halloran (1996). "Do Majority-Minority Districts Maximize Substantive Black Representation in Congress?" *American Political Science Review* 90: 794–812.

Cameron, Charles M., and J. Jung (1992). "Strategic Endorsements." Working Paper, Department of Political Science, Columbia University, New York.

Campbell, A., P. Converse, W. Miller, and D. Stokes (1960). *The American Voter.* New York: Wiley. [Reprinted 1976 by University of Chicago Press.]

Canon, David T. (1993). "Sacrificial Lambs or Strategic Politicians? Political Amateurs in U.S. House Elections." *American Journal of Political Science* 37: 1119–41.

Carmines, Edward G., and James A. Stimson (1981). "Issue Evolution, Population Replacement, and Normal Partisan Change." *American Political Science Review* 75: 107–18.

Carmines, Edward G., and James A. Stimson (1989). *Issue Evolution: Race and the Transformation of American Politics.* Princeton, NJ: Princeton University Press.

Carpenter, Daniel P. (1996). "Adaptive Signal Processing, Hierarchy, and Budgetary Control in Federal Regulation." *American Political Science Review* 90: 283–302.

Carrubba, Cliff (1996). "On the Relevance of Prospect Theory for Rational Choice Modeling." Working Paper, Graduate School of Business, Stanford University.

Carter, John R., and David Schap (1990). "Line Item Veto: Where is Thy Sting?" *Journal of Economic Perspectives* 4: 103–18.

Chapple, Eliot D. (1940). *Measuring Human Relations: An Introduction to the Study of the Interaction of Individuals* (Genetic Psychology Monographs, vol. 22). Providence, MA: Journal Press.

Chari, V. V., Larry Jones, and Ramon Marimon (1998). "The Economics of Split Voting in Representative Democracies." *American Economic Review* 87: 957–76.

Chen, Hsiao Chi, James W. Friedman, and Jacques-Francois Thisse (1997). "Boundedly Rational Nash Equilibrium: A Probabilistic Choice Approach." *Games and Economic Behavior* 18: 32–54.

Chew, S. H. (1983). "A Generalization of the Quasilinear Mean With Applications to the Measurement of Income Inequality and Decision Theory Resolving the Allais Paradox." *Econometrica* 51: 1065–92.

Cho, In-Koo, and David Kreps (1987). "Signalling Games and Stable Equilibria." *Quarterly Journal of Economics* 104: 45–72.

Condorcet, M. J. A. N. C., Marquis de (1785). *Essai sur l'Application de l'Analyse à la Probabilité des Decisions Rendues à la Pluralité des Voix.* Paris: l'Imprimerie Royale.

Conlisk, J. (1989). "Three Variants on the Allais Example." *American Economic Review* 79: 392–407.

Converse, Philip (1969). "Of Time and Partisan Stability." *Comparative Political Studies* 2: 139–71.

Coughlin, Peter (1990). "Candidate Uncertainty and Electoral Equilibria." In James M. Enelow and Melvin J. Hinich (Eds.), *Advances in the Spatial Theory of Voting,* pp. 145–66. Cambridge University Press.

Coughlin, P., and S. Nitzan (1981). "Directional and Local Electoral Equilibria with Probabilistic Voting." *Journal of Economic Theory* 24: 226–39.

Cox, Gary W. (1990a). "Multicandidate Spatial Competition." In James M. Enelow and Melvin J. Hinich (Eds.), *Advances in the Spatial Theory of Voting.* Cambridge University Press.

Cox, Gary W. (1990b). "Centripetal and Centrifugal Incentives in Electoral Systems." *American Journal of Political Science* 34: 903–35.

Cox, Gary W. (1997). *Making Votes Count: Strategic Coordination in the World's Electoral Systems.* Cambridge University Press.

Crawford, Vincent P. (1990). "Explicit Communication and Bargaining Outcomes." *American Economic Review, Papers and Proceedings* 80: 213–19.

Dahl, Robert (1961). "The Behavioral Approach in Political Science: Epitaph for a Monument to a Successful Protest." *American Political Science Review* 55: 763–72.

Davidson, R., and J. G. MacKinnon (1981). "Several Tests for Model Specification in the Presence of Alternative Hypotheses." *Econometrica* 49: 781–93.

Davis, Otto A., Morris DeGroot, and Melvin J. Hinich (1972). "Social Preference Orderings and Majority Rule." *Econometrica* 40: 147–57.

Davis, Douglas D., and Charles A. Holt (1993). *Experimental Economics.* Princeton, NJ: Princeton University Press.

Dawes, Robyn M. (1988). *Rational Choice in an Uncertain World.* Orlando, FL: Harcourt Brace Jovanovich.

de Finetti, B. (1937). "La Prevision: Ses Lois Logiques, Ses Sources Sources Subjectives." *Annales de l'Institut Henri Poincare* 7: 1–68

Denzau, Arthur, and Robert Mackay (1983). "Gatekeeping and Monopoly Power of Committees: An Analysis of Sincere and Sophisticated Behavior." *American Journal of Political Science* 27: 740–61.

Denzau, Arthur T., William Riker, and Kenneth Shepsle (1985). "Farquharson and Fenno: Sophisticated Voting and Home Style." *American Political Science Review* 79: 1117–34.

Diba, Behzad, and Allan M. Feldman (1984). "Utility Functions for Public Outputs and Majority Voting." *Journal of Public Economics* 25: 235–43.

Diermeier, Daniel, and Rebecca B. Morton (1998). "Proportionality versus Perfectness: Experiments in Legislative Bargaining." Working Paper, University of Iowa, Iowa City.

Diermeier, Daniel, and Roger B. Myerson (1994). "Bargaining, Veto Power, and Legislative Committees." Working Paper, Center for Mathematical Studies in Economics and Management Science, Northwestern University, Evanston, IL.

Dion, Douglas (1992). "The Robustness of the Structure-Induced Equilibrium." *American Journal of Political Science* 36: 462–82.

Dion, Douglas (forthcoming). *Turning the Legislative Thumbscrew: Minority Rights and Procedural Change in Legislative Politics.* Ann Arbor: University of Michigan Press.

Dodd, Stuart C. (1948). "A Systematics for Sociometry and for All Science." *Sociometry* 11: 113–30.

Downs, Anthony (1957). *An Economic Theory of Democracy.* New York: Harper and Row.

Duverger, M. (1953). *Political Parties: Their Organization and Activity in the Modern State.* New York: Wiley.

Eichberger, J. (1995). "Bayesian Learning in Repeated Normal Form Games." *Games and Economic Behavior* 11: 254–78.

Eichberger, J., Hans Haller, and F. Milne (1993). "Naive Bayesian Learning in 2 × 2 Matrix Games." *Journal of Economic Behavior and Organization* 22: 69–90.

Einhorn, H. J., and R. M. Hogarth (1987). "Confidence in Judgment: Persistence of the Illusion of Validity." *Psychological Review* 85: 395–416.

Ellison, Glenn (1994). "Cooperation in the Prisoner's Dilemma with Anonymous Random Matching." *Review of Economic Studies* 61: 567–88.

Enelow, James M., and Melvin J. Hinich (1984). *The Spatial Theory of Voting: An Introduction.* Cambridge University Press.

Enelow, James M., and Rebecca B. Morton (1993). "Promising Directions in Public Choice." *Public Choice* 77: 85–93.

Epstein, David, and Peter Zemsky (1995). "Money Talks: A Signaling Approach to Campaign Finance." *American Political Science Review* 89: 295–308.

Epstein, Lee, Jeffrey A. Segal, Harold J. Spaeth, and Thomas G. Walker (1996). *The Supreme Court Compendium: Data, Decisions, and Development,* 2nd ed. Washington, DC: Congressional Quarterly.

Erikson, Robert S., and David W. Romero (1990). "Candidate Equilibrium and the Behavioral Model of the Vote." *American Political Science Review* 84: 1103–26.

Faber, R. J., and M. C. Storey (1984). "Recall of Information from Political Advertisements." *Journal of Advertising* 13: 39–44.

Fair, Ray (1988). "The Effect of Economic Events on Votes for President: 1984 Update." *Political Behavior* 10: 168–79.

Fearon, James (1992). "Threats to Use Force: The Role of Costly Signals in International Crises." Ph.D. Dissertation, University of California, Berkeley.

Fearon, James D. (1994). "Signaling versus the Balance of Power and Interests: An Empirical Test of a Crisis Bargaining Model." *Journal of Conflict Resolution* 38: 236–69.

Fearon, James D., and David D. Laitin (1996). "Explaining Interethnic Cooperation." *American Political Science Review* 90: 715–35.

Feddersen, Timothy J. (1992). "A Voting Model Implying Duverger's Law and Positive Turnout." *American Journal of Political Science* 36: 938–62.

Feldmann, Sven E. (1997). "Do Legislators Maximize Votes?" Mimeo, Harris School of Public Policy, University of Chicago.

Ferejohn, John, and Charles Shipan (1990). "Congressional Influence on Bureaucracy." *Journal of Law, Economics and Organization* 6: 1–20.

Fey, Mark, Richard D. McKelvey, and Thomas R. Palfrey (1996). "An Experimental Study of the Constant-Sum Centipede Games." *International Journal of Game Theory* 25: 269–87.

Filer, John E., Lawrence W. Kenny, and Rebecca B. Morton (1993). "Redistribution, Income, and Voting." *American Journal of Political Science* 37: 63–87.

Fiorina, Morris P. (1997). "Voting Behavior." In Dennis C. Mueller (Ed.), *Perspectives on Public Choice: A Handbook*, pp. 391–414. Cambridge University Press.

Fischer, Stanley (1977). "Long Term Contracts, Rational Expectations, and the Optimal Money Supply Rule." *Journal of Political Economy* 85: 191–206.

Fishburn, Peter C. (1982). " Nontransitive Measurable Utility." *Journal of Mathematical Psychology* 26: 31–67.

Forsythe, Robert, Roger B. Myerson, Thomas A. Rietz, and Robert J. Weber (1993). "An Experiment on Coordination in Multi Candidate Elections: The Importance of Polls and Election Histories." *Social Choice and Welfare* 10: 223–47.

Forsythe, Robert, Roger B. Myerson, Thomas A. Rietz, and Robert J. Weber (forthcoming). "An Experimental Study of Voting Rules and Polls in Three-Way Elections." *International Journal of Game Theory*.

Francis, Wayne L., Lawrence W. Kenny, Rebecca B. Morton, and Amy B. Schmidt (1994). "Retrospective Voting and Political Mobility." *American Journal of Political Science* 38: 999–1024.

Fudenberg, Drew, and David Levine (1997). "The Theory of Learning in Games." Unpublished manuscript.

Fudenberg, Drew, and Jean Tirole (1991). *Game Theory*. Cambridge, MA: MIT Press.

Garramone, G. M. (1984). "Voter Responses to Negative Political Ads." *Journalism Quarterly* 61: 250–8.

Garramone, G. M. (1985). "Effects of Negative Political Advertising: The Roles of Sponsor and Rebuttal." *Journal of Broadcasting and Electronic Media* 29: 147–59.

Gates, Scott, and Brian Humes (1997). *Games, Information, and Politics: Applying Game Theoretic Models to Political Science*. Ann Arbor: University of Michigan Press.

Gerber, Alan (1994). "Campaign Spending and Election Outcomes: Re-estimating the Effects of Campaign Spending." Working Paper, Yale University, New Haven, CT.

Gerber, Alan (1996a). "Rational Voters, Candidate Spending, and Incomplete Information: A Theoretical Analysis with Implications for Campaign Finance Reform." Working Paper, Yale University, New Haven, CT.

Gerber, Elisabeth R. (1996b). "Legislative Response to the Threat of Popular Initiatives." *American Journal of Political Science* 40: 99–128.

Gerber, Elisabeth R., and Rebecca B. Morton (1998). "Primary Election Systems and Representation." *Journal of Law, Economics, and Organization* 14: 304–24.

Gerber, Elisabeth R., Rebecca B. Morton, and Thomas Rietz (1998). "Minority Representation in Multimember Districts." *American Political Science Review* 92: 127–44.

Gibbard, Allan (1973). "Manipulation of Voting Schemes: A General Result." *Econometrica* 41: 587–601.

Gilligan, Thomas, and Keith Krehbiel (1987). "Collective Decisionmaking and Standing Committees: An Informational Rationale for Restrictive Amendment Procedures." *Journal of Law, Economics, and Organization* 3: 287–335.

Gilligan, Thomas, and Keith Krehbiel (1989). "Asymmetric Information and Legislative Rules with a Heterogeneous Committee." *American Journal of Political Science* 33: 459–90.

Gilmour, John B., and Paul Rothstein (1994). "Term Limitation in a Dynamic Model of Partisan Balance." *American Journal of Political Science* 38: 770–96.

Glantz, Stanton A., Alan I. Abramowitz, and Michael P. Burkhart (1976). "Election Outcomes: Whose Money Matters?" *Journal of Politics* 38: 1033–8.

Goldenberg, Edie N., Michael W. Traugott, and Frank R. Baumgartner (1986). "Preemptive and Reactive Spending in U.S. House Races." *Political Behavior* 8: 3–20.

Gould, Roger V. (1991). "Multiple Networks and Mobilization in the Paris Commune, 1871." *American Sociological Review* 56: 716–29.

Gould, Roger V. (1993). "Collective Action and Network Structure." *American Sociological Review* 58: 182–96.

Granato, Jim (1991). "An Agenda for Econometric Model Building." *Political Analysis* 3: 123–54.

Green, Donald P., and Jonathan Krasno (1988). "Salvation for the Spendthrift Incumbent: Reestimating the Effects of Campaign Spending in House Elections." *American Journal of Political Science* 32: 884–907.

Green, Donald P., and Jonathan Krasno (1990). "Rebuttal to Jacobson's 'New Evidence for Old Arguments'." *American Journal of Political Science* 34: 363–72.

Green, Donald P., and Ian Shapiro (1994). *Pathologies of Rational Choice Theory: A Critique of Applications in Political Science.* New Haven, CT: Yale University Press.

Grier, Kevin B. (1989). "Campaign Spending and Senate Elections, 1978–84." *Public Choice* 63: 201–19.

Groseclose, Tim, and James M. Snyder, Jr. (1996). "Buying Supermajorities." *American Political Science Review* 90: 303–15.

Grossman, Gene M., and Elhanan Helpman (1996). "Competing for Endorsements." Discussion Paper, Centre for Economic Policy Research, Tel Aviv.

Harsanyi, J. C. (1967–68). "Games with Incomplete Information Played by 'Bayesian' Players." *Management Science* 14: 159–82, 320-334, 486–502.

Harsanyi, J. C. (1973). "Games with Randomly Disturbed Payoffs: A New Rationale for Mixed-Strategy Equilibrium Points." *International Journal of Game Theory* 2: 1–23.

Heckman, J. (1978). "Dummy Endogenous Variables in a Simultaneous Equation System." *Econometrica* 46: 931–59.

Hey, John D., and C. Orme (1994). "Investigating Generalizations of Expected Utility Theory Using Experimental Data." *Econometrica* 62: 1291–1326.

Hibbs, Douglas (1977). "Political Parties and Macroeconomic Policy." *American Political Science Review* 71: 1467–87.

Hibbs, Douglas (1987). *The American Political Economy: Electoral Policy and Macroeconomics in Contemporary America*. Cambridge, MA: Harvard University Press.

Hinich, Melvin J. (1977). "Equilibrium in Spatial Voting: The Median Voter Result is an Artifact." *Journal of Economic Theory* 16: 208–19.

Hinich, Melvin J., John O. Ledyard, and Peter C. Ordeshook (1972). "Nonvoting and the Existence of Equilibrium under Majority Rule." *Journal of Economic Theory* 4: 144–53.

Hinich, Melvin J., and Michael C. Munger (1989). "Political Investment, Voter Perceptions, and Candidate Strategy: An Equilibrium Spatial Analysis." In Peter C. Ordeshook (Ed.), *Models of Strategic Choice in Politics*, pp. 49–68. Ann Arbor: University of Michigan Press.

Hinich, Melvin J., and Michael C. Munger (1997). *Analytical Politics*. Cambridge University Press.

Hoffman, Elizabeth, J. Marsden, and A. Whinston (1986). "Using Different Economic Data Forms." *Journal of Behavioral Economics* 15: 67–84.

Hoffman, Elizabeth, J. Marsden, and A. Whinston (1990). "Laboratory Experiments and Computer Simulation: An Introduction to the Use of Experimental and Process Model Data in Economic Analysis." In John Kagel and L. Green (Eds.), *Advances in Behavioral Economics*, vol. 2. Norwood, NJ: Ablex.

Hogarth, R. M., and M. W. Reder (Eds.) (1987). *Rational Choice: The Contrast Between Economics and Psychology*. University of Chicago Press.

Holmstrom, Bengt (1982). "Moral Hazard in Teams." *Bell Journal of Economics* 13: 324–40.

Hotelling, H. (1929). "Stability in Competition." *Economic Journal* 39: 41–57.

Huber, John D. (1992). "Restrictive Legislative Procedures in France and the United States." *American Political Science Review* 86: 675–87.

Huckshorn, Robert J., and Robert C. Spencer (1971). *The Politics of Defeat*. Amherst: University of Massachusetts Press.

Huth, P. (1988). *Extended Deterrence and the Prevention of War*. New Haven, CT: Yale University Press.

Huth, P., and B. Russett (1988). "Deterrence Failure and Crisis Escalation." *International Studies Quarterly* 32: 29–46.

Ingberman, Daniel, and John Villani (1993). "An Institutional Theory of Divided Government and Party Polarization." *American Journal of Political Science* 37: 429–71.

Iyengar, Shanto, and Stephen Ansolabehere (1995). *Going Negative.* New York: Free Press.

Jacobson, Gary C. (1976). "Practical Consequences of Campaign Finance Reform: An Incumbent Protection Act?" *Public Policy* 24: 1–32.

Jacobson, Gary C. (1978). "The Effects of Campaign Spending in Congressional Elections." *American Political Science Review* 72: 469–91.

Jacobson, Gary C. (1980). *Money in Congressional Elections.* New Haven, CT: Yale University Press.

Jacobson, Gary C. (1985). "Money and Votes Reconsidered: Congressional Elections, 1972–1982." *Public Choice* 47: 7–62.

Jacobson, Gary C. (1987). *The Politics of Congressional Elections,* 2nd ed. Boston: Little, Brown.

Jacobson, Gary C. (1989). "Strategic Politicians and the Dynamics of House Elections, 1946–1986." *American Political Science Review* 83: 773–93.

Jacobson, Gary C. (1990). "The Effects of Campaign Spending in House Elections: New Evidence for Old Arguments." *American Journal of Political Science* 34: 334–62.

Jacobson, Gary C., and Samuel Kernell (1981). *Strategy and Choice in Congressional Elections.* New Haven, CT: Yale University Press.

Jarque, Carlos M., and Anil Bera (1980). "Efficient Tests for Normality, Homoscedasticity, and Serial Independence of Regression Residuals." *Economic Letters* 6: 255–9.

Johnston, J. (1972). *Econometric Methods,* 2nd ed. New York: McGraw-Hill.

Just, M., A. Crigler, and L. Wallach (1990). "Thirty Seconds or Thirty Minutes: What Viewers Learn from Spot Advertisements and Candidate Debates." *Journal of Communication* 40: 120–33.

Kadera, Kelly (forthcoming). *The Power–Conflict Story: A Dynamic Model of Interstate Rivalry.* Ann Arbor: University of Michigan Press.

Kagel, John H., and Alvin E. Roth (Eds.) (1995). *The Handbook of Experimental Economics.* Princeton, NJ: Princeton University Press.

Kahneman, D., and Amos Tversky (1979). "Prospect Theory: An Analysis of Decision Under Risk." *Econometrica* 47: 263–91.

Kandori, Michihiro (1992). "Social Norms and Community Enforcement." *Review of Economic Studies* 59: 63–80.

Kanthak, Kristin, and Rebecca B. Morton (Eds.) (1998). *Experiments and Models: A Guide to Using Experiments to Test Formal Models.* Unpublished manuscript.

Kazee, Thomas A. (1980). "The Decision to Run for Congress: Challenger Attitudes in the 1970s." *Legislative Studies Quarterly* 5: 79–100.

Kenny, Christopher, and Michael McBurnett (1992). "A Dynamic Model of the Effect of Campaign Spending on Congressional Vote Choice." *American Journal of Political Science* 36: 923–37.

Kessler, Daniel, and Keith Krehbiel (1996). "Dynamics of Cosponsorship." *American Political Science Review* 90: 555–65.

Kiewiet, Roderick D., and Mathew D. McCubbins (1991). *The Logic of Delegation.* University of Chicago Press.

King, Gary (1989). *Unifying Political Methodology: The Likelihood Theory of Statistical Inference.* Cambridge University Press.

King, Gary (1997). *A Solution to the Ecological Inference Problem.* Princeton, NJ: Princeton University Press.

King, Gary, Robert O. Keohane, and Sidney Verba (1994). *Designing Social Inquiry: Scientific Inference in Qualitative Research.* Princeton, NJ: Princeton University Press.

Kollman, Ken, John Miller, and Scott Page (1992). "Adaptive Parties in Spatial Elections." *American Political Science Review* 86: 929–37.

Kollman, Ken, John H. Miller, and Scott E. Page (1998). "Political Parties and Electoral Landscapes." *British Journal of Political Science* 28: 139–58.

Kramer, Gerald H. (1973). "On a Class of Equilibrium Conditions for Majority Rule." *Econometrica* 41: 285–97.

Krasno, Jonathan S., and Donald P. Green (1988). "Preempting Quality Challengers in House Elections." *Journal of Politics* 50: 920–36.

Krehbiel, Keith (1991). *Information and Legislative Organization.* Ann Arbor: University of Michigan Press.

Krelle, W. (1976). *Preistheorie,* part 2. Tübingen: J. C. B. Mohr.

Kreps, David M. (1990). "Corporate Culture and Economic Theory." In James M. Alt and Kenneth A. Shepsle (Eds.), *Perspectives on Positive Political Economy.* Cambridge University Press.

Kreps, David M., and Robert B. Wilson (1982). "Reputation and Imperfect Information." *Journal of Economic Theory* 27: 253–79.

Lacy, Dean (1995). "Nonseparable Preferences, Issue Voting, and Issue Packaging in Elections." Manuscript, Ohio State University, Columbus.

Ladha, Krishna, Gary Miller, and Joe Oppenheimer (1996). "Information Aggregation by Majority Rule: Theory and Experiments." Unpublished manuscript, University of Maryland, College Park.

Lasley, Scott (1996). "Information and Candidate Quality." Working Paper, Department of Political Science, University of Iowa, Iowa City.

Laver, Michael, and Norman Schofield (1990). *Multiparty Government: The Politics of Coalition in Europe.* Oxford University Press.

Laver, Michael, and Kenneth A. Shepsle (1996). *Making and Breaking Governments: Cabinets and Legislatures in Parliamentary Democracies.* Cambridge University Press.

Ledyard, John O. (1984). "The Pure Theory of Large Two-Candidate Elections." *Public Choice* 44: 7–41.

Ledyard, John O. (1995). "Public Goods: A Survey of Experimental Research." In John H. Kagel and Alvin E. Roth (Eds.), *The Handbook of Experimental Economics,* pp. 111–194. Princeton, NJ: Princeton University Press.

Lee, Lung-Fei, and Robert Porter (1984). "Switching Regression Models with Imperfect Sample Separation Information, with an Application on Cartel Stability." *Econometrica* 52: 391–418.

Leuthold, David A. (1968). *Electioneering in a Democracy.* New York: Wiley.

Levitt, Steven (1994). "Using Repeat Challengers to Estimate the Effect of Campaign Spending on Election Outcomes in the U.S. House." *Journal of Political Economy* 102: 777–98.

Leys, Colin (1959). "Models, Theories, and the Theory of Political Parties." *Political Studies* 7: 127–46.

Lijphart, Arend (1994). *Electoral Systems and Party Systems: A Study of Twenty-Seven Democracies, 1945–1990.* Oxford University Press.

Lin, T., James Enelow, and H. Dorussen (1996). "Equilibrium in Multicandidate Probabilistic Spatial Voting." Unpublished manuscript, University of Texas, Austin.

Lodge, M., K. McGraw, and P. Stroh (1989). "An Impression-Driven Model of Candidate Evaluation." *American Political Science Review* 83: 399–419.

Lodge, Milton, Marco R. Steenbergen, and Shawn Brau (1995). "The Responsive Voter: Campaign Information and the Dynamics of Candidate Evaluation." *American Political Science Review* 89: 309–26.

Lodge, M., and P. Stroh (1993). "Inside the Mental Voting Booth." In S. Iyengar and R. McGuire (Eds.), *Political Psychology.* Durham, NC: Duke University Press.

Londregan, John, and Thomas Romer (1993). "Polarization, Incumbency, and the Personal Vote." In William A. Barnett, Melvin J. Hinich, and Norman Schofield (Eds.), *Political Economy: Institutions, Competition, and Representation.* Cambridge University Press.

Luce, R. Duncan (1959). *Individual Choice Behavior: A Theoretical Analysis.* New York: Wiley.

Luce, R. Duncan, and Howard Raiffa (1957). *Games and Decisions.* New York: Wiley.

Luce, R. Duncan, and P. Suppes (1965). "Preference, Utility, and Subjective Probability." In R. Duncan Luce, R. B. Bush, and E. Galanter (Eds.), *Handbook of Mathematical Psychology,* vol. III, pp. 249–410. New York: Wiley.

Lucier, Charles E. (1979). "Changes in the Values of Arms Race Parameters." *Journal of Conflict Resolution* 23: 17–39.

Macdonald, Stuart Elaine, Ola Listhaug, and George Rabinowitz (1991). "Issues and Party Support in Multiparty Systems." *American Political Science Review* 85: 1107–31.

MacCrimmon, K. R. (1965). "An Experimental Study of the Decision Making Behavior of Business Executives." Ph.D. Dissertation, University of California, Los Angeles.

MacCrimmon, K. R., and S. Larson (1979). "Utility Theory: Axioms versus Paradoxes." In M. Allais and O. Hagen (Eds.), *The Expected Utility Hypothesis and the Allais Paradox,* pp. 333–409. Dordrecht: Reidel.

Machina, M. J. (1982). " 'Expected Utility' Analysis without the Independence Axiom." *Econometrica* 50: 277–323.

Machina, M. J. (1989). "Comparative Statics and Non-Expected Utility Preferences." *Journal of Economic Theory* 47: 393–405.

Macy, Michael W. (1991). "Chains of Cooperation: Threshold Effects in Collective Action." *American Sociological Review* 56: 730–47.

Maisel, L. Sandy (1982). *From Obscurity to Oblivion: Congressional Primary Elections in 1978.* Knoxville: University of Tennessee Press.

Maki, Daniel P., and Maynard Thompson (1972). *Mathematical Models and Applications: With Emphasis on the Social, Life, and Management Sciences.* Englewood Cliffs, NJ: Prentice-Hall.

Mann, Thomas E., and Raymond E. Wolfinger (1980). "Candidates and Parties in Congressional Elections." *American Political Science Review* 74: 617–32.

Manski, C. F., and S. R. Lerman (1977). "The Estimation of Choice Probabilities from Choice-Based Samples." *Econometrica* 45: 1977–88.

Marschak, J. (1950). "Rational Behavior, Uncertain Prospects, and Measurable Utility." *Econometrica* 18: 111–41.

Mayhew, David R. (1974). *Congress: The Electoral Connection.* New Haven, CT: Yale University Press.

McCarty, Nolan, and Lawrence Rothenberg (1996). "The Strategic Decisions of Political Action Committees." Paper presented at the 3rd Annual Wallis Institute Conference on Political Economy (Rochester, NY).

McFadden, D. (1974). "Conditional Logit Analysis of Qualitative Choice Behavior." In P. Zarembka (Ed.), *Frontiers of Economics.* New York: Academic Press.

McGraw, Kathleen M. (1996). "Political Methodology: Research Design and Experimental Methods." In Robert Goodin and Hans-Dieter Klingemann (Eds.), *A New Handbook of Political Science,* pp. 769–86. Oxford University Press.

McKelvey, Richard D. (1976). "Intransitivities in Multidimensional Voting Models and Some Implications for Agenda Control." *Journal of Economic Theory* 12: 472–82.

McKelvey, Richard D. (1991). "An Experimental Test of a Stochastic Game Model of Committee Bargaining." In Thomas R. Palfrey (Ed.), *Laboratory Research in Political Economy.* Ann Arbor: University of Michigan Press.

McKelvey, Richard D., and Peter C. Ordeshook (1990). "A Decade of Experimental Research on Spatial Models of Elections and Committees." In James M. Enelow and Melvin J. Hinich (Eds.), *Advances in the Spatial Theory of Voting,* pp. 99–144. Cambridge University Press.

McKelvey, Richard D., and Thomas R. Palfrey (1992). "An Experimental Study of the Centipede Game." *Econometrica* 60: 803–36.

McKelvey, Richard D., and Thomas R. Palfrey (1995). "Quantal Response Equilibria for Normal Form Games." *Games and Economic Behavior* 10: 6–38.

McKelvey, Richard D., and Thomas R. Palfrey (1996). "A Statistical Theory of Equilibrium in Games." *Japanese Economic Review* 47: 186–209.

McKelvey, Richard D., and Thomas R. Palfrey (1998). "Quantal Response Equilibria for Extensive Form Games." *Experimental Economics* 1: 9–41.

Mebane, Walter (1997). "Congressional Campaign Contributions, District Service and Electoral Outcomes in the United States: Statistical Tests of a Formal Game

Model with Nonlinear Dynamics." Working Paper, Cornell University, Ithaca, NY.

Merritt, S. (1984). "Negative Political Advertising: Some Empirical Findings." *Journal of Advertising* 13: 27–38.

Milgrom, Paul, Douglass North, and Barry Weingast (1990). "The Role of Institutions in the Revival of Trade." *Economics and Politics* 2: 1–23.

Miller, Gary J. (1992). *Managerial Dilemmas: The Political Economy of Hierarchy.* Cambridge University Press.

Miller, John, and James Andreoni (1991). "Can Evolutionary Dynamics Explain Free Riding in Experiments?" *Economics Letters* 36: 9–15.

Moraski, Bryon, and Charles Shipan (1998). "The Politics of Supreme Court Nominations: A Theory of Institutional Constraints and Choices." Working Paper, Department of Political Science, University of Iowa, Iowa City.

Morrison, D. G. (1967). "On the Consistency of Preferences in Allais' Paradox." *Behavioral Science* 12: 373–83.

Morrow, James D. (1994). *Game Theory for Political Scientists.* Princeton, NJ: Princeton University Press.

Morton, Rebecca B. (1987). "A Group Majority Voting Model of Public Good Provision." *Social Choice and Welfare* 4: 117–31.

Morton, Rebecca B. (1991). "Groups in Rational Turnout Models." *American Journal of Political Science* 3: 758–76.

Morton, Rebecca B. (1993). "Incomplete Information and Ideological Explanations of Platform Divergence." *American Political Science Review* 87: 382–92.

Morton, Rebecca B. (1996). "Partisan Electoral Cycles and Monetary Policy Games." In Norman Schofield (Ed.), *Collective Decision-Making: Social Choice and Political Economy.* Boston: Kluwer.

Morton, Rebecca B., and Charles M. Cameron (1992). "Elections and the Theory of Campaign Contributions: A Survey and Critical Analysis." *Economics and Politics* 4: 79–108.

Mueller, Dennis C. (1989). *Public Choice II.* Cambridge University Press.

Mueller, Dennis C. (1997). "Public Choice in Perspective." In *Perspectives on Public Choice: A Handbook.* Cambridge University Press.

Myerson, Roger B. (1991). *Game Theory: Analysis of Conflict.* Cambridge, MA: Harvard University Press.

Myerson, Roger B. (1995). "Analysis of Democratic Institutions: Structure, Conduct, and Performance." *Journal of Economic Perspectives* 9: 77–89.

Myerson, Roger B., and Robert J. Weber (1993). "A Theory of Voting Equilibria." *American Political Science Review* 87: 102–14.

Myerson, Roger, Thomas Rietz, and Robert Weber (1993). "Campaign Finance Levels as Coordinating Signals in Three-Way, Experimental Elections." Working Paper no. 150, Department of Finance, Kellogg Graduate School of Management, Northwestern University, Evanston, IL.

Nagler, Jonathan (1994). "Scobit: An Alternative Estimator to Logit and Probit." *American Journal of Political Science* 38: 230–55.

Nixon, D., D. Olomoki, Norman Schofield, and Itai Sened (1995). "Multiparty Probabilistic Voting: An Application to the Israeli Knesset." Working Paper no. 186, Center in Political Economy, Washington University at St. Louis, MO.

Nordhaus, William (1975). "The Political Business Cycle." *Review of Economic Studies* 42: 169–90.

Offerman, Theo (1996). *Beliefs and Decision Rules in Public Good Games: Theory and Experiments* (Tinbergen Institute Research Series no. 124). Amsterdam: Tinbergen Institute.

Offerman, Theo, J. Sonnemans, and Arthur Schram (1996). "Value Orientations, Expectations and Voluntary Contributions in Public Goods." *Economic Journal* 106: 817–45.

Olson, Mancur (1965). *The Logic of Collective Action*. Cambridge, MA: Harvard University Press.

O'Rand, Angela M. (1992). "Mathematizing Social Science in the 1950s: The Early Development and Diffusion of Game Theory." In E. Roy Weintraub (Ed.), *Toward a History of Game Theory: Annual Supplement to Volume 24, History of Political Economy*, pp. 177–204. Durham, NC: Duke University Press.

Osborne, Martin J., and Ariel Rubinstein (1994). *A Course in Game Theory*. Cambridge, MA: MIT Press.

Palfrey, Thomas R. (1984). "Spatial Equilibrium with Entry." *Review of Economic Studies* 51: 139–56.

Palfrey, Thomas R. (1989) "A Mathematical Proof of Duverger's Law." In Peter C. Ordeshook (Ed.), *Models of Strategic Choice in Politics*, pp. 69–92. Ann Arbor: University of Michigan Press.

Palfrey, Thomas R. (1991). "Introduction." In Thomas R. Palfrey (Ed.), *Laboratory Research in Political Economy*, pp. 1–10. Ann Arbor: University of Michigan Press.

Payne, J. W., J. Bettman, and E. Johnson (1992). "Behavioral Decision Research: A Constructive Processing Perspective." *Annual Review of Psychology* 43: 87–131.

Phelan, Peter, and Peter Reynolds (1996). *Argument and Evidence: Critical Analysis for the Social Sciences*. London: Routledge.

Plott, Charles R. (1967). "A Notion of Equilibrium and Its Possibility under Majority Rule." *American Economic Review* 57: 787–806.

Plott, Charles R. (1986). "Rational Choice in Experimental Markets." *Journal of Business* 59: S301–S327.

Potters, Jan, Randolph Sloof, and Frans van Winden (1997). "Campaign Expenditures, Contributions and Direct Endorsements: The Strategic Use of Information and Money to Influence Voter Behavior." *European Journal of Political Economy* 13: 1–31.

Prat, Andrea (1997). "Campaign Advertising and Voter Welfare." Working Paper, Center for Economic Research, Tilburg University, Netherlands.

Quattrone, George A., and Amos Tversky (1988). "Contrasting Rational and Psychological Analyses of Political Choice." *American Political Science Review* 82: 720–36.

Rabin, Matthew (1993). "Incorporating Fairness into Game Theory and Economics." *American Economic Review* 83: 1281–1302.

Rabinowitz, George, and Stuart Elaine Macdonald (1989). "A Directional Theory of Voting." *American Political Science Review* 83: 93–121.

Ramsey, F. (1931). "Truth and Probability." In F. Ramsey (Ed.), *The Foundations of Mathematics and Other Logical Essays*. London: Routledge & Kegan Paul.

Rapoport, Anatol (1950). *Science and the Goals of Man*. New York: Harper & Bros.

Rashevsky, Nicholas (1947). *Mathematical Theory of Human Relations*. Bloomington: Principia Press.

Reiss, Peter C. (1996). "Empirical Models of Discrete Strategic Choices." *American Economic Review* 86: 421–6.

Rhode, David W. (1979). "Risk-Bearing and Progressive Ambition: The Case of Members of the United States House of Representatives." *American Journal of Political Science* 23: 1–26.

Richards, Diana (1992). "Spatial Correlation Test for Chaotic Dynamics in Political Science." *American Journal of Political Science* 36: 1047–74.

Richardson, Lewis F. (1939). *Generalized Foreign Politics* (British Journal of Psychology Monograph Supplement no. 23). Cambridge University Press.

Riker, William (1980). "Implications from the Disequilibrium of Majority Rule for the Study of Institutions." *American Political Science Review* 74: 432–46.

Riker, William H. (1982). *Liberalism Against Populism: A Confrontation between the Theory of Democracy and the Theory of Social Choice*. San Francisco: Freeman.

Riker, William (1992). "The Entry of Game Theory into Political Science." In E. Roy Weintraub (Ed.), *Toward a History of Game Theory: Annual Supplement to Volume 24, History of Political Economy*, pp. 207–224. Durham, NC: Duke University Press.

Riker, William H., and Peter Ordeshook (1968). "A Theory of the Calculus of Voting." *American Political Science Review* 62: 25–42.

Rogoff, K. (1990). "Equilibrium Political Budget Cycles." *American Economic Review* 80: 21–36.

Rogoff, K., and Anne Sibert (1988). "Elections and Macroeconomic Policy Cycles." *Review of Economic Studies*. 55: 1–16.

Rose-Ackerman, Susan (1996). "Altruism, Nonprofits, and Economic Theory." *Journal of Economic Literature* 34: 701–28.

Rosenthal, Robert (1982). "Games of Perfect Information, Predatory Pricing, and the Chain Store Paradox." *Journal of Economic Theory* 25: 92–100.

Roth, Alvin E. (1995). "Bargaining Experiments." In John Kagel and Alvin Roth (Eds.), *The Handbook of Experimental Economics*, pp. 253–348. Princeton, NJ: Princeton University Press.

Roth, Alvin E. (forthcoming). "Comments on Tversky's 'Rational Theory and Constructive Choice'." In K. Arrow, E. Colombatto, M. Perlman, and C. Schmidt (Eds.), *The Rational Foundations of Economic Behavior*, pp. 198–202. New York: Macmillan.

Roth, Alvin E., and Ido Erev (1995). "Learning in Extensive-Form Games: Experimental Data and Simple Dynamic Models in the Intermediate Term." *Games and Economic Behavior* 8: 164–212.

Rothenberg, Thomas J. (1973). *Efficient Estimations with A Priori Information* (Cowles Foundation Monograph no. 23). New Haven, CT: Yale University Press.

Rubinstein, Ariel (1982). "Perfect Equilibrium in a Bargaining Model." *Econometrica* 50: 97–109.

Samuelson, Larry (1984). "Electoral Equilibria with Restricted Strategies." *Public Choice* 43: 307–27.

Sartori, Giovanni (1976). *Parties and Party Systems: A Framework for Analysis,* vol. 1. Cambridge University Press.

Satterthwaite, Mark A. (1975). "Strategy-Proofness and Arrow's Conditions: Existence and Correspondence Theorems for Voting Procedures and Social Welfare Functions." *Journal of Economic Theory* 10: 1–7.

Savage, L. J. (1954). *The Foundations of Statistics.* New York: Wiley.

Schelling, Thomas C. (1960). *The Strategy of Conflict.* Cambridge, MA: Harvard University Press.

Schmidt, Amy B., Lawrence W. Kenny, and Rebecca B. Morton (1996). "Evidence on Electoral Accountability in the U.S. Senate: Are Unfaithful Agents Really Punished?" *Economic Inquiry* 34: 545–67.

Schofield, Norman (1978). "Instability of Simple Dynamic Games." *Review of Economic Studies* 45: 575–94.

Segal, Jeffrey A., Charles M. Cameron, and Albert D. Cover (1992). "A Spatial Model of Roll Call Voting: Senators, Constituents, Presidents, and Interest Groups in Supreme Court Nominations." *American Journal of Political Science* 36: 96–121.

Segal, Jeffrey A., and Albert D. Cover (1989). "Ideological Values and the Votes of U.S. Supreme Court Justices." *American Political Science Review* 83: 557–65.

Sen, Amartya (1970). *Collective Choice and Social Welfare.* San Francisco: Holden-Day.

Shapley, Lloyd, and Martin Shubik (1954). "A Method for Evaluating the Distribution of Power in a Committee System." *American Political Science Review* 48: 787–92.

Shepsle, Kenneth (1979). "Institutional Arrangements and Equilibrium in Multidimensional Voting Models." *American Journal of Political Science* 32: 27–59.

Shepsle, Kenneth A. (1991). *Models of Multiparty Electoral Competition.* Chur: Harwood.

Shepsle, Kenneth A., and Barry Weingast (1981). "Structure-Induced Equilibrium and Legislative Choice." *Public Choice* 37: 503–19.

Shepsle, Kenneth A., and Barry Weingast (1984). "When Do Rules of Procedure Matter?" *Journal of Politics* 46: 206–21.

Shotts, Ken (1997a). "The Effect of Majority-Minority Mandates on Partisan Gerrymandering." Working Paper, Graduate School of Business, Stanford University.

Shotts, Ken (1997b). "Gerrymandering, Legislative Composition, and National Policy Outcomes." Working Paper, Graduate School of Business, Stanford University.

Signorino, Curtis S. (1998). "Estimation and Strategic Interaction in Discrete Choice Models of International Conflict." Working Paper, Department of Political Science, University of Rochester, NY.

Simon, Adam (1998). "The Winning Message? Candidate Behavior, Campaign Discourse and Democracy." Unpublished manuscript, University of Washington, Seattle.

Simon, Herbert (1957). *Models of Man: Social and Rational; Mathematical Essays on Rational Human Behavior in a Social Setting.* New York: Wiley.

Simon, Herbert A. (1976). *Administrative Behavior: A Study of Decision-Making Processes in Administrative Organization,* 3rd ed. New York: Free Press.

Simon, Herbert (1985). "Human Nature in Politics: The Dialogue of Psychology with Political Science." *American Political Science Review* 79: 293–304.

Slovic, P., and A. Tversky (1974). "Who Accepts Savage's Axiom?" *Behavioral Science* 19: 368–73.

Slutsky, Steven M. (1975). "Abstentions and Majority Equilibrium." *Journal of Economic Theory* 11: 292–304.

Slutsky, Steven M. (1977). "A Voting Model for the Allocation of Public Goods: Existence of an Equilibrium." *Journal of Economic Theory* 14: 299–325.

Smith, Vincent L. (1991). "Rational Choice: The Contrast between Economics and Psychology." *Journal of Political Economy* 99: 877–97.

Snyder, James M. (1990). "Campaign Contributions as Investments: The U.S. House of Representatives 1980–86." *Journal of Political Economy* 98: 1195–1227.

Squire, Peverill (1989). "Competition and Uncontested Seats in U.S. House Elections." *Legislative Studies Quarterly* 14: 281–95.

Stahl, I. (1972). *Bargaining Theory.* Stockholm: Economics Research Institute, Stockholm School of Economics.

Sunder, S. (1995). "Experimental Asset Markets: A Survey," In John Kagel and Alvin Roth (Eds.), *The Handbook of Experimental Economics,* pp. 445–500. Princeton, NJ: Princeton University Press,

Swedberg, Richard (1990). *Economics and Sociology Redefining Their Boundaries: Conversations with Economists and Sociologists.* Princeton, NJ: Princeton University Press.

Taagepera, Rein, and Matthew Soberg Shugart (1989). *Seats and Votes.* New Haven, CT: Yale University Press.

Taber, Charles S., and Richard J. Timpone (1996). *Computational Modeling.* Thousand Oaks, CA: Sage.

Taylor, Howard, and Samuel Karlin (1984). *An Introduction to Stochastic Modeling.* Orlando, FL: Academic Press.

Tetlock, Philip E., and Aaron Belkin (Eds.) (1996). *Counterfactual Thought Experiments in World Politics: Logical, Methodological, and Psychological Perspectives.* Princeton, NJ: Princeton University Press.

Tien, Charles (1996). "Towards a Comprehensive Theory of Budgeting: Parties, Deficits, Vetoes, and Spending." Ph.D. Dissertation, University of Iowa, Iowa City.

Trevor, Maggie (1995). "The Implications of Individual-Level Models of Party Identification for Predictions of Change in Party Systems: A Study of the United States and Great Britain." Ph.D. Dissertation, Department of Political Science, University of Chicago.

Truman, David B. (1968). "The Impact on Political Science of the Revolution in the Behavioral Sciences." In May Brodbeck (Ed.), *Readings in the Philosophy of the Social Sciences*, pp. 541–60. New York: Macmillan.

Van Huyck, J., Ray Battalio, and R. Beil (1990). "Tacit Coordination Games, Strategic Uncertainty, and Coordination Failure." *American Economic Review* 80: 234–48.

von Neumann, John, and Oskar Morgenstern (1944). *Theory of Games and Economic Behavior*. Princeton, NJ: Princeton University Press.

Wahlke, John C. (1979). "Pre-Behavioralism in Political Science." *American Political Science Review* 73: 9–31.

Westholm, Anders (1997). "Distance versus Direction: The Illusory Defeat of the Proximity Theory of Electoral Choice." *American Political Science Review* 91: 865–83.

Weyland, Kurt (1996). "Risk Taking in Latin American Economic Restructuring: Lessons from Prospect Theory." *International Studies Quarterly* 40: 185–208.

Wilson, Rick K. (1996). "Disequilibrium and Measurement in Committee Games." Unpublished manuscript, Rice University, Houston, TX.

Wittman, Donald (1977). "Candidates with Policy Preferences: A Dynamic Model." *Journal of Economic Theory* 14: 180–9.

Wittman, Donald (1983). "Candidate Motivation: A Synthesis of Alternative Theories." *American Political Science Review* 77: 142–57.

Wittman, Donald (1990). "Spatial Strategies When Candidates Have Policy Preferences." In James Enelow and Melvin Hinich (Eds.), *Advances in the Spatial Theory of Voting*, pp. 66–98. Cambridge University Press.

Wood, B. Dan, and James E. Anderson (1993). "The Politics of U.S. Antitrust Regulation." *American Journal of Political Science* 37: 1–39.

Wood, B. Dan, and Richard W. Waterman (1993). "The Dynamics of Political-Bureaucratic Adaptation." *American Journal of Political Science* 37: 497–528.

Zaller, John, and Stanley Feldman (1992). "A Simple Theory of the Survey Response: Answering Questions versus Revealing Preferences." *American Journal of Political Science* 36: 579–616.

Zinnes, Dina (1989). "The Study of Conflict Processes: An Intellectual Autobiography." In Joseph Kruzel and James N. Rosenau (Eds.), *Journeys through World Politics: Autobiographical Reflections of Thirty-four Academic Travelers*. Lexington, MA: Lexington Books.

Name Index

Abelson, Robert P., 92n8
Abramowtiz, Alan I., 4
Adams, Greg D., 238–9
Aldrich, John, 26, 58, 77, 168–9, 184–5, 249, 252
Alesina, Alberto, 140, 174–5, 178, 195, 223–32, 237, 271n10
Allais, Maurice, 84, 149–52
Alt, James, 167
Alvarez, R. Michael, 10n3, 11n3, 21, 131–2, 177, 284
Anderson, James, 263
Anderson, Simon P., 125
Andreoni, James, 87n6
Ansolabehere, Stephen, 5–7, 11n3
Arrow, Kenneth, 14, 18, 21, 41–2, 79–80
Austen-Smith, David, 10–11, 47–8, 115, 192, 197–203, 208, 220–2, 235, 237, 249, 267
Axelrod, Robert, 54

Banks, Jeffrey, 34–9, 41, 47–50, 55–9, 77n1, 107, 115, 135, 139, 193–4
Baron, David, 47, 116–18, 134, 237, 243n2
Bartels, Larry, 3, 8–9, 21, 24, 44, 170
Basil, M., 11n3
Bates, Robert, 134–5, 189, 259–61
Battalio, Ray, 193
Baumgartner, Frank, 6n1
Baumol, William, 14
Becker, Gordon M., 174
Bednar, Jenna, 134
Beil, R., 193
Belkin, Aaron, 23n8, 134
Bendor, Jonathan, 263
Bernhardt, M. D., 249
Bernheim, Douglas, 227

Bernholz, P., 189
Bettman, J., 92n8
Bianco, William, 189, 259–61
Binmore, Ken, 23, 83
Black, Duncan, 18
Boettcher, William A. III, 156
Bohm, P., 54
Bowen, Howard R., 18
Bowler, Shawn, 177
Box-Steffensmeier, Janet M., 6n1
Boylan, Richard, 48n8, 86, 231–5, 237
Boynton, G. R., 21–2
Brady, Henry, 3, 8–9, 21, 24, 44, 170
Brandts, Jordi, 193, 198, 247
Brau, Shawn, 92–3
Brehm, John, 130–1, 259–62, 264–6, 275, 284
Bresnaham, Timothy, 135
Brians, C. L., 11n3
Brock, William A., 10
Brophy-Baermann, Bryan, 226n3
Brown, Courtney, 25, 93–4, 96
Buchanan, James, 18
Buckley, Fred, 97
Bueno de Mesquita, Bruce, 26, 126, 268
Burkhart, Michael P., 4

Calvert, Randall, 37, 40, 54, 83, 89, 111, 146, 167, 171n4, 175, 194–5, 249, 252
Camerer, Colin, 84, 89–92, 112, 150n2, 154–5, 193–4
Cameron, Charles, 10, 11, 53, 131, 178, 210–16, 220–2, 235, 239, 243n1, 249, 271
Campbell, A., 20
Canon, David, 57–9, 135, 139
Carmines, Edward G., 20

317

Subject Index